MARKETING INSIGHTS

CONTRIBUTING AUTHORS

ALEXANDER, R. S.
Columbia University

BARTELS, ROBERT
The Ohio State University

BLISS, PERRY
State University of New York at Buffalo

BORCH, F. J.
General Electric Company

BORDEN, NEIL H.
Harvard University

BOYD, HARPER W., Jr.
Stanford University

BURCK, GILBERT
Fortune Magazine

BURNETT, LEO
Leo Burnett Company

CASSADY, RALPH, Jr.
University of California, Los Angeles

DAVIDSON, WILLIAM R.
The Ohio State University

DEAN, JOEL
Joel Dean Associates

DICHTER, ERNEST
Institute for Motivational Research, Inc.

HANCOCK, ROBERT S.
Southern Illinois University

HOLLANDER, STANLEY C.
Michigan State University

KATONA, GEORGE
University of Michigan

KEITH, ROBERT J.
The Pillsbury Company

KLAW, SPENCER
Fortune Magazine

KOCH, EDWARD G.
University of California, Los Angeles

KOTLER, PHILIP
Northwestern University

KUHLMAN, JOHN M.
University of Missouri

LANZILLOTTI, ROBERT F.
Michigan State University

LeKASHMAN, RAYMOND
Knight and Gladieux

LEVITT, THEODORE
Harvard University

LEVY, SIDNEY J.
Northwestern University

MARTINEAU, PIERRE
Late of *Chicago Tribune*

MASON, WILLIAM R.
Celanese Corporation

McDONALD, JOHN G.
McKinsey and Company, Inc.

McGARRY, EDMUND D.
State University of New York at Buffalo

McVEY, PHILLIP
University of Nebraska

NOLEN, HERMAN C.
McKesson Robbins, Inc.

OXENFELDT, ALFRED R.
Columbia University

PARKER, HUGH
McKinsey and Company, Inc.

RIESER, CARL
Fortune Magazine

RUSSELL, JAMES W.
Mack Trucks, Inc.

SCANLAN, BURT K.
University of Wisconsin

SELIGMAN, DANIEL
Fortune Magazine

SMITH, WENDELL R.
University of Massachusetts

STOLLE, JOHN F.
Booz, Allen & Hamilton, Inc.

WASSON, CHESTER R.
Northern Illinois University

WEISS, DOYLE L.
Purdue University

WHITE, IRVING S.
Creative Research Associates, Inc.

R. CLIFTON ANDERSEN
Southern Illinois University

AND

PHILIP R. CATEORA
University of Colorado

Marketing Insights

SELECTED READINGS

 Second Edition

New York

APPLETON-CENTURY-CROFTS

DIVISION OF MEREDITH CORPORATION

ACKNOWLEDGMENTS

Robert J. Keith, "The Marketing Revolution" reprinted from the *Journal of Marketing,* national quarterly publication of the American Marketing Association, Volume 24, No. 3 (January, 1960).

F. J. Borch, "The Marketing Philosophy as a Way of Business Life." An address to the American Marketing Management Association, February 4, 1957.

John G. McDonald & Hugh Parker, "Creating a Strategy for International Growth." McKinsey and Company, Inc., Management Consultants; based on an article that originally appeared in *Business Horizons* (1962).

Theodore Levitt, "Marketing Myopia" reprinted by permission of the publishers from Edward C. Bursk & John F. Chapman, editors, *Modern Marketing Strategy.* Cambridge, Mass.: Harvard University Press, Copyright, 1964, by the President and Fellows of Harvard College.

George Katona, "The Powerful Consumer" reprinted from the *Thirty-second Annual Boston Conference on Distribution,* October 17–18, 1960.

Ernest Dichter, "When Marketing Abroad . . . Remove Your Star-Spangled Glasses" reprinted from the May 2, 1966 issue of *Business Abroad* by special permission. Copyrighted © 1966 by the Dun & Bradstreet Publications Corporation.

John M. Kuhlman, "The Procter and Gamble Decision" from the *Quarterly Review of Economics & Business,* Volume 6, No. 1 (Spring, 1966).

Phillip McVey, "Are Channels of Distribution What the Textbooks Say?" reprinted from the *Journal of Marketing,* national quarterly publication of the American Marketing Association, Volume 24, No. 3 (January, 1960).

Stanley C. Hollander, "Social Pressures and Retail Competition" from *Business Topics,* Volume 13, No. 1 (Winter, 1965), used by permission of the publisher: Bureau of Business and Economic Research, Graduate School of Business Administration, Michigan State University.

Spencer Klaw, "The Soap Wars: A Strategic Analysis" reprinted from the June, 1963 issue of *Fortune* Magazine by special permission; © 1963 Time Inc.

Philip Kotler, "Behavioral Models for Analyzing Buyers" reprinted from the *Journal of Marketing,* national quarterly publication of the American Marketing Association, Volume 29, No. 4 (October, 1965).

Pierre Martineau, "Social Classes and Spending Behavior" reprinted from the *Journal of Marketing,* national quarterly publication of the American Marketing Association, Volume 23, No. 2 (October, 1958).

Daniel Seligman, "The New Masses" reprinted from the May, 1959 issue of *Fortune* Magazine by special permission; © 1959 Time Inc.

Gilbert Burck, "How American Taste Is Changing" reprinted from the July, 1959 issue of *Fortune* Magazine by special permission; © 1959 Time Inc.

iv

ACKNOWLEDGMENTS

Burt K. Scanlan, "Anthropology's Potential Role in Gauging Consumer Desires" reprinted from *Business and Society* (Spring, 1965).

Leo Burnett, "Marketing Snags and Fallacies" reprinted from the *Journal of Marketing,* national quarterly publication of the American Marketing Association, Volume 30, No. 3 (July, 1966).

Harper W. Boyd, Jr. & Sidney J. Levy, "What Kind of Corporate Objectives?" reprinted from the *Journal of Marketing,* national quarterly publication of the American Marketing Association, Volume 30, No. 4 (October, 1966).

Edward G. Koch, "New Organization Patterns for Marketing" reprinted from *Management Review,* publication of the American Management Association, Volume 52, No. 2 (February, 1962).

Raymond LeKashman & John F. Stolle, "The Total Cost Approach to Distribution" from *Business Horizons,* Volume 8, No. 4 (Winter, 1965).

Robert Bartels, "Credit Management as a Marketing Function" reprinted from the *Journal of Marketing,* national quarterly publication of the American Marketing Association, Volume 28, No. 3 (July, 1964).

Philip Kotler, "A Design for the Firm's Marketing Nerve Center" from *Business Horizons,* Volume 9, No. 3 (Fall, 1966).

Doyle L. Weiss, "Simulation for Decision Making in Marketing" reprinted from the *Journal of Marketing,* national quarterly publication of the American Marketing Association, Volume 28, No. 3 (July, 1964).

"Computers Begin to Solve the Marketing Puzzle" reprinted from the April 17, 1965, issue of *Business Week* by special permission. Copyrighted © 1965 by McGraw-Hill, Inc.

Wendell R. Smith, "Product Differentiation and Market Segmentation as Alternative Marketing Strategies" reprinted from the *Journal of Marketing,* national quarterly publication of the American Marketing Association, Volume 21, No. 1 (July, 1956).

Chester R. Wasson, "What Is 'New' About a New Product?" reprinted from the *Journal of Marketing,* national quarterly publication of the American Marketing Association, Volume 25, No. 1 (July, 1960).

Neil H. Borden, "The Growing Problems of Product Line Planning" reprinted from the *Thirty-second Annual Conference on Distribution,* October 17–18, 1960.

James W. Russell, "Developing New Products for Profit" reprinted from *Management Review,* publication of the American Management Association, Volume 47, No. 8 (August, 1958).

R. S. Alexander, "The Death and Burial of 'Sick' Products" reprinted from the *Journal of Marketing,* national quarterly publication of the American Marketing Association, Volume 28, No. 2 (April, 1964).

William R. Mason, "A Theory of Packaging in the Marketing Mix" from *Business Horizons* (Summer, 1958).

Robert S. Hancock, "Factors Motivating Consumer Choice of Private Brands" reprinted from Richard M. Hill, ed., *Marketing Concepts in Changing Times,* Proceedings From the Winter Conference of the American Marketing Association (December, 1959).

William R. Davidson, "Channels of Distribution—One Aspect of Marketing Strategy" from *Business Horizons* (February, 1961).

Perry Bliss, "Schumpeter, the 'Big' Disturbance and Retailing" from *Social Forces,* Volume 39, No. 1 (October, 1960). Copyright ©, 1960, University of North Carolina Press.

Alfred R. Oxenfeldt, "The Retailing Revolution: Why and Whither?" from the *Journal of Retailing,* publication of New York University, Volume 36, No. 3 (Fall, 1960).

Pierre Martineau, "The Personality of the Retail Store," reprinted from the *Harvard Business Review,* Volume 36, No. 1 (January–February, 1958).

Herman C. Nolen, "The Modern Wholesaler and His Adjustment to a Changing Economy" reprinted from W. David Robbins, ed., *Successful Marketing at Home and Abroad,* Proceedings of the 40th National Conference of the American Marketing Association (June, 1958).

Irving S. White, "The Functions of Advertising in Our Culture" reprinted from the *Journal of Marketing,* national quarterly publication of the American Marketing Association, Volume 24, No. 1 (July, 1959).

Edmund D. McGarry, "The Propaganda Function in Marketing" reprinted from the *Journal of Marketing,* national quarterly publication of the American Marketing Association, Volume 23, No. 2 (October, 1958).

Joel Dean, "Does Advertising Belong in the Capital Budget?" reprinted from the *Journal of Marketing,* national quarterly publication of the American Marketing Association, Volume 30, No. 4 (October, 1966).

Carl Rieser, "The Salesman Isn't Dead—He's Different" reprinted from the November, 1962 issue of *Fortune* Magazine by special permission; © 1962 Time Inc.

"Trading Stamp Tumult" reprinted with permission of *Sales Management, The Marketing Magazine* (December 1, 1966).

Joel Dean, "The Role of Price in the American Business System" reprinted from *Pricing: The Critical Decision,* A.M.A. Management Report No. 66, publication of the American Management Association.

Alfred R. Oxenfeldt, "Multi-Stage Approach to Pricing" reprinted from the *Harvard Business Review,* Volume 38, No. 4 (July–August, 1960).

Robert F. Lanzillotti, "Why Corporations Find It Necessary to 'Administer' Prices" reprinted from *Challenge, The Magazine of Economic Affairs,* Volume 8, No. 4 (January, 1960).

Ralph Cassady, Jr., "The Price Skirmish—A Distinctive Pattern of Competitive Behavior" reprinted from the *California Management Review,* Volume VII, No. 2 (Winter, 1964). Copyright 1964 by The Regents of the University of California.

To
CAROLYN AND NANCY

PREFACE

THE REVISED EDITION of *Marketing Insights,* not unlike the first edition, is designed as a supplementary collection of readings for the introductory course in marketing. Its purpose is to provide additional insight into the field of marketing. Twenty-three sources are represented, and there is a natural concentration from publications focused primarily on marketing.

In selecting from among the many worthwhile articles made available since the first edition, two criteria have been used: the extent to which the article covers an area in a perspective not typical of most texts, and the degree to which the content reflects a framework in which marketing is viewed as a dynamic area of business activity.

A major aspect of this framework is that marketing activities take place within a broad operating environment and that marketing decisions are made and implemented within this environment. A discussion of all of the factors which comprise the marketing environment is not included, because a careful effort has been made to avoid unnecessary duplication of text material.

A second factor underlying the organization and selection of the articles is that marketing activities are interdependent and decisions in any one area of marketing should be made a part of a total marketing program.

Part I, The Marketing Philosophy and Management, illustrates how the importance attached to the marketing function affects both marketing activities and the job of the marketing manager. The degree to which top management accepts a marketing viewpoint will be a significant determinant of the scope, importance, and effectiveness of marketing. To an increasing extent, top management is thinking in an international context, with vital implications for marketing management.

The articles included in Part II, The Marketing Environment, depict some of the environmental aspects which shape marketing activities and must be incorporated into marketing decisions. Some of these aspects are internal to the firm, while others comprise an external environment. Because the environment for many American firms is becoming international in scope, articles have been added which relate marketing strategies to this "new" type of environment.

Part III, Integrated Marketing Decisions, is organized into the decision-areas of product, marketing channels, promotion, and price. A new group of selections has been added to illustrate some of the more significant means by which decisions in these areas can be improved. The articles in Part III depict the interrelated nature of marketing activities, as well as the relationship of particular environmental aspects to a specific decision area. In this way, it is possible to perceive marketing activities as a part of a total marketing effort and as a result of environmental conditions.

Our appreciation is extended to the authors and publishers for permission to use the articles. All of the articles are reprinted in their entirety and in their original form. We, of course, assume responsibility for the framework in which the individual selections have been placed.

Carbondale, Illinois
and
Boulder, Colorado

R. Clifton Andersen

Philip R. Cateora

CONTENTS

C. Marketing Channels Decisions

D. Promotion Decisions

E. Price Decisions

ACQUIRING MARKETING INSIGHT

THE SPHERE OF MARKETING ACTIVITY encompasses a broad range of business operations and includes many diverse and complex activities. Acquiring insight into this vital area of business activity can be facilitated by viewing the marketing function as influenced by the philosophy of marketing, by the environment within which marketing activities take place, and by the interdependent nature of these activities. Each of these conditions determines the nature and scope of marketing.

The philosophy underlying the performance of the marketing function is an important determinant of the significance attached to marketing as a part of the firm's total operations. As new developments and concepts have been incorporated into a philosophy of marketing, more attention has been directed toward a marketing viewpoint as a basis for the successful operation of the firm.

Many of the conceptual changes that have influenced the position of marketing are reflected in the Marketing Concept. An historical perspective to the gradual evolution of this concept contributes to a better appreciation of the effect that the Marketing Concept can have upon the operations of the firm and upon the responsibilities of the marketing manager.

The character of marketing also is shaped by the environment within which marketing decisions are made and implemented. A host of factors can be identified as comprising a marketing environment. The key to effective marketing is the successful adaptation to this ever-changing environment.

The elements comprising the marketing environment can be examined in terms of the degree to which their effect upon marketing activities can be controlled by the decision-maker. Some of the environmental aspects can be viewed as internal to the firm, in that greater control can be exerted over their influence upon marketing operations. Other aspects can be considered as external to the firm and represent an influence which basically is beyond the decision-maker's control. Since the customer is the focal point of marketing action, this aspect of the environment is of particular significance. In any case, the effect of the environmental aspects must be studied carefully and must be incorporated into marketing decisions.

A final condition which influences marketing activities is the interdependent nature of these activities. An understanding of this characteristic results in viewing marketing activities as a total, coordinated effort and not merely as a series of specific independent decisions.

Marketing activities can be classified broadly into areas concerned with the product, marketing channels, promotion, and price. Although these areas can be approached individually, the emphasis should be placed upon integration into a coordinated marketing effort which is focused upon the consumer and which reflects the marketing environment.

With an understanding of the conditions affecting marketing activities comes a sharper insight into the field of marketing.

I

THE MARKETING PHILOSOPHY
AND MANAGEMENT

ONE OF THE RECENT DEVELOPMENTS in business which has had important implications for the field of marketing is the changing attitude on the part of top management toward marketing activities. Rather than being regarded as the final phase of business activities, marketing is being recognized as the beginning of business actions.

Rapidly changing markets, new technological developments, and more intense competitive conditions are among the reasons for the re-examination and the re-evaluation of the role of marketing within the firm. In order to sustain and to improve their firm's competitive position, it has been of increasing importance for management to become familiar with the marketing concept.

Information gathered as a part of a recent survey among the five-hundred largest corporations in the United States led the author to conclude: "The adoption of the marketing concept as a *conscious* top management philosophy is a new, all-important, far-reaching *management* revolution that has swept big business in the past five years and is likely to lead to a *total business* revolution in the next decade." [1]

While it is true that some firms have embraced the marketing concept for many years, the past ten years have shown a more frequent and widespread reference on the part of management to the conscious adoption of a marketing philosophy as a decision-making framework for their organizations. Terms such as "marketing concept," "marketing philosophy," and "marketing orientation to business operations," suggest a new emphasis upon marketing and broader responsibilities for the marketing manager.

The central theme of the marketing concept is customer orientation. Customer orientation says simply that decisions *start* with, as well as end with, the customer. From the inception of the product to its consumption, the activities of the firm must be sensitive to the requirements of the customer. This concept has become an operating guide, not only for the marketing manager, but also for those responsible for the total success of the business organization.

Because of rapidly changing markets, the attainment and the implementation of customer orientation is not an easy accomplishment. New and shifting consumer preferences have to be anticipated and the operations of the firm must be planned and adapted accordingly. Not only are marketing activities affected but also activities involving production capacity and techniques, personnel requirements, financial resources, et cetera.

The customer has become a major uncertainty affecting the successful operation of the firm. In order to take advantage of the profit opportunities provided by rapidly changing markets, an increasing number of business executives have considered, and in many instances have adopted, a marketing-oriented managerial philosophy.

[1] Hector Lazo, "Big Business Gives Big OK To Marketing Management," *Sales Management,* November 21, 1958, p. 35. Emphasis is Lazo's.

> Our attention has shifted from problems of production to problems of marketing, from the product we *can* make to the product the consumer *wants* us to make, from the company itself to the market place.

1

The Marketing Revolution

ROBERT J. KEITH

THE CONSUMER, not the company, is in the middle.

In today's economy the consumer, the man or woman who buys the product, is at the absolute dead center of the business universe. Companies revolve around the customer, not the other way around.

Growing acceptance of this consumer concept has had, and will have, far-reaching implications for business, achieving a virtual revolution in economic thinking. As the concept gains ever greater acceptance, marketing is emerging as the most important single function in business.

A Revolution in Science

A very apt analogy can be drawn with another revolution, one that goes back to the sixteenth century. At that time astronomers had great difficulty predicting the movements of the heavenly bodies. Their charts and computations and celestial calendars enabled them to estimate the approximate positions of the planets on any given date. But their calculations were never exact—there was always a variance.

Then a Polish scientist named Nicolaus Copernicus proposed a very simple answer to the problem. If, he proposed, we assume that the sun, and not the earth, is at the center of our system, and that the earth moves

Reprinted from the *Journal of Marketing,* national quarterly publication of the American Marketing Association, Volume 24, No. 3 (January, 1960), pp. 35-38.

around the sun instead of the sun moving around the earth, all our calculations will prove correct.

The Pole's idea raised a storm of controversy. The earth, everyone knew,
was at the center of the universe. But another scientist named Galileo put
the theory to test—and it worked. The result was a complete upheaval in
scientific and philosophic thought. The effects of Copernicus' revolutionary
idea are still being felt today.

A Revolution in Marketing

In much the same way American business in general—and Pillsbury in
particular—is undergoing a revolution of its own today: a marketing revolution.

This revolution stems from the same idea stated in the opening sentence
of this article. No longer is the company at the center of the business
universe. Today the customer is at the center.

Our attention has shifted from problems of production to problems of
marketing, from the product we *can* make to the product the consumer
wants us to make, from the company itself to the market place.

The marketing revolution has only begun. It is reasonable to expect that
its implications will grow in the years to come, and that lingering effects
will be felt a century, or more than one century, from today.

So far the theory has only been advanced, tested, and generally proved
correct. As more and more businessmen grasp the concept, and put it to
work, our economy will become more truly marketing oriented.

Pillsbury's Pattern: Four Eras

Here is the way the marketing revolution came about at Pillsbury. The
experience of this company has followed a typical pattern. There has been
nothing unique, and each step in the evolution of the marketing concept
has been taken in a way that is more meaningful because the steps are, in
fact, typical.

Today in our company the marketing concept finds expression in the
simple statement, "Nothing happens at Pillsbury until a sale is made." This
statement represents basic reorientation on the part of our management.
For, not too many years ago, the ordering of functions in our business
placed finance first, production second, and sales last.

How did we arrive at our present point of view? Pillsbury's progress in the
marketing revolution divides neatly into four separate eras—eras which
parallel rather closely the classic pattern of development in the marketing
revolution.

1ST ERA—PRODUCTION ORIENTED

First came the era of manufacturing. It began with the formation of the company in 1869 and continued into the 1930s. It is significant that the *idea* for the formation of our company came from the *availability* of high-quality wheat and the *proximity* of water power—and not from the availability and proximity of growing major market areas, or the demand for better, less expensive, more convenient flour products.

Of course, these elements were potentially present. But the two major elements which fused in the mind of Charles A. Pillsbury and prompted him to invest his modest capital in a flour mill were, on the one hand, wheat, and, on the other hand, water power. His principal concern was with production, not marketing.

His thought and judgment were typical of the business thinking of his day. And such thinking was adequate and proper for the times.

Our company philosophy in this era might have been stated this way: "We are professional flour millers. Blessed with a supply of the finest North American wheat, plenty of water power, and excellent milling machinery, we produce flour of the highest quality. Our basic function is to mill high-quality flour, and of course (and almost incidentally) we must hire salesmen to sell it, just as we hire accountants to keep our books."

The young company's first new product reveals an interesting example of the thinking of this era. The product was middlings, the bran left over after milling. Millfeed, as the product came to be known, proved a valuable product because it was an excellent nutrient for cattle. But the impetus to launch the new product came not from a consideration of the nutritional needs of cattle or a marketing analysis. It came primarily from the desire to dispose of a by-product! The new product decision was production oriented, not marketing oriented.

2ND ERA—SALES ORIENTED

In the 1930s Pillsbury moved into its second era of development as a marketing company. This was the era of sales. For the first time we began to be highly conscious of the consumer, her wants, and her prejudices, as a key factor in the business equation. We established a commercial research department to provide us with facts about the market.

We also became more aware of the importance of our dealers, the wholesale and retail grocers who provided a vital link in our chain of distribution from the mill to the home. Knowing that consumers and dealers as well were vital to the company's success, we could no longer simply mark them down as unknowns in our figuring. With this realization, we took the first step along the road to becoming a marketing company.

Pillsbury's thinking in this second era could be summed up like this: "We are a flour-milling company, manufacturing a number of products for the consumer market. We must have a first-rate sales organization which can dispose of all the products we can make at a favorable price. We must back up this sales force with consumer advertising and market intelligence. We want our salesmen and our dealers to have all the tools they need for moving the output of our plants to the consumer."

Still not a marketing philosophy, but we were getting closer.

3RD ERA—MARKETING ORIENTED

It was at the start of the present decade that Pillsbury entered the marketing era. The amazing growth of our consumer business as the result of introducing baking mixes provided the immediate impetus. But the groundwork had been laid by key men who developed our sales concepts in the middle forties.

With the new cake mixes, products of our research program, ringing up sales on the cash register, and with the realization that research and production could produce literally hundreds of new and different products, we faced for the first time the necessity for selecting the best new products. We needed a set of criteria for selecting the kind of products we would manufacture. We needed an organization to establish and maintain these criteria, and for attaining maximum sale of the products we did select.

We needed, in fact, to build into our company a new management function which would direct and control all the other corporate functions from procurement to production to advertising to sales. This function was marketing. Our solution was to establish the present marketing department.

This department developed the criteria which we would use in determining which products to market. *And these criteria were, and are, nothing more nor less than those of the consumer herself.* We moved the mountain out to find out what Mahomet, and Mrs. Mahomet, wanted. The company's purpose was no longer to mill flour, nor to manufacture a wide variety of products, but to satisfy the needs and desires, both actual and potential, of our customers.

If we were to restate our philosophy during the past decade as simply as possible, it would read: "We make and sell products for consumers."

The business universe, we realized, did not have room at the center for Pillsbury or any other company or groups of companies. It was already occupied by the customers.

This is the concept at the core of the marketing revolution. How did we put it to work for Pillsbury?

The Brand-Manager Concept. The first move was to transform our small advertising department into a marketing department. The move involved far more than changing the name on organizational charts. It required the introduction of a new, and vitally important, organizational concept—the brand-manager concept.

The brand-manager idea is the very backbone of marketing at Pillsbury. The man who bears the title, brand manager, has total accountability for results. He directs the marketing of his product as if it were his own business. Production does its job, and finance keeps the profit figures. Otherwise, the brand manager has total responsibility for marketing his product. This responsibility encompasses pricing, commercial research, competitive activity, home service and publicity coordination, legal details, budgets, advertising plans, sales promotion, and execution of plans. The brand manager must think first, last, and always of his sales target, the consumer.

Marketing permeates the entire organization. Marketing plans and executes the sale—all the way from the inception of the product idea, through its development and distribution, to the customer purchase. Marketing begins and ends with the consumer. New product ideas are conceived after careful study of her wants and needs, her likes and dislikes. Then marketing takes the idea and marshals all the forces of the corporation to translate the idea into product and the product into sales.

In the early days of the company, consumer orientation did not seem so important. The company made flour, and flour was a staple—no one would question the availability of a market. Today we must determine whether the American housewife will buy lemon pudding cake in preference to orange angel food. The variables in the equation have multiplied, just as the number of products on the grocers' shelves have multiplied from a hundred or so into many thousands.

When we first began operating under this new marketing concept, we encountered the problems which always accompany any major reorientation. Our people were young and frankly immature in some areas of business; but they were men possessed of an idea and they fought for it. The idea was almost too powerful. The marketing concept proved its worth in sales, but it upset many of the internal balances of the corporation. Marketing-oriented decisions resulted in peaks and valleys in production, schedules, labor, and inventories. But the system worked. It worked better and better as maverick marketing men became motivated toward tonnage and profit.

4TH ERA—MARKETING CONTROL

Today marketing is coming into its own. Pillsbury stands on the brink of its fourth major era in the marketing revolution.

Basically, the philosophy of this fourth era can be summarized this way: "We are moving from a company which has the marketing concept to a marketing company."

Marketing today sets company operating policy short-term. It will come

to influence long-range policy more and more. Where today consumer research, technical research, procurement, production, advertising, and sales
swing into action under the broad canopy established by marketing, tomorrow capital and financial planning, ten-year volume and profit goals will
also come under the aegis of marketing. More than any other function,
marketing must be tied to top management.

Today our marketing people know more about inventories than anyone
in top management. Tomorrow's marketing man must know capital financing and the implications of marketing planning on long-range profit forecasting.

Today technical research receives almost all of its guidance and direction
from marketing. Tomorrow marketing will assume a more creative function
in the advertising area, both in terms of ideas and media selection.

Changes in the Future. The marketing revolution has only begun. There
are still those who resist its basic idea, just as there are always those who
will resist change in business, government, or any other form of human
institution.

As the marketing revolution gains momentum, there will be more changes.
The concept of the customer at the center will remain valid; but business
must adjust to the shifting tastes and likes and desires and needs which
have always characterized the American consumer.

For many years the geographical center of the United States lay in a
small Kansas town. Then a new state, Alaska, came along, and the center
shifted to the north and west. Hawaii was admitted to the Union and the
geographical mid-point took another jump to the west. In very much the
same way, modern business must anticipate the restless shifting of buying
attitudes, as customer preferences move north, south, east, or west from
a liquid center. There is nothing static about the marketing revolution, and
that is part of its fascination. The old order has changed, yielding place to
the new—but the new order will have its quota of changes, too.

At Pillsbury, as our fourth era progresses, marketing will become the
basic motivating force for the entire corporation. Soon it will be true that
every activity of the corporation—from finance to sales to production—is
aimed at satisfying the needs and desires of the consumer. When that stage
of development is reached, the marketing revolution will be complete.

> Under marketing the customer
> becomes the fulcrum, the pivot
> point about which the business
> moves in operating for the bal-
> anced best interests of all con-
> cerned.

2

The Marketing Philosophy as a Way of Business Life

F. J. BORCH

GENTLEMEN, I CAN TELL YOU VERY SINCERELY that the combination of this title, the importance of the subject matter of this AMA session, and this outstanding audience has me more than just a little concerned. Marketing is a subject I feel very strongly about, but the prospect of coming before you gentlemen who are so familiar with its ramifications causes me to pause at this point and try to get on the same wave length as our subject—marketing—which seems to mean so many things to so many people.

As we look back over a relatively short time span—say the last 10 years—it is really surprising and somewhat remarkable to note the progress in the choice of words referring to that activity of business which focuses on the customer. "Sales," with its connotation of action, has frequently given way to "distribution," which implies a process, and now more recently we encounter "marketing"—a term in which I sense a striving for some real notion of viewpoint of purpose.

Marketing Is a Philosophy

To get some measure of the degree of the variations which we associate with the term "marketing," a survey was recently conducted by the American Management Association in an effort to get a reading on the various

An address to the American Management Association, February 4, 1957. Reproduced with permission.

11

implications of the term. Some of the responses may be of interest to us today because they show the varying opinions which exist regarding this term "marketing." About one-half the companies surveyed expressed themselves as operating with what was called a "marketing" approach. Of this group, one-fifth did not respond to the request for their definition of what they felt "marketing" really was. Of those that did indicate their companies' definitions, a very substantial majority based their definitions solely on functional operations—such as sales, market research, distribution, and the like.

I am afraid I must disagree in substantial measure with this type of marketing definition. In our Company, we feel that marketing is a fundamental business philosophy. This definition recognizes marketing's functions and methods of organizational structuring as *only the implementation* of the philosophy. These things are not, in themselves, the philosophy.

Let me digress for a moment and clear up the difference I think I see between a philosophy and a concept, because we will be referring frequently to both words and I do not want to give the impression that I am using them interchangeably. A *philosophy* is the broad umbrella that governs the total business life, while a *concept* is a recognized way of operating within the climate that the philosophy umbrella has set.

Believe me, I recognize the risk I run when I make the statement that our definition of marketing is, in reality, so broad as to constitute a business philosophy. Perhaps I can make myself more clear by explaining that fundamental to this philosophy is the recognition and acceptance of a customer-oriented way of doing business. Under marketing the customer becomes the fulcrum, the pivot point about which the business moves in operating for the balanced best interests of all concerned.

The Marketing Philosophy Is Not New

On more than one occasion I get the feeling that what we hear about marketing and customer orientation these days is being looked at as something really new. I do not think that it is. Years ago when our economy was much younger, customer orientation was a built-in feature of a business enterprise. Before the days of mass communication, national markets, and mass production, the business pioneers were cognizant of their customers and their markets. They knew their customers individually, and these individual customers formed their collective market. These predecessors of ours built their relationships through personal contact and got very rapid feedbacks of customer needs and wants. They were their own market researchers, analysts, salesmen, product planners, advertisers, and promoters. Beyond question, their businesses were customer-oriented because they knew this was the only way to run a business!

But mass production could not bring its desired economies to widely-scattered customers without taking away the ability of the maker to know personally each customer. So the maker had to devise a substitute method of contact and observation that was reliable—and this is not to say it was perfectly effective *every* time. For example:

Automobiles were made in just the color the customer wanted, as long as black was the first preference. More than one manufacturer of the old, stiff, high collars nearly went broke trying to sell his product, long after customer preferences had shifted toward today's softer varieties. It took World War II silk shortages to convince many stocking manufacturers that nylons really were preferred to silk.

Those companies that have successfully grown are those which were quick to recognize their departure from a true understanding of the customer. It would certainly be valid to point out that as a company grows in size, its potential ability to drift away from customer orientation grows proportionately. Similarly, as its size increases, so does its necessity for this awareness. What we refer to today as the marketing philosophy is a recognition of just this situation.

Understanding of Two Key Fundamentals Is Necessary

Full appreciation of the marketing philosophy demands an understanding of the two key fundamentals on which it rests:

The first is an understanding of what I call the dual core job of marketing. The initial part of this dual core job is that we in marketing must focus our businesses on the customer's needs and desires, including those needs and desires that the customer is *not* aware of as well as those he knows all too well. It will be only after identification of these needs that marketing people can take the lead for the business in determining what each function of the business should do by way of product and service to satisfy them.

The other half of the dual core job for marketing is one that we are familiar with—namely, the need to persuade the prospective customer through all the arts of selling and advertising, to purchase the products and services which have been developed.

The second fundamental on which the marketing philosophy rests is that it is rooted in the profit concept, not the volume concept. (I am not eliminating the use of volume as a rewarding way of obtaining profits from the efficiency of the service rendered—I am referring to the profitless volume or volume-for-the-sake-of-volume-alone concept.) This is so basic that I am not going to dwell on it, but will simply restate that the acceptance of the profit concept rather than the volume concept as a way of business life is the second part of the marketing philosophy.

Forces Contributing to a Rapid Evolution of the Marketing Philosophy

I think each of us will accept the fact that the marketing philosophy is not coming into being without an interplay of forces from the economic, social, and political environments of our times. A partial listing of these forces would include:

- The three different competitions: Product *vs.* product competition (soap against soap); Cross-line product competition (where the new mink coat competes with the second car); and Cross-line technological competition (where aircraft companies start building canoes).
- Specialization (the expert in a highly vertical type of responsibility who knows everything about his field, little about others).
- Diversification (the move into new and varied product lines).
- Complexity (the faster pace and increased number of functions).
- Automation (the automatic factory which leads to a highly rigidized product).
- The Efficiency Urge (the emphasis on getting the most rewarding return on our investment).

Each of these forces is a contributor to accelerating the development of the marketing philosophy. However, out of these, and others I have not isolated, we can see three problem areas of business where an awareness of the marketing philosophy may help us over what otherwise could be insurmountable hurdles:

First, our rapidly changing customer, whose wants are multiplying at a terrific rate. In the consumer goods businesses this problem is a direct result of our standard of living, which provides an ever-mounting variety of goods, with a constantly diminishing compulsion to purchase any of them. As a result, the sales volume of individual products is being increasingly influenced by competitive pressures, rather than by the consumer's own requirements for survival. In 1800, 75 percent of a working man's expenditures went for food alone, and only 8 percent for products other than housing, fuel, clothing, and food. Today, that 8 percent has grown to 48 percent with half of this increase coming in the last 30 years—and it represents the growing discretionary control of the consumer that makes modern advertising so necessary, and causes mink coats to compete with cars, vacations with appliances, and a host of similar phenomena.

In the producer goods field, the equivalent problem is posed by the

rapid development of our technology and the competitive pressure for reduction of manufacturing costs. This has given rise to alternate product
competition that crosses over former industrial boundaries, so that plastics
and metals, hydraulics and electronics, carbon and atomic fuels vie to dis-
place each other. From the standpoint of marketing, the number of things
to be forecast is infinitely complicated—and the difficulties of getting the
right facts, weighing them in proper balance, and making the best decisions
with respect to product and distribution policy becomes terrific. Yet, if
we work both sides of the street and hedge all bets, the resulting increase
in our costs may ruin us more quickly than the alternate risks that drive
us to cover. Net result is that the most rapidly growing feature of business
is our opportunity for error in planning how to please our ever changing
customer.

The *second* major problem—we cannot fail to notice that the amount
of resources which must be committed to implement marketing decisions
is rising rapidly. All costs are tending to become more fixed—be they costs
of automated plants or costs of national distribution structures. But by
far the more serious side of these trends is not what is happening to our
costs, but what is happening to our freedom of action. We are increasing
our *capacity* to act at the expense of our *freedom* to act when we freeze
the design of the product in the interests of further mechanization, and
when we freeze the distribution structure, the media we use and the message we impart in the interests of achieving a nation-wide impact.

Consequently, the price of errors in basic marketing decisions is not
only the cost of producing the wrong product at the wrong time for the
wrong market, but the loss of our resources and the loss of further capacity
to correct our errors. It is small wonder, then, that the risk-taking vigor
and spirit of our fathers has given way to increasing concern with management decisions and controls which seek to avoid and limit risk—yet the
mounting costs of checking and double-checking and postponing and revising may ruin us more quickly than the consequences of a wrong decision. Net result—the price of the wrong decision is growing at as fast a
rate as the opportunity to make the wrong decision!

The *third* problem—in addition to the steady rise in the opportunities
for error (caused by the mounting alternatives of the customer) and in the
price of error (caused by the mounting cost of plant and distribution
structures) we are plagued with greater difficulties in our internal communication and decision process. When our organizations have to reach
out for more and more customers in order to pass the break-even point in a
competitive market, the structural machinery for getting information delivered and decisions made must be more and more diligently watched to
assure keeping continually in phase with requirements.

In addition to the three problems we have discussed, I would like to touch on a few others—the preparation of new plants, products, and promotions requires increasing decision lead time which certainly adds a burden to accurate forecasting. And as specialization grows, the number of employees who understand any *whole* situation and can make any *whole* decisions keeps shrinking. So it is that an organization unexpectedly discovers that it is in new businesses, that the sales plan in operation seems quite different from anything planned on paper, and that the standing joke in the district office is the one about "it's just policy." Decentralization and divisionalization are the only answers, but unless very carefully planned and timed, they too cost money.

What Management Can Expect from the Marketing Philosophy

We have been covering in more than a little detail the marketing philosophy and its implementation. Understanding of this is important, but now, I would like to depart from the philosophical and discuss the payoff phase—the answer to the question of what the marketing philosophy can produce in terms of creating sounder business management that can better face the problems we have just posed.

Fortunately, we are gaining enough experience to see some answers developing to the question of marketing's contributions to management. They include:

RESPONSIBILITIES

Many functional areas which were previously floaters—or loosely assigned to more than one individual with resultant confusion or lack of action—can be isolated, assigned and measured in terms of effectiveness.

The business' creative planning can be partially delegated into responsible hands, assuring a customer-orientation to business plans and strategies.

DECISIONS

Decisions made without the customer focus can do irreparable harm to a business. And, unfortunately, such decisions usually multiply and additional wrong ones are made in a vain attempt to correct the earlier ones. For example, this happens all too frequently in situations like these:

1. When we protect the losing sales channel at the expense of extra promotion, trying to make water run uphill without any consideration of whether the customer is better served by such action.

2. When we similarly protect the losing technology and fail to shift over to the new technology that better serves the customer.

3. When we try and minimize the risk by combining ventures which really do not fit insofar as their marketing requirements are concerned, involving the extra decision on the cost of ironing out the constant collision of objectives involved in keeping the two activities out of each other's hair at the marketing level.

4. When in an effort to get further specialized attention on the difficult forecasting problems, we make the mistake of duplicating overhead organization on lines that are really the same, without getting any benefit out of the extra cost thus incurred.

COORDINATION

Coordination is brought into play early, when it is *most effective* because functions such as product design, pricing and engineering development must *start* with a clear understanding of the customer situation as it relates to these areas. This market-place understanding can eliminate much of the time an executive spends in reconciling plans for each function of the business because they have not been prepared with a previously understood common objective.

Another distinct advantage which is difficult to categorize might best be called a tightening of the time lag between decision and action. For example, if the marketing strategy is to go all out for volume, market position, or product quality—the *entire force of the business* can be quickly harnessed to support such a decision *if* the business is being operated under customer-orientation.

Indications of the Need for the Marketing Philosophy

I would like to run through just a few questions which we have found we can answer with a surprisingly greater degree of accuracy with a marketing organization that is really operating under the marketing philosophy. You may find these helpful as a check list to determine how many such answers your business has.

- Do I really know the *fundamental* rather than *symptomatic* reasons for declining or increasing trends in my dollar volume?

- What is my market's growth potential? Do I have a clear indication, based on more than educated guessing, on what it will be in five years? In ten years? In twenty years? Will I be prepared facility-wise to meet this future market?

- Is my existing market one that could be quickly eliminated by a major technological breakthrough? If so, what plans do we have if this should happen?

- Do I know whether product diversification would benefit my company? If it would, do I have a *planned* program of diversification by either product and market development, or by acquisition? What criteria do I have to help me decide which product lines and markets I should be in?

- Are my business planning and strategy decisions taking into consideration the knowledge of the people who *really* know and understand my customer?

- Do I make and develop markets?

- Do I predict inventory levels with any degree of success? Or, am I plagued with over and under inventories, layoffs and overtime?

- Do I really make my own business decisions? Or are others making them for me?

I leave you to ponder these—as we do.

How These Trends and Challenges Can Be Translated into Business Opportunities

I should now like to examine with you a couple of real-life situations where a real understanding of the marketing philosophy as a way of business life, plus adherence to sound objectives and willingness to take risks by making sweeping changes focused on the customer, brought results. That these two case histories come from my own Company is no cause for boasting on my part because I only wish that they were more typical. Nevertheless, they do demonstrate that if we are willing to take the risk of thinking the marketing job through from the standpoint of increasing consumable value for the customer, the opportunities for increasing our marketing efficiency in adding to profits are tremendous. I shall start with the story of the vacuum cleaner.

This was the situation faced by our Vacuum Cleaner Department in 1951:

- We were practically unrecognized in the industry, with only a minor percent share of the market.

- We had no unique product identification to form the basis of our advertising and selling appeals. In fact, we had no national advertising.

Certainly, these are not admissions of strength. Equally important, profitable businesses are not built on this sort of foundation.

Our people at this point applied a marketing approach and attempted to identify the difficulties from the customer's viewpoint. This is what they found.

First, vacuum cleaners were priced at levels that were high relative to other appliances, a major factor in keeping the market saturation percentage far below that of other appliances.

Second, distribution was not adequate, with only 30 percent of vacuum cleaners being sold through retailers and the rest door-to-door. From the housewife's standpoint, this meant that when she was in most retail appliance stores, she found practically every other home appliance except the vacuum cleaner.

Third, a large number of models was offered by each manufacturer. This had two serious negative effects—the housewife was confused and manufacturing costs were reflecting the high additional costs of multi-model production.

Our product was a compromise between engineering's ideas on what a vacuum cleaner should do and manufacturing's thinking on how it should be made. Everyone seemingly had a hand in the product *except* the customer.

Our action to overcome these problems was based entirely on the application of the marketing philosophy, and I would like to group the results of these activities in relation to the customer, the dealer, and the management people in this Department.

First, to the *customer:*

- Through product improvements and the decision to concentrate on a single model, rather than the 15 we were previously offering, our prices were lowered. Surveys have shown that even today most housewives do not yet realize that they can buy a good vacuum for under $100. Consequently, we feel that we made a contribution to the consumer in widely advertising our best selling model last year at $49.95.

- Cleaners are now available in practically every retail outlet normally handling home appliances, and product repair service is improved.

- Cleaners are now better-designed, performing household tasks more efficiently under the concept of cleaning the entire home rather than merely the rug.

I should like to point out that these things were by no means accomplished solely by General Electric. We applied the marketing philosophy to this business, and so did others with a resulting increase in competition that really brought about these customer benefits.

To the *dealer,* this change meant, first of all, the addition of a profitable line to his business. Today, the vacuum cleaner is the fifth or sixth largest of all appliance businesses in terms of retail dollars. Broadly speaking, it could not have been considered a dealer business prior to 1946.

It may be interesting to point out here that in spite of the fact that 70 percent of sales had been door-to-door, the sales increases for G.E. and the industry came from new business originating through retailers rather than at the expense of the door-to-door people.

We estimate that vacuum cleaner sales by manufacturers selling door-to-door have increased slightly since 1951, but sales of the total industry have risen an estimated 33 percent from 1951 to 1956. During this period, market saturation has increased from 50 to 65 percent. These changes have been due, we feel, to the efforts of companies like ourselves that have adopted the marketing approach. Planned market growth is one of the major contributions this philosophy can make to the business.

How did the marketing philosophy help this Department's *management?* Let me request that you bear in mind the scope of the decisions these men were facing:

- They were going to make a complete shift in the historical methods of vacuum cleaner distribution, attempting to build a major market with a type of mass distribution that never had been successfully used with this product.

- They were going to eliminate all but one model from their line and face competition with a single model offering. And, on top of this, they were committed to marketing's real responsibility to help run the business in a profitable manner.

The most important single contribution of marketing was to give the people who had to make these decisions the confidence that they were being made on firm understanding of the customer's wants. The shift to customer orientation had convinced these men that they could proceed from a position of knowledge and market-place strength.

All of the management advantages that I have cited earlier apply to this Department, and these specific ones can be added:

- The isolation and assigning of the product planning and market research responsibilities has built leadership in the market, and subsequent decisions are being made on the basis of a sound analysis of what we *knew* was needed by the customer.

- Engineering and manufacturing quickly oriented their activities to the requirements of the customer, with some revolutionary results in terms of new product offerings which had helped expand not only our business, but the total market.

- Planning is now long-range rather than year-to-year or, in some instances, day-to-day.

- The general manager and marketing manager are free to devote more of their time to the *fundamental* problems of the business, because much of the work they previously handled is now the responsibility of the marketing staff.

- Investments in advertising and sales promotion (and they are high in this industry) are made more wisely because the copy and scripts reflect the real sales appeals that market research and customer awareness have proved to be effective.

And, dealers are selling with the same story that advertising tells, because the job of integrating advertising and sales has been made more effective. Equally important, engineers now design the product with the requirements of television advertising and the dealer's showroom in mind.

I should also point out that the acceptance by our engineering and manufacturing people of the need for these changes as they affected the product was tremendous. They rose, in no small way, to the challenge and made these plans realities.

You will note that this case is an illustration of the application of the marketing philosophy to a consumer goods business. At this point, I should state that we feel that the philosophy applies with equal validity to all kinds of business, and I shall illustrate this in my second case history which involves an industrial product. You will note, however, that while the philosophy is the same, the methods of implementation vary quite substantially.

Our Meter Department is a good example of this. In this business we were also fortunate to have made the decision to operate under the marketing philosophy.

Let me quickly describe the kind of business this is. It has one major product—the watt-hour-meter for measuring industrial and consumer electrical power consumption. Fifty-four million units are now in use. It has one primary group of customers—electrical utilities, and the market is relatively inelastic. (Demand is in relation to new homes and plants plus some replacement business.) It has an abnormally high engineering content in the product. And, perhaps most important for this discussion— product advantages constitute the major brand preference motivation.

We believe we have held a position of leadership in this field, but about two years ago we were quite surprised to find that on more-than-what-could-be-considered a normal number of occasions, our competitors were making some of our important product decisions for us. This situation came about, frankly, because to a degree we were losing our cognizance of the customer's needs. In recognizing this, we put the marketing philosophy to a severe test.

In a business where success depends almost solely on knowing precisely what the customer needs, and the subsequent satisfaction of those needs, there could be no substitute for the real knowledge the marketing way of operation gave us. The people managing this business got us back on the track in a hurry—and this year, in a business that has historically never announced more than one product innovation annually, we will be announcing several. And, we were able to bridge the gap between identifying customer's real wants and translating these into product innovations within less than two years.

As with the vacuum cleaner business, I am sure that the customer orientation of the key men in the department is responsible for our having in two years changes which normally would have taken much longer. Certainly this is a departure from the old make-it, sell-it days which we have all lived through. Today, the engineering and manufacturing managers in the Department recognize fully that their contributions must be in terms of product innovations which are incorporated into our watt-hour-meters before a competitor introduces them.

Because these product changes are not all yet announced, I'd like to refer to a previous example to show the type of integration the marketing philosophy can help bring to a business. Not long ago it took us more than 18 months to redesign our watt-hour-meter to increase capacity from 60 to 100 amps. We recently raised the capacity of these same meters from 100 to 200 amps. This was a much more difficult job than the original incremental raise, and it was accomplished in less than 12 months, pointing out again the tremendous cooperation demonstrated by the engineering and manufacturing people in helping to really make this work.

These higher ratings have answered a very definite utility need, and had it not been for the superimposition of the customer awareness and closely integrated type of operation the marketing philosophy had given this department, they could well be lagging their competitors. I should like to emphasize that competition in this field is very heavy in terms of alertness and ability. One does not doze off and retain leadership for very long in any phase of the electrical industry with which I'm familiar. (In fact, there aren't many businesses today where this can be done!)

In addition to the advantages we have already discussed, the management people in this Department realized many others. (For the sake of brevity, I shall not repeat any which we have discussed earlier with the Vacuum Cleaner Department.) The others worthy of note include:

With responsibility for finished goods inventories and production requirements in the hands of the marketing manager, production is closely tied to the real needs of the market and excessive inventories are kept at a minimum. This also assures more employment stability through a definite dampening effect on personnel increases and decreases due to poorly forecasted production requirements.

The marketing manager operates as a business manager assuming his share of the responsibility of setting the required business strategies and objectives.

A concept has been developed of selling not the product, but the function that the product performs. To be specific, these men do not consider themselves in the device business; they are in the business of measuring electrical power revenue for utilities.

These two case histories have demonstrated the fundamentals we discussed earlier and they show clearly that the decisions that increase value to the customer also increase sales. They also show the impact that the philosophy can make by contributing to the strategy decisions and, concurrently, by augmenting the sales concept. To me—and to put it quite simply—the sales concept alone concerns itself primarily with volume. Marketing means customer orientation—a true alliance with the fellow at the other end of the pipeline, but it insists upon a course of action of mutual benefit.

Gentlemen, if we organize our policies around these factors which are mutually important to the customer and to our profits, we will find a real community of interest between the producer and the consumer. This is the Marketing philosophy, and its realization and practice can change the way of life in the world no less than did the industrial revolution of many years ago.

Leadership in American marketing is no guarantee of leadership abroad.

3

Creating a Strategy for International Growth

JOHN G. McDONALD

&

HUGH PARKER

GROWING NUMBERS of American companies are spreading their wings abroad. The roster includes not just small- and medium-size manufacturing companies, but some of the largest and most powerful firms in the country. "By 1970, some 50 percent of our profit will come from overseas operations," predicts the chief of a large diversified company. Du Pont, which once restricted production to this continent, is now producing in Holland, Belgium, and Northern Ireland. The Campbell Soup Company has launched a $30 million assault aimed at capturing a major share of the growing European food market, and I.B.M. World Trade is growing even faster than its ebullient U.S. parent.

The blue-ribbon list goes on and on. Some one thousand American companies have established postwar operations in Europe, most within the past four years. A recent McGraw-Hill survey indicates that the investment plans of American companies called for a $1.7 billion addition to plant and equipment overseas in 1961, 25 percent more than in 1960. The census of private U.S. investments abroad, recently released by the Department of Commerce, shows that during the year of the census (1957) U.S. firms

McKinsey and Co., Inc., Management Consultants; based on an article that originally appeared in *Business Horizons,* 1962.

abroad paid wages and salaries of nearly $7 billion, employed about 3 million people, and spent about $17 billion for materials and services. This international flow of funds and goods is becoming one of the most important economic forces in the world today.

Companies set up manufacturing facilities abroad for a variety of reasons. Some want to enjoy the rapid growth offered by expanding foreign markets. Others seek to reduce their production costs with an eye to worldwide exports—including exports to the United States.

Not long ago, the stay-at-home competitors of these "internationalists" would have been unconcerned with these moves, but things have changed. Today many stay-at-homes see a threat to their home market position and the possibility of being blocked out of increasingly interesting foreign markets. Some companies are already being harassed in their domestic markets by low-cost goods produced abroad by their U.S. rivals (the 1957 census showed imports of $1 billion from overseas enterprises of U.S. companies). And there is now the prospect of tax and tariff changes that may further cloud their futures.

As a reaction to these threats, actual or potential, many companies are establishing beachheads of their own abroad. Thus for many reasons, some offensive, others defensive, the flood of American companies overseas continues to grow.

Here, based on our own experience and the experience of others, is a report on what these companies find in the way of risks and opportunities, and how they create strategies to minimize these risks.

Special Problems in Moving Abroad

Setting up a new production base and marketing organization abroad is far more risky than establishing a new business at home. Manufacture abroad means that large sums of money are invested in plant and equipment for a long period of time in an alien, often changing environment. Management effort and personnel problems take on new dimensions, and profits can sometimes have a long lead time in a new land.

In his home market, the executive moves with ease and confidence; he knows the ground rules. Distribution patterns, trade terms, nuances of consumer tastes and preferences, and competitors' strengths and weaknesses are second nature to him; his judgment in this familiar environment is usually sound, since he operates under a set of fairly stable economic and political conditions. But many of the comfortable assumptions that the executive uses at home may not hold true overseas. In some ways, this is to the good. It permits him to view situations with different eyes and thus grasp opportunities that others do not see. Drawing from domestic experience, he may spot the early signs of a trend for convenience items, packaged foods, or new appliances; or he may see the chance to apply a proven technique in a new situation. But he may also stub his toe. He may assume that foreign consumers react in the American pattern, or he may assume that practices that were successful at home will work equally well abroad. As a result, both the risks and opportunities resulting from executive action abroad are often greater than they would be at home. (See special section, *Keys to Marketing Success Abroad,* at end of article.)

Risk comes in many guises and varies from country to country. The political situation, governmental control, or a market unready for a product may be all-important. Several years ago, General Motors, whose European and Australian subsidiaries are currently booming, shut down an expensive assembly plant in India. A prime factor in this painful decision was the unforeseen political climate and the effect of governmental control. In another instance, an American consumer-goods producer moved too soon; after establishing a plant in Belgium, he then found the market was not ready for its product. As a result, he has been conducting an expensive holding operation for the past three years.

Most companies have moved abroad too recently to know how well they will do in the long run, but reports are beginning to filter back. Some companies have been eminently successful, others have run into trouble, and still others have had both successes and failures in different countries. Clearly, long-term success or failure depends on the way a company moves into its overseas adventure. Once a company decides to move and invest abroad, it faces a basic problem: How does it plan its moves to take advantage of obvious opportunities at minimum risk?

Stages of Foreign Involvement

The evolution of a domestic company into a functioning world enterprise normally follows four distinct but overlapping stages.

- *Stage one:* Export-import activity with a minimum of change in management outlook, company organization, or product line.
- *Stage two:* Foreign licensing and the international movement of technical know-how, still with little impact on domestic operations or management outlook.
- *Stage three:* Establishment of overseas operations. At this point the company makes substantial international investments in funds and management time, and begins to develop special international skills. But still the domestic operations remain essentially unaffected.
- *Stage four:* Emergence as a world enterprise with an integrated global approach encompassing both domestic and overseas operations.

These stages may be passed through one at a time, or any one can be bypassed. It is even possible to find a company with its various parts involved in all four at once. But as a rule, the take-off point for moving abroad occurs when a company makes the decision to risk large investments on the prospects of becoming a world enterprise.

It is important that a company re-examine its position at take-off, for it may well have some built-in obstacles to a successful launching of an overseas manufacturing operation. One company, about to enter stage three, fortunately identified such an obstacle in its organizational pattern in time to avoid any delays in achieving its goal. At the take-off point, the company had a group of "international" specialists organized in two departments—exporting and licensing—under one international executive. Ironically, the project team responsible for studying the feasibility of moving abroad found most resistance from the place it expected most support, the export and licensing departments. With the export department already feeling the squeeze from competition built up by the license department, it naturally resisted schemes to squeeze its profits further. Similarly, the licensing department was not cooperating since it foresaw some adverse effects on its profits if single subsidiaries were to replace its numerous licenses in various countries. To surmount this obstacle, changes had to be made in organization and profit responsibility.

Earlier licensing agreements or exclusive distribution rights can also cripple moves overseas. One manufacturer of marine equipment is doing fairly well in Europe, but is encountering tough competition from a German company, which was "educated" with patent exchanges and a licensing agreement several years ago. Many companies that would now like to move abroad are locked out of certain countries by exclusive licensing agreements that seemed wise, low-risk profitable decisions just a few years ago.

When top management is alert to some of these environmental and strategic problems, it can develop sound organizational plans and safeguards in advance of a move abroad. Step-by-step international experience can became a major asset if it gives a company this foresight. But if top management does not plan its business ahead, existing international activities and agreements can be a major obstacle.

How Companies Make Their Moves Abroad

Some companies have been content to move abroad without much planning and have done well; some have been disappointed. Other companies have evolved standard and, in some cases, fairly sophisticated approaches.

THE UNPLANNED APPROACH

The decision to move into a given country at any time may be based almost entirely on chance. Perhaps the company president has been to the country and likes it, or he may know businessmen there. Many such moves are made in response to an invitation. One successful electronic relay company, with little interest in foreign adventures, was recently approached by a European company about setting up a joint venture. Intrigued by the possibility, the American company joined the enterprise and decided other moves would be made "after we've experimented a bit." A company with a patented line was recently approached by a Wall Street finance group with this suggestion: "We have been contacted by a company that is convinced there's a real opportunity for your product in Europe. If you are ever interested in moving, let us know."

An increasing number of companies have gone abroad recently in response to just such random opportunities. Reasons given include: "Our competitors have done so," or "our suppliers are moving," or "we've been offered an interesting opportunity, but it won't be available for long."

Sometimes this random and essentially "one shot" approach works quite well. Dozens of companies that are now successfully established overseas virtually tumbled into their present spots. But, as the following examples show, the inherent risks are numerous.

Some companies have experimented with moving idle production equipment and setting up shop in another country. Certainly there is a worldwide market for much secondhand U.S. manufacturing equipment, but setting up a subsidiary with an obsolete plant can backfire. Local companies are equipping themselves with the latest devices and can sometimes outproduce and outprice a U.S. subsidiary saddled with old machinery. This is happening in electronics, where rising European manufacturers are using the latest automated equipment.

One Midwestern heavy equipment manufacturer, spotting what looked like a fine opportunity to enter the European market, bought up a good-sized French company in the same field. The French concern looked good on paper, but it was actually a high-cost operation on the verge of losing important markets. The Americans apparently looked at past performance, not at future trends. They took over just as the new property started down the roller coaster and have poured in over a million dollars trying to salvage it.

An American hospital equipment firm without experience in Europe was approached by a small Dutch manufacturer. By bidding for U.S. military supply contracts, the Dutch company had obtained plans and specifications for special equipment identical to that made by the American company, and was producing this equipment—with improvements. The Dutch owner asked the Americans whether they were interested in a joint venture in Europe. The Americans were impressed by the man; they were not only interested in the idea of growth abroad, but were anxious to avoid further competition in a saturated home market. They took a minority interest in the Dutch venture—and watched their cash investment sink out of sight. It turned out that the European company, which had been a very low-cost producer before the U.S. investment, used the added capital to convert from a "garage operation" to a plant operation. The company thereby became a high-cost producer in a beautiful home, but found it could not break even on its low sales volume. With little likelihood of gaining more volume in a hurry, the joint venture developed an insatiable demand for dollars. In addition, the joint venture agreement prevented the American company, now wiser, from tackling the European market on its own.

COUNTRY-BY-COUNTRY ANALYSIS

Unplanned approaches have sometimes paid off, but their often fatal drawback is the absence of any analysis of alternatives. As companies realize this, a number who have already made some moves overseas have evolved a more systematic approach.

An overseas veteran has a standard approach for analyzing the feasibility of manufacturing in a specific country. Basically, this involves three steps taken in the order listed:

- The home office conducts desk research on the market, briefly reviewing reference material available in the U.S., plus its own past international experience and intelligence. This step gives top management a quick reading on the investment required and the possible financial returns. (It also gives management an estimate of the budget, in terms of time, men, and money, required to complete the investigation.)
- If the investment looks profitable, a marketing man makes an on-the-spot investigation. In addition to studying the market, he obtains answers to questionnaires supplied by the manufacturing and financial people. This results in a "first approximation," or feasibility, report.
- An on-the-spot confirmation study by a small task force (including a senior member of management) results in the "second and final approximation" report and, later, actual investment, postponement, or rejection of a project.

This type of approach—a study of key information at home followed by on-the-spot investigation of special factors in the target country—is becoming common. It is a useful, and almost textbook-perfect approach. Unfortunately, it can yield critically misleading results. The reason is that no country is so self-sufficient that it is not affected by trends in world trade; therefore, the optimum decision for a single country might be fatal in view of capabilities and economic trends in other countries. If one looks at each country individually, for example, it may seem perfectly sensible to establish manufacturing plants in Italy, Germany, and France. In view of the

increasing integration of European economies, a better solution might be to
build one large plant.

A New Approach—Global Planning

A few companies, some American and some European, are building new
approaches that minimize the risks of moving abroad. Generally, these
approaches begin with one of the fundamentals of good planning—understanding the ultimate goal—and come under the term "global planning."

Global planning assumes that the ultimate objective of any company
taking the first move overseas is to expand later without encountering any
obstacles created by its first move. It also assumes that the chief executive
is willing to extend the scope of his responsibility. Before making any move,
he will ask: Where in the world should I invest my company's time, manpower, and funds for the best long-term interests of our stockholders?

A CASE EXAMPLE

Here is a step-by-step account of how one major company went about
global planning.

Phase one. The company appointed a select executive committee to formulate the company's worldwide policies and strategic plans. This global
planning committee began by making decisions to:

1. Familiarize all members of corporate management with the principles of a
   world enterprise so that they would all know the company's ultimate international goals.
2. Concentrate the company's initial expansion in countries that were already developed industrially.
3. Consider the world as four basic areas: North America, South America,
   Europe (and Africa), and the Far East.
4. Assign priority to study of the whole European area—since Europe represents the bulk of the industrial free world outside the U.S.—to identify
   opportunities and ways of capitalizing on them.
5. Place a moratorium on all foreign licensing and joint-venture opportunities throughout the world until this study was complete.

Then, one of the senior executives from the global planning committee
was named vice president for European operations and was assigned the
task of developing a strategy for the company's entry into Europe. After
getting approval of a set of ground rules (the amount of money the company was willing to invest, a policy on bringing European products into
the U.S., and so forth), he then appointed a task force to lay out a plan of
action and prepare a budget.

Phase two. The task force laid out the plan of action for the next three phases. During *phase two* the committee examined the export and licensing agreements to see if any exclusive selling or manufacturing rights had been granted that would prevent the company from operating in certain European countries. Also, from data available in the U.S., the committee identified countries with potential markets and laid its plans for European field work. This preparatory work included developing interview guides (standardized to facilitate later consolidation of individual interviewers' results) based on the market indicators used in the U.S.; studying the history of industry in the U.S. in order to identify the stage of maturity that the industry had reached in Europe; determining the factors governing the success of various products in the ·U.S., in preparation for checking to see whether the same factors applied in Europe; and, finally, working out a detailed schedule of fact-finding.

Phase three. Next came fact-finding in Europe. The objectives were to review general economic and political conditions in Europe as a whole and then in each major country; to perform an economic study of the company's industry in Europe as a whole, and then a more detailed study of the countries identified with major investments in this industry; and to analyze how well the company's strengths and position had already been established in the area through previous export and licensing activities.

The economic analysis of the firm's industry in Europe showed that the countries producing this equipment could be divided into those of major importance and those of minor importance. The major producers—England, West Germany, France, and Italy—had large local markets. The major producers were also the major suppliers for the minor producers and the nonproducing countries. The industry in each of the four major-producer countries was then studied in depth, and two representative countries in the minor-producer group were examined to see what factors were essential for success in such a market.

The economic analysis of the industry in each of the four major-producer countries included growth trends and potential markets for local production, exports, and imports, plus the structure, relative importance, and trends of the major sectors. It also included the relative importance and trends in product groups in each sector and in their end-user industries, as well as key factors for success—importance of local service and installation facilities, and the need for a corporate image as an indigenous company. The study looked at any obstacles to entry and the general requirements of the field—large investment, unique patented product, and long established engineering reputation.

Phase four. The stage was now set for *phase four,* the development of a long-term operational strategy for capitalizing on the opportunities defined in the fact-finding phase and for sidestepping any adverse effects of economic interaction between the countries. Separate strategies were developed for the major-producer countries and minor-producer countries. Major-producer countries, where local production was likely to offer serious competition, demanded strategy involving the establishment or acquisition of local production facilities. The strategy for the minor and nonproducer countries, which offered no sizable local markets, was to rely on imports from the U.S. or from European sources.

Another part of phase four was development of a statutory plan, once the operational strategy and organization had been defined. The operational strategy defined what had to be done, where companies had to be set up, and where distribution or licensing had to be performed. With the operational organization defined, it was possible to mold a statutory organization—that is, a system of ownership links—that would provide the most effective cash flow. In this case, the statutory organization consisted of a headquarters in Switzerland, with the ownership of various subsidiaries linked so that the company could capitalize on tax and other statutory advantages. Since tax laws and regulations are subject to constant change, the statutory plans were recognized as temporary; actions that could endanger flexibility were avoided.

Plans for establishing the European operations also involved company-wide changes. Organization patterns, management information and control systems, and procedures for evaluating new investment proposals had to be reoriented so that, in major company deliberations, Europe was always considered as a possible alternative. Once these changes were agreed upon—and only then—positive moves were made to establish new activities abroad.

MAJOR ADVANTAGES

Some of the major advantages of global planning are these:

- Setting long-range objectives and developing a long-term strategy before moving abroad enables a company to coordinate all the interim moves so that they do not cancel each other.

- Investigating a whole area in depth enables a company to take action in as many countries as desired, so that later integration can be achieved with a minimum of expensive overlapping and duplication.

- Developing statutory plans ahead of time gives a company a framework for making country-by-country decisions that will permit later shifts in cash flow without serious consequences (for example, capital gains tax on transfer of appreciated equity ownership).

In effect, the global approach has provided the essential key to long-range planning in the internationalization of American business.

PITFALLS IN GLOBAL PLANNING

Like any technique, global planning has its dangers; these stem mainly from some form of misapplication.

One case of superficial application occurred when a billion-dollar corporation, with a few haphazardly placed overseas activities, decided to use the global planning technique to assess the feasibility of its conversion to a world enterprise. Its international division in New York was very powerful politically and, as a peace offering, was allowed to retain all existing remote control powers over foreign subsidiaries. In other words, the company went through the motions of appointing area managers for the various regions of the world, but they were virtually powerless since every decision still had to be referred back to corporate executives in New York.

The new area manager for Europe was not given a budget to perform a fact-finding study that would enable him to reappraise and coordinate the company's existing activities, which were spread thinly across Europe. As a result, it was not long before he found that many of the company's subsidiaries were launching new products just because "New York had advised them to do so" and not because they were appropriate for Europe. In effect, therefore, the company had remained domestically oriented while giving lip service to global planning.

Another company ostensibly adopted global planning but continued to allow its domestic divisions to encourage visits from foreign buyers of their products. As a result, the man assigned to set up operations in the European area was constantly being sidetracked in order to chase down special situations for the strong domestic divisions.

Cases of misapplication of global planning also result when a company succumbs to "international fever." This reportedly happened in one Midwestern consumer company. Shortly after a special team had been selected to set up operations in Europe, the team's attractive itinerary caught the eyes of other firm members. Soon letters from hitherto unknown distributors began reaching the company from Asia and South America—each letter suggesting that the company send a man to look over the "fabulous" opportunities in the writer's country. As it turned out, random opportunities did exist in Hong Kong and Brazil. In effect, the global planning technique had been applied partially—that is, in Europe—while plans for the rest of the world resulted from the old unplanned approach. This led to a conflict of interest. One of the European companies that had been selected for acquisition had subsidiaries in the Far East that competed with a property the international division was negotiating for in Hong Kong.

In summary, too often corporate moves overseas are motivated more than a little by the fad to go abroad. Admittedly, real pressures to move overseas are mounting, but the consequences of poor analysis and false moves in this rapidly changing world can be painful. Approaches based on short-term thinking are not sufficient. Any move overseas must be looked upon as an integral part of a clearly defined long-range goal.

There is no magic formula for successful global planning, but companies that do it well do possess and make use of one open secret. This is the understanding that only the company president or chief executive officer can successfully implement a series of moves abroad. Only a company president can effectively persuade a board of directors of the value of a move abroad. Only a company president can effectively control and channel the inevitable rivalries and seeming contradictions in policy that simultaneous operation in several countries creates. Only a company president can successfully create the new marketing and financial controls needed for the new kind of company he will head if he creates a world enterprise.

Keys to Marketing Success Abroad

ADAPTING DOMESTIC SKILLS TO FOREIGN MARKETS

Leadership in American marketing is no guarantee of leadership in marketing abroad. Some outstandingly successful American firms have been able to duplicate in foreign markets their domestic success with ease and speed. For others success has come slowly and expensively. And for others not at all.

An analysis of the experience of leading American firms in major markets of the world has identified four characteristics of the outstanding marketer. These characteristics describe his fundamental approach to marketing decision-making, which, even in the short run, appears far more important than advantages in price or product.

1. The outstanding marketer exports his approaching marketing decision-making rather than his domestic practices. Foreign competitors are often alert, tough, and aggressive; but many are relatively inexperienced in analyzing marketing techniques. This experience—the ability to diagnose the problem, identify the best alternatives, and choose wisely among them—is the American competitor's real advantage. The marketing practices he now employs in the U.S. may be totally inappropriate in the rest of the world, but his technique for developing these practices has application everywhere.

2. The outstanding marketer is keenly aware of the variation from one market to another. He never thinks solely in terms of "the European market," "the Latin American market," or even "the Common Market." He knows that countries, and even sections of countries, differ enormously in almost every factor critical to his market planning:

- Distribution Channels: In Italy and France, chain stores are in the ascendant. In Germany, wholesaler groups are growing rapidly. Distribution practices in the north of the United Kingdom are very different from those in the south.
- Consumer Attitudes: In Germany, utility may be more important than style; in France, advertising and brand name may play larger roles. Hence product design and promotion have to be tailored to individual markets.
- Competitive Environment: In one country, the market for a product may be dominated by a single company; in a neighboring country many firms scramble for their shares.
- Market Size, Maturity, and Rate of Growth: An American power tool manufacturer found only replacement opportunities in one market but a completely untapped potential in a country nearby. Within the Common Market, per capita sales of widely used products vary enormously, and rates of growth for the same product differ by as much as 100 percent.

3. The outstanding marketer is sensitive to differences in his competitive position. American companies heavily committed to foreign markets are often industry leaders at home. In the U.S., they have become accustomed to the privileges and responsibilities of leadership. They may have a powerful influence on the industry pricing practices. They may be able to avoid discounts and deals. They can limit their distribution to carefully selected outlets. But their domestic position does not travel with them like a passport. The competitive structure of an industry varies widely from one economy to another and so does the industry position of a corporation that competes in several markets around the world. A company that has 30 percent of the American market may have to fight for 3 percent of a foreign market. And the company that gets 3 percent and more does so with a strategy appropriate for its position in that market.

4. The outstanding marketer combines policy-making at home with tactical decision-making abroad. Only corporate management is in a position to make broad policy decisions and to integrate local plans into a company-wide program. Without this kind of leadership, the most knowledgeable and skilled local marketing people can be only partly effective. But broad policies and plans are implemented best when the tactical decisions are made by local people in each market. There are three reasons for this:

- Referral of every problem to the U.S. invites poor decisions and involves unavoidable delay.
- Policy-level executives in the U.S. cannot know enough about foreign markets to make every detailed decision.
- Information required for operating decisions is often almost impossible to transmit.

A short time ago American corporations found things easier and more profitable abroad than at home; but today margins are shrinking, rates of return are declining, and competition is everywhere more intense. How American companies will fare depends greatly on the way they approach the new problems of international marketing.[1]

[1] Parts of this article are from "Minimizing Risks of Moving Abroad," by John G. McDonald, *Business Horizons* (Spring 1961), Indiana University, Bloomington, Indiana.

II

THE
MARKETING ENVIRONMENT

THE PLANNING AND DIRECTING of marketing activities should reflect an awareness and understanding of various operating conditions such as competition, consumer preference, production costs and capabilities, and a host of other factors which collectively comprise a marketing environment. Changes in this environment contribute to the dynamic nature of marketing.

The elements making up the marketing environment can be viewed as either external or internal to the firm. The external aspects are those over which little, if any, direct control can be exercised. Those aspects which might be considered as internal to the firm are subject to more direct control.

This classification does not imply any degree of absolute control or complete lack of control nor does it suggest a relative importance in terms of a greater or lesser effect upon marketing. The emphasis is upon recognizing that an environment does exist and that it is within this environment that marketing activities take place.

Included among the external elements are conditions such as the structure of competition and the marketing strategies of competitors, the legal framework, the current operating state of the economy, the level and nature of demand, governmental attitudes and policies, et cetera. Although these factors may not be subject to direct control, it does not follow that marketing practices are adapted passively to the external aspects. The active adaptation to the external elements of the environment presents some of the more challenging problems and opportunities confronting the decision-maker.

Among the internal aspects are top management goals and policies, production requirements, financial criteria and policies, personnel requirements, et cetera. Marketing is but one part of the firm's operations, and marketing activities have to be adjusted to be consistent with the requirements for the over-all success of the business. As one of the firm's key executives, however, the marketing manager often is in a position to accomplish changes in the internal aspects which would improve both the marketing program and the total operations of the firm.

The relationship of the environment to marketing activities should be reviewed continuously because changes in the environment alter the requirements of effective marketing.

A. EXTERNAL ASPECTS

> **Management must think of itself not as producing products but as providing customer-creating value satisfactions. It must push this idea (and everything it means and requires) into every nook and cranny of the organization.**

4

Marketing Myopia

THEODORE LEVITT

EVERY MAJOR INDUSTRY was once a growth industry. But some that are now riding a wave of growth enthusiasm are very much in the shadow of decline. Others which are thought of as seasoned growth industries have actually stopped growing. In every case the reason growth is threatened, slowed, or stopped is *not* because the market is saturated. It is because there has been a failure of management.

Fateful Purposes

The failure is at the top. The executives responsible for it, in the last analysis, are those who deal with broad aims and policies. Thus:

> The railroads did not stop growing because the need for passenger and freight transportation declined. That grew. The railroads are in trouble today not because the need was filled by others (cars, trucks, airplanes, even telephones), but because it was *not* filled by the railroads themselves. They let others take customers away from them because they assumed themselves to be in the railroad business rather than in the transportation business.

Reprinted from the *Harvard Business Review,* Volume 38, No. 4 (July-August, 1960), pp. 45-56.

The reason they defined their industry wrong was because they were railroad-oriented instead of transportation-oriented; they were product-oriented instead of customer-oriented.

Hollywood barely escaped being totally ravished by television. Actually, all the established film companies went through drastic reorganizations. Some simply disappeared. All of them got into trouble not because of TV's inroads but because of their own myopia. As with the railroads, Hollywood defined its business incorrectly. It thought it was in the movie business when it was actually in the entertainment business. "Movies" implied a specific, limited product. This produced a fatuous contentment which from the beginning led producers to view TV as a threat. Hollywood scorned and rejected TV when it should have welcomed it as an opportunity—an opportunity to expand the entertainment business.

Today TV is a bigger business than the old narrowly defined movie business ever was. Had Hollywood been customer-oriented (providing entertainment), rather than product-oriented (making movies), would it have gone through the fiscal purgatory that it did? I doubt it. What ultimately saved Hollywood and accounted for its recent resurgence was the wave of new young writers, producers, and directors whose previous successes in television had decimated the old movie companies and toppled the big movie moguls.

There are other less obvious examples of industries that have been and are now endangering their futures by improperly defining their purposes. I shall discuss some in detail later and analyze the kind of policies that lead to trouble. Right now it may help to show what a thoroughly customer-oriented management *can* do to keep a growth industry growing, even after the obvious opportunities have been exhausted; and here there are two examples that have been around for a long time. They are nylon and glass—specifically, E. I. duPont de Nemours & Company and Corning Glass Works:

Both companies have great technical competence. Their product orientation is unquestioned. But this alone does not explain their success. After all, who was more pridefully product-oriented and product-conscious than the erstwhile New England textile companies that have been so thoroughly massacred? The DuPonts and the Cornings have succeeded not primarily because of their product or research orientation but because they have been thoroughly customer-oriented also. It is constant watchfulness for opportunities to apply their technical know-how to the creation of customer-satisfying uses which accounts for their prodigious output of successful new products. Without a very sophisticated eye on the customer, most of their new products might have been wrong, their sales methods useless.

Aluminum has also continued to be a growth industry, thanks to the efforts of two wartime-created companies which deliberately set about creating new customer-satisfying uses. Without Kaiser Aluminum & Chemical Corporation and Reynolds Metals Company, the total demand for aluminum today would be vastly less than it is.

ERROR OF ANALYSIS

Some may argue that it is foolish to set the railroads off against aluminum or the movies off against glass. Are not aluminum and glass naturally so versatile that the industries are bound to have more growth opportunities than the railroads and movies? This view commits precisely the error I have been talking about. It defines an industry, or a product, or a cluster of know-how so narrowly as to guarantee its premature senescence. When we mention "railroads," we should make sure we mean "transportation." As transporters, the railroads still have a good chance for very considerable growth. They are not limited to the railroad business as such (though in my opinion rail transportation is potentially a much stronger transportation medium than is generally believed).

What the railroads lack is not opportunity, but some of the same managerial imaginativeness and audacity that made them great. Even an amateur like Jacques Barzun can see what is lacking when he says: "I grieve to see the most advanced physical and social organization of the last century go down in shabby disgrace for lack of the same comprehensive imagination that built it up. [What is lacking is] the will of the companies to survive and to satisfy the public by inventiveness and skill." [1]

Shadow of Obsolescence

It is impossible to mention a single major industry that did not at one time qualify for the magic appellation of "growth industry." In each case its assumed strength lay in the apparently unchallenged superiority of its product. There appeared to be no effective substitute for it. It was itself a runaway substitute for the product it so triumphantly replaced. Yet one after another of these celebrated industries has come under a shadow. Let us look briefly at a few more of them, this time taking examples that have so far received a little less attention:

Dry Cleaning. This was once a growth industry with lavish prospects. In an age of wool garments, imagine being finally able to get them safely and easily clean. The boom was on.

Yet here we are 30 years after the boom started and the industry is in trouble. Where has the competition come from? From a better way of cleaning? No. It has come from synthetic fibers and chemical additives that have cut the need for dry cleaning. But this is only the beginning. Lurking in

[1] Jacques Barzun, "Trains and the Mind of Man," *Holiday,* February 1960, p. 21.

the wings and ready to make chemical dry cleaning totally obsolescent is that powerful magician, ultrasonics.

Electric Utilities. This is another one of those supposedly "no-substitute" products that has been enthroned on a pedestal of invicible growth. When the incandescent lamp came along, kerosene lights were finished. Later the water wheel and the steam engine were cut to ribbons by the flexibility, reliability, simplicity, and just plain easy availability of electric motors. The prosperity of electric utilities continues to wax extravagant as the home is converted into a museum of electric gadgetry. How can anybody miss by investing in utilities, with no competition, nothing but growth ahead?

But a second look is not quite so comforting. A score of nonutility companies are well advanced toward developing a powerful chemical fuel cell which could sit in some hidden closet of every home silently ticking off electric power. The electric lines that vulgarize so many neighborhoods will be eliminated. So will the endless demolition of streets and service interruptions during storms. Also on the horizon is solar energy, again pioneered by nonutility companies.

Who says that the utilities have no competition? They may be natural monopolies now, but tomorrow they may be natural deaths. To avoid this prospect, they too will have to develop fuel cells, solar energy, and other power sources. To survive, they themselves will have to plot the obsolescence of what now produces their livelihood.

Grocery Stores. Many people find it hard to realize that there ever was a thriving establishment known as the "corner grocery store." The supermarket has taken over with a powerful effectiveness. Yet the big food chains of the 1930's narrowly escaped being completely wiped out by the aggressive expansion of independent supermarkets. The first genuine supermarket was opened in 1930, in Jamaica, Long Island. By 1933 supermarkets were thriving in California, Ohio, Pennsylvania, and elsewhere. Yet the established chains pompously ignored them. When they chose to notice them, it was with such derisive descriptions as "cheapy," "horse-and-buggy," "cracker-barrel storekeeping," and "unethical opportunists."

The executive of one big chain announced at the time that he found it "hard to believe that people will drive for miles to shop for foods and sacrifice the personal service chains have perfected and to which Mrs. Consumer is accustomed." [2] As late as 1936, the National Wholesale Grocers convention and the New Jersey Retail Grocers Association said there was nothing to fear. They said that the supers' narrow appeal to the price buyer limited the size of their market. They had to draw from miles around. When imitators came, there would be wholesale liquidations as volume fell. The current high sales of the supers was said to be partly due to their novelty. Basically people wanted convenient neighborhood grocers. If the neighborhood stores "cooperate with their suppliers, pay attention to their costs, and

2 For more details see M. M. Zimmerman, *The Super Market: A Revolution in Distribution* (New York, McGraw-Hill, 1955), p. 48.

improve their service," they would be able to weather the competition until it blew over.[3]

It never blew over. The chains discovered that survival required going into the supermarket business. This meant the wholesale destruction of their huge investments in corner store sites and in established distribution and merchandising methods. The companies with "the courage of their convictions" resolutely stuck to the corner store philosophy. They kept their pride but lost their shirts.

SELF-DECEIVING CYCLE

But memories are short. For example, it is hard for people who today confidently hail the twin messiahs of electronics and chemicals to see how things could possibly go wrong with these galloping industries. They probably also cannot see how a reasonably sensible businessman could have been as myopic as the famous Boston millionaire who 50 years ago unintentionally sentenced his heirs to poverty by stipulating that his entire estate be forever invested exclusively in electric streetcar securities. His posthumous declaration, "There will always be a big demand for efficient urban transportation," is no consolation to his heirs who sustain life by pumping gasoline at automobile filling stations.

Yet, in a casual survey I recently took among a group of intelligent business executives, nearly half agreed that it would be hard to hurt their heirs by tying their estates forever to the electronics industry. When I then confronted them with the Boston streetcar example, they chorused unanimously, "That's different!" But is it? Is not the basic situation identical?

In truth, *there is no such thing* as a growth industry, I believe. There are only companies organized and operated to create and capitalize on growth opportunities. Industries that assume themselves to be riding some automatic growth escalator invariably descend into stagnation. The history of every dead and dying "growth" industry shows a self-deceiving cycle of bountiful expansion and undetected decay. There are four conditions which usually guarantee this cycle:

1. The belief that growth is assured by an expanding and more affluent population.

2. The belief that there is no competitive substitute for the industry's major product.

3. Too much faith in mass production and in the advantages of rapidly declining unit costs as output rises.

4. Preoccupation with a product that lends itself to carefully controlled scientific experimentation, improvement, and manufacturing cost reduction.

I should like now to begin examining each of these conditions in some

[3] *Ibid.,* pp. 45-47.

detail. To build my case as boldly as possible, I shall illustrate the points with reference to three industries—petroleum, automobiles, and electronics —particularly petroleum, because it spans more years and more vicissitudes. Not only do these three have excellent reputations with the general public and also enjoy the confidence of sophisticated investors, but their managements have become known for progressive thinking in areas like financial control, product research, and management training. If obsolescence can cripple even these industries, it can happen anywhere.

Population Myth

The belief that profits are assured by an expanding and more affluent population is dear to the heart of every industry. It takes the edge off the apprehensions everybody understandably feels about the future. If consumers are multiplying and also buying more of your product or service, you can face the future with considerably more comfort than if the market is shrinking. An expanding market keeps the manufacturer from having to think very hard or imaginatively. If thinking is an intellectual response to a problem, then the absence of a problem leads to the absence of thinking. If your product has an automatically expanding market, then you will not give much thought to how to expand it.

One of the most interesting examples of this is provided by the petroleum industry. Probably our oldest growth industry, it has an enviable record. While there are some current apprehensions about its growth rate, the industry itself tends to be optimistic. But I believe it can be demonstrated that it is undergoing a fundamental yet typical change. It is not only ceasing to be a growth industry, but may actually be a declining one, relative to other business. Although there is widespread unawareness of it, I believe that within 25 years the oil industry may find itself in much the same position of retrospective glory that the railroads are now in. Despite its pioneering work in developing and applying the present-value method of investment evaluation, in employee relations, and in working with backward countries, the petroleum business is a distressing example of how complacency and wrongheadedness can stubbornly convert opportunity into near disaster.

One of the characteristics of this and other industries that have believed very strongly in the beneficial consequences of an expanding population, while at the same time being industries with a generic product for which there has appeared to be no competitive substitute, is that the individual companies have sought to outdo their competitors by improving on what they are already doing. This makes sense, of course, if one assumes that sales are tied to the country's population strings, because the customer can compare products only on a feature-by-feature basis. I believe it is significant, for example, that not since John D. Rockefeller sent free kerosene lamps to China has the oil industry done anything really outstanding to create a demand for its product. Not even in product improvement has it showered itself with eminence. The greatest single improvement, namely, the development of tetraethyl lead, came from outside the industry, specifically from General Motors and DuPont. The big contributions made by the industry itself are confined to the technology of oil exploration, production, and refining.

ASKING FOR TROUBLE

In other words, the industry's efforts have focused on improving the *efficiency* of getting and making its product, not really on improving the generic product or its marketing. Moreover, its chief product has continuously been defined in the narrowest possible terms, namely, gasoline, not energy, fuel, or transportation. This attitude has helped assure that:

- Major improvements in gasoline quality tend not to originate in the oil industry. Also, the development of superior alternative fuels comes from outside the oil industry, as will be shown later.

- Major innovations in automobile fuel marketing are originated by small new oil companies that are not primarily preoccupied with production or refining. These are the companies that have been responsible for the rapidly expanding multipump gasoline stations, with their successful emphasis on large and clean layouts, rapid and efficient driveway service, and quality gasoline at low prices.

Thus, the oil industry is asking for trouble from outsiders. Sooner or later, in this land of hungry inventors and entrepreneurs, a threat is sure to come. The possibilities of this will become more apparent when we turn to the next dangerous belief of many managements. For the sake of continuity, because this second belief is tied closely to the first, I shall continue with the same example.

IDEA OF INDISPENSABILITY

The petroleum industry is pretty much persuaded that there is no competitive substitute for its major product, gasoline—or if there is, that it will continue to be a derivative of crude oil, such as diesel fuel or kerosene jet fuel.

There is a lot of automatic wishful thinking in this assumption. The trouble is that most refining companies own huge amounts of crude oil reserves. These have value only if there is a market for products into which oil can be converted—hence the tenacious belief in the continuing competitive superiority of automobile fuels made from crude oil.

This idea persists despite all historic evidence against it. The evidence not only shows that oil has never been a superior product for any purpose for very long, but it also shows that the oil industry has never really been a growth industry. It has been a succession of different businesses that have gone through the usual historic cycles of growth, maturity, and decay. Its over-all survival is owed to a series of miraculous escapes from total obsolescence, of last-minute and unexpected reprieves from total disaster reminiscent of the Perils of Pauline.

PERILS OF PETROLEUM

I shall sketch in only the main episodes:

First, crude oil was largely a patent medicine. But even before that fad ran out, demand was greatly expanded by the use of oil in kerosene lamps. The prospect of lighting the world's lamps gave rise to an extravagant promise of growth. The prospects were similar to those the industry now holds for gasoline in other parts of the world. It can hardly wait for the underdeveloped nations to get a car in every garage.

In the days of the kerosene lamp, the oil companies competed with each other and against gaslight by trying to improve the illuminating characteristics of kerosene. Then suddenly the impossible happened. Edison invented a light which was totally nondependent on crude oil. Had it not been for the growing use of kerosene in space heaters, the incandescent lamp would have completely finished oil as a growth industry at that time. Oil would have been good for little else than axle grease.

Then disaster and reprieve struck again. Two great innovations occurred, neither originating in the oil industry. The successful development of coal-burning domestic central-heating systems made the space heater obsolescent. While the industry reeled, along came its most magnificent boost yet—the internal combustion engine, also invented by outsiders. Then when the prodigious expansion for gasoline finally began to level off in the 1920's, along came the miraculous escape of a central oil heater. Once again, the escape was provided by an outsider's invention and development. And when that market weakened, wartime demand for aviation fuel came to the rescue. After the war the expansion of civilian aviation, the dieselization of railroads, and the explosive demand for cars and trucks kept the industry's growth in high gear.

Meanwhile centralized oil heating—whose boom potential had only recently been proclaimed—ran into severe competition from natural gas. While the oil companies themselves owned the gas that now competed with their oil, the industry did not originate the natural gas revolution, nor has it to this day greatly profited from its gas ownership. The gas revolution was made by newly formed transmission companies that marketed the product with an aggressive ardor. They started a magnificent new industry, first against the advice and then against the resistance of the oil companies.

By all the logic of the situation, the oil companies themselves should have made the gas revolution. They not only owned the gas; they also were the only people experienced in handling, scrubbing, and using it, the only people experienced in pipeline technology and transmission, and they understood heating problems. But, partly because they knew that natural gas would compete with their own sale of heating oil, the oil companies pooh-poohed the potentials of gas.

The revolution was finally started by oil pipeline executives who, unable to persuade their own companies to go into gas, quit and organized the spectacularly successful gas transmission companies. Even after their success became painfully evident to the oil companies, the latter did not go into gas transmission. The multibillion dollar business which should have been theirs went to others. As in the past, the industry was blinded by its narrow preoccupation with a specific product and the value of its reserves. It paid little or no attention to its customers' basic needs and preferences.

The postwar years have not witnessed any change. Immediately after World War II the oil industry was greatly encouraged about its future by the rapid expansion of demand for its traditional line of products. In 1950 most companies projected annual rates of domestic expansion of around 6% through at least 1975. Though the ratio of crude oil reserves to demand in the Free World was about 20 to 1, with 10 to 1 being usually considered a reasonable working ratio in the United States, booming demand sent oil men searching for more without sufficient regard to what the future really promised. In 1952 they "hit" in the Middle East; the ratio skyrocketed to 42 to 1. If gross additions to reserves continue at the average rate of the past five years (37 billion barrels annually), then by 1970 the reserve ratio will be up to 45 to 1. This abundance of oil has weakened crude and product prices all over the world.

UNCERTAIN FUTURE

Management cannot find much consolation today in the rapidly expanding petrochemical industry, another oil-using idea that did not originate in the leading firms. The total United States production of petrochemicals is equivalent to about 2% (by volume) of the demand for all petroleum products. Although the petrochemical industry is now expected to grow by about 10% per year, this will not offset other drains on the growth of crude oil consumption. Furthermore, while petrochemical products are many and growing, it is well to remember that there are nonpetroleum sources of the basic raw material, such as coal. Besides, a lot of plastics can be produced with relatively little oil. A 50,000-barrel-per-day oil refinery is now considered the absolute minimum size for efficiency. But a 5,000-barrel-per-day chemical plant is a giant operation.

Oil has never been a continuously strong growth industry. It has grown by fits and starts, always miraculously saved by innovations and developments not of its own making. The reason it has not grown in a smooth progression is that each time it thought it had a superior product safe from the possibility of competitive substitutes, the product turned out to be inferior and notoriously subject to obsolescence. Until now, gasoline (for motor fuel, anyhow) has escaped this fate. But, as we shall see later, it too may be on its last legs.

The point of all this is that there is no guarantee against product obsolescence. If a company's own research does not make it obsolete, another's will. Unless an industry is especially lucky, as oil has been until now, it can easily go down in a sea of red figures—just as the railroads have, as the buggy whip manufacturers have, as the corner grocery chains have, as most of the big movie companies have, and indeed as many other industries have.

The best way for a firm to be lucky is to make its own luck. That requires knowing what makes a business successful. One of the greatest enemies of this knowledge is mass production.

Production Pressures

Mass-production industries are impelled by a great drive to produce all they can. The prospect of steeply declining unit costs as output rises is more than most companies can usually resist. The profit possibilities look spectacular. All effort focuses on production. The result is that marketing gets neglected.

John Kenneth Galbraith contends that just the opposite occurs.[4] Output is so prodigious that all effort concentrates on trying to get rid of it. He says this accounts for singing commercials, desecration of the countryside with advertising signs, and other wasteful and vulgar practices. Galbraith has a finger on something real, but he misses the strategic point. Mass production does indeed generate great pressure to "move" the product. But what usually gets emphasized is selling, not marketing. Marketing, being a more sophisticated and complex process, gets ignored.

The difference between marketing and selling is more than semantic. Selling focuses on the needs of the seller, marketing on the needs of the buyer. Selling is preoccupied with the seller's need to convert his product into cash; marketing with the idea of satisfying the needs of the customer by means of the product and the whole cluster of things associated with creating, delivering, and finally consuming it.

In some industries the enticements of full mass production have been so powerful that for many years top management in effect has told the sales departments, "You get rid of it; we'll worry about profits." By contrast, a truly marketing-minded firm tries to create value-satisfying goods and services that consumers will want to buy. What it offers for sale includes not only the generic product or service, but also how it is made

[4] *The Affluent Society* (Boston, Houghton Mifflin, 1958), pp. 152-160.

available to the customer, in what form, when, under what conditions, and at what terms of trade. Most important, what it offers for sale is determined not by the seller but by the buyer. The seller takes his cues from the buyer in such a way that the product becomes a consequence of the marketing effort, not vice versa.

LAG IN DETROIT

This may sound like an elementary rule of business, but that does not keep it from being violated wholesale. It is certainly more violated than honored. Take the automobile industry:

> Here mass production is most famous, most honored, and has the greatest impact on the entire society. The industry has hitched its fortune to the relentless requirements of the annual model change, a policy that makes customer orientation an especially urgent necessity. Consequently the auto companies annually spend millions of dollars on consumer research. But the fact that the new compact cars are selling so well in their first year indicates that Detroit's vast researches have for a long time failed to reveal what the customer really wanted. Detroit was not persuaded that he wanted anything different from what he had been getting until it lost millions of customers to other small car manufacturers.

How could this unbelievable lag behind consumer wants have been perpetuated so long? Why did not research reveal consumer preferences before consumers' buying decisions themselves revealed the facts? Is that not what consumer research is for—to find out before the fact what is going to happen? The answer is that Detroit never really researched the customer's wants. It only researched his preferences between the kinds of things which it had already decided to offer him. For Detroit is mainly product-oriented, not customer-oriented. To the extent that the customer is recognized as having needs that the manufacturer should try to satisfy, Detroit usually acts as if the job can be done entirely by product changes. Occasionally attention gets paid to financing, too, but that is done more in order to sell than to enable the customer to buy.

As for taking care of other customer needs, there is not enough being done to write about. The areas of the greatest unsatisfied needs are ignored, or at best get stepchild attention. These are at the point of sale and on the matter of automotive repair and maintenance. Detroit views these problem areas as being of secondary importance. That is underscored by the fact that the retailing and servicing ends of this industry are neither owned and operated nor controlled by the manufacturers. Once the car is produced, things are pretty much in the dealer's inadequate hands. Illustrative of Detroit's arm's-length attitude is the fact that, while servicing holds enormous sales-stimulating, profit-building opportunities, only 57 of Chevrolet's 7,000 dealers provide night maintenance service.

Motorists repeatedly express their dissatisfaction with servicing and their apprehensions about buying cars under the present selling setup. The anxieties and problems they encounter during the auto buying and maintenance processes are probably more intense and widespread today than 30 years ago. Yet the automobile companies do not *seem* to listen to or take their cues from the anguished consumer. If they do listen, it must be through the filter of their own preoccupation with production. The marketing effort is still viewed as a necessary consequence of the product, not vice versa, as it should be. That is the legacy of mass production, with its parochial view that profit resides essentially in low-cost full production.

WHAT FORD PUT FIRST

The profit lure of mass production obviously has a place in the plans and strategy of business management, but it must always *follow* hard thinking about the customer. This is one of the most important lessons that we can learn from the contradictory behavior of Henry Ford. In a sense Ford was both the most brilliant and the most senseless marketer in American history. He was senseless because he refused to give the customer anything but a black car. He was brilliant because he fashioned a production system designed to fit market needs. We habitually celebrate him for the wrong reason, his production genius. His real genius was marketing. We think he was able to cut his selling price and therefore sell millions of $500 cars because his invention of the assembly line had reduced the costs. Actually he invented the assembly line because he had concluded that at $500 he could sell millions of cars. Mass production was the *result* not the cause of his low prices.

Ford repeatedly emphasized this point, but a nation of production-oriented business managers refuses to hear the great lesson he taught. Here is his operating philosophy as he expressed it succinctly:

> Our policy is to reduce the price, extend the operations, and improve the article. You will notice that the reduction of price comes first. We have never considered any costs as fixed. Therefore we first reduce the price to the point where we believe more sales will result. Then we go ahead and try to make the prices. We do not bother about the costs. The new price forces the costs down. The more usual way is to take the costs and then determine the price, and although that method may be scientific in the narrow sense; it is not scientific in the broad sense, because what earthly use is it to know the cost if it tells you that you cannot manufacture at a price at which the article can be sold? But more to the point is the fact that, although one may calculate what a cost is, and of course all of our costs are carefully calculated, no one knows what a cost ought to be. One of the ways of discovering . . . is to name a price so low as to force everybody in the place to the highest point of efficiency. The low price makes everybody dig for profits. We make more

discoveries concerning manufacturing and selling under this forced method than by any method of leisurely investigation.

PRODUCT PROVINCIALISM

The tantalizing profit possibilities of low unit production costs may be the most seriously self-deceiving attitude that can afflict a company, particularly a "growth" company where an apparently assured expansion of demand already tends to undermine a proper concern for the importance of marketing and the customer.

The usual result of this narrow preoccupation with so-called concrete matters is that instead of growing, the industry declines. It usually means that the product fails to adapt to the constantly changing patterns of consumer needs and tastes, to new and modified marketing institutions and practices, or to product developments in competing or complementary industries. The industry has its eyes so firmly on its own specific product that it does not see how it is being made obsolete.

The classical example of this is the buggy whip industry. No amount of product improvement could stave off its death sentence. But had the industry defined itself as being in the transportation business rather than the buggy whip business, it might have survived. It would have done what survival always entails, that is, changing. Even if it had only defined its business as providing a stimulant or catalyst to an energy source, it might have survived by becoming a manufacturer of, say, fanbelts or air cleaners.

What may some day be a still more classical example is, again, the oil industry. Having let others steal marvelous opportunities from it (e.g., natural gas, as already mentioned, missile fuels, and jet engine lubricants), one would expect it to have taken steps never to let that happen again. But this is not the case. We are now getting extraordinary new developments in fuel systems specifically designed to power automobiles. Not only are these developments concentrated in firms outside the petroleum industry, but petroleum is almost systematically ignoring them, securely content in its wedded bliss to oil. It is the story of the kerosene lamp versus the incandescent lamp all over again. Oil is trying to improve hydrocarbon fuels rather than to develop *any* fuels best suited to the needs of their users, whether or not made in different ways and with different raw materials from oil.

Here are some of the things which nonpetroleum companies are working on:

> Over a dozen such firms now have advanced working models of energy systems which, when perfected, will replace the internal combustion engine and eliminate the demand for gasoline. The superior merit of each of these sys-

[5] Henry Ford, *My Life and Work* (New York, Doubleday, 1923), pp. 146-147.

tems is their elimination of frequent, time-consuming, and irritating refueling stops. Most of these systems are fuel cells designed to create electrical energy directly from chemicals without combustion. Most of them use chemicals that are not derived from oil, generally hydrogen and oxygen.

Several other companies have advanced models of electric storage batteries designed to power automobiles. One of these is an aircraft producer that is working jointly with several electric utility companies. The latter hope to use off-peak generating capacity to supply overnight plug-in battery regeneration. Another company, also using the battery approach, is a medium-size electronics firm with extensive small-battery experience that it developed in connection with its work on hearing aids. It is collaborating with an automobile manufacturer. Recent improvements arising from the need for high-powered miniature power storage plants in rockets have put us within reach of a relatively small battery capable of withstanding great overloads or surges of power. Germanium diode applications and batteries using sintered-plate and nickel-cadmium techniques promise to make a revolution in our energy sources.

Solar energy conversion systems are also getting increasing attention. One usually cautious Detroit auto executive recently ventured that solar-powered cars might be common by 1980.

As for the oil companies, they are more or less "watching developments," as one research director put it to me. A few are doing a bit of research on fuel cells, but almost always confined to developing cells powered by hydrocarbon chemicals. None of them are enthusiastically researching fuel cells, batteries, or solar power plants. None of them are spending a fraction as much on research in these profoundly important areas as they are on the usual run-of-the-mill things like reducing combustion chamber deposit in gasoline engines. One major integrated petroleum company recently took a tentative look at the fuel cell and concluded that although "the companies actively working on it indicate a belief in ultimate success . . . the timing and magnitude of its impact are too remote to warrant recognition in our forecasts."

One might, of course, ask: Why should the oil companies do anything different? Would not chemical fuel cells, batteries, or solar energy kill the present product lines? The answer is that they would indeed, and that is precisely the reason for the oil firms having to develop these power units before their competitors, so they will not be companies without an industry.

Management might be more likely to do what is needed for its own preservation if it thought of itself as being in the energy business. But even that would not be enough if it persists in imprisoning itself in the narrow grip of its tight product orientation. It has to think of itself as taking care of customer needs, not finding, refining, or even selling oil.

Once it genuinely thinks of its business as taking care of people's transportation needs, nothing can stop it from creating its own extravagantly profitable growth.

"CREATIVE DESTRUCTION"

Since words are cheap and deeds are dear, it may be appropriate to indicate what this kind of thinking involves and leads to. Let us start at the beginning—the customer. It can be shown that motorists strongly dislike the bother, delay, and experience of buying gasoline. People actually do not buy gasoline. They cannot see it, taste it, feel it, appreciate it, or really test it. What they buy is the right to continue driving their cars. The gas station is like a tax collector to whom people are compelled to pay a periodic toll as the price of using their cars. This makes the gas station a basically unpopular institution. It can never be made popular or pleasant, only less unpopular, less unpleasant.

To reduce its unpopularity completely means eliminating it. Nobody likes a tax collector, not even a pleasantly cheerful one. Nobody likes to interrupt a trip to buy a phantom product, not even from a handsome Adonis or a seductive Venus. Hence, companies that are working on exotic fuel substitutes which will eliminate the need for frequent refueling are heading directly into the outstretched arms of the irritated motorist. They are riding a wave of inevitability, not because they are creating something which is technologically superior or more sophisticated, but because they are satisfying a powerful customer need. They are also eliminating noxious odors and air pollution.

Once the petroleum companies recognize the customer-satisfying logic of what another power system can do, they will see that they have no more choice about working on an efficient, long-lasting fuel (or some way of delivering present fuels without bothering the motorist) than the big food chains had a choice about going into the supermarket business, or the vacuum tube companies had a choice about making semiconductors. For their own good the oil firms will have to destroy their own highly profitable assets. No amount of wishful thinking can save them from the necessity of engaging in this form of "creative destruction."

I phrase the need as strongly as this because I think management must make quite an effort to break itself loose from conventional ways. It is all too easy in this day and age for a company or industry to let its sense of purpose become dominated by the economies of full production and to develop a dangerously lopsided product orientation. In short, if management lets itself drift, it invariably drifts in the direction of thinking of itself as producing goods and services, not customer satisfactions. While it probably will not descend to the depths of telling its salesmen, "You get rid of it; we'll worry about profits," it can, without knowing it, be practicing precisely that formula for withering decay. The historic fate of one growth industry after another has been its suicidal product provincialism.

Dangers of R & D

Another big danger to a firm's continued growth arises when top management is wholly transfixed by the profit possibilities of technical research and development. To illustrate I shall turn first to a new industry—electronics—and then return once more to the oil companies. By comparing a fresh example with a familiar one, I hope to emphasize the prevalence and insidiousness of a hazardous way of thinking.

MARKETING SHORTCHANGED

In the case of electronics, the greatest danger which faces the glamorous new companies in this field is not that they do not pay enough attention to research and development, but that they pay *too much* attention to it. And the fact that the fastest growing electronics firms owe their eminence to their heavy emphasis on technical research is completely beside the point. They have vaulted to affluence on a sudden crest of unusually strong general receptiveness to new technical ideas. Also, their success has been shaped in the virtually guaranteed market of military subsidies and by military orders that in many cases actually preceded the existence of facilities to make the products. Their expansion has, in other words, been almost totally devoid of marketing effort.

Thus, they are growing up under conditions that come dangerously close to creating the illusion that a superior product will sell itself. Having created a successful company by making a superior product, it is not surprising that management continues to be oriented toward the product rather than the people who consume it. It develops the philosophy that continued growth is a matter of continued product innovation and improvement.

A number of other factors tend to strengthen and sustain this belief:

1. Because electronic products are highly complex and sophisticated, managements become top-heavy with engineers and scientists. This creates a selective bias in favor of research and production at the expense of marketing. The organization tends to view itself as making things rather than satisfying customer needs. Marketing gets treated as a residual activity, "something else" that must be done once the vital job of product creation and production is completed.

2. To this bias in favor of product research, development, and production is added the bias in favor of dealing with controllable variables. Engineers and scientists are at home in the world of concrete things like machines,

test tubes, production lines, and even balance sheets. The abstractions to which they feel kindly are those which are testable or manipulatable in the laboratory, or, if not testable, then functional, such as Euclid's axioms. In short, the managements of the new glamour-growth companies tend to favor those business activities which lend themselves to careful study, experimentation, and control—the hard, practical, realities of the lab, the shop, the books.

What gets shortchanged are the realities of the *market*. Consumers are unpredictable, varied, fickle, stupid, shortsighted, stubborn, and generally bothersome. This is not what the engineer-managers say, but deep down in their consciousness it is what they believe. And this accounts for their concentrating on what they know and what they can control, namely, product research, engineering, and production. The emphasis on production becomes particularly attractive when the product can be made at declining unit costs. There is no more inviting way of making money than by running the plant full blast.

Today the top-heavy science-engineering-production orientation of so many electronics companies works reasonably well because they are pushing into new frontiers in which the armed services have pioneered virtually assured markets. The companies are in the felicitous position of having to fill, not find, markets; of not having to discover what the customer needs and wants, but of having the customer voluntarily come forward with specific new product demands. If a team of consultants had been assigned specifically to design a business situation calculated to prevent the emergence and development of a customer-oriented marketing viewpoint, it could not have produced anything better than the conditions just described.

STEPCHILD TREATMENT

The oil industry is a stunning example of how science, technology, and mass production can divert an entire group of companies from their main task. To the extent the consumer is studied at all (which is not much), the focus is forever on getting information which is designed to help the oil companies improve what they are now doing. They try to discover more convincing advertising themes, more effective sales promotional drives, what the market shares of the various companies are, what people like or dislike about service station dealers and oil companies, and so forth. Nobody seems as interested in probing deeply into the basic human needs that the industry might be trying to satisfy as in probing into the basic properties of the raw material that the companies work with in trying to deliver customer satisfactions.

Basic questions about customers and markets seldom get asked. The latter occupy a stepchild status. They are recognized as existing, as having to be taken care of, but not worth very much real thought or dedicated attention. Nobody gets as excited about the customers in his own backyard as about the oil in the Sahara Desert. Nothing illustrates better the neglect of marketing than its treatment in the industry press:

The centennial issue of the *American Petroleum Institute Quarterly*, published in 1959 to celebrate the discovery of oil in Titusville, Pennsylvania, contained 21 feature articles proclaiming the industry's greatness. Only one of these talked about its achievements in marketing, and that was only a pictorial record of how service station architecture has changed. The issue also contained a special section on "New Horizons," which was devoted to showing the magnificent role oil would play in America's future. Every reference was ebulliently optimistic, never implying once that oil might have some hard competition. Even the reference to atomic energy was a cheerful catalogue of how oil would help make atomic energy a success. There was not a single apprehension that the oil industry's affluence might be threatened or a suggestion that one "new horizon" might include new and better ways of serving oil's present customers.

But the most revealing example of the stepchild treatment that marketing gets was still another special series of short articles on "The Revolutionary Potential of Electronics." Under that heading this list of articles appeared in the table of contents:

- "In the Search for Oil"
- "In Production Operations"
- "In Refinery Processes"
- "In Pipeline Operations"

Significantly, every one of the industry's major functional areas is listed, *except* marketing. Why? Either it is believed that electronics holds no revolutionary potential for petroleum marketing (which is palpably wrong), or the editors forgot to discuss marketing (which is more likely, and illustrates its stepchild status).

The order in which the four functional areas are listed also betrays the alienation of the oil industry from the consumer. The industry is implicitly defined as beginning with the search for oil and ending with its distribution from the refinery. But the truth is, it seems to me, that the industry begins with the needs of the customer for its products. From that primal position its definition moves steadily backstream to areas of progressively lesser importance, until it finally comes to rest at the "search for oil."

BEGINNING & END

The view that an industry is a customer-satisfying process, not a goods-producing process, is vital for all businessmen to understand. An industry begins with the customer and his needs, not with a patent, a raw material,

or a selling skill. Given the customer's needs, the industry develops backwards, first concerning itself with the physical *delivery* of customer satisfactions. Then it moves back further to *creating* the things by which these
satisfactions are in part achieved. How these materials are created is a
matter of indifference to the customer, hence the particular form of manufacturing, processing, or what-have-you cannot be considered as a vital
aspect of the industry. Finally, the industry moves back still further to
finding the raw materials necessary for making its products.

The irony of some industries oriented toward technical research and
development is that the scientists who occupy the high executive positions
are totally unscientific when it comes to defining their companies' over-all
needs and purposes. They violate the first two rules of the scientific method
—being aware of and defining their companies' problems, and then developing testable hypotheses about solving them. They are scientific only about
the convenient things, such as laboratory and product experiments. The
reason that the customer (and the satisfaction of his deepest needs) is not
considered as being "the problem" is not because there is any certain
belief that no such problem exists, but because an organizational lifetime
has conditioned management to look in the opposite direction. Marketing
is a stepchild.

I do not mean that selling is ignored. Far from it. But selling, again, is
not marketing. As already pointed out, selling concerns itself with the
tricks and techniques of getting people to exchange their cash for your
product. It is not concerned with the values that the exchange is all about.
And it does not, as marketing invariably does, view the entire business
process as consisting of a tightly integrated effort to discover, create, arouse,
and satisfy customer needs. The customer is somebody "out there" who,
with proper cunning, can be separated from his loose change.

Actually, not even selling gets much attention in some technologically
minded firms. Because there is a virtually guaranteed market for the
abundant flow of their new products, they do not actually know what a
real market is. It is as if they lived in a planned economy, moving their
products routinely from factory to retail outlet. Their successful concentration on products tends to convince them of the soundness of what they have
been doing, and they fail to see the gathering clouds over the market.

Conclusion

Less than 75 years ago American railroads enjoyed a fierce loyalty
among astute Wall Streeters. European monarchs invested in them heavily.
Eternal wealth was thought to be the benediction for anybody who could
scrape a few thousand dollars together to put into rail stocks. No other
form of transportation could compete with the railroads in speed, flexibility,

durability, economy, and growth potentials. As Jacques Barzun put it, "By the turn of the century it was an institution, an image of man, a tradition, a code of honor, a source of poetry, a nursery of boyhood desires, a sublimest of toys, and the most solemn machine—next to the funeral hearse—that marks the epochs in man's life." [6]

Even after the advent of automobiles, trucks, and airplanes, the railroad tycoons remained imperturbably self-confident. If you had told them 60 years ago that in 30 years they would be flat on their backs, broke, and pleading for government subsidies, they would have thought you totally demented. Such a future was simply not considered possible. It was not even a discussable subject, or an askable question, or a matter which any sane person would consider worth speculating about. The very thought was insane. Yet a lot of insane notions now have matter-of-fact acceptance —for example, the idea of 100-ton tubes of metal moving smoothly through the air 20,000 feet above the earth, loaded with 100 sane and solid citizens casually drinking martinis—and they have dealt cruel blows to the railroads.

What specifically must other companies do to avoid this fate? What does customer orientation involve? These questions have in part been answered by the preceding examples and analysis. It would take another article to show in detail what is required for specific industries. In any case, it should be obvious that building an effective customer-oriented company involves far more than good intentions or promotional tricks; it involves profound matters of human organization and leadership. For the present, let me merely suggest what appear to be some general requirements.

VISCERAL FEEL OF GREATNESS

Obviously the company has to do what survival demands. It has to adapt to the requirements of the market, and it has to do it sooner rather than later. But mere survival is a so-so aspiration. Anybody can survive in some way or other, even the skid-row bum. The trick is to survive gallantly, to feel the surging impulse of commercial mastery; not just to experience the sweet smell of success, but to have the visceral feel of entrepreneurial greatness.

No organization can achieve greatness without a vigorous leader who is driven onward by his own pulsating *will to succeed*. He has to have a vision of grandeur, a vision that can produce eager followers in vast numbers. In business, the followers are the customers. To produce these customers, the entire corporation must be viewed as a customer-creating and customer-satisfying organism. Management must think of itself not as

[6] *Op. cit.*, p. 20.

producing products but as providing customer-creating value satisfactions. It must push this idea (and everything it means and requires) into every nook and cranny of the organization. It has to do this continuously and with the kind of flair that excites and stimulates the people in it. Otherwise, the company will be merely a series of pigeonholed parts, with no consolidating sense of purpose or direction.

In short, the organization must learn to think of itself not as producing goods or services but as *buying customers,* as doing the things that will make people *want* to do business with it. And the chief executive himself has the inescapable responsibility for creating this environment, this viewpoint, this attitude, this aspiration. He himself must set the company's style, its direction, and its goals. This means he has to know precisely where he himself wants to go, and to make sure the whole organization is enthusiastically aware of where that is. This is a first requisite of leadership, for *unless he knows where he is going, any road will take him there.*

If any road is okay, the chief executive might as well pack his attaché case and go fishing. If an organization does not know or care where it is going, it does not need to advertise that fact with a ceremonial figurehead. Everybody will notice it soon enough.

. . . numerous studies over the past fifteen years have demonstrated that consumer demand does not depend on ability to buy alone. Ability to buy is important, but people do not always buy just because they have money.

5

The Powerful Consumer

GEORGE KATONA

WHAT USE does the American consumer make of his economic power? Does he exercise his influence in a way that exaggerates economic fluctuations so that boom years alternate with years of severe recession? Does consumer behavior make for inflationary price increases? Does consumer action promote growth or stagnation of our economy? These are crucial questions because the impact of consumers on the economy has been growing during the past twenty years and is bound to increase further.*

Statements that the purpose of all production is consumption or that the consumer is king are as old as economics. And yet during the past fifty years most economists have assigned the consumer a minor role in the economy. It has been argued that consumers' expenditures depend on their incomes, and incomes depend on what the other sectors of the economy, business and government, pay out. Therefore, new trends were assumed to originate exclusively in those other sectors. Consumers were thought of as uninfluential transmitters of trends.

There may have been some truth in these theories several decades ago, and even today in many lesser developed societies. But in the American

Reprinted from the *Thirty-second Annual Boston Conference on Distribution*, October 17-18, 1960, pp. 86-89.
* My book, *The Powerful Consumer,* published a few months ago by McGraw-Hill, New York, contains findings supporting the major arguments developed in this paper.

economy there have been structural changes which have enhanced consumer latitude of action. First, there has been what some analysts call the income revolution. We now have broad middle and upper-middle income groups rather than masses of poor people and a few very rich ones. Millions of families have supernumerary income. The annual income of more than one-third of the 54 million American family units lies between $6,000 and $15,000. These families are in a position to spend money on things other than necessities. If they so choose, they can increase or decrease their rate of spending.

Next, there is the fact that buying on credit is today a generally accepted and widely practiced form of behavior. The easy availability of credit and the psychological acceptance of installment buying mean, of course, that consumers may, if they so choose, spend more than what they have.

Finally, over the past fifty years a significant portion of consumer expenditures have shifted to durable goods. When a society spends most of its income on perishable goods or on services used up over short periods of time, its discretion in postponing purchases or in buying in advance of immediate needs is severely limited. But today in America most automobiles and electrical appliances are not bought by the have-nots nor by those whose cars or appliances have broken down or are in a technologically bad condition. These expenditures are discretionary, as are expenditures on travel and vacation, on innumerable hobby items, and on repairs and improvements of housing. We have every reason to speak of consumer investments which are of similar importance for the business cycle as business investments.

What makes consumers step up or reduce their investment expenditures? If consumer demand were a function of consumer income—in other words, if consumers' sentiment and inclinations to buy improved after their income had risen and deteriorated after their income had fallen—then, in spite of all that has been said, we would have to rule out consumers as a major factor in the economy. But numerous studies over the past fifteen years have demonstrated that consumer demand does not depend on ability to buy alone. Ability to buy is important, but people do not always buy just because they have money. In the economy, marginal decisions matter. Stepping up discretionary expenditures by 10 per cent or reducing them by 10 per cent may make the difference between prosperity and recession, inflation and price stability. Such changes depend on willingness to buy in addition to ability to buy. People's sentiment and buying inclinations may improve even when their income has not gone up, and may deteriorate when their income has not gone down.

Up to now I have spoken on a qualitative, descriptive plane. But science is quantitative. The demonstration that changes in consumer willingness to buy are measurable represents significant progress. It is not correct to assume that income, amounts spent, or amounts saved are exact quantities, while expectations, optimistic or pessimistic attitudes, feelings of security or anxiety are vague or not quantifiable notions. Psychological states, or more correctly, changes in psychological states are susceptible to exact measurement. Modern sampling methods enable us to draw fairly small samples which are representative of all American consumers or of such important subgroups as the young or old, the rich or poor. In sample interview surveys conducted every few months we ask questions on optimism or pessimism, confidence or anxiety regarding personal finances, the business outlook, and market conditions. Thereby, we find out whether or not consumer willingness to buy has changed, and if so, whether it has improved or deteriorated.

Such measurements have proved their value over the past fifteen years. To mention only a few relevant findings, the Survey Research Center of the University of Michigan reported in June, 1954, when business activity and incomes were at a low point, that consumer optimism and confidence had improved substantially. A few months later, in the winter of 1954-55, automobile sales rose sharply, which development, in turn, ushered in three prosperous years. Early in 1957 and especially in the summer of 1957 consumer optimism weakened. Doubts, uncertainties and anxieties on the part of consumers were observed several months before the 1958 recession, which consisted both of reduced business expenditures and reduced expenditures on consumer durable goods. During the last two years we have had a modest recovery, rather than buoyant business activity, under the influence of fairly substantial fluctuations of consumer sentiment.

Now we are ready to discuss the question with which I began my paper. Is the way American consumers exercise their power beneficial or harmful to our economy? At first appraisal, an unfavorable conclusion suggests itself. Occasionally changes in consumer sentiment have amplified the fluctuations in the sales of automobiles and household appliances. It has also been argued that the masses of consumers are uninformed, suggestible, subject to manipulation and therefore inclined toward excessive behavior. If so, the fact that the control of economic developments no longer is exercised by a fairly small number of entrepreneurs and by the government, but now is shared by millions of middle and upper-middle income consumers, would contribute to a decrease in the stability of our economy.

Alternatively, however, one may argue that consumers are inherently conservative and sane and that the unorganized masses are more resistant to the spread and exaggeration of rumors than cohesive groups. Consumers are less aware of what other consumers do than business leaders are of their competitors, whose actions they watch and often follow. In sum, the errors of overexuberance during a boom and of overcaution during a depression are more characteristic of business action than of consumer action.

Studies carried out by the Survey Research Center of the University of Michigan during the past twelve years support the second view. To be sure, certain consumer attitudes and expectations do change frequently and substantially and make for fluctuations in consumers' discretionary expenditures which are much greater than the fluctuations in consumer expenditures for necessities or convenience goods. Also, it is possible for the consumers to lose their sanity under the influence of repeated severe shocks. Then what psychologists call catastrophic behavior is adopted, and mass hysteria characterized by cumulative and self-justifying expectations spreads widely. But most commonly consumer sentiment is governed by certain fairly stable features. Let me describe them.

1. *In Time People Are Satiated with Good News as Well as With Bad News.* For most people only what is *new* is news. When, over two or three years, production, sale, and profit figures continue to show increases, the news tends to become less and less salient. People get accustomed to a certain type of news, do not notice it, and do not react to it. Furthermore, after a few years of continuous good news people are apt to notice slight divergent tendencies and watch for them. Similarly in the recession. When the tempo of decline no longer accelerates and unemployment stops growing, many people get accustomed to the bad news and are more sensitive to good news.

2. *Levels of Aspiration Are Only Slightly above Levels of Achievement.* Achievement does not fully satisfy people. A person who has finally reached a goal which, a few months ago, seemed to him ideal, will soon raise his sights and strive for further advancement. After a consumer has bought a house, a car, a washing machine, or clothes dryer, other previously suppressed needs and desires arise.

This tendency to raise our sights following accomplishment or to lower them after failure or frustration seldom leads to excesses. Usually it follows closely the actual accomplishment level. We want a little more income, a few additional goods, and a somewhat better house; our desires and fancies are reality-bound and reality-tested.

3. *People Change Their Convictions Slowly.* Even contrary personal experiences do not necessarily shake a consumer's opinions. For instance, masses of people believe today that high expenditures for rearmament are not good for the economy because the money is, as they say, wasted rather than serving to raise the standard of living. This belief is widely held even though thousands of people had the best years of their lives when rearmament expenditures were high.

The same is true of the conviction that inflation is bad. Even people whose income automatically keeps pace with prices, or those who profit from inflation, do not attribute their income gains to inflation. Income gains are thought to be the result of one's own accomplishments or, occasionally, of lucky breaks. Inflation, on the other hand, is considered detrimental to the enjoyment of the fruits of one's labor.

Such broad generalizations as "inflation is bad," "what goes up must come down," "trees don't grow to heaven" are inherently conservative. Because of such beliefs, people react to inflationary news by restricting their discretionary purchases. This is the case when small and gradual price increases are expected: Here is one of the crucial differences between creeping and runaway inflation! Buying more freely when prices are stable and buying less when prices are rising helps reduce fluctuations rather than make them excessive.

4. *Consumers Are Conservative.* Diversification is a widely prevailing practice. Even people who do not argue consciously that it is wrong to put all your eggs in one basket do not back the most probable course with all their means.

Many people who are convinced that, over a decade or two, sizable price increases are inevitable still keep some money in savings accounts. They know that what appears probable still is not certain and they take into consideration that some risks are involved in the stocks they may buy as hedges against inflation. Most people have only one important hedge against inflation—the house they own.

People like to buy on time and look at the amount of monthly payments rather than the size of the carrying charges. This has occasionally been cited as indicating that consumers are impulsive or irrational. But paying while using is not a new idea and seems right. What matters most, financially, is the relation of monthly charges to the family income. In this area many families prepare accurate estimates. They calculate the size of the monthly payments they can afford to make. This serves as an effective budgetary device which restrains impulse buying.

It is rather generally accepted that the character of the business cycle has changed. The three post-war recessions were all fairly short and mild. The new business cycle is not due exclusively to automatic stabilizers or to anti-recession action by the government. The last fifteen years have witnessed not only a change in the nature of the business cycle, but also a change in the power exercised by the consumer. The two developments are interrelated. The much maligned, often misunderstood and unorganized consumer is a stabilizing force in our economy. His conservative and sane behavior does not suffice to rule out the recurrence of recessions or to arrest inflation, but does help to lessen the scope of economic fluctuations and to reduce inflationary pressures.

Up to now I have discussed the size rather than the composition of demand. How to increase the size of the pie represents a crucial question for students of distribution. Yet the other question, about the share of different businesses in the pie, should not be neglected either. In this respect the American consumer did not have a good press during the last few years. It has been frequently and persuasively argued that the consumer exercises his influence in a socially undesirable manner. It has been deplored that the consumers choose gadgets rather than books, or spend more on liquor and cosmetics than on health and education. Furthermore, it has been said that, under the influence of consumers, our society as a whole devotes an unduly great share of its resources to consumer goods.

There have been, of course, few periods in history in which consumer choices were not deplored by social critics. That America wastes its resources is an old argument. Conspicuous consumption and luxurious living by the rich were criticized especially toward the end of the last and the beginning of this century. In this respect there has been some change. Today it is not the very rich whose purchases and tastes dominate the economy. The upper-middle income groups—families with an annual income between, say, $6,000 and $15,000—buy most of the cars and appliances. Their tastes and preferences, for shopping in supermarkets and traveling in the family car and staying in motels, for instance, bring forth new trends in living which represent comfort and fun, and not extravagance and splurging.

American standards of living are high. Compared with Western Europe and, of course, with communist and underdeveloped countries, the number of rooms, cars, and refrigerators owned per family in this country represents a very high standard. But the standard of living we have is not good enough for most of us. We desire more and better goods and services and strive for them. Should we deplore this? Or should we recognize that in people's wanting more and better things lies one of the most powerful incentives to work hard and to stimulate production, efficiency, and economic growth? Economists teach that consumption is a function of income. Today, to a large extent, income is a function of expenditures; because we need more and better things, we strive to earn more. And the goods and services we feel we need are not luxuries and waste, but means toward security and comfort.

How about the great social purposes and goals? Because of our preoccupation with cars and appliances we do not have enough schools, missiles, and satellites, so says the critic. Let us not forget that never in the past did we devote a larger share of our income to the government—that is, for distribution through community decisions rather than by individual fancies and wishes. For the past twenty years the proportion of income taken away by taxes has been larger than ever before. To be sure, most of the tax money is spent on defense. Nevertheless, it remains true that the American people approve of a very substantial reduction of their disposable income for common rather than personal goals.

But we ought to do more, so we hear often, in order to have better health, less delinquency, improved schools, and faster scientific progress. Naturally, the allocation of national resources is never ideal, and it would be foolish to argue that allocation could not be improved. Whose responsibility is it to do so? On the one hand the consumer, or the consumption orientation and thing-mindedness of the American people, are blamed. On the other hand, we are told that the consumer is a puppet, manipulated by marketers, advertisers, and even hidden persuaders. Influence is hardly ever a one-way process. There is interaction between businessmen and consumers. Advertisers and marketers watch carefully for every sign of change in consumer preferences and try to utilize incipient tendencies for business purposes. Thus, if we are dissatisfied with the allocation of our resources—the manner in which the pie is divided—we should blame both consumers and business. And the responsibility for improving the allocation rests on both and, also, on leaders of public opinion.

From this point of view, the recent widespread criticism of consumers and of consumer tastes is useful, even if not fully justified. For consumers can learn. Learning, again, is a process of interaction between teacher and pupil. Social learning—a change in the beliefs, attitudes, and preferences of the masses—is a slow process but something which we have experienced repeatedly. The attitudes and notions prevailing today among American consumers, which I have described before and characterized as conservative and contributing to economic growth without excessive fluctuations, have been learned over the past few decades. Similarly, progress can be made toward a better allocation of national resources through social learning. The goals held in highest esteem by the American people are susceptible to change rather than being rigid. Maybe the consumer is not "manipulated" enough. More guidance and education of the consumer is needed, especially about the best ways of utilizing his leisure time. We have every reason to expect that the powerful consumer, with the great latitude of action he now has, will react to such guidance. He will learn from the advice given by leaders of public opinion.

Of all national stereotypes, the most important for Americans to recognize is their own national superiority complex.

6

When Marketing Abroad ... Remove Your Star-Spangled Glasses

ERNEST DICHTER

MANY AMERICANS HAVE some blind spots when it comes to marketing abroad. In automatically applying their U.S. experience to foreign markets, too often they fail to consider fairly simple differences in psychology. Here are a few of the most common mistakes made:

Because everybody wants to be different, lumping foreigners together not only leads to inaccurate thinking, it offends them. Europeans, for example, today are intensely conscious of national differences, regional differences, even local differences. The French point out: "We're not German, not Italian, not Spanish, but French." Germans draw painstaking distinctions between people living in Schleswig-Holstein and in Bavaria, and even between the north side of Düsseldorf and the south side.

This wish to retain their identity leads to erroneous stereotypes, sometimes promoted by the Europeans themselves. I was told in France, for example, that although American women might be interested in educational and political issues, French women are not. The old saw that French women would never abandon the local food shop because they liked to talk for

Reprinted from the May 2, 1966 issue of *Business Abroad*, pp. 14-15, 18, by special permission. Copyrighted © 1966 by the Dun & Bradstreet Publications Corporation.

two hours has now been disproved by the success of supermarkets in France. The myth that they are extremely fashion conscious can be disproved by studies which show they are even more economy minded, and ready-to-wear sales are beginning to lend support. The success of "Le Snack Bar" and the American Drug Store on the Champs Elysées also have flown in the face of the stereotype.

It is important to probe stereotypes like these in depth before accepting them. Just asking a Frenchman won't do. Most nationals—Frenchmen or Americans—know the least about their own mentality.

Of all national stereotypes, the most important for Americans to recognize is their own national superiority complex. Many U.S. businessmen sincerely believe American things, processes, and ideas are generally the best. Marketing men are particularly prone to view the world through star-spangled glasses, and it can get in the way of their work.

One Italian candy manufacturer is now studying the oral dissatisfactions of Europeans today. "What are they dreaming about?" he asks. "Do they want to suck, crack, crunch, or chew? We can make any kind of product. We can give them one which supplies all four satisfactions at the same time. What do they want?" This is as sophisticated a piece of market research as any.

Distortion aside, the star-spangled glasses can lead Americans into important marketing errors. One company spoiled its international sales meeting by using for favors a simulated gold coin with "$1 billion" printed on it. Some foreign participants were annoyed. "Why not 'DM 4 billion'?" they said. "Why does everything have to be under the dollar sign?" Some martial music was played, as it usually is at a U.S. sales meeting. "This is familiar," a German told me in German. "It's not much different from what we had under Hitler."

The opposite of American superiority complex is a deep-seated feeling of inferiority in the minds of many foreigners. This may express itself in a revulsion against U.S. marketing methods or in a bitter cry of "Yankee go home!" We found that Venezuelans smoke American cigarettes because they taste good, but feel they really should smoke the local product out of a sense of duty. Sales of Venezuelan rum improved when the sales pitch shifted away from chauvinism to emphasize that the product was sold successfully even in the U.S.

We also discovered one reason Europeans don't visit the U.S. as often as they could afford—they don't like to go back with feelings of inferiority. It shows them a world which they fear as part of their own future. It threatens their well established past.

A study we made for the German laundry industry a few years ago showed that 80% of Germans change their shirts once a week. The industry's initial advertising campaign fell flat when it emphasized American cleanliness. "Americans change their shirts three times a week, and you Germans—80% of you—change yours only once a week," it said in effect. The message boomeranged. "Yes, but we are morally clean," was the reaction. "Americans may be outwardly clean, but what about Little Rock?"

One of the most common marketing mistakes of U.S. firms overseas is the condescending message that foreigners finally have been invited to enjoy the benefits of American civilization. "Look at what we've done in the U.S.," runs this line, "and now it's available for you!" The reaction, our studies tell us, is likely to be: "Well, keep it." It is important to avoid the impression the dish you are serving consists of crumbs from the American table.

Selling the past is generally bad business, anyway. Talking to the voters of Puerto Rico, we found the political slogans that emphasized all the things Governor Muñoz had done for his people got a cool reception, especially from the young people. "So what?" was the reaction, "Now we have cars, TV sets, cleaner homes. Everybody has these things. They are nothing to be proud about. What is he going to do for us in the future?" The same psychology applies to product advertising.

A better approach is to tell the people in the markets you are opening what you intend to do for them in the future. Emphasize the ways you are going to modify—especially for them—the particular product or service. Remind them the American product really had its origin in Europe. Often this is the truth.

Culture is important. Businessmen accustomed to the U.S. market have a tendency to underrate the importance of culture and humanism to many foreigners. Europeans may or may not be more cultured, less materialistic than Americans. The point is, they think they are.

In the past years we have found that a very useful approach to weave in with your promise of bigger sales and product advantages is some real or imagined cultural kind of advantage. This is, in my opinion, one of the most important and interesting developments we have been witnessing and it could help considerably in establishing better relations between the U.S. and foreign countries.

An occasional reference to a Greek philosopher, quoting a good book, or the inclusion of real art or history in sales and promotion literature are not considered out of place in Europe. For example, the history of the baker, of baking as a profession became a successful sales tool for a German bread company. A large number of business leaders in Europe have a Ph.D., and they expect people dealing with them to be at least equally well educated.

Modern business has a certain obligation which goes beyond purely commercial and mercenary goals. Individual business leaders, once they have made their money, often become personally interested in charity, politics or cultural pursuits. They may do this out of a feeling of frustration, a feeling that life consists of more than selling soap and toothpaste. The same desire for compensation exists for businesses, too. A company takes on a better psychological balance by acknowledging the "other world" of sophistication, elegance, and culture.

Looking beneath the surface of foreign attitudes can yield unexpected— and profitable—results. For example, a U.S. manufacturer of paper products learned that Europeans feel guilty about throwing things away. This showed not only in a resistance to disposable plates and tablecloths, but even in their attitude toward soft, high-quality toilet paper. The more luxury, the greater the guilt feeling and the less likelihood of their using the product.

Different values can suggest different marketing approaches. Hatmakers supposed Germans would respond to the approach: "You're a real man when you wear a hat. When you wear a hat, you've arrived!" But Germans apparently do not want to arrive these days. They want to keep growing. So an entirely different marketing approach was indicated.

Englishmen feel they are the best dressed men in the world, and Americans the worst. Yet many Englishmen prefer lightweight suits. This annoys them because the Americans seem to have preempted the market. We recommended our client make lightweight clothes, but make some modification that would give them an English value system.

This is a bit like the cafeteria in Paris. That it is a U.S. idea is freely admitted, "but we are still serving good French food." In other words, understand we've improved on the original idea.

It is even worthwhile to examine the dreams of a market. In a study for the German detergent firm, Henkel, we found that 80% of Italian housewives do their laundry by hand. This concrete statistic would dictate one marketing philosophy. Yet we also found that most Italian housewives dream of owning washing machines. This suggested a different philosophy and a new product which recognizes cycles in the washing process. The Italian housewife is still washing her linens by hand, but the new detergent is bringing her closer to her dream.

These examples simply illustrate that the gap between the image and the reality is sometimes large, and a successful marketing philosophy ought to take cognizance of both. To the extent that U.S. businessmen question the stereotypes, find the facts, and understand the psychology of a market, they are likely to avoid the most important mistakes.

Is it to society's interest to permit firms to grow through merger, if growth through internal expansion is a likely alternative?

7

The Procter and Gamble Decision

JOHN M. KUHLMAN

THE FEDERAL TRADE COMMISSION challenged the merger of the Procter and Gamble Company and the Clorox Chemical Company on the basis that the probable effect of the merger would be a lessening of competition.[1] In law, the case was an initial venture for the antitrust agencies into the area of conglomerate mergers. To the economist it was a challenge of the power of conglomerate firms as distinct from a challenge of monopoly power. Does a conglomerate firm have a peculiar kind of power resulting not from its monopoly position in any particular field but from the fact that it produces a number of products in different fields and as a result has a degree of power which is inconsistent with social well-being? [2]

The Decision of the Federal Trade Commission

THE FACTS AND THE BACKGROUND

Household liquid bleach, a 5¼ percent sodium hypochlorite solution, is

Quarterly Review of Economics & Business, Volume 6, No. 1 (Spring, 1966), pp. 29-36.

[1] *In the Matter of the Procter and Gamble Company,* Docket No. 6901. All page references are to the mimeographed copy of the decision.

[2] Corwin D. Edwards, "Conglomerate Bigness as a Source of Power," in *Business Concentration and Price Policy,* George Stigler, ed. (Princeton: Princeton University Press, 1955).

71

a homogeneous commodity produced by more than 200 firms in the United States. The Clorox Chemical Company, the producer of Clorox, had nearly half of the market at the time of the merger and Purex, the second-largest producer, had 15 percent of the market. The six largest firms controlled nearly 80 percent of the total. The techniques of production are not complicated; there is no problem of patents or trade secrets; and a relatively small capital investment is required to undertake production.

Liquid bleach is marketed locally or regionally because of the weight of the finished product and its low sales price per unit. Clorox, with 13 plants, was the only firm which sold in a national market; Purex did not sell in the Northeast or the Middle Atlantic States, and the remaining producers operated in local markets.

Procter and Gamble, one of the nation's 50 largest firms (and the largest single advertiser) acquired the Clorox Chemical Company in 1957. Since the two firms did not manufacture the same product, the merger could not be classed as a horizontal merger; and since the output of one was not used by the other, it could not be classed as a vertical merger. It approximated a conglomerate merger, although the Federal Trade Commission (FTC) referred to it as a "product extension" merger because the products of the two firms were "functionally closely related." [3]

GENERAL PRINCIPLES IN THE INTERPRETATION AND APPLICATION OF SECTION 7

The FTC, in arriving at its decision, had a decade of experience under the amended Section 7 of the Clayton Antitrust Act to draw upon, but there were no specific or authoritative precedents to cite. Since it was a decision on a conglomerate merger, even though it was not so described, previous decisions involving horizontal and vertical mergers were not appropriate.

In the absence of specific precedents, the commission found the following five principles in the legislative history of the 1950 amendment, court decisions, and legal and economic writings. (1) All mergers are to be tested against the same standard. Congress intended that every merger—horizontal, vertical, or conglomerate—be tested by its tendency to substantially lessen competition or to create a monopoly. (2) Competition is the fundamental national policy. It is the (preferred) alternative to private cartelization or extensive government regulation. (3) The appropriate concept of competition is neither simple nor obvious. The commission interpreted the commitment to competition to imply a specific type of industry structure rather than a particular type of market behavior. The significant structural characteristics would include the absence of undue concentration, minimal

3 In the Matter of the Procter and Gamble Company, p. 15.

barriers to entry, and a freedom from domination by large firms. (4) The appropriate concept of competition is socioeconomic rather than purely economic and emphasizes the social importance of local (rather than absentee) control of business and the protection of small firms. (5) Since the Clayton Act (including the amended Section 7) is preventive, it follows that the standard of proof is less stringent than for Sherman Act cases.

In effect, it was only necessary to make a prediction of the probable future performance and conduct resulting from the change in structure. If the merger indicated a probable lessening of competition, then the remedy would involve restructuring in the form of divestiture. The post-merger market behavior was irrelevant.

THE EFFECT OF THE INSTANT MERGER ON COMPETITION

Prior to the merger, the Clorox Chemical Company was the dominant firm in the household liquid bleach industry. Because of a substantial consumer preference for Clorox, resulting largely from extensive advertising and promotional campaigns, the price of Clorox was several cents a quart above that of other bleaches. This position of dominance meant that barriers to entry were significant, as were barriers to further expansion by firms already in the industry. There were no firms, either existing or potential, in a position to become fully effective competitors in the industry.

The FTC, in addition to finding the premerger structure of the industry unsatisfactory, found that further undesirable results would flow from the merger.

1. Substitution of a large multiproduct firm for a small single-product firm would permit the latter to achieve "substantial cost savings and other advantages in advertising and promotion, especially in television advertising." [4] Such advantages would include cumulative discounts, joint-product promotion by the multiproduct firm, more effective use of advertising time, the substitution of a direct sales force for a system of independent brokers, and an improved bargaining position vis-à-vis the independent dealers.

2. Substitution of Procter and Gamble for the Clorox Chemical Company would mean the replacement of a relatively small firm by a much larger firm with financial strength and experience unmatched in the bleach industry. The merged firm would enjoy a degree of flexibility in pricing not enjoyed by other firms. The greater financial strength of the merged firm would permit it to engage in price-cutting to an extent beyond the capacity of its competitors.

3. And lastly, the intangible effect of Procter and Gamble's reputation as a well-managed and aggressive firm upon present and potential producers of bleach had to be considered. The commission observed that since "mar-

[4] *Ibid.,* p. 43.

ket behavior is determined by the state of mind of the firms in the market, Procter's history of success, its general size and its prowess, which loom large in the eyes of the small liquid bleach firms, must for that reason alone be reckoned significant competitive factors." [5]

Thus, the commission concluded that the merger would raise barriers to entry, make expansion by existing firms still more difficult, and, in general, further enhance the dominance of the industry by Clorox.

THE SUBSTANTIALITY OF THE INSTANT MERGER'S ANTICOMPETITIVE EFFECTS

In the absence of precise quantitative measuring techniques, it was necessary to devise other means for estimating the "substantiality of the merger's probable adverse effect." [6] There were five such factors of significance.

1. The merger, in replacing a relatively small firm by a large firm, would increase the size disparity of the firms in the industry with the following adverse effects: it would result in substantial cost advantages to the merged firm, it would further enhance the advertising advantage of Clorox, and it would be inconsistent with the Congressional aim of maintaining competitive opportunities for small firms.

2. The high degree of concentration and the barriers to entry made for an unhealthy premerger structure. Any merger which restricts freedom of entry in such a market is "highly suspect under Section 7." [7] The merger would permit the merged company to use the monopoly profits in one market to impair competition in others. And lastly, the merger would, in effect, capitalize the monopoly gains of Clorox; and the commission felt that its approval of such action would encourage further anticompetitive developments in the private sector of the economy.

3. Procter and Gamble's entrance into the industry through the merger eliminated that firm as a potential entrant through internal expansion. Whether or not it would have entered is immaterial, for its potential entrance was a limiting factor for the existing firms.

4. Procter and Gamble's strong market position in other products gives it an inherent advantage over any single-product firm with which it competes. The power of a conglomerate firm is not dependent upon its monopoly power in any particular market but results from the sum of its position in many markets. "The short of it is that a conglomerate merger involving firms which have dominant power in their respective markets tends to reinforce and augment such power" [8] and "Congress was expressing its special concern with those acquisitions which result in the mutual entrenchment of

---

[5] *Ibid.*, p. 49.
[6] *Ibid.*, p. 53.
[7] *Ibid.*, p. 58.
[8] *Ibid.*, p. 63.

unhealthy market situations, and thus bear grave consequences for the future of our competitive economy." [9]

5. Lastly, the FTC found no reason to conclude that economies of scale were to be given greater weight than the maintenance of competition. The ultimate effect of the economies of scale, in this case, was to increase barriers to entry.

"In sum, the undue emphasis on advertising which characterizes the liquid bleach industry is itself a symptom of and a contributing cause to the sickness of competition in the industry. Price competition, beneficial to the consumer, has given way to brand competition in a form beneficial only to the seller. In such an industry, cost advantages that enable still more intensive advertising only impair price competition further; they do not benefit the consumer." [10]

The Economics of the Decision

The decision raised three significant economic issues. The first, the nature of firm growth, is basic to all merger decisions. The second was the nature and significance of the economies associated with advertising and product promotion. And lastly, there was the question of conglomerate power which has, to date, not often been raised in merger decisions but promises to become a more frequent issue as firms expand into new product lines and diversify rather than expand in present product lines.

THE STRATEGY OF FIRM GROWTH

Merger decisions can be viewed as a selection by management of one of several alternative strategies of firm growth. A management may select growth through a program of internal expansion including the development of new products, or it may select growth through mergers with existing firms including those producing unrelated products. Consideration of the alternative strategies will involve a comparison of costs and returns for each alternative and a selection of that particular strategy which has the most promise of meeting management's goals. In the case of firm growth, however, there are differences in social costs associated with the alternative strategies available to the firm, and these social costs may be, in some instances, of such magnitude that they are unacceptable to society.

Economists generally take for granted the desirability of economic growth —an increasing real per capita output. Such growth will require a more efficient utilization of existing resources, improved technology, or the development and utilization of new resources. Internal firm growth contributes

9 *Ibid.*, p. 64.
10 *Ibid.*, p. 67.

to aggregate growth if such growth takes the form of new investment and increased output unless, of course, such expansion is at the expense of some other firm. But expansion through merger does not necessarily contribute to aggregate growth. In an accounting sense, there is no increase in society's assets, since the growth in assets of the merged firms is just offset by the decline in the assets of the acquired and no longer independent firm(s).

If, instead of the accounting concepts, one uses the present value of the income stream, then the value of the merged firm's assets will exceed the value of the assets of the formerly independent firms. (If this were not so, there would seem to be little reason for the merger unless one includes such motives as the management's power motive.) This increase in the present value of the income stream generated by the assets may represent either economies resulting from the merging of the firms or increased monopoly power. In the present case, the purchase price of Clorox was $30,000,000, whereas the assets were said to be worth $12,600,000.[11] The decision indicated that the difference represented the price of Clorox's dominant position in the industry. However, it also reflected the economies which would result from the increased advertising budget as well as anticipated monopoly gains.

The social desirability of one or the other of the two strategies of growth are certainly important aspects of merger decisions. Unfortunately, however, the "state of the art" relative to the economics of firm growth is comparatively underdeveloped and is of limited usefulness in antitrust litigation. Its most important limitation is the lack of criteria to be used to measure such variables as freedom of entry and exit or the impact of potential entrants. No precise means exist for measuring the impact of barriers to entry and how much is lost (or gained) when they are raised (or lowered). There is no way to judge that barriers are sufficiently low or how much they should be lowered. How can the loss to society be determined when an existing firm enters an industry through merger and thus is no longer a potential competitor? What happens to the demand schedule of existing producers when such a potential firm entrant acquires the assets of a firm already in the industry as compared with entrance through the construction of new facilities? These are the sorts of questions for which nice precise answers are not available, but they are the questions which will be raised in the challenge of a merger such as the one being considered.

In the case at hand, the acquiring company was a potential entrant in the bleach industry until its acquisition of Clorox. But that acquisition did not represent a new entry, for it was merely a change of control over existing production facilities. If Procter and Gamble had elected to enter through the construction of new production facilities and the use of Procter and Gamble management, some of the advantages of entry would have accrued to the public in the form of increased supply, more competitors (by one), and (possibly) lower prices. But even though the criteria for evaluation are absent, the relative desirability of Procter and Gamble's selection of this particular method of entry over that of internal expansion remains an important part of this case.

ECONOMIES OF SCALE

The commission's analysis of economies of scale associated with advertising and sales promotion was a crucial part of the decision. The commission argued that the merger would result in certain economies, "but the cost savings made possible by the instant merger serves . . . not to promote competition, but only to increase the barriers to new entry into the relevant market, and thereby impair competition." [12] These economies were weighed against such social values as the dispersal of private power and the desirability of small locally owned businesses and were found wanting.

The critical role of these economies warrants a somewhat more extensive investigation and analysis than that made in the decision. First, the nature of the economies should be mentioned. The advertising budget of Clorox was so small that it was "virtually certain that (it) . . . did not entitle Clorox to discounts of any substance." [13] After the merger, "for the same amount of money Clorox spent on network television advertising prior to the merger, at least 33⅓ percent more network television can now be obtained." [14] This resulted from the practice of those firms in advertising of granting cumulative discounts instead of computing the discount on the basis of a single sale, a particular product, or an individual plant. A multiple-product firm, for example, receives a discount based on its total advertising for all products on a given network or station or in a given magazine. In this case, the new lower rate for Clorox reflected the much larger volume of advertising done by Procter and Gamble for all of its products.

At a more analytical level, the economies associated with the advertising input offer a greater degree of difficulty than those associated with other inputs. This arises from the fact that the advertising input affects both the cost and revenue functions, whereas other inputs affect only the former. Advertising costs may change either as the proportion of advertising input changes relative to other inputs or the amount of total advertising input changes along with all other inputs. This is, of course, the traditional dichotomy between variable proportions and returns to scale.

In reference to changing proportions, if the price of a single input is lowered, for example, more of that input will be used and the cost function

[12] *Ibid.*, p. 65.
[13] *Ibid.*, p. 44.
[14] *Ibid.*, p. 45.

will be lowered and will change its shape because of the change in proportions. There is no reason to believe that, in the short run, the advertising
inputs behave in accordance with laws of production which are different
from those applicable to other inputs. In the long run, it is generally accepted that the advertising input may not have to be increased so fast as
other inputs, thus indicating that advertising is subject to increasing returns
to scale. Such economies result from a more effective use of time, joint
promotions with other products, and so forth. These are the true economies
of scale.

Decreasing average costs resulting from changing proportions or from
changing scale may be either technological (i.e., real) or pecuniary. To the
extent that the cost functions shift downward from price discounts which
exceed gains in efficiency, such economies would be classed as internal
pecuniary economies; and to the extent that such economies reflect increased
efficiency, they would be classed as real or technological economies.

Economies of either a pecuniary or a technological nature associated
with the advertising and sales promotion input are of a different nature from
those associated with other productive inputs. It is not unreasonable to
assume independence between the demand functions and the factors of production with the exception of the advertising input. In the latter case, to
assume independence is to assume that the productivity of the input is zero
and thus none of that input would be used. For any input except advertising,
a lower price for the input will result in a lower price and a larger output
if there is no change in the product demand function and if that function
is less than perfectly inelastic.

But this is not the case when advertising is considered. A reduction in
the price of advertising causes the cost functions to shift downward, and,
as advertising becomes relatively cheaper, it will be substituted for other
inputs—product improvement activities, for example. Hence a fall in the
cost of sales promotion activities means that it becomes relatively cheaper
to attempt to influence the firm's sales schedule and thus relatively cheaper
to maintain or raise barriers to entry and thus promote or enhance the
firm's monopoly power.

If the price of the input and the demand function are not independent,
it is impossible to predict what the effect of changes in the input price will
be on the price and quantity of the output of the firm. The final impact will
reflect the relative changes in the input price and the change in the demand
schedules. There is no reason to believe, however, that all of the cost reduction will be passed on to the consumer in the form of either lower prices or
increased outputs.

In the present case, then, there are several unanswered questions which
were not explored in the decision of the FTC. Although it is generally

agreed that there are certain economies associated with increased advertising, there was no attempt to explain the division of those gains between the advertising firms and the firms purchasing the advertising. Furthermore, there was no attempt to compare the real economies in the industry with the actual discounts granted to the large advertisers. And finally, there was no exploration of the economies of cumulative discounts. Cumulative discounts which cover a time span of 12 months and a wide variety of products probably cannot be explained in terms of traditional economies. The consequences of cumulative discounts merited considerably more attention than was given them in this decision.[15]

THE CONGLOMERATE FIRM

The concept of the conglomerate firm does not, as yet, have a secure position in economic analysis. Professor Edwards argues that a conglomerate firm acquires a peculiar type of economic power resulting from its aggregate role in a large number of markets—even though it may have no monopoly power in any individual market.[16] To permit the merger, according to this view, would still further enhance the position of Procter and Gamble in the many markets in which it operates, and, in particular, the power of the conglomerate firm would now be an overwhelming factor in the household liquid bleach industry.

The nature of the cumulative quantity discounts in the advertising media does cast new light on the nature of the conglomerate firm. In a single-product firm, a fall in the price of the advertising input will cause that input to be substituted for other inputs in the production of that product alone. Since there is the interdependent relationship between costs and demand, no prediction can be made regarding the effect of such economies on the final price and output. There would be no reason to believe, however, that such economies would be passed on to the consumer.

In the conglomerate firm, the situation is even less well defined. Suppose that the firm produces a number of different products, each one of which competes with those of a number of single-product firms. None of the latter are large enough to obtain quantity discounts in their purchase of advertising. If the conglomerate firm has not exhausted all possible quantity discounts, then as it adds additional product lines, it will receive additional discounts on the advertising inputs for all of its products. Advertising becomes relatively cheaper in each product line instead of only in the last one acquired. Thus, if Procter and Gamble was not receiving the maximum discount in all advertising outlets when it acquired Clorox, the merger would

---

[15] The Federal Trade Commission is presently investigating the effects of cumulative discounts. See *Advertising Age,* Vol. 36 (August 30, 1965).

[16] Edwards, *op. cit.*

not only have affected the small producers of bleach but also the small producers of peanut butter, toothpaste, and so on.

The impact of a conglomerate-type merger, then, extends beyond the single product of the acquired firm; it extends to all of the products of the various industries represented by the acquiring conglomerate firm. In each, further quantity discounts will result in advertising becoming relatively cheaper and then being substituted for other inputs. The result may be an enhancement of the monopoly power as well as a raising of the barriers to entry in each of the product lines. It not only becomes more difficult to enter the bleach industry, but also the peanut butter industry. The presence and utilization of cumulative quantity discounts available to the conglomerate firm certainly casts some new light on such an organization.

In this case, as in the metal container case,[17] the real culprit appears to have been an industry practice—only in this case, it was a practice associated with a seller of one of the inputs. In the container decision, restrictions were imposed upon cumulative discounts and requirements contracts. The result was a substantial change in the structure of the industry. Cumulative quantity discounts in the purchase of the advertising input would seem to have little justification so far as public policy is concerned.

As a matter of fact, cumulative discounts work in a fashion which is contrary to that policy advocated by many economists. It is often recommended that a progressive tax be imposed on advertising expenditures in order to discourage large-scale advertising and thus facilitate entry into industries in which product differentiation is presently a formidable barrier. Simply eliminating cumulative quantity discounts would, in effect, impose a tax of considerable progressivity over a wide range of advertising expenditures and lessen the power of the conglomerate firm.

Conclusion

The basic issue in merger decision is as follows: Is it to society's interest to permit firms to grow through merger, if growth through internal expansion is a likely alternative? The latter will result in an increased number of competitors in the industry involved as well as in additional capacity. A merger replaces one controlling interest with another, without a necessary increase in capacity. A merger will increase the disparity in the size distribution of the firms in the industry and it may enhance the monopoly position of the merged firms.

The relative desirability of these alternative methods of firm growth is a difficult question to answer both in economics and in law. It does not readily fit into the traditional tests of promoting or impairing competition. It raises

[17] *United States of America v. American Company,* 87 F. Supp. 18 (1949).

issues which may be beyond the competence of the Federal Trade Commission, the Antitrust Division, and the courts.[18]

The FTC, instead of basing its decision on the relative desirability of the alternative methods of firm growth, based its decision upon the nature of the economies of scale and the conflict between such economies and the diffusion of economic power. This was, in a sense, a false dichotomy, for the alleged economies were of such a nature and existed in an industry structure that made it difficult, if not impossible, to predict any gain to society in the form of increased efficiency.

[18] John M. Kuhlman, "The Changing Role of Antitrust Agencies," *The Antitrust Bulletin,* Vol. 9 (November-December, 1964) and "Incremental Decision-Making and Antitrust Policy," *The Southwestern Social Service Quarterly,* Vol. 45 (December, 1964).

The middleman is not a hired link in a chain forged by a manufacturer, but rather an independent market, the focus of a large group of customers for whom he buys. Subsequent to some market analysis of his own, he selects products and suppliers, thereby setting at least one link in the channel.

8

Are Channels of Distribution

What the Textbooks Say?

PHILLIP McVEY

PERHAPS WROE ALDERSON said as much as is safe to say when he described a marketing channel as a group of firms which "constitute a loose coalition engaged in exploiting joint opportunity in the market." [1]

Theory and Actuality

Certainly too much is said about channel relationships in many published textbooks for businessmen and students, if one is to look for proof in current marketing practice. The picture usually given is one of long lists of various types of middlemen and facilitating agencies, which differ minutely but precisely in functions performed. Alignments of particular types are presented as "right" or "customary" for a given commodity or type of

Reprinted from the *Journal of Marketing*, national quarterly publication of the American Marketing Association, Volume 24, No. 3 (January, 1960), pp. 61-65.

[1] Wroe Alderson, "The Development of Marketing Channels," in Richard M. Clewett (editor), *Marketing Channels for Manufactured Products* (Homewood, Illinois; Richard D. Irwin, Inc., 1954), p. 30.

producer. Furthermore, it is often implied that it is the producer who selects all the links in the channel and establishes the working arrangements with them, down to and including the outlet which sells his goods to the final user.

Several popular college textbooks in marketing illustrate this manufacturer-oriented approach to channel planning.[2] One reason for fairly standard treatment of channel-building is that the growth of marketing knowledge has proceeded from a description of the activities of existing business firms, leaning heavily on data provided by the U. S. Censuses of Wholesale and Retail Trade. The framework appears orderly and well planned. But little recognition is given to the probability that some channel sequences "just grew" like Topsy, without direction or intent of known parents.

The Census method of counting, whereby each separate establishment is assigned to a single traditional category on the basis of a *major-portion-of-dollar-volume* rule, tends to produce more orderliness in the picture than probably exists. It tends to obscure a great deal of "promiscuous distribution" and channel-jumping. The Census rule, like the Procrustean bed of Greek mythology, effectively reduces the number of categories into which firms are sorted, and avoids hybrid, nondescript classifications.

Yet hybridity is too common among marketing firms to be ignored. For example, almost any wholesaler will do some business at retail; similarly, it is not uncommon for a broker to find himself holding title to a given lot of goods, thus becoming temporarily a merchant middleman. A realistic classification may require the use of relative terms to identify types of operation, according to a range of variables—for example, the *degree* to which a firm caters to a given customer group, or the *frequency* with which a function is performed.

Further study of marketing textbooks may lead a reader to conclude that: (a) middlemen of many types are available to any manufacturer in any market to which he wishes to sell, and within each type there is an ample selection of individual firms; (b) the manufacturer habitually controls the selection and operation of individual firms in his channel; and (c) middlemen respond willingly as *selling agents* for the manufacturer rather than as *purchasing agents* for a coveted group of customers to whom the middlemen sell.

Yet none of these conclusions is entirely valid.

In a product line such as fashion apparel, a garment maker may have

[2] Examples are found in: T. N. Beckman, H. H. Maynard, and W. R. Davidson, *Principles of Marketing,* sixth edition (New York, Ronald, 1957), pp. 44-45. C. F. Phillips and D. J. Duncan, *Marketing Principles and Methods,* third edition (Homewood, Illinois; Richard D. Irwin, 1956), p. 562. M. P. McNair, M. P. Brown, D. S. R. Leighton, and W. B. England, *Problems in Marketing,* second edition (New York, McGraw-Hill, 1957), p. 66.

an extremely limited choice of types of middlemen: the selling agent, the broker, the direct-buying retailer, or the chain store buying office. The general absence of service wholesalers from this line of trade is not correctible by manufacturers' *fiat*.

In a particular market area, the choice may be even more limited. Of individual firms of a given type, there may be no choice at all. These limitations arise, of course, because of the free choices made by the middlemen as to locations, customer groups, and product assortments they elect to sell.

Is the "Channel" an Academic Concept?

Integrated action up and down a channel is a rare luxury in marketing. Why? It may be that the "channel of distribution" is a concept that is principally academic in usage and unfamiliar to many firms selling to and through these channels.

Instead of a channel, a businessman is likely to concern himself merely with suppliers and customers. His dealings are not with all of the links in the channel but only with those immediately adjacent to him, from which he buys and to which he sells. He may little know nor care what becomes of his products after they leave the hands of some merchant middleman who has paid him for them and released him to return to problems involving his special functions. A manufacturer may not even consider himself as standing at the head of a channel, but only as occupying a link in a channel that begins with his suppliers.

POLICIES

Choice of a channel is not open to any firm unless it has considerable freedom of action in matters of marketing policy. Other areas of policy seem to be treated with more respect. For example, it is well recognized that a *price* policy is an authoritarian privilege open only to those sellers who possess power to withhold goods from the market in considerable quantities, or who have the choice of alternative markets and the means to solicit them. Usually a differentiated product is necessary. Therefore, a wheat farmer can seldom have anything resembling a price policy.

Likewise, a *design* policy is meaningful only when variations in product characteristics have been understood and accepted by customers to be of significance. Manufacturers of semi-finished or component parts, or of textile "gray goods" cannot enjoy this luxury in most cases.

Similarly, the selection of a multi-stage channel is not the prerogative of a manufacturer unless his franchise is coveted by the middlemen he seeks, as being more valuable to them than their franchise would be to him.

Names such as Sears Roebuck & Company, Macy's, or Kroger mean a great deal more to the customers of these retailers than do the brand names of most of the items sold in their stores. These firms control the channels for many products, even to the point of bringing into existence some manufacturing firms needed to fill gaps in their assortments. In the same manner some national wholesalers, holding the reins of a huge distributive system, are more powerful than either their suppliers or their customers. In such extreme cases the power position is obvious. The big company, regardless of its position in the channel, tries to make its plans and policies effective by taking the initiative for co-ordinated action.

Uncertainty Among Smaller Firms

As to the many thousands of middle-size and small companies that truly characterize American marketing, the power position is speculative, vacillating, and ephemeral. Strength in certain market areas, the temporary success of a product, ability to perform a certain needed type of financing or promotional effort—these and similar factors enable companies to assume power.

On the other hand, financial reverses, an unfortunate sales campaign, or even the lack of accurate market news—these factors can shift power elsewhere, possibly to another link in the channel or to another firm in the same link. In any case, the opportunity of any firm is contingent upon the willingness of others to use it as a link in the channel.

COMPARISON WITH ADVERTISING MEDIA

Selection of middlemen has been likened to the selection of advertising media. In both instances the task is to find a vehicle which has an existing coverage (or circulation) which coincides with the market desired. A region blanketed with a neat mosaic of distributors' territories will appear on a map much like the same region covered by television stations.

However, there is an important difference. Seldom does an advertising medium restrict its availability. The advertiser's product need not be sold first to the medium on the grounds of self-interest. Only occasionally will a middleman accept any product he is offered. The requirement that he invest his own money and effort forces him to be selective in terms of probable outcome or profit. No seller can afford to neglect the task of selling *to* the middlemen he seeks, as well as *through* them. Nearly every comprehensive campaign of consumer advertising allots substantial effort to dealer promotion and distributor promotion. Indeed, much consumer advertising is undertaken primarily for the stimulating effect it will have upon middlemen.

MIDDLEMEN'S REACTIONS

Middlemen's reactions to new-product offerings probably deserve more attention from manufacturers than usual. Wholesalers and retailers, as well as agent middlemen, enjoy an excellent position from which to make keen judgments of a product's probable successes within local markets. Free from the manufacturer's proclivity to "fall in love with the product," but not primarily concerned with its ultimate usage characteristics, middlemen who are alert merchandisers can look at the product with an eye to salability alone.

Yet it is common practice for manufacturers to force acceptance with a heavy barrage of consumer advertising, introductory high-markup offers, free merchandise, combination deals, co-operative advertising schemes, and the like. These may have the effect of "mesmerizing" middlemen, and of clouding the issue of the product's own rate of initial acceptance.

Lack of effective vertical communication in most channels is a serious deterrent. Possibly no other proof of the weakness of manufacturers' control over channels is so convincing as their inability to obtain facts from their own ultimate and intermediate markets. Information that could be used in product development, pricing, packaging, or promotion-planning is buried in non-standard records of middlemen, and sometimes purposely secreted from suppliers.

Channels research is one of the most frustrating areas of marketing investigation, since it requires access to data collected by firms which are independent, remotely situated, and suspicious. Unless given incentive to do so, middlemen will not maintain separate sales records by brands sold. Extracting the needed figures by preferred units of measure is often a hopeless task. To get such data, one producer of pipe tools adopted a device commonly used with electric appliances: a "warranty registration" questionnaire attached to the tools. Ostensibly designed to validate users' damage claims, its true purpose was to discover where, when, how, and by whom the tools had been sold.

Communication downward from the manufacturer is also faulty, placing in doubt the claim that all links in the channel are bound together by common objectives. For example, it is seldom practical to disclose a forthcoming promotional plan in all its details and to ask the middlemen whether the plan will be timely, acceptable, and supportable by their efforts. To do so would jeopardize the advantage of surprise, usually a significant competitive stratagem. Yet the value of synchronized, co-ordinated action on any new plan by all firms in the channel is obvious.

Middlemen's Views

CHANNEL BUILDING

To the extent that any middleman can do so, he should think of himself primarily as a purchasing agent for his customers, and only secondarily as a selling agent for his suppliers. The planning of his product line will proceed from an analysis of a finite customer group in which he is interested . . . to the selection of goods capable of satisfying those needs . . . and then to the choice of available suppliers who can provide those goods. Of course, he may actually begin his assortment with one or more basic products, chosen by him as a way of defining the area of customer needs in which he elects to deal.

From that point on, however, his chief stock in trade becomes not the franchises of important suppliers, but rather his customer group. He is interested in selling any product which these customers desire to buy from him. The attractiveness of any new offering by a supplier is not to be judged by the size of the markup or commission, nor the unusual nature of the product, nor details of its manufacture, nor the promises of manufacturer's advertising support.

The key question is: Does it fit the line? That is, does it complement the other products that he sells, in terms of salability to precisely the same group of buyers? His list of customers is probably less subject to intentional revision than are many other aspects of his business. Is it not at this point, then, that channel building starts?

Some unusual product combinations may result from this approach. A manufacturers' agent selling baby garments in the Southwest took on a line of printed business forms, which the small retailers on whom he called were seeking. An Omaha wholesaler successfully added grocery products to his liquor business. A Cleveland distributor of welding equipment rejected a portable farm welder offered by his principal supplier, since he had no contact with farmers, but was interested in carrying a line of warehouse tractors and lift trucks.

APPROACH TO NEW PROSPECTS

In some cases a middleman may deem it worthwhile to shift from his current customer group to a new list of prospects, in order to find a market for a particularly promising new product. In the main, however, he will not do so. His approach to new prospects is based on their close similarity to those now on his customer list. To all these persons he attempts to become known as a helpful specialist in a well-defined set of recurring needs. The scope of his line, and the interrelation of products in it, must be known to the bulk of his customers. Scrambled merchandising, or stocking of unrelated items, will tend to split his market into many small groups.

ASSORTMENT SALES

Furthermore, the middleman attempts to weld all of his offerings into a family of items which he can sell in combination, as a packaged assortment, to individual customers. His selling efforts are directed primarily at obtaining orders for the assortment, rather than for individual items. Naturally the greatest *numbers* of his transactions will seldom be made in this way; but often his greatest volume and more profitable sales to "blue-chip" accounts will be assortment sales.

Catering to assortment sales has considerable significance to channel operation, because the kind of sales service which a middleman can offer a single-product supplier is affected thereby. Since he is relatively disinterested in pushing individual items, the middleman is criticized for failure to stress a given brand, or for the poor quality of his salesmen's product knowledge, his disuse of suppliers' advertising materials, his neglect of certain customers (who may be good prospects for individual items but not for the assortment), and even for his unrefined systems of record keeping, in which brand designations may be lost.

The Middleman as an Independent Market

The middleman is not a hired link in a chain forged by a manufacturer, but rather an independent market, the focus of a large group of customers for whom he buys. Subsequent to some market analysis of his own, he selects products and suppliers, thereby setting at least one link in the channel.

After some experimentation, he settles upon a method of operation, performing those functions he deems inescapable in the light of his own objectives, forming policies for himself wherever he has freedom to do so. Perhaps these methods and policies conform closely to those of a Census category of middleman, but perhaps they do not.

It is true that his choices are in many instances tentative proposals. He is subject to much influence from competitors, from aggressive suppliers, from inadequate finances and faulty information, as well as from habit. Nonetheless, many of his choices are independent.

As he grows and builds a following, he may find that his prestige in his market is greater than that of the suppliers whose goods he sells. In some instances his local strength is so great that a manufacturer is virtually unable to tap that market, except through him. In such a case the manufacturer can have no channel policy with respect to that market.

. . . the most pervasive and
potent forces that control retail
competition are custom, consumer expectations, and social
pressure.

9

Social Pressures and Retail Competition

STANLEY C. HOLLANDER

THE MOST AMBIGUOUS, the most accommodating and changeable, and yet the most pervasive and potent forces that control retail competition are custom, consumer expectations, and social pressure. Suppliers frequently try to direct their dealers' behavior. Retail unions and other worker groups have sought, sometimes successfully, to influence store hours, services, and operating methods. The market in many ways limits what retailers can do. The wares that merchants offer must be adjusted to customer needs and tastes: the sale of antifreeze at the equator and of bathing suits at the Arctic Circle usually are not viable merchandising alternatives. Similarly, price policies must be adapted to the incomes and spending habits of the market. But in some sense even more fundamental than the market is the set of ideas that both merchants and the public share as to what is the proper way for a retail business to be conducted.

In some cases the public's concept of what is appropriate retail action becomes crystallized in legislation. Legislative action may result when the behavior of some retailers differs substantially from what an influential segment of the public believes to be fitting and proper conduct. Aside and apart from formal legislative codes, however, custom and expectations create very

Material from *Business Topics,* Volume 13, No. 1 (Winter, 1965), pp. 7-14, used by permission of the publisher: Bureau of Business and Economic Research, Graduate School of Business Administration, Michigan State University.

real, even if somewhat vague, limits on the competitive alternatives that the retailers can successfully adopt.

The relationship between retailing and its environment is complex. It is difficult for us to perceive that relationship as it operates within our own culture, since our questions and expectations of retailing are very largely determined by that same culture. A sort of cross-cultural anthropological economic analysis is needed to discover the social determinants of retailing. In the past few years marketing specialists and anthropologists alike have become increasingly interested in that sort of analysis; and so we have recently had, for example, some fascinating studies of the social forces that determine trading relationships, the use of credit, and merchandising practices in Indonesian villages. British economists have tried to establish statistical relationships between socioeconomic variables, on one hand, and, on the other, the number and kind of stores that will operate within a given community. Many other interesting studies are becoming available,[1] and while they still are exploratory rather than definitive, they do much to suggest society's role in shaping the limits of competition.

Societal Controls

Most merchants are even unlikely to conceive or consider alternatives outside those limits, a fact that in turn reinforces the original impact of the social controls. Few merchants in America today, for example, would consider as a competitive tool the use of a "puller-in," that is, a man stationed at the doorway to coax window shoppers into the store. The use of these men was once a common competitive tactic, yet today it is simply outside the average merchant's frame of reference.

The August fur sale illustrates the self-reinforcing nature of many retail customs. At one time very few furs were sold in August, which is what one would expect to have been the case in the days before air-conditioning. Apparently some furriers tried offering drastic price inducements to offset this normal seasonal slump in business. Their competitors followed suit, and eventually a large, price-conscious segment of the market began to do its fur shopping in August. Consequently, the merchants who wanted to attract this segment had to offer their more attractive specials that month, before the customers purchased elsewhere. The concentration of specials, in turn, tended to strengthen the consumers' belief that August was the time to buy, and so on in circular fashion.

[1] See the sources cited in Stanley C. Hollander, "Retailing: Cause or Effect," in William S. Decker (ed.), *Emerging Concepts in Marketing* (Chicago: American Marketing Association, 1962), pp. 220-232. Also see Robert Bartels, *Comparative Marketing* (Homewood, Illinois: Richard D. Irwin, Inc., for the American Marketing Association, 1963), pp. 1-6, 283-308, for a discussion of comparative analysis in wholesaling.

A similar illustration of self-reinforcement appears in the recommendations that the American Newspaper Publishers' Association offered to the retail trade for many years. Although the Association's Bureau of Advertising has recently modified its position somewhat, it used to suggest that retailers concentrate their advertising of each type of merchandise in those months when the consumer purchases of that merchandise were greatest.

Of course, societal forces shape all businesses, not merely retailing alone. As one economist has put it:

> No less important is the unconscious influence provided by the mores, folklore, customs, institutions, social ideals, and myths of a society which lay the foundation for formal organization. More immediately relevant to any one firm's behavior are the standards and values of the groups with which it comes into contact as an organization, as well as the groups, communities and organizations to which its members belong. It should be clear that the preference system of the firm, as well as the attitudes of the participants in the firm's organization toward such things as co-operation, efficiency, innovation, etc. must be profoundly affected by the broader community within which the firm operates.[2]

The totally public nature of retailing and of some of the service trades does nevertheless create some special problems for businessmen in those fields. Often a factory or a wholesale establishment in an isolated or unfrequented location, for example, may operate at full force on Sunday subject to possible resentment only among its own employees and their families. The storekeeper who opens on Sunday, however, is more likely to come to the attention of, and to irritate, segments of the general public that may include both voters and potential customers. Local sentiments, which vary from place to place, determine whether clothing merchants must cover their windows when changing the garments on the display dummies.

In an entirely different sense as well, dealing with the ultimate consumer probably leaves the retailer more susceptible to the influence of custom and tradition than most other businessmen. For over two hundred years economists, marketing specialists, and psychologists have debated whether habit and past practice are more important in guiding the purchases of consumer buyers than those of the supposedly more rational industrial and commercial buyers. This debate has often centered around the supposedly more crucial role of customary prices in consumer markets than in commercial ones. The argument is by no means settled, but the only question in all the debate has been whether consumer dependence on tradition is greater than or only equal to that of business buyers. No one has ever seriously urged that it is less. The retailer's problem is that his public is indeed *the* public.

[2] Andreas G. Papandreou, "Some Basic Problems in the Theory of the Firm," in Bernard F. Haley (ed.), *A Survey of Contemporary Economics* (Homewood, Illinois: Richard D. Irwin, Inc., 1952), II, 192.

Caplow has argued that the prevailing customs and expectations influence the retailer's entire relationship to his customers and, to a considerable extent, even his behavior outside the store. In contrasting the occupation of shopkeeper with that of factory worker, he says:

> the control of occupational behavior is entirely different, being at once much wider and much more diffuse. Indeed, it is the popular belief that self employment in a small business carries with it freedom from personal coercion which constitutes the principal appeal of retail trade, just as it is often the impact of impersonal coercion which subsequently disillusions the neophyte proprietor.

He describes the coercion as originating with suppliers, creditors, and customers. Then he goes on to say:

> [Compared to the rigid system of control exercised by suppliers and other creditors], the control which the customer exerts upon the occupational comportment of the merchants is very informal. It is none the less important. Particularly since the restrictions of price and quality competition, personal relations with customers are often the decisive factor in the history of a retail business.
>
> The "rules" are essentially these:
>
> 1. The merchant is expected to minimize his status and exaggerate that of the customer by exaggerated forms of deference, by yielding in minor arguments, by expressing more interest in the customer's personal affairs than the customer is expected to show in his, and by small personal services.
> 2. Under this ritual, it becomes essential that the habits of the customer be identified and protected. A strain is thus produced on the merchant to maintain nearly absolute consistency in his manners, his purchasing routines, and his hours of work. . . .
>
> The norms of deference imposed on the shopkeeper prevent him from displaying a distinctly higher status than his customers [in life style], while his aspirations toward the role of businessman impel him to do so.[3]

This picture is somewhat overdrawn, particularly if it is used to depict all retailer-customer relations. Certainly many of the most successful mass-retailers exhibit little of the deference suggested by the first "rule" cited above. And the smaller merchants who have succeeded without much servility are also numerous. But in spite of these and other criticisms of Caplow's picture, we must grant that a retailer in the typical American community today cannot long behave like the operator of a trading post on the Navaho reservation who says: "The important thing is to show the

---

[3] Theodore Caplow, *The Sociology of Work* (Minneapolis: University of Minnesota Press, 1954), pp. 118-19, 128-29. Caplow, it should be made clear, directs his remarks specifically to small shopkeepers.

Indians who is boss." [4] Nor can he expect to take on the general role of social, economic, financial, and technical advisor to the community, as did so many pioneer merchants of the Western frontier. In short, society has dictated the general limits of the retailer's role. It also dictates many of the details of his operation.

Pricing

As any one retailer faces his world, he finds that it tells him a number of things about what it considers appropriate pricing policies. Our society, for example, regards haggling and bargaining as permissible in some retail situations and improper in others. Automobile dealers are expected to bargain, haberdashers are not. Of course, the explanation can be offered that the size of the automobile transaction and the unstandardized condition of the trade-in are conducive to bargaining in the car dealership, while different conditions obtain in the haberdashery. This is perfectly reasonable, and true. But the point is that in other times, and at other places, haberdashers have been expected to bargain, while in our society they definitely are not expected to do so. Also, we generally feel that such professional men as architects and physicians, whose output is also unstandardized and sometimes of substantial size, should not bargain, although under some conditions they may discriminate between patrons.

Some patterns of discriminatory prices have become so widely accepted in the sale of some, *but not all,* goods and services that it requires a conscious effort of mind to appreciate that these patterns do, in fact, discriminate between customers. These conventional discriminations are often based upon age, and occasionally upon sex. Children's rates, lower than those for adults, are frequently offered in the sale of transportation, amusement, and other services. In cases such as the provision of restaurant meals and haircuts, it can properly be argued that the child receives a different, albeit perhaps more troublesome, service than the adult. This is not so in the case of many amusement and transportation services in which the child, charged the lower rate, receives exactly the same privileges as the higher rated adult. Some aspects of family-plan airline and railroad fares, and the free admission of women to baseball parks on Ladies' Day are examples of similar discriminations based upon sex.

Some discriminatory practices based on the patronage status of the pur-

---

[4] William Y. Adams, *Shonto: A Study of the Role of the Trader in a Modern Navaho Community,* Smithsonian Institution, Bureau of American Ethnology, Bulletin 188 (Washington: U.S. Government Printing Office, 1963), pp. 210-12, 278-90. The traders cited by Adams reverse every one of the rules of deference indicated above, and in order to discourage automobile ownership among the Indians, go so far as to deliberately create disorder and uncertainty in the marketing of gasoline.

chaser seem to be of general acceptability. Special introductory rates for new subscribers are very frequently used in building magazine subscription lists. Department store private sales for the benefit of old customers cast the discriminatory advantage in the opposite direction. While magazine introductory rates usually are actually restricted to new subscribers, many so-called private sales are much less impregnable. In many stores the term is used to describe the practice of giving charge customers notice of approaching sales before the advertisements appear in the newspaper. Rational justifications can be offered for each of these discriminations. But again the point is that each of these sets of price differentials seems to be regarded as acceptable only within a particular context. Clothing merchants usually find that extra alteration charges are more readily accepted in the sale of women's clothing than in menswear. Generally however, commodity retailers, unlike service trade operators, usually do not think in terms of age or sex-based price differentials and the public doesn't seem to expect them to do so, although there is as much social justification for a child's discount on toothpaste as on movie admissions. A department store sale that was confined to non-customers would engender waves of ill will, and no department store executive would dream of such a sale. Yet magazine publishers do it every day, with apparently very little criticism.

Another curious way in which public expectations, reinforced by retail practice, limit the retailer's freedom to select among competitive pricing alternatives is in the matter of "customary prices." This is the popular belief that only certain prices or price endings are appropriate for certain types of goods. The use of these prices has been condemned as a mechanism that forces price increases into unnecessarily large steps, and praised as a device that facilitates consumer comparisons. Whether desirable or not, most retailers feel that the public's expectation that these traditional price endings should be used is a very real force that must be considered in setting prices. Very few studies attempting to measure the strength of consumer attachment to customary prices have been reported. The best known one started with a hypothesis on the part of the researcher and his mail-order house sponsors that the whole thing was a myth. The only conclusion was that the dangers of testing outweighed the possible benefits of the test.[5] And finally the public often seems to have some vague sense of what it considers as unfair or fair prices. An experienced retailer puts it this way:

> It is generally accepted as poor policy to charge what the traffic will bear. Whenever an article is priced higher than eye-value would seem to justify, the retailer is at pains to explain that the fault is not his, but the high price

[5] Eli Ginzberg, "Customary Prices," *American Economic Review*, XXVI (June 1936), 296.

of the manufacturer. Indeed, he may often shade his mark-on in order to avoid criticism.[6]

Merchandise

The public also has some expectations as to the type and nature of the merchandise that each type of retailer will carry. Such expectations are in fact necessary, if shopping is not to be a matter of haphazard searching. The importance of these traditional expectations about merchandise offerings is denied to some extent by recent developments of "scrambled merchandising," i.e., the sale of many types of goods in non-traditional outlets —for example, the introduction of non-foods into grocery supermarkets. Yet it is interesting to note that some commodity lines, which the public apparently considers too different from the usual grocery stock, such as clothing accessories, have encountered considerable customer resistance in many supermarkets. On the other hand, soap is considered so traditional a grocery line that no one ever refers to it as a "non-food," even though it is hardly edible; and consequently, no grocer would dare exclude it from his stocks.

A very different sort of public pressure arises if the retailer handles goods that come from sources that are objectionable to some portion of his public. The reaction may take the form of picketing, boycotts, or attempts to secure some type of controlling legislation. Most recently this sort of reaction has occurred in connection with the sale of goods originating in the communist-bloc countries. At various times, similar responses have been evoked by the sale of low-priced Japanese textiles, products made by firms that practice racial discrimination, prison-made and non-union-made goods, and items from Nazi Germany and elsewhere.

And, of course, the public or a segment may protest if it considers the merchandise itself objectionable. Again, apparently, the reaction will often be directed with different strength against different types of retailers. At least one book distributor reports that the public seems to tolerate more lurid paperbacks in drugstores than it will in supermarkets.

Services

When the Twentieth Century Fund sponsored its classic study of distribution costs a number of years ago, it also asked a distinguished panel to prepare recommendations on ways of reducing those costs. Among other things, the panel recommended that retailers separate the charge for each service rendered the customer from the basic price of the merchandise

[6] Oswald Knauth, "Considerations in the Setting of Retail Prices," *Journal of Marketing,* XIV (July 1949), 7.

itself.[7] This suggestion was based upon the belief that the general practice of quoting a single price for the item and the attendant services leads many consumers to use more services than they really want or would be willing to pay for in a free market. The panel felt that many consumers would like the option of choosing between service and price savings. Also charging for services in proportion to use would be more equitable than the prevailing practice. The idea seems thoroughly reasonable. Yet many merchants, and especially the ones to whom this suggestion was particularly addressed, were, and to a great extent still are, extremely reluctant to adopt it.

Their reluctance has been based upon a strong feeling that the public associates a particular bundle of services with each type of store, and that any attempt to reduce those bundles will create a sense of outrage. Again, the public expectations seem to have a differential impact. As a very perceptive analyst points out, what is considered appropriate will vary with the store's price-policy and with the socioeconomic class it seeks to attract.[8] Department store operators claim that their comparatively long history as operators of full service institutions makes them subject to consumer expectations of expensive delivery, credit, exchange, return, and miscellaneous other privileges. Yet, they allege, the same consumers will patronize such competitive outlets as discount houses, chain stores, and mail-order house retail shops without demanding any of the services whose discontinuance by department stores would be vigorously resented. Undoubtedly the harshness of the situation is sometimes exaggerated by department store people as an excuse for poor profit performance, but nevertheless the problem does exist.

One aspect of retail services about which many people, including both customers and non-customers, have strong feelings is the matter of store hours, and particularly the question of Sunday openings. In many areas local pharmacists' associations have detected some public dissatisfaction with the hours observed by drug stores and have formulated plans under which there will always be at least one pharmacy open in the community at any hour to handle emergency needs. In contrast, an increasing trend toward Sunday sales on the part of roadside clothing, hardware, furniture, general merchandise stores, and automobile dealers has induced a call for some type of control in many parts of the country. The issue is complicated by the varying economic interests of the retailers and the communities involved, the diverse desires of retail workers, and the thorny question of the proper position of government in matters that have religious overtones.

    [7] Paul W. Stewart and J. Frederick Dewhurst, *Does Distribution Cost Too Much?* (New York: Twentieth Century Fund, 1939), pp. 351-52.
    [8] W. T. Tucker, *The Social Context of Economic Behavior* (New York: Holt, Rinehart & Winston, Inc., 1964), pp. 73-81.

But it is clear that a number of people in this country do believe that at least some types of stores should close on Sunday.

Impact of Social Pressure

The strength of the social forces that we have just looked at can easily be overestimated. The merchants who are affected by these forces may be particularly likely to see more power than is actually there. Customs may persist, not because of any inherent vitality, but because of inertia and the absence of any strong incentive for change. Department store merchants who have been beset by discount house competition have found that they could, in many cases, move to self-service, to the elimination of some frills, and to separation of commodity and service charges. Possibly this increased freedom to compete has been due to changes in the consumer between 1935 and 1950 and 1964. Some of it probably is. But at least some of the change probably is a correction of an erroneous impression as to the amount of service the consumer really wanted. Katona mentions another instance of failure to judge what was permissible among the many apparel merchants who offered totally unnecessary seasonal reductions during the wartime shortage years of 1942 and early 1943.[9] Other such examples could be cited.

Yet in spite of all such instances, the fact remains that the retailer is in the business of dealing with the public, and so he must be responsive to the public's demands upon him. Frequently, as in the case of the mail-order firm that wanted to question the strength of customary pricing, attempts to test those demands involve risks of lost sales or of customer alienation. The risks are greatest, although sometimes the rewards also may be greatest, when an individual retailer tries to move independently, counter to the practices of his competitors. Thus, for example, two authors who generally favor independence and competitiveness in retailing, urge group action to reduce the returned goods rate:

Although the individual store can do much to reduce its returns, group action of the retailers within a given shopping area is often necessary for best results. The group can afford to do many things which the individual store cannot do. Also, some of the steps the individual retailer might take would merely drive his customers to competitors, where they would still return as much merchandise, so that the returned-goods problem of the community would be as important as before. Group action, therefore, has the major advantage of making it easier to establish a sound educational program on the costliness of returns and of making it less difficult for in-

[9] George Katona, *Psychological Analysis of Economic Behavior* (New York: Mc-Graw-Hill Book Company, Inc., 1951), p. 51. See also John K. Galbraith, *The Theory of Price Control* (Cambridge: Harvard University Press, 1952), p. 12.

dividual stores to refuse returns because of the established "law" in the community governing such matters.

Realizing the advantages of group action, merchants in such cities as Dallas, Los Angeles, Kansas City and Milwaukee have joined together to reduce returns. Such action usually involves agreement on one or more of the following points: establishing uniform time limits, setting up a standard policy of refusing to pick up certain merchandise for return, standardizing extra charges for return pickups, framing sanitary provisions and obtaining local ordinances involving sanitary considerations, activating educational campaigns and providing material for publicity drives, exchanging information about customers with records of excessive returns, and exchanging return-ratio data.[10]

Anyone who is dedicated to a classical "hard-core" antitrust position might question the propriety of some of the actions outlined above, although several of them are similar to recommendations of the Twentieth Century Fund's distribution cost panel. But they do also illustrate the difficulty of making individual changes in the established way of dealing with the public.

[10] Delbert J. Duncan and Charles F. Phillips, *Retailing: Principles and Methods* (6th ed.; Homewood, Illinois: Richard D. Irwin, Inc., 1963), pp. 591-92.

. . . and it is for the privilege
of supplying the American
housewife with laundry products that the big companies
wage their costly and bitter
wars.

10

The Soap Wars:
A Strategic Analysis

SPENCER KLAW

FEW SECRETS in American business are more closely guarded than the
strategy and tactics of selling soap. It is no secret, of course, that advertising is the ammunition on which the big U.S. soap companies mainly
rely in their perpetual wars with one another. Colgate-Palmolive, Lever
Brothers, and Procter & Gamble, the three companies that make close to
85 percent of all the soap and synthetic-detergent products consumed in
the U.S.—they also make some non-soap products, like shortening and
toothpaste—spend approximately $250 million a year to advertise their
wares. They spend an additional $150 million or so on sales promotion—
e.g., on prize contests, price-off coupons, distributing free samples. But the
broad strategies that underlie the firing of all this ammunition are ordinarily invisible to the neutral observer. Such reports as find their way into
the pages of the trade press are inaccurate at worst and sketchy at best.
One learns that detergent X, which Cleans Everything Washable, has been
routed by detergent Y, a similar product that Cleans Like a White Tor-
nado. The maneuvers that led to victory, the enemy weaknesses that were
exploited, the cost of the victory, and its effect on the balance of power
among the big soap companies—all these remain obscure.

Reprinted from the June, 1963 issue of *Fortune* Magazine by special permission;
© 1963 Time Inc., pp. 123 ff.

Last January, however, the secrecy surrounding some of the great battles of recent years was at least partially dispelled. The occasion was the trial, in New York, of an antitrust case arising out of a 1957 deal in which Lever Brothers obtained from Monsanto Chemical the right to market a product called "All"—a laundry detergent of the variety known as low-sudser, that Monsanto had developed and had been selling in competition with the big soap companies. The government's contention was that the deal tended to lessen competition in the detergent business, and therefore violated Section 7 of the Clayton Act. At the trial Lever made two main arguments in opposing the government's demand that it divest itself of All. One was that All's sales had been falling off in 1957, and that Lever had actually served the cause of competition by taking the product over and marketing it more effectively than Monsanto could. The second argument was that Lever, having recently suffered a series of defeats at the hands of Procter & Gamble, needed a best-selling detergent like All if it was to remain a serious competitor in the laundry-products business.

These arguments evidently impressed the court, and several weeks ago the government's suit against Lever and Monsanto was dismissed. But the record of the trial will stand as a document of extraordinary interest. For days Lever executives testified in rich detail about the strategy of the soap-and-detergent business, and about the humiliations inflicted on them by Procter & Gamble. Moreover, at Lever's request—though over the strong protests of Procter & Gamble's chairman, former Defense Secretary Neil H. McElroy—the court forced P. & G. to reveal certain facts about *its* operations as well. These included figures showing how much P. & G. had spent to advertise and promote certain brands, and how much money it had made in certain years from the sale of its laundry soaps and detergents—information that the big soap companies often deny even to their own advertising agencies.

The trial dealt with only one class of soap products: so-called heavy-duty soaps and detergents that are used mainly for washing clothes. The big soap companies also sell toilet soap, shampoos, all-purpose liquid cleaners, light-duty liquid detergents for washing dishes and delicate fabrics, and other kinds of cleaning products. But the heavy-duty products are the heart of the soap business: of the five billion pounds of soap and detergents that Americans will consume this year, well over three billion pounds, costing about $900 million at retail, will be consumed in washing machines, and it is for the privilege of supplying the American housewife with laundry products that the big companies wage their most costly and bitter wars. Last winter's trial not only shed light on the way these wars are fought; it also made clear some of the reasons why they have so consistently been won in recent years by Procter & Gamble.

Miraculous Tide vs. No-Rinse Surf

The balance of power among the big soap companies has, in fact, shifted radically in favor of P. & G. since World War II. The shift began with that company's introduction, in 1946, of a product called Tide, which was billed as a "revolutionary washday miracle." Tide was not a soap, but a synthetic detergent—i.e., it was made by chemical synthesis, not by the simple processing of animal fats. While there had been detergent powders on the market for years, Tide was the first one strong enough for washing clothes as well as dishes. It did such a good job, in fact, that before the end of 1949 one out of every four women was doing her laundry with Tide.

Confronted with this flight from old-fashioned soap powders, both Colgate and Lever Brothers hastily introduced heavy-duty detergents of their own. Colgate's was called Fab, and in time it sold moderately well. But Lever's entry, Surf, did such a mediocre washing job that it was withdrawn from the market. In 1949 a new, reformulated Surf was introduced, which was said to be so efficient that it obviated the need for rinsing clothes after they had been washed. This impressed housewives to such an extent that very soon Procter & Gamble advertisements were proclaiming that Tide, too, "washes clothes so miracle clean NO RINSING NEEDED." The claim was also appropriated by Colgate, and since Tide and Fab were available in almost every grocery store in the U.S., while Surf had up to then been introduced in only a few markets, almost all the benefits of the no-rinse story, as it was known in the trade, accrued to P. & G. and Colgate. Whether any benefit at all accrued to housewives is another question; the FTC insisted that rinsing did make clothes cleaner, even if they had been washed with a detergent, and eventually all three companies agreed not to make any further claims to the contrary.

By the end of 1953, according to evidence given at last winter's trial, about all that Lever had to show for six years of effort on behalf of Surf was a $24-million loss. The company was still bent on having a best-seller in the laundry-detergent field. But the feeling was strong, a Lever executive testified, that "we couldn't make that soufflé [i.e., Surf] come up for a second time," and so a decision was made to start over again and try promoting a new detergent called Rinso Blue instead. Lever's hopes for Rinso Blue were based in part on the results of blind tests, a procedure in which consumers are asked to try two different products, each in an unmarked box, and to say which one they prefer. While Surf appears not to have shown up too well in such tests, a Lever witness testified that housewives seemed to like Rinso Blue just as well as Tide, and even better than a second Procter & Gamble detergent called Cheer.

When one of the big soap companies launches a new product, it must, as a rule, commit itself to a huge outlay for advertising and promotion; otherwise, grocery stores are loath to stock the product. The amount of such investment spending, as it is called, is determined partly by the level of sales the new product is expected to reach after it has been on the market for a few months: the bigger the expected sales volume, of course, the bigger the investment that can be risked. Encouraged by Rinso Blue's showing in blind tests, Lever was confident that its sales would eventually hit at least $70 million a year, at which level the gross profits would amount to between $20 million and $25 million. On this assumption, the company felt justified in investing a very large sum—nearly $22 million— to get Rinso Blue into national distribution as quickly as possible.

When Rinso Blue reached the market, Procter & Gamble reacted with unexpected vigor. In the two areas where the new detergent was first placed on sale—the West Coast and the middle Atlantic states—P. & G. increased by hundreds of thousands of dollars its local advertising budget for Tide and Cheer. At the same time, it took other and more direct steps to neutralize any effect of Lever's introductory sales campaign. While Lever handed out millions of free sample packages of Rinso Blue, P. & G. handed out coupons good for the purchase, at reduced prices, of Tide and other P. & G. products. In Baltimore and Philadelphia, a Lever executive testified, P. & G. adopted the "highly unusual practice for them of delivering coupons on a door-to-door basis . . . they came in so hard and heavy that as our sampling crews were going up one side of the block, the Procter men were coming down the other side handing out the Tide coupons." P. & G. also used straight price-off deals to accomplish the classic defensive maneuver known as "loading the customer." Vast quantities of merchandise were put on sale at big price discounts, so that a woman who had tried her free sample of Rinso Blue, and had gone to the supermarket intending to buy a box, would be tempted to load up on Tide or Cheer instead.

Partly as a result of these countermeasures, by the end of 1955 Lever had lost more than $7 million on Rinso Blue, in addition to the $24 million it had already lost on Surf; and in those areas where the new detergent had been introduced, its sales had leveled out, not at 10 percent of the market for detergents, as Lever had hoped, but a little over 4 percent. The J. Walter Thompson agency, to which the Rinso Blue advertising account had just been shifted, studied the situation and reported gloomily that it was unlikely to improve. Tide and Cheer were so profitable, the agency pointed out, and P. & G. could therefore afford to spend so much money in their defense, that Lever would be able to achieve its sales goal for Rinso Blue only at a ruinous cost. Thompson underlined its conviction that Lever's situation was all but hopeless by gallantly proposing a 60 percent cut in the Rinso Blue advertising budget. The proposal was accepted, and Lever's executives did some painful thinking. "This led to the conclusion," the company's chairman, William H. Burkhart, testified last winter, "that we were facing apparently a hopeless task to get a real entry, a winner, into this field [and] we came to the conclusion that we would give up any further attempt to force our way into a winning position in the heavy-duty field."

The full dimensions of P. & G.'s triumph and Lever's defeat emerged clearly at the trial. Before the war, the two companies had been fairly evenly matched in the laundry-soap business. But between 1940 and 1956, P. & G.'s estimated share of the market rose from 34 percent to nearly 57 percent, while Lever's share fell from 30 percent to 17 percent. (Colgate's share was unchanged at approximately 11 percent.) This shift naturally had a profound effect on the earnings of the big soap companies. From 1951 through 1956, according to figures reluctantly provided by P. & G., the sale of Tide and its other laundry soaps and detergents yielded profits totaling about a quarter of a billion dollars before taxes. In the same period, Lever and Colgate were *losing* money in the laundry-products field. P. & G.'s net earnings nearly tripled in the postwar decade, rising to $59 million in 1956 on sales of just over $1 billion. Meanwhile, Colgate's earnings on its domestic business declined from $16 million in 1946 to $5 million ten years later. Lever's record was even worse: in the early 1950's the company barely broke even, and the $3 million that it earned in 1956, on sales of $282 million, was only about a third of what Lever had earned in a good prewar year.

That Old Blue Magic

While the Rinso Blue fiasco had impressed on Lever Brothers the folly of making frontal assaults on entrenched positions, the company's management did not intend simply to abandon the field to P. & G. When Lever was given the opportunity to acquire All, and thereby to occupy an entrenched position of its own, it gladly seized the chance. Before turning, however, to the new series of battles into which Lever Brothers was plunged, it may be useful to consider in a general way the evolution of marketing strategy in the soap industry since World War II.

Probably no event in this period has more greatly influenced the strategy of the big companies than the successful launching by Procter & Gamble of its second heavy-duty detergent, Cheer. By 1950, four years after the introduction of Tide, Procter & Gamble had at least two good reasons for wanting to market another laundry detergent. One was that it might appeal to housewives who just didn't like Tide. The other was that it would get P. & G. a larger share of the limited shelf space in the grocery stores.

Often the big soap companies contrive to get additional "facings" for a brand by bringing it out in a variety of different-sized packages. But Tide was already being sold in three sizes—regular, medium, and giant—and there was obviously not much more that could be done along this line.

Although Cheer was not a bad product—in cool water, for instance, it was considered by P. & G. to perform better in some ways than Tide—the company could not at first get women interested in buying it. Then it tried a scheme for giving Cheer a new and distinctive personality. Like other detergents on the market, Cheer contained an optical bleach—a dye, that is, that made clothes look very white in sunlight by causing them to reflect some of the sun's ultraviolet rays in the form of blue light. The scheme was to add blue coloring matter to Cheer, which had been sold up to then as a white powder, and to make a great point of the "blue whiteness" it imparted to shirts and sheets. This worked so well that by 1953 the new Cheer ("It's New! It's Blue! . . . *only* Cheer has the Blue-Magic Whit-ener!") was outselling every other brand of laundry soap or detergent except Tide.

If It Isn't "New," It's "Improved"

The success of Tide had shown the enormous benefits to be reaped from a basic improvement in a soap product. The lesson soap men drew from Cheer was that even what they call a "me-too product"—i.e., one essen-tially similar to others on the market—can be marketed successfully if it at least *looks* new and different. This discovery has led the big soap com-panies to put much less emphasis than they did before the war on devising new claims for old products—inventing B.O., for example, and announc-ing that Lifebuoy would cure it, or suggesting that the way to avoid "undie odor" was to use Lux Flakes. The emphasis today is on making constant changes, often of a fairly superficial kind, in the products them-selves.

Soap products are constantly being brought out in new colors and new forms, or at least in new containers. Light-duty liquid detergents have successively been marketed in bottles, in cans, and in plastic containers, and they are now sold in three different colors. P. & G., for example, offers the housewife her choice of Creamy Pink Thrill, Ivory Liquid ("the gentle white detergent"), and New Sparkling Clear Joy. Elsewhere in the soap-products section, the shopper is confronted with a rich variety of laundry powders and laundry liquids; of all-purpose cleaners with ammonia, and all-purpose cleaners without ammonia; of toilet soaps that contain bacteri-ostatic additives, and toilet soaps that contain cold cream; of low-sudsers that are "condensed," and low-sudsers that are "fluffy"; of detergents that come in small, soluble packets, and detergents that come in the form of large tablets. Most items are labeled "New!" or "Improved!" As a Colgate executive observed recently, "If the package doesn't say 'New' these days, it better say 'Seven Cents off.' "

The fact that soap companies are putting more stress on product changes does not mean that they are putting any less stress these days on advertising. On the contrary, the rise of the self-service store has caused soap manufacturers to cut back on promotional efforts aimed at storekeepers, and to concentrate even more single-mindedly than in the past on selling the consumer directly. As a group, the big soap companies today spend more money on advertising, in proportion to their total sales, than they did twenty years ago; P. & G. salesmen are informed when they sign on with the company that "nearly one billion Procter & Gamble messages are delivered to the housewives of America each week."

It is hard to find new things to say about a soap product (apart from the fact that it is "new"), and as a result the advertising claims that are made on behalf of competing brands in any given category of products— e.g., laundry powders—tend to sound a lot alike. In 1953 the Chicago *Tribune* commissioned a study, by a firm called Social Research, Inc., of women's feelings about laundry soaps and detergents, and their feelings about the way these products were advertised. The resulting report listed a number of advertising slogans that were current at the time, and observed, "For a woman to learn to distinguish between product claims like these requires her to become a scholar in the subtle evaluation of textual difference . . . to decide whether a wash is whiter when it is 'whiter *without* a bleach' or when it is 'whiter *than* bleach.' " Most women, the report added, simply stop paying attention to the claims.

Puralin Plus and New Germaseptic Dreft

Since 1953, there have been some changes in soap advertising. Humor is in vogue, and soap commercials abound with humorous lady plumbers and humorous washing-machine repairmen; P. & G. even has a commercial featuring an Oriental houseboy, who says, "Lady know Joy not hurt pretty little hands . . . Joy mild as lotus blossom." But the specific advertising claims sound pretty much the same, and there is evidence that many women find them just as hard to sort out—and to take seriously—as ever. Oxydol "bleaches as it washes," New Super Suds offers "a *brighter* wash, a *whiter* wash than ever before," Dreft is "New Germaseptic Dreft," Cascade has Chloro-Sheen, Lifebuoy has Puralin Plus, Spic-and-Span contains Germ-Fite, Salvo is "the *fortified* detergent," Tide is "New Improved Tide," and offers "the cleanest, freshest smelling wash in Tide history," while Fab has "five extra launderatives" and produces "a wash that's not just detergent clean—but clean right through."

But whatever they think about such advertising claims, housewives seem to have a special confidence in detergents that *are* advertised. One evidence of this is the relatively poor sales record of private-label soaps and detergents. Private-label laundry detergents, which have been found by independent testing organizations to perform, in general, about as well as brands like Fab or Cheer or Tide or Rinso Blue, are now available in most supermarkets. But nine out of ten women prefer to buy a nationally advertised brand, even though it may cost them as much as 40 to 45 percent more.

The big soap companies themselves, it is true, frequently offer their own products at bargain prices. In a particular store, on a particular day, half a dozen different brands of soap products may be on sale in boxes prominently marked "Five Cents Off Regular Price!" Cents-off deals of this kind are initiated by the manufacturer, who offers retailers for a limited time a chance to buy a particular brand at a big price reduction if the retailer will agree to pass the saving on in full to his customers. But the fact that a soap company can resort to this maneuver again and again is in itself proof of the power of advertising, since it is on advertising that the manufacturer mainly relies to persuade housewives that the product they were offered at 27 cents a box last week is still a pretty good value now that it is back at its regular price of 32 cents.

If a new product is to be profitably marketed by one of the big soap companies, it must normally meet certain basic requirements. It must fill a real need—or one that can be demonstrated by advertising to be a real need—and it must work reasonably well. All together, the Big Three are now spending around $30 million a year on efforts to develop such products. In addition, a product must strike consumers as giving good value—although this does not necessarily mean that it must be sold at the same price as similar products already on the market. In 1959, for example, P. & G. introduced its liquid cleaner Mr. Clean in a twenty-eight-ounce bottle, and charged as much for it as the makers of Lestoil, a similar and very popular product, got for a thirty-two-ounce bottle. However, since Mr. Clean had some inherent advantages (unlike Lestoil, it was non-inflammable), and since the Mr. Clean bottle was not only more conveniently shaped than the Lestoil bottle but was cleverly designed so that it looked just as big or even bigger, consumers overlooked the discrepancy, and within two years Mr. Clean was outselling Lestoil two to one.

Muddying the Test Waters

But even if a product performs well and seems to offer a good value, it is impossible to tell a priori what the actual demand for it will be. Overestimating its potential sales can cost many millions of dollars, as Lever's experience with Rinso Blue demonstrated, and soap companies ordinarily test the market very carefully before launching a new brand. Colgate, for example, will spend over $16 million this year on market tests.

Putting a product on sale in a test market has one obvious risk, however. While the test may furnish a good line on the potential sales of the product, and on the amount of advertising and promotion that will be required to sustain that volume, it is very hard to keep this information secret. If Lever Brothers puts a new product on sale in, say, Grand Rapids, P. & G. and Colgate will be among the first to buy it. Often they will not only analyze the product in their laboratories, but try it out on consumer panels in blind tests. Furthermore, by keeping a close watch on what Lever is doing to advertise and promote the new product, and by auditing its sales in a few Grand Rapids grocery stores, Lever's rivals can learn almost as much as Lever does about the product's potentialities.

Actually, market tests in the soap business often more nearly resemble a poker game than a scientific experiment. When player A puts a new product on sale in a certain market, player B, who has a similar product already in national distribution, may raise the stakes—that is, he may triple his advertising of that product in the area where player A is making his test. This confronts player A with a difficult question: Does player B intend to triple his *national* advertising budget if player A puts his new product on sale nationally? Or is player B bluffing? He may only be engaged in what is commonly known as "muddying the test waters."

A classic demonstration of water-muddying was staged some years ago by the Toni Corp., then the leading producer of home-permanent preparations. When Colgate began a market test of a product called Lustre Creme Home Permanent, Toni launched a counteroffensive referred to, in intracompany memoranda, as Operation Snafu. Toni already had three home permanents on the market, Toni, Prom, and Bobbi; in addition to stepping up greatly its local advertising of all three of these brands, the company introduced a fourth brand, called Epic, in the cities Colgate had chosen for its test. The object was to scare Colgate off entirely or, failing that, to make Colgate underestimate the potential sales of its new product, and therefore to launch it with a relatively small advertising and promotion budget—which would, of course, make life easier for Toni. Whether or not Operation Snafu was the deciding factor, Colgate did in fact drop its plans to market Lustre Creme Permanent nationally.

Why Nobody Wanted All

When Lever Brothers acquired All in 1957, no market test was needed to find out if there was a big demand for it. All had been on the market for more than ten years, and recently it had been selling a lot better than either Rinso Blue or Surf. It was, in fact, outselling every other brand of packaged soap or detergent apart from Tide and Cheer and Colgate's Fab.

All's popularity was doubtless an irritation to the big soap companies. Although they expect stiff competition when marketing toiletry items like shampoos and home permanents, they have, for some forty years, almost completely dominated the market for basic soap products. The only important exception to this rule, apart from Monsanto's success with All, has been Armour's success in marketing Dial soap. For years, the Big Three did not consider the market for a high-priced deodorant soap like Dial big enough to be interesting. Then, when they realized their mistake, Armour was so solidly entrenched in the soap business that not even an all-out offensive by P. & G., which in 1958 introduced a deodorant soap of its own, called Zest, was able to dislodge Dial more than temporarily from its position as the best-selling toilet soap on the market.

But if Armour has shown that the big soap companies can be beaten in their own territory, the story of Monsanto's venture shows how great are the dangers that threaten an invader. The history of All goes back to the early 1940's, soon after the development by Westinghouse of a device it called the Laundromat. The Laundromat was an automatic washing machine of the kind known as a front-loader, in which the clothes are washed by being tossed around in a revolving drum. In a washer of this type, the cleaning action is impeded by too many suds, and Westinghouse asked Monsanto if it could develop a synthetic detergent that would wash well without making a lot of foam. In 1945, Monsanto came up with a low-sudsing product, called Sterox, that did the trick, and began looking around for a company that would be interested in putting it on the market.

But very few automatic washers were in use as yet, and none of the companies first approached by Monsanto—they included all three of the big soap manufacturers—was interested in a product for which the demand would presumably be so limited. The deal that Monsanto finally made was with a new company called Detergents, Inc. It had been formed, with the encouragement of Westinghouse, for the specific purpose of buying Sterox in bulk from Monsanto and selling it to consumers under the trade name of All.

In 1946, when All first went on sale, many of the new automatic washers then coming onto the market were of the top-loading variety, in which the clothes were swished around by a mechanical agitator, or paddle. In most such machines there was no harm in having lots of suds; ordinary soap powders, or high-sudsing synthetic detergents like Tide, worked well in them, just as they did in old-fashioned nonautomatic washing machines. Detergents, Inc., however, promoted All as the ideal product to use in *any* automatic washer, not just in front-loaders, and as the number of automatics in use rose into the millions, sales of All grew rapidly. They grew so rapidly, in fact, that Detergents, Inc., soon had more business on its hands than it could cope with. The company had been formed with very little capital, and by 1951 it was strapped for working funds and heavily in debt to Monsanto. Monsanto decided it had better buy out the company's stockholders and market All itself.

For two years everything went beautifully. Then, in 1954, P. & G. introduced a low-sudsing detergent of its own, called Dash, and Colgate soon followed with a product called Ad. While Colgate's efforts on behalf of Ad were modest, Dash was launched with heavy expenditures for advertising and promotion. Some of the money spent by P. & G. went into tie-in deals with washing-machine manufacturers. Detergents, Inc., had hit on the notion of promoting All by persuading manufacturers of automatic washers to put a sample box of All in every machine they sold. P. & G. now offered the manufacturers large amounts of free advertising on its television programs if they would agree to stop packing All in their machines and pack P. & G. products instead. Specifically, P. & G. proposed to manufacturers of top-loading machines that they pack Tide, and to manufacturers of front-loaders that they pack Dash. By 1957, every manufacturer had deserted All and gone to Tide or Dash.

The Horrifying Ad Budget

At first, Monsanto tried slugging it out with P. & G. In 1955 the company spent what Monsanto's chairman, Dr. Charles Allen Thomas, described at the trial as the "rather horrifying" sum of $12 million to advertise and promote All. But even so, sales fell off, and Monsanto's Consumer Products Division, which had been organized to market All, reported a $3-million loss for the year.

It was obvious that part of the difficulty arose from the fact that All was the only consumer product Monsanto had. There was talk of adding a conventional, high-sudsing detergent to the company's line. Nothing came of this, however, partly because the big soap companies were good customers of Monsanto—in 1956, they bought some $27 million worth of its phosphates and other chemicals—and the company's management was reluctant to antagonize them. Monsanto also considered buying the Clorox Corp., the largest U.S. producer of household bleach, but nothing came of this either. Monsanto's estimate was that it would take at least $22 million to buy Clorox, and Thomas testified that "being of technical background we thought it rather ridiculous to pay this much money for water to which some chlorine and caustic soda had been added."

Meanwhile, P. & G.'s campaign was continuing to cut into the sales of All, and Monsanto soon concluded that the best thing to do was to sell off the All business before it was too late—that is, to turn the All trademark over to some company that could market the product successfully, and that would therefore be in the market for lots of Sterox. Talks were held with several companies, and for a time a deal with Armour seemed likely. But after several months negotiations broke down—mainly, it appears, over the question of how much Armour should pay for the Sterox.

Then, early in 1957, Monsanto approached Lever Brothers. Two years before, Lever had put a low-sudsing detergent of its own into test markets. But the product had been withdrawn in the face of complaints that it solidified when it was left standing too long, and Lever was delighted at the prospect of acquiring All. It was agreed that for five years Lever would buy the finished product (that is, Sterox) from Monsanto, and that during the same period it would buy an additional $80 million worth of Monsanto chemicals. Monsanto, congratulating itself on having withdrawn from the field in fairly good order and with no serious losses, handed the All trademark over to Lever.

"Makes White Clothes Greener!"

At the trial Lever witnesses gave a number of explanations for Monsanto's unimpressive showing against P. & G. They pointed out that Monsanto had been selling All through food brokers, and allocating 12 to 13 percent of the net sales receipts to direct selling expenses. By contrast, a Lever executive testified, his company (or P. & G.), having a big sales force of its own, was in a position to do a much better selling job for only about 3 percent of sales. Lever also argued that the ability to get volume discounts in buying network television time gave P. & G. a significant advantage that was not available to Monsanto. (For very big buyers, like P. & G. and Lever, these discounts amount to as much as 25 or 30 percent off the card rate.) Thomas Carroll, Lever's vice president of marketing, testified that Monsanto, partly because of inexperience, had in any case made a mistake by concentrating too much of its advertising in newspapers, where, he said, "the delivery of messages to homes is very expensive" compared to television.

Another cause of Monsanto's difficulties, Lever witnesses said, was that All had had some serious deficiencies as a product in the days when Monsanto was marketing it. According to tests made by Lever in 1957, a good many women didn't think it smelled as nice as Dash. More important, All had a tendency to cake, it sometimes left sandlike grains in the bottom of a washing machine, and in cities where the air was badly polluted it was apt to turn white shirts and sheets an apple-green color. "Dash was a superior product," Carroll testified. "It was being introduced with vast quantities of television advertising. . . . Their selling was good. They introduced it with sampling. They would go from door to door, and knock on the door, and ask a woman if she owned an automatic washing machine. And if she did they gave her a sample of Dash . . ." Carroll added, "They followed it up with couponing, price packs, and other very strong promotions. They had a sales force that numbered nearly a thousand men . . . and, in short, they were coming in and it was pretty clear that All was going to suffer the ravages of this warfare."

When Lever took over All, the tide of battle began to turn. The market for low-sudsing detergents was expanding rapidly, and between 1956 and 1959 Lever was able to increase All's sales from $30 million to $44 million. This was brought about, moreover, with an annual outlay for advertising and promotion amounting to only about half of what Monsanto had spent on All in 1955. As a result, profits on All rose to more than $8,500,000 (before taxes) in 1959.

This was the first decent piece of business Lever had done for many years in the laundry-products field. Since 1956, it is true, the company had been making around $4 million a year before taxes on the sale of its four conventional high-sudsing detergents. (Besides Rinso Blue and Surf, they included two other low-volume brands called Breeze and Silver Dust Blue.) But these profits had been made possible only by reducing advertising and promotional expenses so drastically that sales had begun to decline, and Lever's management was unhappily aware that the four brands were gradually being milked dry.

In 1960, Lever introduced "New *Active* All," which smelled nicer than the old All and didn't have the same tendency to cake or to turn shirts green. Up to this time, sales of Dash had been increasing even faster than sales of All. But in 1961, even though P. & G. appeared to be spending more money (figured on a dollars-per-case basis) to advertise and promote Dash than Lever was spending on All, the trend was reversed. For the first time since the introduction of Dash, its share of the market fell, while All's share rose. Lever's joy at this development was mingled with apprehension, however. A Lever executive recalled at the trial that "we, for once in our life, had a reversal of the classic position . . . and we were observing Procter & Gamble spending on a much higher per-case basis, and it was our conjecture as to just how long they would be willing to play this game . . ."

As it turned out, P. & G. had already thought up a new game. Lever and P. & G. had both been testing the market for a low-sudsing detergent to be sold in tablet form, and in 1961 both companies began to put their products into national distribution. P. & G., however, appeared to be investing a lot more money in the introduction of its product, Salvo, than Lever felt it could afford to invest in Vim, its own low-sudsing tablet.

It was obvious that Procter's strategy was to shift the battle of the low-sudsers to new ground, where Lever would not have the advantage of an entrenched position; by the end of last year, it was also obvious that the strategy was working. While Lever's Vim had captured only 8.5 percent of the total market for low-sudsing detergents, Procter's Salvo had captured 20 percent. Although Dash still lagged behind All, sales of Dash *plus* Salvo were running well ahead of sales of All plus Vim. P. & G. had thus succeeded, at last, in becoming the leader in the low-sudsing field.

While these facts were being recited to the court by a Lever witness, the trial judge, Archie O. Dawson, broke in impatiently at one point to ask what they all added up to. He added, "I can see that the witness is annoyed with Procter, there is a competitive feeling there, and all that, and this is the poor little boy with the rich relative or rich uncle who's got lots of money to spend, but what has that to do with this case?" In reply, Lever's principal trial attorney, William L. McGovern, said that he assumed the government would contend that Lever, in acquiring All, had acquired the power to lessen competition. He went on to say, "The purpose of this testimony, Your Honor, is to show that not only did we not lessen any competition, but with all of our own talents and skills and funds we have been scarcely able to keep our head above the water."

The Fruits of Victory

It can be argued that P. & G. is not quite so irresistible a force as Lever Brothers made it out to be at the trial. Lever's toilet soaps—Lux, Lifebuoy, Dove, and Praise—have, for instance, been giving P. & G.'s Ivory, Camay, and Zest a very good run for their money. And Colgate's Liquid Ajax has recently replaced P. & G.'s Mr. Clean as the best-selling brand in the $100-million-a-year market for liquid cleaners.

But while P. & G. may lose now and then, its batting average is still very high. More than half of all the cleaning products sold in the U.S. are manufactured by P. & G., and last year, as the following table shows, it made more than three times as much money as its two big competitors made between them; if foreign earnings are excluded, it made seven times as much:

	Net sales (000 omitted)	Net income (000 omitted)
Procter & Gamble		
Domestic and foreign	$1,619,000	$109,300
Domestic only	N.A.	89,100
Lever Brothers	413,000	10,200
Colgate		
Domestic and foreign	673,800	22,900
Domestic only	327,300	2,400

These figures, coupled with some of the evidence given at last winter's trial, raise an interesting question: Why doesn't P. & G. go after an even bigger share of the soap-and-detergent business by cutting substantially the price of Tide and of its other heavy-duty detergents? Within the industry, P. & G.'s restraint is sometimes attributed to fear of the Department of Justice's antitrust division. But P. & G. may well figure that it can make more money by keeping the price of its laundry detergents at a high enough level to assure a copious flow of profits, and by investing a portion of those profits in fields outside the soap-and-detergent business.

Another Secret Weapon: Toothpaste

In any case, P. & G. in the past ten years has added to its product line such non-soap items as scouring powder, bleaches, facial and toilet tissue, peanut butter, and cake mixes. It has also added toothpaste, and sales of its two brands, Crest and Gleem, now account for almost half of all U.S. toothpaste sales. Crest and Gleem have benefited P. & G. in two ways. Besides contributing handsomely to company profits, their success has cut into the profits that Lever and Colgate had been making in the toothpaste business, and has thereby deprived them of money they might have been able to use against P. & G. in the soap-and-detergent business.

As the evidence at last winter's trial demonstrated, to play the kind of game the big soap companies play takes a lot of money, and the fact that P. & G. has so much more money than its competitors has certainly been one important reason for its long winning streak. Ever since its early triumphs in the synthetic-detergent field, P. & G. has been able to invest the kind of money in the launching of a new product—Salvo, for example— that its rivals find it difficult to match.

But it is not just P. & G.'s ability to outspend its rivals that makes it so formidable a competitor. The fact is that it is also an extremely well managed company. At various times since World War II both Lever and Colgate have had difficulty in finding capable top executives. By contrast, P. & G.'s managers have been successful in recruiting and training successors as tough and able as they are themselves, with the same natural flair for poker, and the same willingness to play as a member of a big team. As P. & G.'s president, Howard Morgens, has said, "Everything we do is created, adjusted, and tested by the team." This way of doing business is not everybody's dish of tea, but there is no doubt about the fact that it sells a lot of soap.

B. CUSTOMER ASPECTS

. . . uncovering *why* people buy is an extremely difficult task. The answer will tend to vary with the investigator's behavioral frame of reference.

11

Behavioral Models for Analyzing Buyers

PHILIP KOTLER

IN TIMES PAST, management could arrive at a fair understanding of its buyers through the daily experience of selling to them. But the growth in the size of firms and markets has removed many decision-makers from direct contact with buyers. Increasingly, decision-makers have had to turn to summary statistics and to behavioral theory, and are spending more money today than ever before to try to understand their buyers.

Who buys? How do they buy? And why? The first two questions relate to relatively overt aspects of buyer behavior, and can be learned about through direct observation and interviewing.

But uncovering *why* people buy is an extremely difficult task. The answer will tend to vary with the investigator's behavioral frame of reference.

The buyer is subject to many influences which trace a complex course through his psyche and lead eventually to overt purchasing responses. This conception of the buying process is illustrated in Figure 11.1. Various influences and their modes of transmission are shown at the left. At the right are the buyer's responses in choice of product, brand, dealer, quantities, and frequency. In the center stands the buyer and his mysterious psycho-

Philip Kotler, reprinted from the *Journal of Marketing,* national quarterly publication of the American Marketing Association, Volume 29, No. 4 (October, 1965), pp. 37-45.

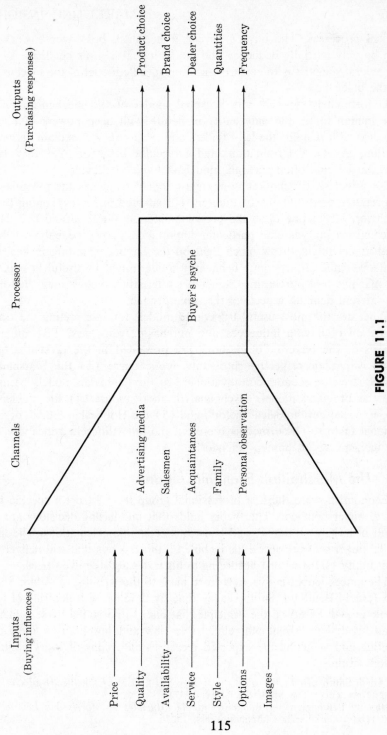

FIGURE 11.1

The Buying Process Conceived as a System of Inputs and Outputs

115

logical processes. The buyer's psyche is a "black box" whose workings can be only partially deduced. The marketing strategist's challenge to the behavioral scientist is to construct a more specific model of the mechanism in the black box.

Unfortunately no generally accepted model of the mechanism exists. The human mind, the only entity in nature with deep powers of understanding, still remains the least understood. Scientists can explain planetary motion, genetic determination, and molecular behavior. Yet they have only partial, and often partisan, models of *human* behavior.

Nevertheless, the marketing strategist should recognize the potential interpretative contributions of different partial models for explaining buyer behavior. Depending upon the product, different variables and behavioral mechanisms may assume particular importance. A psychoanalytic behavioral model might throw much light on the factors operating in cigarette demand, while an economic behavioral model might be useful in explaining machine-tool purchasing. Sometimes alternative models may shed light on different demand aspects of the same product.

What are the most useful behavioral models for interpreting the transformation of buying influences into purchasing responses? Five different models of the buyer's "black box" are presented in the present article, along with their respective marketing applications: (1) the Marshallian model, stressing economic motivations; (2) the Pavlovian model, learning; (3) the Freudian model, psychoanalytic motivations; (4) the Veblenian model, social-psychological factors; and (5) the Hobbesian model, organizational factors. These models represent radically different conceptions of the mainsprings of human behavior.

The Marshallian Economic Model

Economists were the first professional group to construct a specific theory of buyer behavior. The theory holds that purchasing decisions are the result of largely "rational" and conscious economic calculations. The individual buyer seeks to spend his income on those goods that will deliver the most utility (satisfaction) according to his tastes and relative prices.

The antecedents for this view trace back to the writings of Adam Smith and Jeremy Bentham. Smith set the tone by developing a doctrine of economic growth based on the principle that man is motivated by self-interest in all his actions.[1] Bentham refined this view and saw man as finely calculating and weighing the expected pleasures and pains of every contemplated action.[2]

[1] Adam Smith, *An Inquiry into the Nature and Causes of the Wealth of Nations,* 1776 (New York: The Modern Library, 1937).
[2] Jeremy Bentham, *An Introduction to the Principles of Morals and Legislation,* 1780 (Oxford, England: Clarendon Press, 1907).

Bentham's "felicific calculus" was not applied to consumer behavior (as opposed to entrepreneurial behavior) until the late 19th century. Then, the "marginal-utility" theory of value was formulated independently and almost simultaneously by Jevons [3] and Marshall [4] in England, Menger [5] in Austria, and Walras [6] in Switzerland.

Alfred Marshall was the great consolidator of the classical and neoclassical tradition in economics; and his synthesis in the form of demand-supply analysis constitutes the main source of modern micro-economic thought in the English-speaking world. His theoretical work aimed at realism, but his method was to start with simplifying assumptions and to examine the effect of a change in a single variable (say, price) when all other variables were held constant.

He would "reason out" the consequences of the provisional assumptions and in subsequent steps modify his assumptions in the direction of more realism. He employed the "measuring rod of money" as an indicator of the intensity of human psychological desires. Over the years his methods and assumptions have been refined into what is now known as *modern utility theory:* economic man is bent on maximizing his utility, and does this by carefully calculating the "felicific" consequences of any purchase.

As an example, suppose on a particular evening that John is considering whether to prepare his own dinner or dine out. He estimates that a restaurant meal would cost $2.00 and a home-cooked meal 50 cents. According to the Marshallian model, if John expects less than four times as much satisfaction from the restaurant meal as the home-cooked meal, he will eat at home. The economist typically is not concerned with how these relative preferences are formed by John, or how they may be psychologically modified by new stimuli.

Yet John will not always cook at home. The principle of diminishing marginal utility operates. Within a given time interval—say, a week—the utility of each additional home-cooked meal diminishes. John gets tired of home meals and other products become relatively more attractive.

John's *efficiency* in maximizing his utility depends on the adequacy of his information and his freedom of choice. If he is not perfectly aware of costs, if he misestimates the relative delectability of the two meals, or if he is barred from entering the restaurant, he will not maximize his potential utility. His choice processes are rational, but the results are inefficient.

[3] William S. Jevons, *The Theory of Political Economy* (New York: The Macmillan Company, 1871).

[4] Alfred Marshall, *Principles of Economics,* 1890 (London: The Macmillan Company, 1927).

[5] Karl Menger, *Principles of Economics,* 1871 (Glencoe, Illinois: Free Press, 1950).

[6] Leon Walras, *Elements of Pure Economics,* 1874 (Homewood, Illinois: Richard D. Irwin, Inc., 1954).

MARKETING APPLICATIONS OF MARSHALLIAN MODEL

Marketers usually have dismissed the Marshallian model as an absurd figment of ivory-tower imagination. Certainly the behavioral essence of the situation is omitted, in viewing man as calculating the marginal utility of a restaurant meal over a home-cooked meal.

Eva Mueller has reported a study where only one-fourth of the consumers in her sample bought with any substantial degree of deliberation.[7] Yet there are a number of ways to view the model.

From one point of view the Marshallian model is tautological and therefore neither true nor false. The model holds that the buyer acts in the light of his best "interest." But this is not very informative.

A second view is that this is a *normative* rather than a *descriptive* model of behavior. The model provides logical norms for buyers who want to be "rational." Although the consumer is not likely to employ economic analysis to decide between a box of Kleenex and Scotties, he may apply economic analysis in deciding whether to buy a new car. Industrial buyers even more clearly would want an economic calculus for making good decisions.

A third view is that economic factors operate to a greater or lesser extent in all markets, and, therefore, must be included in any comprehensive description of buyer behavior.

Furthermore, the model suggests useful behavioral hypotheses such as: (a) The lower the price of the product, the higher the sales. (b) The lower the price of substitute products, the lower the sales of this product; and the lower the price of complementary products, the higher the sales of this product. (c) The higher the real income, the higher the sales of this product, provided that it is not an "inferior" good. (d) The higher the promotional expenditures, the higher the sales.

The validity of these hypotheses does not rest on whether *all* individuals act as economic calculating machines in making their purchasing decisions. For example, some individuals may buy *less* of a product when its price is reduced. They may think that the quality has gone down, or that ownership has less status value. If a majority of buyers view price reductions negatively, then sales may fall, contrary to the first hypothesis.

But for most goods a price reduction increases the relative value of the goods in many buyers' minds and leads to increased sales. This and the other hypotheses are intended to describe average effects.

The impact of economic factors in actual buying situations is studied

---

[7] Eva Mueller, "A Study of Purchase Decisions," Part 2, *Consumer Behavior, The Dynamics of Consumer Reaction,* edited by Lincoln H. Clark (New York: New York University Press, 1954), pp. 36-87.

through experimental design or statistical analyses of past data. Demand equations have been fitted to a wide variety of products—including beer, refrigerators, and chemical fertilizers.[8] More recently, the impact of economic variables on the fortunes of different brands has been pursued with significant results, particularly in the case of coffee, frozen orange juice, and margarine.[9]

But economic factors alone cannot explain all the variations in sales. The Marshallian model ignores the fundamental question of how product and brand preferences are formed. It represents a useful frame of reference for analyzing only one small corner of the "black box."

The Pavlovian Learning Model

The designation of a Pavlovian learning model has its origin in the experiments of the Russian psychologist Pavlov, who rang a bell each time before feeding a dog. Soon he was able to induce the dog to salivate by ringing the bell whether or not food was supplied. Pavlov concluded that learning was largely an associative process and that a large component of behavior was conditioned in this way.

Experimental psychologists have continued this mode of research with rats and other animals, including people. Laboratory experiments have been designed to explore such phenomena as learning, forgetting, and the ability to discriminate. The results have been integrated into a stimulus-response model of human behavior, or as someone has "wisecracked," the substitution of a rat psychology for a rational psychology.

The model has been refined over the years, and today is based on four central concepts—those of *drive, cue, response,* and *reinforcement.*[10]

Drive. Also called needs or motives, drive refers to strong stimuli internal to the individual which impels action. Psychologists draw a distinction between primary physiological drives—such as hunger, thirst, cold, pain, and sex—and learned drives which are derived socially—such as cooperation, fear, and acquisitiveness.

Cue. A drive is very general and impels a particular response only in relation to a particular configuration of cues. Cues are weaker stimuli in the environment and/or in the individual which determine when, where,

---

[8] See Erwin E. Nemmers, *Managerial Economics* (New York: John Wiley & Sons, Inc., 1962), Part II.

[9] See Lester G. Telser, "The Demand for Branded Goods as Estimated from Consumer Panel Data," *Review of Economics and Statistics,* Vol. 44 (August, 1962), pp. 300-324; and William F. Massy and Ronald E. Frank, "Short Term Price and Dealing Effects in Selected Market Segments," *Journal of Marketing Research,* Vol. 2 (May, 1965), pp. 171-185.

[10] See John Dollard and Neal E. Miller, *Personality and Psychotherapy* (New York: McGraw-Hill Book Company, Inc., 1950), Chapter III.

and how the subject responds. Thus, a coffee advertisement can serve as a cue which stimulates the thirst drive in a housewife. Her response will depend upon this cue and other cues, such as the time of day, the availability of other thirst-quenchers, and the cue's intensity. Often a relative change in a cue's intensity can be more impelling than its absolute level. The housewife may be more motivated by a 2-cents-off sale on a brand of coffee than the fact that this brand's price was low in the first place.

Response. The response is the organism's reaction to the configuration of cues. Yet the same configuration of cues will not necessarily produce the same response in the individual. This depends on the degree to which the experience was rewarding, that is, drive-reducing.

Reinforcement. If the experience is rewarding, a particular response is reinforced; that is, it is strengthened and there is a tendency for it to be repeated when the same configuration of cues appears again. The housewife, for example, will tend to purchase the same brand of coffee each time she goes to her supermarket so long as it is rewarding and the cue configuration does not change. But if a learned response or habit is not reinforced, the strength of the habit diminishes and may be extinguished eventually. Thus, a housewife's preference for a certain coffee may become extinct if she finds the brand out of stock for a number of weeks.

Forgetting, in contrast to extinction, is the tendency for learned associations to weaken, not because of the lack of reinforcement but because of nonuse.

Cue configurations are constantly changing. The housewife sees a new brand of coffee next to her habitual brand, or notes a special price deal on a rival brand. Experimental psychologists have found that the same learned response will be elicited by similar patterns of cues; that is, learned responses are *generalized.* The housewife shifts to a similar brand when her favorite brand is out of stock. This tendency toward generalization over less similar cue configurations is increased in proportion to the strength of the drive. A housewife may buy an inferior coffee if it is the only brand left and if her drive is sufficiently strong.

A counter-tendency to generalization is *discrimination.* When a housewife tries two similar brands and finds one more rewarding, her ability to discriminate between similar cue configurations improves. Discrimination increases the specificity of the cue-response connection, while generalization decreases the specificity.

MARKETING APPLICATIONS OF PAVLOVIAN MODEL

The modern version of the Pavlovian model makes no claim to provide a complete theory of behavior—indeed, such important phenomena as perception, the subconscious, and interpersonal influence are inadequately treated. Yet the model does offer a substantial number of insights about some aspects of behavior of considerable interest to marketers.[11]

An example would be in the problem of introducing a new brand into a highly competitive market. The company's goal is to extinguish existing brand habits and form new habits among consumers for its brand. But the company must first get customers to try its brand; and it has to decide between using weak and strong cues.

Light introductory advertising is a weak cue compared with distributing free samples. Strong cues, although costing more, may be necessary in markets characterized by strong brand loyalties. For example, Folger went into the coffee market by distributing over a million pounds of free coffee.

To build a brand habit, it helps to provide for an extended period of introductory dealing. Furthermore, sufficient quality must be built into the brand so that the experience is reinforcing. Since buyers are more likely to transfer allegiance to similar brands than dissimilar brands (generalization), the company should also investigate what cues in the leading brands have been most effective. Although outright imitation would not necessarily effect the most transference, the question of providing enough similarity should be considered.

The Pavlovian model also provides guide lines in the area of advertising strategy. The American behaviorist, John B. Watson, was a great exponent of repetitive stimuli; in his writings man is viewed as a creature who can be conditioned through repetition and reinforcement to respond in particular ways.[12] The Pavlovian model emphasizes the desirability of repetition in advertising. A single exposure is likely to be a very weak cue, hardly able to penetrate the individual's consciousness sufficiently to excite his drives above the threshold level.

Repetition in advertising has two desirable effects. It "fights" forgetting, the tendency for learned responses to weaken in the absence of practice. It provides reinforcement, because after the purchase the consumer becomes selectively exposed to advertisements of the product.

The model also provides guide lines for copy strategy. To be effective as a cue, an advertisement must arouse strong drives in the person. The strongest product-related drives must be identified. For candy bars, it may be hunger; for safety belts, fear; for hair tonics, sex; for automobiles, status. The advertising practitioner must dip into his cue box—words, colors, pictures—and select that configuration of cues that provides the strongest stimulus to these drives.

[11] The most consistent application of learning-theory concepts to marketing situations is found in John A. Howard, *Marketing Management: Analysis and Planning* (Homewood, Illinois: Richard D. Irwin, Inc., revised edition, 1963).

[12] John B. Watson, *Behaviorism* (New York: The People's Institute Publishing Company, 1925).

The Freudian Psychoanalytic Model

The Freudian model of man is well known, so profound has been its impact on 20th century thought. It is the latest of a series of philosophical "blows" to which man has been exposed in the last 500 years. Copernicus destroyed the idea that man stood at the center of the universe; Darwin tried to refute the idea that man was a special creation; and Freud attacked the idea that man even reigned over his own psyche.

According to Freud, the child enters the world driven by instinctual needs which he cannot gratify by himself. Very quickly and painfully he realizes his separateness from the rest of the world and yet his dependence on it.

He tries to get others to gratify his needs through a variety of blatant means, including intimidation and supplication. Continual frustration leads him to perfect more subtle mechanisms for gratifying his instincts.

As he grows, his psyche becomes increasingly complex. A part of his psyche—the id—remains the reservoir of his strong drives and urges. Another part—the ego—becomes his conscious planning center for finding outlets for his drives. And a third part—his super-ego—channels his instinctive drives into socially approved outlets to avoid the pain of guilt or shame.

The guilt or shame which man feels toward some of his urges—especially his sexual urges—causes him to repress them from his consciousness. Through such defense mechanisms as rationalization and sublimation, these urges are denied or become transmuted into socially approved expressions. Yet these urges are never eliminated or under perfect control; and they emerge, sometimes with a vengeance, in dreams, in slips-of-the-tongue, in neurotic and obsessional behavior, or ultimately in mental breakdown where the ego can no longer maintain the delicate balance between the impulsive power of the id and the oppressive power of the super-ego.

The individual's behavior, therefore, is never simple. His motivational wellsprings are not obvious to a casual observer nor deeply understood by the individual himself. If he is asked why he purchased an expensive foreign sports-car, he may reply that he likes its maneuverability and its looks. At a deeper level he may have purchased the car to impress others, or to feel young again. At a still deeper level, he may be purchasing the sports-car to achieve substitute gratification for unsatisfied sexual strivings.

Many refinements and changes in emphasis have occurred in this model since the time of Freud. The instinct concept has been replaced by a more careful delineation of basic drives; the three parts of the psyche are regarded now as theoretical concepts rather than actual entities; and the behavioral perspective has been extended to include cultural as well as biological mechanisms.

Instead of the role of the sexual urge in psychic development—Freud's discussion of oral, anal, and genital stages and possible fixations and traumas—Adler [13] emphasized the urge for power and how its thwarting manifests itself in superiority and inferiority complexes; Horney [14] emphasized cultural mechanisms; and Fromm [15] and Erikson [16] emphasized the role of existential crises in personality development. These philosophical divergencies, rather than debilitating the model, have enriched and extended its interpretative value to a wider range of behavioral phenomena.

MARKETING APPLICATIONS OF FREUDIAN MODEL

Perhaps the most important marketing implication of this model is that buyers are motivated by *symbolic* as well as *economic-functional* product concerns. The change of a bar of soap from a square to a round shape may be more important in its sexual than its functional connotations. A cake mix that is advertised as involving practically no labor may alienate housewives because the easy life may evoke a sense of guilt.

Motivational research has produced some interesting and occasionally some bizarre hypotheses about what may be in the buyer's mind regarding certain purchases. Thus, it has been suggested at one time or another that

- Many a businessman doesn't fly because of a fear of posthumous guilt—if he crashed, his wife would think of him as stupid for not taking a train.
- Men want their cigars to be odoriferous, in order to prove that they (the men) are masculine.
- A woman is very serious when she bakes a cake because unconsciously she is going through the symbolic act of giving birth.
- A man buys a convertible as a substitute "mistress."
- Consumers prefer vegetable shortening because animal fats stimulate a sense of sin.
- Men who wear suspenders are reacting to an unresolved castration complex.

There are admitted difficulties of proving these assertions. Two prominent motivational researchers, Ernest Dichter and James Vicary, were employed independently by two separate groups in the prune industry to determine why so many people dislike prunes. Dichter found, among other

---

13 Alfred Adler, *The Science of Living* (New York: Greenberg, 1929).

14 Karen Horney, *The Neurotic Personality of Our Time* (New York: W. W. Norton & Co., 1937).

15 Erich Fromm, *Man For Himself* (New York: Holt, Rinehart & Winston, Inc., 1947).

16 Erik Erikson, *Childhood and Society* (New York: W. W. Norton & Co., 1949).

things, that the prune aroused feelings of old age and insecurity in people, whereas Vicary's main finding was that Americans had an emotional block about prunes' laxative qualities.[17] Which is the more valid interpretation? Or if they are both operative, which motive is found with greater statistical frequency in the population?

Unfortunately the usual survey techniques—direct observation and interviewing—can be used to establish the representativeness of more superficial characteristics—age and family size, for example—but are not feasible for establishing the frequency of mental states which are presumed to be deeply "buried" within each individual.

Motivational researchers have to employ time-consuming projective techniques in the hope of throwing individual "egos" off guard. When carefully administered and interpreted, techniques such as word association, sentence completion, picture interpretation, and role-playing can provide some insights into the minds of the small group of examined individuals; but a "leap of faith" is sometimes necessary to generalize these findings to the population.

Nevertheless, motivation research can lead to useful insights and provide inspiration to creative men in the advertising and packaging world. Appeals aimed at the buyer's private world of hopes, dreams, and fears can often be as effective in stimulating purchase as more rationally-directed appeals.

The Veblenian Social-Psychological Model

While most economists have been content to interpret buyer behavior in Marshallian terms, Thorstein Veblen struck out in different directions.

Veblen was trained as an orthodox economist, but evolved into a social thinker greatly influenced by the new science of social anthropology. He saw man as primarily a *social animal*—conforming to the general forms and norms of his larger culture and to the more specific standards of the subcultures and face-to-face groupings to which his life is bound. His wants and behavior are largely molded by his present group-memberships and his aspired group-memberships.

Veblen's best-known example of this is in his description of the leisure class.[18] His hypothesis is that much of economic consumption is motivated not by intrinsic needs or satisfaction so much as by prestige-seeking. He

[17] L. Edward Scriven, "Rationality and Irrationality in Motivation Research," in Robert Ferber and Hugh G. Wales, editors, *Motivation and Marketing Behavior* (Homewood, Illinois: Richard D. Irwin, Inc., 1958), pp. 69-70.

[18] Thorstein Veblen, *The Theory of the Leisure Class* (New York: The Macmillan Company, 1899).

emphasized the strong emulative factors operating in the choice of conspicuous goods like clothes, cars, and houses.

Some of his points, however, seem overstated by today's perspective. The leisure class does not serve as everyone's reference group; many persons aspire to the social patterns of the class immediately above it. And important segments of the affluent class practice conspicuous underconsumption rather than overconsumption. There are many people in all classes who are more anxious to "fit in" than to "stand out." As an example, William H. Whyte found that many families avoided buying air conditioners and other appliances before their neighbors did.[19]

Veblen was not the first nor the only investigator to comment on social influences in behavior; but the incisive quality of his observations did much to stimulate further investigations. Another stimulus came from Karl Marx, who held that each man's world-view was determined largely by his relationship to the "means of production." [20] The early field-work in primitive societies by social anthropologists like Boas [21] and Malinowski [22] and the later field-work in urban societies by men like Park [23] and Thomas [24] contributed much to understanding the influence of society and culture. The research of early Gestalt psychologists—men like Wertheimer,[25] Köhler,[26] and Koffka [27]—into the mechanisms of perception led eventually to investigations of small-group influence on perception.

MARKETING APPLICATIONS OF VEBLENIAN MODEL

The various streams of thought crystallized into the modern social sciences of sociology, cultural anthropology, and social psychology. Basic to them is the view that man's attitudes and behavior are influenced by several levels of society—culture, subcultures, social classes, reference groups, and face-to-face groups. The challenge to the marketer is to determine which of these social levels are the most important in influencing the demand for his product.

[19] William H. Whyte, Jr., "The Web of Word of Mouth," *Fortune,* Vol. 50 (November, 1954), pp. 140 ff.

[20] Karl Marx, *The Communist Manifesto,* 1848 (London: Martin Lawrence, Ltd., 1934).

[21] Franz Boas, *The Mind of Primitive Man* (New York: The Macmillan Company, 1922).

[22] Bronislaw Malinowski, *Sex and Repression in Savage Society* (New York: Meridian Books, 1955).

[23] Robert E. Park, *Human Communities* (Glencoe, Illinois: Free Press, 1952).

[24] William I. Thomas, *The Unadjusted Girl* (Boston: Little, Brown and Company, 1928).

[25] Max Wertheimer, *Productive Thinking* (New York: Harper & Brothers, 1945).

[26] Wolfgang Köhler, *Gestalt Psychology* (New York: Liveright Publishing Co., 1947).

[27] Kurt Koffka, *Principles of Gestalt Psychology* (New York: Harcourt, Brace and World, 1935).

CULTURE

The most enduring influences are from culture. Man tends to assimilate his culture's mores and folkways, and to believe in their absolute rightness until deviants appear within his culture or until he confronts members of another culture.

SUBCULTURES

A culture tends to lose its homogeneity as its population increases. When people no longer are able to maintain face-to-face relationships with more than a small proportion of other members of a culture, smaller units or subcultures develop, which help to satisfy the individual's needs for more specific identity.

The subcultures are often regional entities, because the people of a region, as a result of more frequent interactions, tend to think and act alike. But subcultures also take the form of religions, nationalities, fraternal orders, and other institutional complexes which provide a broad identification for people who may otherwise be strangers. The subcultures of a person play a large role in his attitude formation and become another important predictor of certain values he is likely to hold.

SOCIAL CLASS

People become differentiated not only horizontally but also vertically through a division of labor. The society becomes stratified socially on the basis of wealth, skill, and power. Sometimes castes develop in which the members are reared for certain roles, or social classes develop in which the members feel empathy with others sharing similar values and economic circumstances.

Because social class involves different attitudinal configurations, it becomes a useful independent variable for segmenting markets and predicting reactions. Significant differences have been found among different social classes with respect to magazine readership, leisure activities, food imagery, fashion interests, and acceptance of innovations. A sampling of attitudinal differences in class is the following:

> Members of the *upper-middle* class place an emphasis on professional competence; indulge in expensive status symbols; and more often than not show a taste, real or otherwise, for theater and the arts. They want their children to show high achievement and precocity and develop into physicists, vice-presidents, and judges. This class likes to deal in ideas and symbols.
>
> Members of the *lower-middle* class cherish respectability, savings, a college education, and good housekeeping. They want their children to show self-control and prepare for careers as accountants, lawyers, and engineers.
>
> Members of the *upper-lower* class try to keep up with the times, if not with

the Joneses. They stay in older neighborhoods but buy new kitchen appliances. They spend proportionately less than the middle class on major clothing articles, buying a new suit mainly for an important ceremonial occasion. They also spend proportionately less on services, preferring to do their own plumbing and other work around the house. They tend to raise large families and their children generally enter manual occupations. This class also supplies many local businessmen, politicians, sports stars, and labor-union leaders.

REFERENCE GROUPS

There are groups in which the individual has no membership but with which he identifies and may aspire to—reference groups. Many young boys identify with big-league baseball players or astronauts, and many young girls identify with Hollywood stars. The activities of these popular heroes are carefully watched and frequently imitated. These reference figures become important transmitters of influence, although more along lines of taste and hobby than basic attitudes.

FACE-TO-FACE GROUPS

Groups that have the most immediate influence on a person's tastes and opinions are face-to-face groups. This includes all the small "societies" with which he comes into frequent contact: his family, close friends, neighbors, fellow workers, fraternal associates, and so forth. His informal group memberships are influenced largely by his occupation, residence, and stage in the life cycle.

The powerful influence of small groups on individual attitudes has been demonstrated in a number of social psychological experiments.[28] There is also evidence that this influence may be growing. David Riesman and his coauthors have pointed to signs which indicate a growing amount of *other-direction,* that is, a tendency for individuals to be increasingly influenced by their peers in the definition of their values rather than by their parents and elders.[29]

For the marketer, this means that brand choice may increasingly be influenced by one's peers. For such products as cigarettes and automobiles, the influence of peers is unmistakable.

---

[28] See, for example, Solomon E. Asch, "Effects of Group Pressure Upon the Modification & Distortion of Judgments," in Dorwin Cartwright and Alvin Zander, *Group Dynamics* (Evanston, Illinois: Row, Peterson & Co., 1953), pp. 151-162; and Kurt Lewin, "Group Decision and Social Change," in Theodore M. Newcomb and Eugene L. Hartley, editors, *Readings in Social Psychology* (New York: Henry Holt Co., 1952).

[29] David Riesman, Reuel Denney, and Nathan Glazer, *The Lonely Crowd* (New Haven, Connecticut: Yale University Press, 1950).

The role of face-to-face groups has been recognized in recent industry campaigns attempting to change basic product attitudes. For years the milk industry has been trying to overcome the image of milk as a "sissified" drink by portraying its use in social and active situations. The men's-wear industry is trying to increase male interest in clothes by advertisements indicating that business associates judge a man by how well he dresses.

Of all face-to-face groups, the person's family undoubtedly plays the largest and most enduring role in basic attitude formation. From them he acquires a mental set not only toward religion and politics, but also toward thrift, chastity, food, human relations, and so forth. Although he often rebels against parental values in his teens, he often accepts these values eventually. Their formative influence on his eventual attitudes is undeniably great.

Family members differ in the types of product messages they carry to other family members. Most of what parents know about cereals, candy, and toys comes from their children. The wife stimulates family consideration of household appliances, furniture, and vacations. The husband tends to stimulate the fewest purchase ideas, with the exception of the automobile and perhaps the home.

The marketer must be alert to what attitudinal configurations dominate in different types of families, and also to how these change over time. For example, the parent's conception of the child's rights and privileges has undergone a radical shift in the last 30 years. The child has become the center of attention and orientation in a great number of households, leading some writers to label the modern family a "filiarchy." This has important implications not only for how to market to today's family, but also on how to market to tomorrow's family when the indulged child of today becomes the parent.

THE PERSON

Social influences determine much but not all of the behavioral variations in people. Two individuals subject to the same influences are not likely to have identical attitudes, although these attitudes will probably converge at more points than those of two strangers selected at random. Attitudes are really the product of social forces interacting with the individual's unique temperament and abilities.

Furthermore, attitudes do not automatically guarantee certain types of behavior. Attitudes are predispositions felt by buyers before they enter the buying process. The buying process itself is a learning experience and can lead to a change in attitudes.

Alfred Politz noted at one time that women stated a clear preference for G.E. refrigerators over Frigidaire, but that Frigidaire continued to outsell

G.E.[30] The answer to this paradox was that preference was only one factor entering into behavior. When the consumer preferring G.E. actually undertook to purchase a new refrigerator, her curiosity led her to examine the other brands. Her perception was sensitized to refrigerator advertisements, sales arguments, and different product features. This led to learning and a change in attitudes.

The Hobbesian Organizational-Factors Model

The foregoing models throw light mainly on the behavior of family buyers.

But what of the large number of people who are organizational buyers? They are engaged in the purchase of goods not for the sake of consumption, but for further production or distribution. Their common denominator is the fact that they (1) are paid to make purchases for others and (2) operate within an organizational environment.

How do organizational buyers make their decisions? There seem to be two competing views. Many marketing writers have emphasized the predominance of rational motives in organizational buying.[31] Organizational buyers are represented as being most impressed by cost, quality, dependability, and service factors. They are portrayed as dedicated servants of the organization, seeking to secure the best terms. This view has led to an emphasis on performance and use characteristics in much industrial advertising.

Other writers have emphasized personal motives in organizational buyer behavior. The purchasing agent's interest to do the best for his company is tempered by his interest to do the best for himself. He may be tempted to choose among salesmen according to the extent they entertain or offer gifts. He may choose a particular vendor because this will ingratiate him with certain company officers. He may shortcut his study of alternative suppliers to make his work day easier.

In truth, the buyer is guided by both personal and group goals; and this is the essential point. The political model of Thomas Hobbes comes closest of any model to suggesting the relationship between the two goals.[32] Hobbes held that man is "instinctively" oriented toward preserving and enhancing his own well-being. But this would produce a "war of every man against every man." This fear leads men to unite with others in a corporate body. The corporate man tries to steer a careful course between satisfying his own needs and those of the organization.

[30] Alfred Politz, "Motivation Research—Opportunity or Dilemma?," in Ferber and Wales, same reference as footnote 17, at pp. 57-58.

[31] See Melvin T. Copeland, *Principles of Merchandising* (New York: McGraw-Hill Book Co., Inc., 1924).

[32] Thomas Hobbes, *Leviathan*, 1651 (London: G. Routledge and Sons, 1887).

MARKETING APPLICATIONS OF HOBBESIAN MODEL

The import of the Hobbesian model is that organizational buyers can be appealed to on both personal and organizational grounds. The buyer has his private aims, and yet he tries to do a satisfactory job for his corporation. He will respond to persuasive salesmen and he will respond to rational product arguments. However, the best "mix" of the two is not a fixed quantity; it varies with the nature of the product, the type of organization, and the relative strength of the two drives in the particular buyer.

Where there is substantial similarity in what suppliers offer in the way of products, price, and service, the purchasing agent has less basis for rational choice. Since he can satisfy his organizational obligations with any one of a number of suppliers, he can be swayed by personal motives. On the other hand, where there are pronounced differences among the competing vendors' products, the purchasing agent is held more accountable for his choice and probably pays more attention to rational factors. Short-run personal gain becomes less motivating than the long-run gain which comes from serving the organization with distinction.

The marketing strategist must appreciate these goal conflicts of the organizational buyer. Behind all the ferment of purchasing agents to develop standards and employ value analysis lies their desire to avoid being thought of as order-clerks, and to develop better skills in reconciling personal and organizational objectives.[33]

Summary

Think back over the five different behavioral models of how the buyer translates buying influences into purchasing responses.

- Marshallian man is concerned chiefly with economic cues—prices and income—and makes a fresh utility calculation before each purchase.
- Pavlovian man behaves in a largely habitual rather than thoughtful way; certain configurations of cues will set off the same behavior because of rewarded learning in the past.
- Freudian man's choices are influenced strongly by motives and fantasies which take place deep within his private world.
- Veblenian man acts in a way which is shaped largely by past and present social groups.
- And finally, Hobbesian man seeks to reconcile individual gain with organizational gain.

[33] For an insightful account, see George Strauss, "Tactics of Lateral Relationship: The Purchasing Agent," *Administrative Science Quarterly*, Vol. 7 (September, 1962), pp. 161-186.

Thus, it turns out that the "black box" of the buyer is not so black after all. Light is thrown in various corners by these models. Yet no one has succeeded in putting all these pieces of truth together into one coherent instrument for behavioral analysis. This, of course, is the goal of behavioral science.

Income has always been the
marketer's handiest guide to
family consumption standards.
But it is a far from accurate
index. . . . Social-class position
and mobility-stability dimensions will reflect in much greater
depth each individual's style of
life.

12

Social Classes
and Spending Behavior

PIERRE MARTINEAU

ALL SOCIETIES place emphasis on some one structure which gives form to
the total society and integrates all the other structures such as the family,
the clique, voluntary association, caste, age, and sex groupings into a social
unity.

Social stratification means any system of ranked statuses by which all
the members of a society are placed in some kind of a superordinate and
subordinate hierarchy. While money and occupation are important in the
ranking process, there are many more factors, and these two alone do not
establish social position. The concept of social class was designed to include this process of ranking people in superior and inferior social position
by any and all factors.

Reprinted from the *Journal of Marketing,* national quarterly publication of the
American Marketing Association, Volume 23, No. 2 (October, 1958), pp. 121-130.

Class System

It has been argued that there cannot be a class system existent in America when most individuals do not have the slightest idea of its formal structure. Yet in actuality every individual senses that he is more at home with and more acceptable to certain groups than to others. In a study of department stores and shopping behavior, it was found that the Lower-Status woman is completely aware that, if she goes into High-Status department stores, the clerks and the other customers in the store will punish her in various subtle ways.

"The clerks treat you like a crumb," one woman expressed it. After trying vainly to be waited on, another woman bitterly complained that she was loftily told, "We thought you were a clerk."

The woman who is socially mobile gives considerable thought to the external symbols of status, and she frequently tests her status by shopping in department stores which she thinks are commensurate with her changing position. She knows that, if she does not dress correctly, if she does not behave in a certain manner to the clerks, if she is awkward about the proper cues, then the other customers and the clerks will make it very clear that she does not belong.

In another study, very different attitudes in the purchase of furniture and appliances involving this matter of status were found. Middle-class people had no hesitancy in buying refrigerators and other appliances in discount houses and bargain stores because they felt that they could not "go wrong" with the nationally advertised names. But taste in furniture is much more elusive and subtle because the brand names are not known; and, therefore, one's taste is on trial. Rather than commit a glaring error in taste which would exhibit an ignorance of the correct status symbols, the same individual who buys appliances in a discount house generally retreats to a status store for buying furniture. She needs the support of the store's taste.

In a very real sense, everyone of us in his consumption patterns and style of life shows an awareness that there is some kind of a superiority-inferiority system operating, and that we must observe the symbolic patterns of our own class.

Lloyd Warner and Paul Lunt have described a six-class system: the Upper-Upper, or old families; Lower-Upper, or the newly arrived; Upper-Middle, mostly the professionals and successful businessmen; Lower-Middle, or the white collar salaried class; Upper-Lower, or the wage earner, skilled worker group; and Lower-Lower, or the unskilled labor group.[1] For practical purposes, in order to determine the individual's class position, Warner and his associates worked out a rating index, not based on amount of income but rather on type of income, type of occupation, house type, and place of residence.

Although the Warner thesis has been widely used in sociology, it has not generally been employed in marketing. As a matter of fact, some critics in the social sciences have held that, since Warner's thesis rested essentially on studies of smaller cities in the 10,000-25,000 class, this same system might not exist in the more complex metropolitan centers, or might not be unravelled by the same techniques. Furthermore, many marketers did not see the application of this dimension to the individual's economic behavior, since the studies of Warner and his associates had mostly been concerned with the differences in the broad patterns of living, the moral codes, etc.

Social Class in Chicago

Under Warner's guidance, the *Chicago Tribune* has undertaken several extensive studies exploring social class in a metropolitan city, and its manifestations specifically in family buying patterns. The problem was to determine if such a social-class system did exist in metropolitan Chicago, if the dimensions and the relationships were at all similar to the smaller cities which were studied before the far-reaching social changes of the past fifteen years. The studies were undertaken to see if there were any class significances in the individual family's spending-saving patterns, retail store loyalties, and his expressions of taste in typical areas such as automobiles, apparel, furniture, and house types.

It seems that many an economist overlooks the possibility of any psychological differences between individuals resulting from different class membership. It is assumed that a rich man is simply a poor man with more money and that, given the same income, the poor man would behave exactly like the rich man. The *Chicago Tribune* studies crystallize a wealth of evidence from other sources that this is just not so, and that the Lower-Status person is profoundly different in his mode of thinking and his way of handling the world from the Middle-Class individual. Where he buys and what he buys will differ not only by economics but in symbolic value.

It should be understood, of course, that there are no hard and fast lines between the classes. Implicit in the notion of social class in America is the possibility of movement from one class to another. The "office boy-

[1] W. Lloyd Warner and Paul Lunt, *The Social Life of a Modern Community* (New Haven, Yale University Press, 1950). Also, W. Lloyd Warner, Marchia Meeker, and Kenneth Eells, *Social Class in America* (Chicago, Science Research Associates, 1949).

to-president" saga is a cherished part of the American dream. Bobo Rocke-feller illustrates the female counterpart: from coal miner's daughter to socialite. As a corollary of the explorations in class, the study also tried to be definitive about the phenomenon of social mobility—the movement from one class to another.

There are numerous studies of vertical mobility from the level of socio-logical analysis, mostly by comparing the individual's occupational status to that of his father. There are also studies at the level of psychological analysis. This study attempted to combine the two levels, to observe the individual's progress and also to understand something of the dynamics of the mobile person as compared to the stable individual. The attempt was to look both backward and forward: tracing such factors as occupation, place of residence, and religion back to parents and grandparents, and then where the family expected to be in the next five or ten years, what were the educational plans for each son, each daughter, a discussion of future goals.

Because this article is confined primarily to social class, this section may be concluded by saying that the studies show a very clear relationship between spend-saving aspirations and the factors of mobility-stability.

Framework of Study

Following are Warner's hypotheses and assumptions for the study:

I. ASSUMPTIONS ABOUT SYMBOLS AND VALUES AND ABOUT SAVING OF MONEY AND ACCUMULATION OF OBJECTS

Our society is acquisitive and pecuniary. On the one hand, the values and beliefs of Americans are pulled toward the pole of the accumulation of money by increasing the amount of money income and reducing its outgo. On the other hand, American values emphasize the accumulation of objects and products of technology for display and consumption. The self-regard and self-esteem of a person and his family, as well as the public esteem and respect of a valued social world around the accumulator, are increased or not by such symbols of accumulation and consumption.

The two sets of values, the accumulation of product symbols and the accumulation (saving) of money, may be, and usually are, in opposition.

General working hypotheses stemming from these assumptions were: (1) People are distributed along a range according to the two-value com-ponents, running from proportionately high savings, through mixed cate-gories, to proportionately high accumulation of objects. (2) These value variations conform to social and personality factors present in all Ameri-cans.

II. ASSUMPTIONS ABOUT PRODUCT SYMBOLS, SAVERS, AND ACCUMULATIONS

American society is also characterized by social change, particularly technological change that moves in the direction of greater and greater production of more kinds and more numerous objects for consumption and accumulation.

Hypothesis: New varieties of objects will be most readily accepted by the accumulators, and most often opposed by the savers.

III. ASSUMPTIONS ABOUT THE SOCIAL VALUES OF ACCUMULATORS AND SAVERS

American society is characterized by basic cultural differences, one of them being social status. Social class levels are occupied by people, some of whom are upward mobile by intent and fact. Others are non-mobile, by intent and fact. The values which dictate judgments about actions, such as the kinds of objects which are consumed and accumulated, will vary by class level and the presence or absence of vertical mobility.

IV. ASSUMPTIONS ABOUT THE PERSONAL VALUES OF ACCUMULATORS AND SAVERS

The personality components are distributed through the class levels and through the mobility types. By relating the social and personality components, it is possible to state a series of hypotheses about accumulators and savers as they are related to the object world around them, particularly to objects which are new and old to the culture, those which are imposing or not and those which are predominantly for display or for consumption.

At the direct, practical level, all of these theoretical questions can be summarized by one basic question: *What kinds of things are people likely to buy and not buy if they are in given class positions and if they are or are not socially mobile?* In other words, what is the effect on purchasing behavior of being in a particular social class, and being mobile or non-mobile?

If this is the crucial question, theoretically grounded, then a whole series of hypotheses can be laid out concerning values about money and values about buying various kinds of objects for consumption and for display. Some of these are:

1. There will be a relationship between values held by a particular subject and the extent to which particular products exemplify those values.
2. There is a differential hierarchy of things for which it is worth spending money.
3. Veblen's theory that conspicuous expenditure is largely applied to the Upper Class is erroneous. It runs all the way through our social system.

From these statements certain other hypotheses follow:

4. At different class levels, symbols of mobility will differ.

There is a differential hierarchy of things on which it is worth spending money. Class and mobility will be two of the dimensions that will differentiate—also personality and cultural background.

5. The place in the home where these symbols will be displayed will shift at different class levels.

The underlying assumption here is that there is a hierarchy of importance in the rooms of the house. This hierarchy varies with social class, mobility, age, ethnicity. The studies also revealed clear-cut patterns of taste for lamps, furnishings, house types, etc.

6. The non-mobile people tend to rationalize purchases in terms of cost or economy.

In other words, non-mobile people tend to be oriented more toward the pole of the accumulation of money. Purchases, then, are rationalized in terms of the savings involved.

The basic thesis of all the hypotheses on mobility is this: Whereas the stable individual would emphasize saving and security, the behavior of the mobile individual is characterized by spending for various symbols of upward movement. All of the evidence turned up indicates that this difference in values does exist, and furthermore that notable differences in personality dynamics are involved. For instance, the analysis of how families would make investments shows that stable people overwhelmingly prefer insurance, the symbol of security. By contrast, the mobile people at all levels prefer stocks, which are risk-taking. In Warner's words, the mobile individual acts as if he were free, white, and twenty-one, completely able to handle the world, and perfectly willing to gamble on himself as a sure bet to succeed.

Class Placement

Returning to the factor of social class, in this study class placement was based on a multi-state probability area sample of metropolitan Chicago, involving 3,880 households. It was found that the matter of placement could not be done by the relatively simple scoring sufficient for the smaller cities. To secure house typings, it was necessary to provide the field investigators with photographs covering a wide range of dwelling types, all the way from exclusive apartments to rooms over stores. Because of the very complexity of metropolitan life, occupations provided the biggest problem. To solve this operational problem, it was necessary to construct an exhaustive list of occupational types involving degree of responsibility and training required by each. The data finally used to calculate the Index of Status Characteristics (ISC) were:

(weighted by 5)
　　Occupation (from 1 to 7 broad categories)

(weighted by 4)
　　　　Sources of Income (from 1 to 7 types)

(weighted by 3)
　　　　Housing Type (from 1 to 7 types)

The sum of the individual's weighted scores was used to predict his social class level as follows: [2]

ISC Scores	Predicted Social Class Placement
12-21	Upper Class
22-37	Upper-Middle Class
38-51	Lower-Middle Class
52-66	Upper-Lower Class
67-84	Lower-Lower Class

The study very clearly shows that there is a social-class system operative in a metropolitan area which can be delineated. Furthermore, class membership is an important determinant of the individual's economic behavior, even more so than in the smaller city. The one department store in the smaller city may satisfy almost everyone, whereas in the metropolitan city the stores become sharply differentiated.

This is the social-class structure of Metropolitan Chicago, typifying the transformation of the formerly agrarian Midwestern cities from Pittsburgh to Kansas City into a series of big mill-towns.

Upper and Upper-Middle	8.1%
Lower-Middle	28.4%
Upper-Lower	44.0%
Lower-Lower	19.5%

While the Old Families and the Newly Arrived are still recognizable as types, they constitute less than 1 per cent of the population. A similar study in Kansas City turned up so few that they could not be counted at all. On the other hand, we see the emergence of a seventh class, the Upper-Lower "Stars" or Light-Blue Collar Workers. They are the spokesmen of the Upper-Lower Class groups—high income individuals, who have the income for more ostentatious living than the average factory

[2] Dr. Bevode McCall helped to solve the ISC scoring problem for Metropolitan Chicago.

worker but who lack the personal skills or desire for high status by social mobility.

There is certainly a rough correlation between income and social class. But social class is a much richer dimension of meaning. There are so many facets of behavior which are explicable only on a basis of social class dynamics. For instance, this analysis of the purchase of household appliances in Chicago over a four-year period shows a very different picture by income and by class:

Nine Appliance Types—Four-Year Period

By Income

Over $7,000	36.2%
4,000-6,999	46.0%
Under 4,000	17.8%

By Social Class

Upper and Upper-Middle	16.6%
Lower-Middle	29.2%
Upper-Lower	45.7%
Lower-Lower	8.5%

Income analysis shows that the lowest income group represents an understandably smaller market, but nevertheless a market. Social-class analysis highlights a fundamental difference in attitudes toward the home between the two lower classes. The Upper-Lower Class man sees his home as his castle, his anchor to the world, and he loads it down with hardware—solid heavy appliances—as his symbols of security. The Lower-Lower Class individual is far less interested in his castle, and is more likely to spend his income for flashy clothes or an automobile. He is less property-minded, and he has less feeling about buying and maintaining a home.

Several *Tribune* studies have explored the way of life and the buying behavior in many new suburbs and communities. All of them quickly become stratified along social-class and mobility dimensions, and, therefore, differ tremendously among themselves. *Fortune* has reported on Park Forest, Illinois, a middle-class suburb of 30,000 and only ten years old. It is characterized by high degrees of both upward and geographical mobility. The people are overwhelmingly those who had moved from other parts of the United States, who had few local roots, and who consequently wanted to integrate themselves in friendship groups. But this was not typical of the new Lower-Status suburbs where the women did relatively little fraternizing. It was not typical of the new Upper-Middle Class mobile suburbs where the people were preoccupied with status symbols, not in submerging themselves in the group.

One new community had crystallized as being for Higher-Status Negroes. This was a resettlement project with relatively high rents for Negroes. Eighty-five per cent of them had come from the South where social class was compressed. But, as soon as they came to Chicago, the class system opened up and they were anxious to establish a social distance between themselves and other Negroes. Almost all of them said they enjoyed the "peace and quiet" of their neighborhood, which was their way of insisting that they were not like the "noisy" lower-class Negroes. They deliberately avoided the stores patronized by other Negroes.

Choice of Store

All of these studies reveal the close relation between choice of store, patterns of spending, and class membership. In the probability sample delineating social class, such questions were asked in the total metropolitan area as:

"If you were shopping for a good dress, at which store would you be most likely to find what you wanted?"

"For an everyday dress?"

"For living room furniture?"

"At which store do you buy most of your groceries?"

To assume that all persons would wish to shop at the glamorous High-Status stores is utterly wrong. People are very realistic in the way they match their values and expectations with the status of the store. The woman shopper has a considerable range of ideas about department stores; but these generally become organized on a scale ranking from very High-Social Status to the Lowest-Status and prestige. The social status of the department store becomes the primary basis for its definition by the shopper. This is also true of men's and women's apparel stores, and furniture stores, on the basis of customer profiles. The shopper is not going to take a chance feeling out of place by going to a store where she might not fit.

No matter what economics are involved, she asks herself who are the other customers in the store, what sort of treatment can she expect at the hands of the clerks, will the merchandise be the best of everything, or lower priced and hence lower quality? Stores are described as being for the rich, for the average ordinary people, or for those who have to stretch their pennies.

The most important function of retail advertising today, when prices and quality have become so standard, is to permit the shopper to make social-class identification. This she can do from the tone and physical character of the advertising. Of course, there is also the factor of psychological identification. Two people in the same social class may want different stores. One may prefer a conservative store, one may want the most advanced styling. But neither will go to stores where they do not "fit," in a social-class sense.

In contrast to the independent food retailer, who obviously adapts to the status of the neighborhood, the chain grocers generally invade many income areas with their stores. Nevertheless, customer profiles show that each chain acquires a status definition. The two largest grocery chains in the Chicago area are A. & P. and Jewel; yet they draw very different customer bodies. A. & P. is strong with the mass market, whereas Jewel has its strength among the Middle Class.

While the national brand can and often does cut across classes, one can think of many product types and services which do have social class labels. The Upper-Middle Class person rarely travels by motor coach because none of his associates do so, even though there is certainly nothing wrong with this mode of transportation. On the other hand, even with low air-coach fares, one does not see many factory workers or day laborers on vacation around airports. Such sales successes as vodka and tonic water, and men's deodorants and foreign sports cars, were accomplished without benefit of much buying from this part of the market.

Communication Skills

There is also a relation between class and communication abilities which has significance for marketing. The kind of super-sophisticated and clever advertising which appears in the *New Yorker* and *Esquire* is almost meaningless to Lower-Status people. They cannot comprehend the subtle humor; they are baffled by the bizarre art. They have a different symbol system, a very different approach to humor. In no sense does this imply that they lack intelligence or wit. Rather their communication skills have just been pressed into a different mold.

Here again, style of advertising helps the individual to make class identification. Most of the really big local television success stories in Chicago have been achieved by personalities who radiate to the mass that this is where they belong. These self-made businessmen who do the announcing for their own shows communicate wonderfully well with the mass audience. While many listeners switch off their lengthy and personal commercials, these same mannerisms tell the Lower-Status individual that here is someone just like himself, who understands him.

Social Research, Inc., has frequently discussed the class problem in marketing by dividing the population into Upper-Middle or quality market;

the middle majority which combines both the Lower-Middle and Upper-Lower; and then the Lower-Lower. The distinction should be drawn between the Middle Classes and the Lower-Status groups. In several dozen of these store profiles, there is scarcely an instance where a store has appeal to the Lower-Middle and Upper-Lower classes with anything like the same strength.

It would be better to make the break between the Middle Class, representing one-third of the population and the Lower-Status or Working-Class or Wage-Earner group, representing two-thirds of metropolitan Chicago. This permits some psychological distinctions to be drawn between the Middle-Class individual and the individual who is not a part of the Middle-Class system of values. Even though this is the dominant American value system, even though Middle-Class Americans have been taught by their parents that it is the only value system, this Lower-Status individual does not necessarily subscribe to it.

Who Saves, Who Spends?

Another important set of behavioral distinctions related to social class position was revealed in the "save-spend aspiration" study. The question was asked: "Suppose your income was doubled for the next ten years, what would you do with the increased income?" This is a fantasy question taken out of the realm of any pressing economic situation to reflect aspirations about money. The coding broke down the answers to this question into five general categories: (1) the mode of saving, (2) the purpose of saving, (3) spending which would consolidate past gains, meet present defensive needs, prepare for future self-advancement, (4) spending which is "self-indulgent-centered," (5) spending which is "house-centered."

Here are some of our findings: [3] The higher the individual's class position, the more likely is he to express some saving aspirations. Conversely, the lower his class position, the more likely is he to mention spending only. Moreover, the higher the status, the more likely is the individual to specify *how* he will save his money, which is indicative of the more elaborate financial learning required of higher status.

Proceeding from the more general categories (such as saving versus spending only) to more specific categories (such as non-investment versus investment saving and the even more specific stock versus real estate investment, etc.) an increasingly sharper class differentiation is found. It is primarily *non-investment* saving which appeals to the Lower-Status person. Investment saving, on the other hand, appeals above all to the Upper-Status person.

[3] The saving-spending aspiration analysis was carried out by Roger Coup, graduate student at the University of Chicago.

Investors almost always specify how they will invest. And here in mode of investment are examples of the most sharply class-differentiated preferences. Intangible forms of investment like stock and insurance are very clearly distinguished as Upper-Status investments. Nearly four times as many Upper-Middles select insurance as would be expected by chance, whereas only one-fifth of the Lower-Lowers select it as would be expected by chance. By contrast, Lower-Status people have far greater preference for tangible investments, specifically ownership of real estate, a farm, or a business.

To sum up, Middle-Class people usually have a place in their aspirations for some form of saving. This saving is most often in the form of investment, where there is a risk, long-term involvement, and the possibility of higher return. Saving, investment saving, and intangible investment saving —successively each of these become for them increasingly symbols of their higher status.

The aspirations of the Lower-Status person are just as often for spending as they are for saving. This saving is usually a non-investment saving where there is almost no risk, funds can be quickly converted to spendable cash, and returns are small. When the Lower-Status person does invest his savings, he will be specific about the mode of investment, and is very likely to prefer something tangible and concrete—something he can point at and readily display.

Turning from mode of saving to purpose of saving, very significant class relationships are likewise evident. Consider the verbalization of saving purpose. Lower-Status people typically explain why one should save—why the very act of saving is important. On the other hand, Middle-Class people do not, as if saving is an end-in-itself, the merits of which are obvious and need not be justified.

Spending is the other side of the coin. Analysis of what people say they will spend for shows similar class-related desires. All classes mention concrete, material artifacts such as a new car, some new appliance. But the Lower-Status people stop here. Their accumulations are artifact-centered, whereas Middle-Class spending-mentions are experience-centered. This is spending where one is left typically with only a memory. It would include hobbies, recreation, self-education and travel. The wish to travel, and particularly foreign travel, is almost totally a Middle-Class aspiration.

Even in their fantasies, people are governed by class membership. In his daydreaming and wishful thinking, the Lower-Status individual will aspire in different patterns from the Middle-Class individual.

Psychological Differences

This spending-saving analysis has very obvious psychological implications to differentiate between the classes. Saving itself generally suggests foresightedness, the ability to perceive long-term needs and goals. Noninvestment saving has the characteristics of little risk-taking and of ready conversion, at no loss, into immediate expenditures—the money can be drawn out of the account whenever the bank is open. Investment spending, on the other hand, has the characteristics of risk-taking (a gamble for greater returns) and of delayed conversion, with possible loss, to expenditures on immediate needs.

Here are some psychological contrasts between two different social groups:

Middle-Class

1. Pointed to the future
2. His viewpoint embraces a long expanse of time
3. More urban identification
4. Stresses rationality
5. Has a well-structured sense of the universe
6. Horizons vastly extended or not limited
7. Greater sense of choice-making
8. Self-confident, willing to take risks
9. Immaterial and abstract in his thinking
10. Sees himself tied to national happenings

Lower-Status

1. Pointed to the present and past
2. Lives and thinks in a short expanse of time
3. More rural in identification
4. Non-rational essentially
5. Vague and unclear structuring of the world
6. Horizons sharply defined and limited
7. Limited sense of choice-making
8. Very much concerned with security and insecurity
9. Concrete and perceptive in his thinking
10. World revolves around his family and body

Conclusions

The essential purpose of this article was to develop three basic premises which are highly significant for marketing:

I. *There is a social-class system operative in metropolitan markets, which can be isolated and described.*

II. *It is important to realize that there are far-reaching psychological differences between the various classes.* They do not handle the world in the same fashion. They tend not to think in the same way. As one tries to communicate with the Lower-Status group, it is imperative to sense that their goals and mental processes differ from the Middle-Class group.

III. *Consumption patterns operate as prestige symbols to define class membership, which is a more significant determinant of economic behavior than mere income.* Each major department store, furniture store, and chain-grocery store has a different "pulling power" on different status groups. The usual customers of a store gradually direct the store's merchandising policies into a pattern which works. The interaction between store policy and consumer acceptance results in the elimination of certain customer groups and the attraction of others, with a resulting equilibration around a reasonably stable core of specific customer groups who think of the store as appropriate for them.

Income has always been the marketer's handiest index to family consumption standards. But it is a far from accurate index. For instance, the bulk of the population in a metropolitan market today will fall in the middle-income ranges. This will comprise not only the traditional white collar worker, but the unionized craftsman and the semi-skilled worker with their tremendous income gains of the past decade. Income-wise, they may be in the same category. But their buying behavior, their tastes, their spending-saving aspirations can be poles apart. Social-class position and mobility-stability dimensions will reflect in much greater depth each individual's style of life.

... the complaints seem to miss a crucial point about the new society—a point that most marketing men have not missed. The point is that while our society is more homogeneous, the individual's own opportunities to live in diverse fashions have been expanded considerably.

13

The New Masses

DANIEL SELIGMAN

ONLY TEN YEARS AGO, the following description of an American family's style of life would have enabled one to form some fairly firm impressions about the father's occupation and the general social "rank" of the family:

The parents, who are about forty, live with their two boys in a comfortable six-room suburban house outfitted with a full line of appliances, a television set that is in more or less constant use, and a car in which the father drives to work. The car is also used for camping trips during the summer. The mother shops at a local supermarket and at several local department stores; the boys attend the good local public schools; and on weekends the family often goes swimming at a local beach, although recently the father and mother and their older son have begun to take an interest in golf.

Given these facts in 1950, one might have inferred, quite reasonably, that the head of the house was a lower or middle-echelon executive, or salesman, or the proprietor or part owner of some small business, or a professional man, and that the family's position in society was solidly middle class.

Reprinted from the May, 1959 issue of *Fortune* Magazine by Special Permission; ©, 1959, Time Inc., pp. 106ff.

Given these same facts in 1960, one could deduce practically nothing about the family's social rank or the father's occupation. For the fact is that in the past few years the broad style of life described above has become available, not only to an identifiable "middle class," but to a great mass of Americans, perhaps even a majority. The family head today might be a truck driver earning $5,500, a college professor earning $7,000, a life-insurance salesman earning $8,000, a skilled production worker earning $9,000, an airline pilot earning $15,000, or an executive earning $18,000. In the new American society, it is increasingly difficult to tell the players apart without subpoenaing their tax returns.

Many otherwise alert Americans continue to think and talk of their countrymen as though all of them could be sorted out into three clear-cut classes. The biggest of these, of course, would be a low-income *working class,* or simply *workers* ("lower class" has never come easily to American lips), symbolized most aptly by the "blue collars" in manufacturing but also including farmers. Then there would be the middle-income *middle class,* whose prototype is the small proprietor, or the professional or white-collar employee. And at the top there would be a small layer of important businessmen, prominent professionals, government officials, etc. Europeans would forthrightly call this the American *upper class;* Americans themselves are more likely to speak of *rich people, society people, big shots,* etc., and of course nobody is more reluctant to say "upper class" than a qualified member.

These traditional class concepts still have a kind of shorthand utility in connoting various styles of life, but when they are used to denote a neatly layered social pyramid they are today simply a source of confusion. For one thing, the shape is all wrong. What we have in the U.S. today, by income standards at least, more nearly resembles a diamond than a pyramid—i.e., there are more people in the middle than there are at the top or bottom.

Aside from the shape of the income structure, it is increasingly difficult to "layer" a society of such great flux and diversity. It was never easy to diagram the "class structure" of the U.S. as a matter of fact, and most sociologists have usually been obliged to limit their descriptive efforts to relatively small, self-contained communities like Weirton, West Virginia, or like Newburyport, Massachusetts (whose inhabitants were divided, by W. Lloyd Warner and Paul S. Lunt in a study starting in the 1930's, into *six* classes, ranging from upper-upper to lower-lower). But as we enter the 1960's it is increasingly difficult to find even small communities in which classes are clearly separable.

Russell Lynes, a witty amateur sociologist who is an editor of *Harper's* magazine, has suggested that we visualize the new U.S. society as a series of independent pyramids, each with its own interests, hierarchies, and rewards. That is, one pyramid for business executives, and others for scien tists, labor-union officials, the military, sports figures, etc.—even one for criminals. (An ex-convict named Lewis Dent has described the criminal pyramid in some detail: in prison, the professionals who live entirely by the criminal code are held in highest regard, then come the gifted amateurs who can show some genuine antisocial accomplishments, e.g., rapists, and at the bottom are the "creeps" who are ostracized because they reject the mores of the underworld.) But the pyramids also present difficulties when one tries to relate them to the realities of American life. There are too many pyramids, and all have different shapes. Some of them, in fact, are not really pyramids—e.g., among professional baseball players there are more men in the major leagues than in class B. Furthermore, too many Americans have different positions on several pyramids, and on any one pyramid there is the problem that insiders and outsiders often evaluate individuals differently; the young "comer" may have more prestige within a corporation than many of the executives who apparently outrank him.

But the basic reason for the increased confusion about class in the U.S is the steady growth in the number of Americans who can afford at leas some of the amenities once associated with the highest positions in our society. If most "workers" still cannot afford $110 suits, boats, Thunder birds, *and* trips to Florida, they have at least enough discretionary income so that they can have some of these things some of the time. As much a six years ago, in *The Changing American Market,* FORTUNE noted that 4. per cent of all nonfarm families had become concentrated in the middle income range—i.e., they had cash income after taxes of $4,000 to $7,500 (in 1953 dollars); and it also noted that almost 60 per cent of these families were actually headed by blue-collar workers. This bunching around-the-middle has persisted in the years since 1954, with the note worthy difference that the "middle" keeps moving higher up on the money scale. By 1959 about 43 per cent of all nonfarm families had after-tax cash incomes between $5,000 and $10,000 (in 1959 dollars).

The Modern Maggies

The most conspicuous breakdown of class lines is the one that has taken place just in the past few years as the ex- "proletarians," who are now the heart of the middle-income class, began finally to adopt a middle class style of life. This phenomenon, portentous in its implications for the markets of the 1960's, is hard to express statistically, but there can no longer be any doubt about the broad facts of the case. Nelson Foote, a dis tinguished sociologist who recently left academic life to work for General Electric, says that he has observed the change even in Detroit, a city where class consciousness dies hard. "During the war," Foote says, "you could sit on a streetcar and tell at a glance who were the defense workers and who were the white collars. Then, while the war was still on, the companies did something which has had a profound effect on our society: they installed cafeterias and lockers in the plants. After a while, you stopped seeing lunch boxes and work clothes on the streetcars, and today you just can't tell who's who. The city is full of auto workers whose wives shop at Hudson's—who wouldn't be caught dead buying a pair of shoes at Sears."

Foote is convinced, in fact, that it is the wives of the blue-collar workers who are instrumental in changing their families' style of life, and he has observed at least some blue-collar families in which the familiar old American saga of Jiggs and Maggie is being re-enacted—though in the modern version Maggie is more concerned with "bringing up father" to be an active P.T.A. member than to be a society swell. In some respects, of course, the blue-collar husbands accept middle-class ways with enthusiasm; many suburban shopping-center proprietors argue that the husband is an easier prospect than the wife when a couple are pondering something of a splurge, especially when the splurge promises greater comfort or just plain fun. The wives, however, are closer to the children, hence closer to the real or fancied social pressures the children are under in the suburban schools. Moreover, many of the wives of blue-collar workers have themselves held white-collar jobs in offices, which brought them into contact with longer-established members of the middle class and their style of life.

A Foothold in Levittown

How many blue-collar families have arrived in the suburbs? Even if no sociologists had observed the phenomenon, it can be inferred from available government data that a sizable number of blue collars [1] *have to be* in suburban, or semi-suburban, areas. Families headed by blue collars comprise about 60 per cent of nonfarm families today. It is manifest that they cannot all be in the metropolitan areas' inner cities (which have about 25 per cent of the nonfarm population) and in the smaller cities and towns (which have about 30 per cent).

In an effort to gauge more precisely the impact of the blue-collar families on suburbia, and vice versa, in 1959 FORTUNE surveyed real-estate agents and developers, bankers, school officials, as well as some sociologists, in the suburbs of seven major metropolitan areas. There was almost unanimous agreement among these observers that the blue collars have moved increasingly into suburban homes, especially those in the $10,000-to-$15,000 price range—though there are sizable numbers of sales all the

[1] Blue collars include foremen, skilled and semiskilled workers in manufacturing, building, mining, and transportation, service workers, and laborers. In all, there are some 30 million (including 6 million women).

way up to $21,000. An agent in northeastern Philadelphia guessed that about half the $15,000-to-$20,000 homes he sold in 1958 went to skilled blue-collar workers; and near Dallas there is a development of some 200 homes in the same price range that are almost entirely occupied by production workers for Texas Instruments. On the other hand, an agent near Atlanta who has also sold many homes to skilled workers—especially to airline mechanics and Ford assembly-plant employees—finds that not many of them break through the $10,000 price barrier. An estimate by Charles M. Fink, an attorney and realtor who has been directly involved in the sale or rental of some 4,000 homes in the Levittown, Pennsylvania, suburban development, offers this picture of the blue-collar foothold there:

Price	Number of houses	Proportion of blue-collar occupany
Over $17,500	1,200	Under 5 per cent
About $15,000	750	About 5-10 per cent
$10,000-$12,500	12,500	About 50 per cent
Under $10,000	2,700	About 65 per cent

This breakdown corresponds closely to the figures and impressions obtained from the other suburban areas. In 1954, FORTUNE estimated that about 30 million Americans lived in communities that were "strictly suburban" in character. The figure is in the neighborhood of 40 million today, and comprises about one-quarter of all nonfarm families. FORTUNE's survey suggests that perhaps a quarter of these are now blue-collar families, and in the newer suburban developments the proportion may be over a third.

Blue-and-White Values

In several interesting respects the blue and white collars still play different roles in the suburbs, and still have different reasons for moving there. There have always been some blue-collar families in suburbia, of course, but until recently they tended to be the local service and construction workers who, in middle-class communities, lived on the other side of the tracks. The newer blue-collar suburbanites are characteristically the skilled production workers who man the new industrial plants on the outskirts of metropolitan areas. (Between 1952 and 1957, the suburbs accounted for 80 per cent of all new jobs in the New York metropolitan area.) Unlike the white-collar man, who characteristically moves *away* from his job when he migrates to the suburbs, the blue-collar man is usually moving closer to his job, and is much preoccupied with traffic conditions and driving time between his suburban home and his suburban factory.

The white collar is often acutely conscious of the prestige thought to attach to some particular suburban town or neighborhood. He may load an extra commuting burden on himself to live in such a place—indeed, he may feel that commuting itself is invested with a kind of upper-middle-class prestige value. The blue collar, however, tends to see commuting time simply as an extension of his working day.

The young white collar usually regards his first suburban home as a temporary lodgment on the way to a better one. The blue collar sees it as security for his old age, and for this reason, perhaps, is much more concerned with getting a durable physical property than the white collar is.

But the significant fact is that, while these differences persist, the living habits of the blue and white collars have been converging in many respects; indeed, one might regard the suburbs today as the new American melting pot. A community leader in Royal Oak, a Detroit suburb, notes that the auto workers who followed the plants out of town were "swallowed up" when they lived in Detroit. "When they come out here, they seem hungry for community affairs." Indeed, the fact that they regard their first suburban homes as permanent living places often gives the blue collars a stake in local government that the more transient white collars do not feel they have. A real-estate developer who built a community of $16,000-to-$17,000 houses northwest of Chicago says that about half the community is blue collar, and that he has been "amazed and pleased to see how they've taken hold and run the community. I've sat in on some committees they have, and I'll tell you they make a hell of a lot more sense than some of the junior-executive types I've seen." Even in Park Forest, the Chicago suburb that has been much discussed (in FORTUNE and elsewhere) as a prototypical junior-executive community, there is now a blue-collar minority verging on 10 per cent, and in two recent years the Little League baseball chairmen have been blue collars. With a few exceptions, the people surveyed by FORTUNE reported that the new blue-collar suburbanites are *not* segregated socially.

The breakdown of the older class distinctions can be seen in an extreme form in southern California, especially in and around Los Angeles—an area that is not exactly suburban in character, but not exactly urban either. Nathan Glazer, a young Bennington College sociologist who recently spent a year in California, came away marveling at Los Angeles. "First of all, so many of the people have come from somewhere else that 'backgrounds' have less meaning; nobody cares about your family, or your religion, or the schools you went to. Then the outdoor living tends to make everyone live alike. Everyone uses the same communal facilities, especially the national parks and beaches. In the East, you feel it's kind of immoral to go swimming at four o'clock Wednesday afternoon, but out there you get used to it pretty fast—and the people there on the beach with you are aircraft workers, bellhops, pensioners, intellectuals, and even businessmen. We're used to defining people in terms of their jobs, but around Los Angeles there's a strange lack of emphasis on jobs. There's no central business district, and working hours tend to be quite irregular, principally because there are so many part-time workers, so many service employees who work odd hours, and so many professionals—and pensioners—who are able to keep their own hours. The traffic into and out of the city is heavy morning and evening but it is always going both ways, and you can never be sure who is going to the beach, to the supermarket, to Disneyland, or to work. The result of it all is that you don't identify people with their occupations, as you naturally do in the East, and class distinctions become further blurred."

What the Difference Is

While the older class lines are losing their meaning, it would be wildly unrealistic to argue that the U.S. is developing into a society of equals. Instead of having a fairly clear position in an oversimplified but still identifiable "class," the American of the 1960's is seen by the sociologists as a man with a "status." There are dozens of shadings of status—of a man's standing in the eyes of others. Status is more easily changed, obviously, than class. A family's status may jump a notch not only with the father's promotion at the office, but with the mother's election to the chairmanship of a suburban charity drive, or the son's enrollment at the state university.

Spending and status are still intimately related, of course, but in such diverse and sometimes paradoxical ways that novel opportunities and hazards are continually cropping up in the consumer markets. On the one hand, as more and more Americans have been enabled to adopt some form of the middle-class style of life, they have also become increasingly aware of, and more finely attuned to, the nuances that can disclose "the difference"—the difference between those with more and with less income and responsibility. In an age when millions of Americans live in superficially similar suburban developments, the flagstone walk the developer has given his more expensive houses is attentively noted.

The nuances involve much more than displays of income and raw purchasing power, however, since status is importantly bound up with education—which implies, among other things, the exercise of good taste in consumption. In an age when millions can travel abroad, the difference between a three-week economy trip to London-Paris-Rome and a six-week trip taking in Athens and Istanbul is not just the difference in cost but also in sophistication of the itinerary. Then there is the "keeping-down-with-the-Joneses" phenomenon so often seen in modern suburbia, which is not so much a pressure against heavy spending as a pressure to spend money as educated men are supposed to spend it—i.e., on fine high-fidelity sets and good wines rather than expensive fur coats and cars. And yet— just to complicate things still more—there has been such a proliferation of interesting, sophisticated, or chic things to spend money on that it is increasingly difficult to say that any two or three of these things are *the* badges of status.

The preoccupation with status is a phenomenon whose origins are interesting—especially, perhaps, to marketing and advertising men who are increasingly obliged to think of products as status symbols. The preoccupation is related in part to the fact that since 1940 over 20 million adult Americans have spent a good deal of time in the armed forces, where one is obliged constantly to think about "rank." It is also related to the fact that more and more Americans work for large organizations: something like 38 per cent of the labor force is employed in organizations that have over 500 employees. The figure (which includes all government employees) was only 28 per cent in 1940. In the nature of the case, large organizations are status-ridden: titles and responsibilities are carefully defined in job descriptions, and relationships are carefully plotted on organization charts.

Of all corporate employees, the blue collars have been traditionally the least concerned about status, because their status seemed quite unambiguous. Their wages, job descriptions, even their vacation privileges and other fringes have generally been matters of public record (in a union contract). And whatever his dreams for his son, the future of the blue-collar man himself has been fairly predictable, for he moves up in accordance with seniority rosters that are posted publicly; he has no important opportunities to advance by pulling wires or gaining favor with his superiors. Hence he has taken his job position as something "fixed"; he has not dwelt on the social implications of his job, but has seen it as a means to make money.

The New Strivers

There are some signs, however, that the blue collars are becoming more preoccupied with status: in part because they are now living with white collars in the suburbs, and having their first prolonged exposure to the latter's values; and in part because of the changing nature of blue-collar work. To some extent, the skilled blue-collar worker, eating now in the same company cafeteria as the white collar, working now in shirtsleeves instead of "work clothes," driving home from work to a middle-class suburban community, is beginning to feel the first twinges of concern about his status in society. Nelson Foote, commenting on these changes, says that "it would be a shame, in a way, if the old hard-headed blue-collar values disappeared, and nothing were left in this country except success-strivers."

The corporate white-collar workers, especially the men in the middle and higher reaches of the corporation, have a more ambiguous and volatile status position, and they are prone to develop what the sociologists call "status anxieties." (A number of sociologists have demonstrated that "upwardly mobile" families have a disproportionately high incidence of psychosomatic diseases.) Their preoccupation with status symbols—e.g., with the size and physical trappings of their offices—has been a recurrent theme in business fiction and satire in recent years. (In the movie, *A Face in the Crowd,* an advertising-agency executive suffers a heart attack after realizing he will lose a crucial account. He gasps out to the entertainer who is taking the account away from him: "You've seen my office. A corner office with four windows. Do you know how long it takes at Browning, Schlagel & McNally to get a corner office?" And then he slumps to the floor.)

In the years ahead, status will almost certainly hinge on education more than it has in the past. Indeed, the U.S. may now be moving into a period in which education will make and break men in a totally new fashion. It is a well-publicized fact that undergraduate enrollments, now running around 3,500,000, may come close to doubling by 1970. What is not so well appreciated is the fact that the number of living Americans who *have been to college* will also grow furiously during the 1960's—probably by about a third. Right now, something like 16,500,000 Americans have attended college for at least a year. By 1970, the figure will be in the vicinity of 22 million, of whom about 11 million will have graduated. (A rule of thumb that has held up pretty well in recent years is that of all those who go to college about half graduate.) At that point there are likely to be serious difficulties in finding enough "top jobs" for the college-trained.

Room at the Top?

The problem can be seen in sharp focus if we limit it to men in their twenties and early thirties. In 1950 there were 2,200,000 men between twenty-five and thirty-four who had completed at least a year of college. Today, the figure is about 2,900,000, and by 1970, the Census Bureau estimates, it will be about 3,800,000, and will represent almost a third of all the men in this age band (vs. less than a fifth in 1950). What kinds of job opportunities are these growing numbers of college men encountering?

It would appear that their opportunities to move toward the top jobs have already been narrowed considerably. At present, the number of men between twenty-five and thirty-four who are employed (in Census Bureau terminology) as "professional, technical, and kindred workers," or as "managers, officials, and proprietors," or as "sales workers," is three million—i.e., it is only a little higher than the number of college men in this age band. Virtually all the jobs that are at the top, or that can lead to the top, are in these three Census categories; but it should be noted that the categories also include a lot of "bottom jobs" we do not normally link with college education—e.g., the proprietors include marginal news dealers, and the sales workers include clerks in the five-and-dime stores as well as high-paid life-insurance salesmen. Hence it is obvious that a fair number of college-trained men must already be working at jobs to which no high status attaches.

The trend can be seen in a study prepared by the Bureau of Applied Social Research at Columbia University, working in cooperation with *Time,* and also in a study of U.S. consumers conducted for *Life* by the Alfred Politz research organization. Though the data in the two studies are not exactly comparable, they suggest that college training is increasingly unlikely to lead automatically to top jobs. The *Time* study, based on 1947 data, showed that 5 per cent of male college graduates were holding blue-collar jobs. The *Life* study, based on 1955-56 data, showed that almost 20 per cent of employed "household heads" (mostly male, of course) who had any college training were blue collars.

One partial solution to the job problems of the "educated many" would be to give professional or managerial status to the broad band of corporate and government employees who at present hover uneasily between the clerical and executive layers or, in manufacturing, between the skilled workers and the technical staff. In an age preoccupied with status, a lot can be done simply by changing titles. A lot is being done already, in fact, and at all levels. The janitors in schools are often designated "custodial engineers," though in some industries the term "sanitors" is preferred. Girls who type letters for $70 a week are billed as "Gal Fridays"—there are usually a hundred-odd listings under this heading in the help-wanted section of the Sunday New York *Times*—and thereby gain a kind of executive-assistant status. The U.S. Labor Department ruled recently that any "executive" who earned less than $80 a week had to be paid time and a half for overtime. A part of the recent and prospective increase in the ranks of the professional and managerial groups represents not a true increase in the number of such jobs, but an inflation of titles. This depreciation of managerial status has contributed further to the blurring of the old class lines, and to the preoccupation with the symbols that help one to determine a man's real status.

The Ups and Downs

One fairly certain consequence of the great proliferation of college graduates will be an increase in social and occupational mobility. Education has always been the principal path by which sons gained higher positions than their fathers had; and though the Horatio Alger legend dies hard, numerous studies of the American "business elite" make it plain that the top jobs have *always* gone to the relatively well educated. A recent study by S. M. Lipset and Reinhard Bendix shows that even in the first half of the nineteenth century, when only about 5 per cent of Americans went to high school, 22 per cent of the "elite" [2] had graduated from college, another 10 per cent had attended college, 51 per cent had attended some kind of high school, and only 17 per cent had not gone beyond elementary school. The same authors show that in a more recent generation of elite businessmen (those born between 1891 and 1920) 84 per cent had gone to college and only 5 per cent had not gone beyond elementary school.

It is possible that the value of college degrees will undergo some depreciation, as more and more Americans get them. But at the same time, the degree is becoming an almost universal requirement for admission to the managerial group, and the fact that corporate managers are no longer divided into men with and men without a college education makes for greater mobility within the group. This mobility is fostered by the increasing tendency of corporations to select their managers "scientifically," e.g., with the aid of aptitude and personality tests. The tests may represent invasions of privacy, they may be based on misconceptions about managerial qualities, and they may not even be successful in finding the qualities they are set up to detect, but they attempt at least to put promotions on a more *objective* basis, and make the candidate's background (his college, national origins, religion, father's occupation, etc.) much less relevant. In short, they make it easier for a clerk's son to become a vice president—and vice versa. (Talk about social mobility often seems to proceed on the assumption that mobility is only upward, but in any generation there is always a substantial minority of sons whose positions are lower than their fathers'. Data collected by the Michigan Survey Research Center suggested that, in 1952, of all employed persons whose fathers were "managers, officials, and proprietors," 25 per cent were skilled or semiskilled workers, and 8 per cent were actually laborers.)

[2] Any businessman prominent enough to be mentioned in the *National Cyclopedia of American Biography*—the authors' principal source of information on educational backgrounds—was taken to be of the "elite."

The Homogeneous Life

The increased bunching of Americans around the middle-income levels, the increased blurring of occupational distinctions, and the increased adoption of middle-class living styles by families of diverse occupational background, have all tended to make the U.S. a much more homogeneous society. At this point it may be interesting to observe that we have been "homogenized" in several other respects as well:

National backgrounds have less meaning than they used to. About 95 per cent of all Americans today are native-born (vs. 87 per cent in 1920), and about 80 per cent of them are at least "third generation" Americans (vs. 65 per cent in 1920)—i.e., both their parents were also native-born. With immigration averaging only about 250,000 a year, about 85 per cent of the U.S. population will be at least third generation by 1970. And though the point cannot be verified statistically, it is nonetheless clear that Americans are less prone than they once were to think of other Americans as "Swedes," or "Irishmen," or "Italians"—in part because the old-country ways and languages are largely unknown to the third and fourth generations, and in part because these generations so often have hopelessly *mixed* national backgrounds.

Religious differences are also less meaningful. A number of theologians have remarked, with some bitterness, that while Americans are more interested than they used to be in having a religion, they are much less interested in the *content* of religion, or in religious differences. Americans are increasingly being admonished, on television, for example, to "attend your place of worship this weekend"—and the inference is plain that it doesn't matter which one you attend. In *Religion and the Free Society,* a pamphlet published by the Fund for the Republic, William Lee Miller of the Yale Divinity School has complained of "the drive toward a shallow and implicitly compulsory common creed. . . . The kind of religion that results from this common civic faith is a religion-in-general, superficial and syncretistic, destructive of the profounder elements of faith." William Clancy, educational director of the Church Peace Union, commented in the same pamphlet, "The 'religion' that is accepted as a part of our public life is largely a matter of good fellowship and good works." Where religion once divided Americans on strongly felt sectarian lines, the new good fellowship and good works tend to emphasize nonsectarian activities (e.g., running nursery schools open to children of all religious backgrounds).

Political differences are also becoming blurred. American political debate is increasingly conducted in a bland, even-tempered atmosphere, and extremists of any kind are becoming rarer. The political expression of the new society, in which more and more families are bunched around the middle-income levels and adapting to middle-class ways, is a Congress in which more and more politicians are bunched around the middle of the road, in which both parties are increasingly dominated by "reasonable" liberals who were called, in a December, 1958, article in *Commentary* by Karl E. Meyer, the "Smooth Dealers." Many of them—e.g., Nelson Rockefeller, John F. Kennedy—could fit plausibly into either the Republican or the Democratic party; and as their numbers have grown, American voters increasingly cross party lines to vote for them. In short, the old party divisions are less meaningful.

The New Ivy Leaguer

The net of these "homogenizing" trends is that we all seem to live alike —or, at least, a great many of us live and think and dress more nearly alike than we used to. Many Americans appear to be disturbed by this trend, and to detect in it a threat to their own sense of individuality; they are endlessly complaining about all the "conformity" and "togetherness" in American life.

But the complaints seem to miss a crucial point about the new society— a point that most marketing men have *not* missed. The point is that while our society is more homogeneous, the individual's own opportunities to live in diverse fashions have been expanded considerably. The man in the Ivy League suit may be a millionaire or a skilled machinist, and so may the man at the wheel of the sports car and the man on the beach in Miami. To the spectator, this may look like a new uniformity; to the machinist, it involves a new diversity—a diversity that, it may safely be presumed, he is enjoying immensely.

Not so long ago American taste was the concern chiefly of the country's architects, artists, writers, and intellectual leaders. Now it is also the concern of its business leaders—of anyone, that is, who sells consumer goods and services.

14

How American Taste Is Changing

GILBERT BURCK

NOT SO LONG AGO American taste was the concern chiefly of the country's architects, artists, writers, and intellectual leaders. Now it is also the concern of its business leaders—of anyone, that is, who sells consumer goods and services. Price is important and always will be, but in a society looking forward to an average family income approaching $7,500 a year after taxes, price becomes relatively less important. Just as a woman who can afford to spend $50 for a frock will pay $65 for one that delights her, but begrudges $35 for one that does not, so American consumers as a group today tend more and more to let their senses make up their minds.

As with price, so with the utility and efficiency of products. In these days when consumer testing services are hard pressed to find important technical differences between brands of similar products, what counts more and more is the aesthetic quality of the products.

Business' growing concern with American taste is intensifying the intellectuals' concern about it. Taste is perhaps best defined as the capacity to discern fitness, beauty, order, congruity, or whatever constitutes excel-

Reprinted from the July, 1959 issue of *Fortune* Magazine by Special Permission; ©, 1959, Time Inc., pp. 114ff.

lence. When patterns of taste are dictated by purely commercial considerations, one argument goes, this capacity is stunted, and nearly all taste must conform to the average. Creative talent is diverted from writing novels or composing sonatas into such tasks as confecting advertising slogans; and intellects that are capable of unlocking the secrets of the universe are diverted into such pursuits as designing better cigarette-making machinery.

What *is* the state of American taste? In this essay, FORTUNE puts aside statistics to argue a speculative and controversial thesis: it is that American taste, at least by prevailing standards, is changing for the better, and will continue to do so. The change will be pervasive, encompassing nearly all social and income groups, and will be evident not only in the things people buy, but in the ways people use their leisure. And despite the apprehensions of the intellectuals, the part that business plays in forming tastes will tend not to corrupt but to improve them.

About Taste There Is Much Dispute

But is it possible to talk about absolute standards of taste? A lot of cagey thinkers, from the dawn of civilization, have maintained that anybody laying down such standards is simply describing his personal inclinations. It is certainly true that taste cannot be analyzed and graded to close standards, like aluminum alloys, or internal-combustion engines. Moreover, taste is often the cloak of the intellectual snob who automatically defines as bad anything that is popular. Yet there appear to be some fundamentals of fitness, proportion, and beauty. Give a group of people a series of pictures of objects and tell them to pick the best and the worst, and they agree remarkably on the extremes of both good and bad. What is more, a nation's taste is the measure of its culture, and to deny the reality of qualitative differences in taste is to slam the door on all inherited cultural values. If those values mean anything at all, there is an important difference between J. D. Salinger and Mickey Spillane, between the *Eroica* and *Pink Shoe Laces,* between O'Neill and soap opera, between the Parthenon and a hotdog stand.

Perhaps the most practical approach to taste values is simply to observe that "good" taste is usually the taste of the "upper" classes, the artistically proficient, or the learned. But the arbiters or makers of taste are not only educators, the *avant-garde,* the intellectuals, the writers, the designers. They are also, as we shall see, often manufacturers and merchandisers. These arbiters, of course, don't always agree among themselves, but whether they agree or not, they do set standards. So let us say that "good" taste in the U.S. is represented by the preferences of its tastemakers.

Four major forces are working to elevate American taste: (1) rising real income; (2) more education, both formal and informal; (3) the efforts of the tastemakers to spread their own gospel; and (4) the old American striving for self-betterment.

The effect of rising real income on U.S. taste is not merely that it enables people to buy more. It usually enables business to provide consumers with a steadily wider range of choices, thus making mass production the agent not of uniformity but of constantly widening variety. And along with more money, Americans are getting more leisure in which to develop their taste.

But income and leisure without education are like force without direction. As the excesses of America's own newly rich suggest, more leisure and more money for masses of Americans without more and better education could produce a temporary decline in public taste. Immediately after World War II, for example, warplant workers splurged on the elaborate, overstuffed "borax" furniture they had set their hearts on years before.

Not that formal education necessarily improves anyone's taste. But it does help; in fact it is probably the most powerful single factor in the improvement process. And never in American history has education expanded so fast as it is now expanding. The number of adult Americans who have completed high school rose from 27 million, or 33 per cent of the adult population, in 1947 to 39 million, or 40 per cent of the adult population, in 1957; during the 1960's it will surely rise to about 55 million, or 50 per cent of the adult population. During the past decade the number of youths attending college has risen around 50 per cent; during the decade ahead it is expected to double, reaching perhaps seven million. According to the U.S. Office of Education, 35 million to 40 million adults are "interested" in after-hours study programs, and some nine million are actually enrolled in organized courses.

Surely not far behind the formal educators as molders of taste are the informal educators or tastemakers. They have always existed, but never in such quantity. In the past they consisted of a tiny aristocracy, who so to speak administered a nation's culture; today America probably supports the largest taste-conscious *haute bourgeoisie* in history, expressing itself through an extraordinary variety of communications. People who think they possess good taste, like people who believe they possess the one true religion, often harbor a missionary's urge to convert others; and the American people, for the good of their taste, are being subjected to a constant drumfire of instruction, persuasion, and information. The so-called shelter or home-service magazines, for example, play an enormous role in creating the demand for houses and furnishings gratifying to behold. The mass magazines have made such subjects as America's Arts and Skills and Adventures of the Mind interesting to millions of people without talking down or unduly oversimplifying.

What People Don't Know Helps Them

And then there are the corporate managers and their designers, who are extraordinarily powerful tastemakers. Most of the time, some opinion notwithstanding, this business influence on taste is for the good. Precisely because businessmen are so often at a loss to know just how public taste is going to shift, they tend to let their corporate and personal self-esteem line them up on the side of good, or at least professional, design. And for their part, even the most mercenary practitioners of the "We'll design you any damn thing you want" school would rather turn out something they regard as good than something pandering to bad taste. Most good designers, indeed, take the view that the public's frequent uncertainty about its taste offers the opportunity of turning out something better than they might if the public knew exactly what it wanted.

The preference of corporate executives for "good" design is sometimes a matter of self-esteem; perhaps goaded by their wives, they feel sheepish about making stuff their friends regard as cheap or junky. Frequently their preference is more sophisticated: they want to create a high-class image of their company and its products. As David Ogilvy of Ogilvy, Benson & Mather puts it. "It pays to give a product a high-class image instead of a bargain-basement image. Also, you can get more for it." Or executives believe that taste is changing for the better and the wise policy is to anticipate it. "We try to design just ahead of the market," says Arthur BecVar, manager of General Electric's Industrial Design Operation in Louisville, "so that when public taste advances we are ready for it."

The "Aspiration" Drive

The phenomenon that springs from these forces and at the same time strengthens them all, of course, is the old American urge for self-betterment and self-expression. The currently popular theory of how this urge works has been developed by what might be called the status-symbol school of sociologists, who hold that: (1) people constantly express their personalities not so much in words as in symbols (i.e., mannerisms, dress, ornaments, possessions); (2) most people are increasingly concerned about what other people think of them, and hence about their social status. Thus the taste of many Americans is expressed in symbols of various social positions.

Sociological classification into status groups—based chiefly on occupation and education—with more or less common traits and tastes, has been useful to advertising and marketing men trying to draw an accurate bead on their markets. But the group boundaries, the status-symbol sociologists hasten to add, are not necessarily the boundaries of people's aspirations.

The urge for self-expression and self-betterment, shared by nearly all Americans, takes the form of aspiring to higher status. Thus people tend to buy things that symbolize their aspirations—a certain make of car, a certain style of house, a certain mode of dress. Their very status aspiration, in other words, drives them to emulate "better" taste and so upgrade their own.

But this does not yet mean, says Dr. Burleigh B. Gardner, founder of the motivation-research firm of Social Research, Inc. (which pioneered the status-symbol concept in advertising), that a workingman's wife wants to emulate the wealthy matron far above her, or that a steelworker wants to emulate the chairman of the board. A beer advertising campaign featuring a fox hunter in a pink coat flopped because the hunter symbolized nothing relevant to the ordinary people who drank the beer. The brewer aimed too high. As a rule, the sociologists point out, consumers emulate taste within reach.

The Shifting Symbols

Sometimes a product loses its efficacy as a status symbol; a good example, says Dr. Gardner, is the automobile. Because the U.S. motorcar industry has built its cars more and more alike, the old American custom of upgrading from one make to another has virtually disappeared. Many consumers took to foreign cars not so much because they were cheap to operate but because they were different. What has been happening, many status-symbol theorists agree, is that houses and furnishings are replacing motorcars as status symbols.

Nevertheless, the furniture industry has not yet enjoyed the fruits of this shift in status symbols. Kroehler, the largest U.S. furniture maker, hired Social Research to find out what the trouble was. The American housewife, Social Research reported, obviously does not choose furniture as she chooses can openers. She wants furniture she likes, but she also wants furniture in good taste—furniture that will proclaim her family status. The trouble is that she does not know for sure what good taste in furniture is, and the furniture industry has confounded her with a plethora of styles. Consequently she spends too much time just "looking around" at furniture instead of buying it. More and more stores are now hiring professional decorators to help customers with their frustration.

The "High Mobiles"

Who are the people who first adopt the tastes that others follow? The evidence is strong that these innovators are not necessarily the people with the most money. As a group, they are the "new suburbanites," a status with an obviously strong appeal. A Chicago *Tribune* survey recently gave respondents a choice of twenty-one characterizations of themselves and their lives. Most of them, even some tenement dwellers, identified themselves with the "new young suburbanites" and indicated that they aspired to their kind of life.

It would be foolish, of course, to say that all young suburbanites are pioneers in taste, but the group apparently does contain the important innovators. Opinion Research Corp. of Princeton, New Jersey, trying to identify the dynamic Americans, made a study of 105 suburban households. The "early adopters," it found, included about a quarter of the suburban families it interviewed. They are people who are moving upward in economic status, who are moving around geographically, who are active intellectually, who have acquired a good deal of education, and whose work and play throw them into contact with a wide variety of people. Opinion Research calls them "High Mobiles." The High Mobiles were the first to buy electric blankets, low-calorie beverages, dining credit cards, food freezers, colored sheets, wall-to-wall carpeting, and other things that later became popular. Opinion Research, naturally, argues that business can get a reliable indication of the future trend of consumer tastes by watching the preferences of the High Mobiles.

A "Differentiation" Trend?

But even when emulating others, consumers do make innumerable choices in which status plays little or no part. Although the American urge for self-expression and self-betterment is as strong as ever, its manifestation in the form of status seeking actually may be declining. In *Housing Choices and Housing Constraints,* soon to be published by ACTION, sociologist Nelson Foote suggests that even occupational and educational differences in the future will carry less and less weight, and people will bother less with proclaiming status.[1]

Foote reasons that rising discretionary income will force people to "differentiate" as well as emulate. Just as the newly rich in time become prudent and discriminating buyers, so ordinary Americans who suddenly find themselves with more money to spend will become more discriminating about the way they spend it. They will tend to expand their individuality, says Foote, and will begin to regard life as "a pursuit of meaning." The theory seems fortified by group income trends: the disposable income of

---

[1] *The Status Seekers,* the best-seller by Vance Packard, gives the absurd impression that almost every human reaction in the U.S. is heavily, not to say totally, conditioned by status and status symbols. Packard comes to the sensational conclusion that class lines in the U.S. are growing more rigid, although much of the evidence he himself brings forward actually argues the other way.

the lower income groups is rising faster than that of the upper income groups, and the lower income groups may be confronted with so many more opportunities for emulating the upper groups that emulation itself will become pointless.

At all events, Foote predicts that people will "differentiate" mainly in their leisure pursuits—in such activities as travel, theatregoing, gardening, crafts, participation in public affairs and voluntary associations. To put it another way, people will achieve status by being different—or by being themselves. Perhaps, as Dr. Ernest Dichter, president of the Institute for Motivational Research, has remarked, "social status is coming closer to self-realization."

Something of the sort, as a matter of fact, can be observed among Americans whose social position or self-esteem is so secure that the thought of striving for status amuses more than it worries them. Their tastes are diverse, and dominated by no authority, traditional or contemporary. They casually install a Victorian love seat and a Barcelona chair in the same room. They do not try to emulate or surpass their neighbors, but, if anything, go out of their way to be a little different from their neighbors. And they do not rush out to translate a salary rise into a status symbol.

The Lower Mobiles

But most of these people, so far, are probably the High Mobiles. Meantime, what is happening to the taste of the ordinary American consumer? Few designers of rank would be willing to argue that it is fine, but most would grant that it is improving measurably, if sporadically. To be sure, some designers and architects are depressed by the recent vogue for "Cinderella" or "Hansel and Gretel" houses—essentially simple dwellings decorated with atavistic gimcrackery like scallop-trimmed gables, "leaded" windows, and garages with artificial haylofts. But these confections seem to be prized most by people whose incomes have been rising faster than their taste standards; and anyhow they seem to be better to look at than the bleak bungalows of forty or fifty years ago. More important, the dwellings being built by the High Mobile taste setters usually meet the approval of the experts.

Automobiles, reflecting changing taste, seem headed for simpler, "cleaner" lines, with much less superfluous ornamentation. Appliances, despite such aberrations as clothes washers with instrument panels more dazzling than those on autos, are moving toward better design. "You can no longer design a thing so 'bad' it will sell," says Donald L. McFarland, head of General Electric's small-appliance design division, "or so 'good' it won't sell."

Furniture given to gross stylistic excesses seems actually to be growing scarce. "The broadening of consumer credit has helped a lot," says J. Chalmers O'Brien, vice president of Carson Pirie Scott & Co. in Chicago. "The only place many people could afford to buy a bedroom suite fifteen years ago was one of the borax houses. Now they can buy good furniture on time at the better stores."

"She Must Be American"

Improvements in Americans' taste show up strikingly in their choice of food and clothes. American food preferences are becoming astonishingly sophisticated. Dishes that could be found only in the *haute cuisine* of New York and a few other cities thirty years ago are now fairly common in millions of middle-class homes. Small-town hotel dining rooms and restaurants whose victuals were once an ordeal to even an undiscriminating drummer now turn out food that is not only edible but even appetizing. And the sale of dry table wine has increased no less than 64 per cent in the past decade.

And by the almost unanimous consent of all who pretend to know anything special about the subject, no women in the modern world have ever been so tastefully dressed as American women are today. "When you see a *really* well-dressed woman abroad today," says David Ogilvy, "you think, she must be an American." Precisely because women's clothes can be copied quickly and mass-produced cheaply, the general level of taste in clothing is high and still rising. What is more, all this mass production and style imitation, far from stifling individual expression, have actually encouraged and enabled the American woman to exercise it to a greater degree.

Here may lie a lesson for those who deplore the fact that so much of the advance in American taste amounts to imitation of others. To a considerable extent, of course, all taste must be learned. Even a genius must usually absorb a great deal of conventional knowledge before he can express himself with genuine originality. Yet American women and their clothes demonstrate that ordinary people can discriminate when they have learned enough.

From Extreme to Extreme

The elevation of American taste, however, is surely not a gradual, even process. Business can look forward to frequent and extreme changes in style and fashion, probably to an endless and rapid series of fads. (Sociologists distinguish fad from fashion as something with a touch of the unexpected or irresponsible.) Such changes, of course, are an old story. Fashions in women's clothes have often been carried to faddish excess, whereupon they disappear quickly—as did the hoopskirt, the leg-of-mutton sleeve, the Empress Eugénie hat, the sack dress. Architectural and industrial fashion, which cannot be so quickly imitated as clothes fashion, does not change so rapidly, but even it tends to run from extreme to extreme. The two-story house gives way to the ranch house, the ranch house to the split-level; the long low look in motorcars to comfort, commodiousness, and perhaps even an upright look; the ornamented public building to the starkly simple one, the starkly simple one to the "subjective" style of Edward Stone. "American taste," says William Snaith, managing partner of Raymond Loewy Associates, "is probably now going into a vigorous kind of romanticism—an effort to escape from starkness."

Extremes of fashion, far from being reprehensible, are both natural and psychologically useful. They are the result of money and leisure, and the desire to express or achieve status, sometimes complicated by a yearning for notoriety. They enable people to revolt from custom discreetly, to participate in extremes of taste they would be embarrassed to indulge in all by themselves. "Fashion," sociologist Edward Sapir has written, "is custom in the guise of departure from custom."

The American people, with their rapidly rising discretionary income and leisure, seem likely to humor their "sideline" impulses more than ever, and so will intensify and accelerate the swings of fashion and fad. The lesson for business is clear. In an article in the *Harvard Business Review,* November-December, 1958, Dwight E. Robinson of the University of Washington wrote that "all of the fame and bulk of a leading textile, appliance, construction, or automobile company will not save it from fashion's dustbin. . . . She [fashion], and not the so-called fashion dictator . . . is the true autocrat; and only in a totalitarian state, where the consumer's taste is legislated by government edict, does she meet her match." She bids fair to be a power in the U.S. of the 1960's, and the designers who can intuitively divine what people want before they are fully aware of it themselves will come into their own.

Kitsch Culture

A good many intellectuals, as already noted, take a dim view of American taste. Consider *Mass Culture,* a recent anthology of essays on current American culture. Of its forty-nine articles, only seven were favorable to or optimistic about U.S. taste. Ernest van den Haag, professor at the New School for Social Research, for instance, argues that mass production, creating more leisure and wealth, is at the root of the trouble. Not that business aims at the lowest common denominator of taste, he says, but the trouble is that a mass-produced article or service, while reflecting everybody's taste to some extent, is unlikely to embody anybody's tastes fully. This matters particularly in education and entertainment, van den Haag goes on. Moreover, all culture is becoming homogenized by catering to the masses, and mass culture drives out high culture and folk culture because it tends to suck in the talents that might produce good things.

In the same volume Dwight Macdonald argues even more strongly that what the Germans call *Kitsch* or junk culture tends to drive out high culture. Because mass culture is so easy to produce, he says, it overwhelms by its very quantity, and people's taste sinks to that of the least sensitive and most ignorant: "There are just too many people." The future of high culture is dark, Macdonald concludes; the future of mass culture is even darker, and we will be lucky if it doesn't get worse.

The Audience Is There

The main defect common to such talk is that it disregards social and economic forces such as those FORTUNE is describing and so underrates the nation's capacity both for self-criticism and for high culture. The U.S., indeed, probably gives ear to more criticism of its culture than any other nation in history. Although it does not automatically guarantee a large income to anyone who cries its shortcomings, it will endure and even reward name calling and invective provided that they contain some sense and are rendered in clear and vivid English.

And it is merely recording the obvious to say that high culture in the U.S. is not only very much alive but is growing fast. The American artistic output, as the whole world testifies, is both sizable and respectable. American writing, painting, sculpture, architecture, and music were once merely imitations and extensions of European culture; today they influence the culture of the rest of the world as much as it influences them.

If, as Walt Whitman once observed, it takes great audiences to produce great art, the U.S. should very soon be launching a great new era of musical composition. There are today forty-two major American symphony orchestras, against six in 1905 and thirty-two in 1956. Counting those in colleges and smaller communities, the total is more than 1,100, and at least 275 of them were formed between 1951 and 1957.

A growing number of Americans are not put off by "difficult" listening. Alban Berg's atonal opera *Wozzeck,* which was expected to be a flop when introduced at the Metropolitan Opera last year, played to sold-out houses. When it was put on the air on a Saturday afternoon, several out-of-town newspapers assigned their music critics to review the broadcast. One reason for this broadening of U.S. musical taste is that the sale of serious music on records has been increasing at least as fast as the sale of all records. The fact is that many Americans with a record player today listen to more musical works in a year than even professional musicians once could in dozens of years.

The Rising Demand for Books

Although Americans may not read as many books per capita as the British, Scandinavians, and French, the astonishing fact, considering the competition of other diversions such as radio and television, is that they read as many as they do, and that many of them are as good as they are. Americans are buying some 630 million books a year (including paperbacks and juveniles but not textbooks), up from 330 million ten years ago. The success of the paperbacks, which are selling several hundred million copies a year, is enormously significant. A large percentage of the total is trash, but paperback versions of *The Iliad* and *The Odyssey* have together sold more than a million copies. So has J. D. Salinger's *The Catcher in the Rye* and George Orwell's *1984* (which argues, ironically, that the mass media of today will pave the way for the "double-think" of 1984). "The paperbacks," as Clifton Fadiman has noted, "are democratizing reading. They are conferring upon it the simple, healthy status of a normal habit."

What is also relevant, one of the most successful newspaper columns of recent origin, is Mortimer Adler's feature dealing with philosophical questions suggested by readers. Inaugurated October 19, 1958 (in the Chicago *Sun-Times*), it has been syndicated in newspapers from one end of the country to the other.

Radio and television, which have received their share of criticism, cannot be excluded from any inventory of American cultural media. Although they thrive on mass production, they also cater to special audiences. One can sometimes see or hear on them works one might never have seen or heard in a country with an aristocratic high culture and no mass media, such as Britain and Germany fifty years ago.

All this, of course, does not mean that the masses, for the first time in history, are rushing to embrace high culture. What is significant is that millions of the kind of Americans who make the nation's tastes have clung to or taken up the values of high culture *voluntarily,* uncoerced by state or other cultural authority, in a tolerably free market, and in the face of powerful competition from a multitude of mundane leisure activities. What millions have thus found good, millions more, if past behavior means anything, will almost surely find good.

More Quality and Variety

Taking everything together, then, it is reasonable to say that the forces changing American taste are changing it for the better. Thus business can look forward to a demand for "quality," for more choice and fashion, and for the uncommon or unusual. The large mass producers will probably have to provide more variety—as indeed the auto industry is doing today. And the small businessman with a product that isn't geared to the average will doubtless have a bright future.

Business will still be able to sell junk to a lot of Americans. But it surely will be able to make more money operating on the assumption that people want something "better," not only functionally but aesthetically.

What is needed now is a greater
degree of understanding and cooperation between markers
and anthropologists so that both
may benefit from mutual exchange.

15

Anthropology's Potential
Role in Gauging
Consumer Desires

BURT K. SCANLAN

PRACTITIONERS AND TEACHERS alike have recognized that advance knowledge of consumer behavior is of great importance to marketing. The idea
that psychology and sociology can play important roles in gaining this
much needed information has been widely accepted. There has been tacit
assumption that anthropology could be similarly useful, but if it has so
served its contributions have gone unheralded. Areas of potential contribution on the part of anthropologists need discussion as a prelude to action.

The most significant contribution that the physical anthropologist can
make to business lies in the area of product design. This is particularly
true in clothing and furniture but would also be of importance to such
firms as automobile manufacturers, appliance manufacturers, and those
dealing in specialized equipment such as dental chairs. With the many
measurements of the human body which he has at his disposal, the physical
anthropologist can shed light on what styles of clothing will be the most
comfortable and best fitting, the type of shoe which is best from a health

Reprinted from *Business and Society* (Spring, 1965), pp. 28-32.

171

standpoint, the contour of chairs or other furniture which will most appeal to consumers, the amount of leg and head room needed to provide comfort in an automobile, the width and depth of seats for ease in driving, the location of instruments on the dash panel and the design and location of handles or other operative devices on appliances.

Of less tangible significance are the contributions the physical anthropologist can make by developing more finite measures of potential demand in terms of sizes and styles for various sections of the country. Brues has succeeded in delineating certain physical types particularly characteristic of indicated regions and dominant national extractions. These regional or local types arise from the ethnic origins of the main inbreeding populations. While national origins may explain to a large extent why a particular style of clothing, for example, never takes hold in a specific region the physical types which prevail may be of equal significance. An illustration of this point is the very narrow brimmed, small crown hat which became so popular among the smaller types in the New England area and required some modification before being accepted in the west north-central area where the typical physical type is greater width of face and head.

Cultural Anthropology

The area of cultural anthropology has potential import in the two main areas, consumer appeal and behavioral characteristics. Consumer appeal involves the content of advertising appeals, packaging, and the general approach to the consuming public.

The behavior characteristics delineate those things which the cultural anthropologist knows, or is in a position to find out, about people that will better explain how they will react to certain products or situations; and even beyond this what specifically will capture their attention.

In his study of cultures and subcultures the anthropologist pays particular attention to three things which are of value to marketers in formulating appeals to customers. These are language, the significance of symbols, and the presence of taboos and/or prohibitions.

With respect to language he is interested in the language level, structure of speech, and the learned meaning of various words or phrases. All of these are important if successful communication is desired, that is, if advertising is to accomplish its objectives.

Language symbols influence and reflect varying kinds of behavior because of different meanings attached to words and phrases. The denotative meaning of a word is the same for all people while the connotative meaning is a unique reaction which each individual attaches to a word. Connotative differences are learned phenomena and therefore fall under the scrutiny of the anthropologist. Studies of word meaning have shown that the associations which people make to verbal stimuli vary and will elicit different responses according to language level and the relative importance placed on things.

Learned Aspects of Language

Thus, with his knowledge of the learned aspects of a language the anthropologist is in a position to help the marketer communicate with consumers. More specifically, he knows the language level and various meanings attached to words and phrases by different cultures and subcultures. These are vital keys in successful communication. "As we gain understanding of how very subtle points of our communication process affect our behavior and thought we can develop our use of language as a more powerful selling tool."

Every culture and the subcultures within it have symbols which hold significance for its members. These may take many forms although two of the most common are colors and shapes. To the extent that the anthropologist can successfully associate certain symbols with a given culture or subculture he can help the marketer in making his product more appealing. This would hold true particularly in the case of packaging design but is also of importance in choosing the basic colors or shapes for use as trade marks or in advertising. In America black is a symbol of mourning while white denotes purity. In Japan just the opposite is true. Thus, while a product or package using white as the basic color might be received well in this country, in Japan it may not.

It has been found that beyond the quality of the product itself the package is very important because it symbolizes the character of the product. On the other hand, the consumer is rarely aware of the fact that he is influenced by color and design. Through the use of unconscious level tests psychologists have been able to distinguish certain colors and geometric images which elicit favorable consumer reactions.

With his knowledge of the many types of symbols and their meaning for people in different cultures it would seem that the anthropologist could add considerable depth to these psychological studies. Not only is he in a position to identify in advance those colors and images which are likely to receive unfavorable responses but he can pinpoint the underlying reasons. This, of course, leads to a greater degree of understanding of consumer reactions much of which may be valuable in other decision areas. Of prime importance here is the idea that understanding the "why" of behavior is of more significant value than just knowing what the behavior is.

Taboos and Prohibitions

Closely related to the matter of symbols is the presence of taboos or prohibitions in every culture. These may be cultural, religious, or political in nature. The danger for the marketer is that he may unwittingly violate these taboos because of no prior knowledge that they exist. While of principal importance when selling in foreign markets, taboos or prohibitions become important to the strictly domestic firm when it is trying to cultivate a particular segment of a broad market. Any firm which is seeking to expand sales in a given section or smaller region of the country may profit by consulting an anthropologist for information on the subcultures of the people in that area. It is quite likely that such consultation will prevent the violation of taboos peculiar to the region in question. Here are some examples of taboos present in other cultures:

Latin Americans disapprove of purple because of its association with death. Blue is for mourning in Iran. To show pairs of anything is disapproved of on the Gold Coast in Africa. In Thailand feet are considered despicable.

Winick cites a very interesting example of the violations of taboos. This involved a manufacturer of canned fish who was promoting sales in the Province of Quebec. The advertisement showed a woman in shorts playing golf with her husband. The copy noted that she could be gone all day and still prepare dinner that evening if she used the product advertised. Every element of the ad was in violation of French Canadian culture; the wife would not be wearing shorts, she would not be golfing with her husband, and she would not be serving that particular kind of fish as a main course.

A second major area where anthropology can take on importance is in explaining certain behavioral characteristics which arise out of culture.

The most obvious area where the anthropologist can make distinctions between peoples is with respect to the cultures of two different nations. The area of greatest value is probably his ability to distinguish between the subcultures which make up the national culture.

Technological Levels

The anthropologist gives considerable attention to observing the level of technology of a culture and the effect of this technology on the culture. Thus, he is keenly aware of changes which have taken place and also those forces which are working toward change. Modern cultures are essentially dynamic in character with much of this due to the influence of technological development. To be sure, there are some aspects of culture which offer more resistance to change than others and consequently give a certain degree of stability to the whole. The anthropologist is in a position to identify these areas as well as the degree of stability which is present and the rapidity and likelihood of change.

The importance of this point is somewhat self evident from the standpoint of the marketer. To the extent that he has insight into the changing nature of society he can be the innovator and not the follower. The anthropologist can furnish valuable information concerning the possible acceptability of new products, new and different approaches to advertising, and styling. This is the type of information which helps distinguish the very successful from the moderately successful or unsuccessful firm. Even more important could be the anthropologist's insights into why something may not succeed and what would have to be done to make it do so.

From a domestic standpoint the anthropologist's contributions in these areas are the more significant to the extent that they deal with subcultures rather than broad cultures. This in turn implies that the marketer who is interested in market segmentation will derive more benefit from anthropological knowledge in these areas than the one who is still trying to increase sales in a larger general market by product differentiation.

From his studies of subcultures and individual family units the anthropologist can detect rather comprehensive patterns of living. These patterns will include detailed information on food, drink, and housing preferences as well as other tastes and preferences. In addition to these prevailing patterns he studies how the culture rubs off on other members of the cultural unit. More important, he knows to what extent the younger generation is carrying over those things practiced by and learned from the older ones. Said another way, the anthropologist is aware of degrees of transfer of preferences from one generation to another.

This type of information has marketing value for two reasons. First, it denotes the degree of permanency of various products or ideas concerning living and second, it sets forth those which are undergoing varying degrees of change and more precisely, what direction the change is taking and what the nature of the new preferences are.

Family Relationships

As part of his study of culture the anthropologist takes an interest in the family unit. His primary concern is with the relationship between various members of the unit as they pertain to age, sex, and traditional roles. This type of information is significant to the marketer when making decisions concerning consumer appeals. For example in selling an automobile should the advertising be directed toward the husband or wife? The answer to this question lies in which of the two traditionally makes the decisions for this type of purchase. If one were to contrast automobile advertising in 1960 with that of 1962 he will note an obvious change of thinking. That of 1960 emphasized interior fabrics, driving conveniences, and other factors which were designed to capture the lady's interest while 1962 emphasized rugged construction, maintenance advantages, and those qualities which have more meaning for the man. Anthropological studies which yield information concerning these traditional decision-making roles can help the marketer make sure he is channeling his efforts in the right direction.

The final area where the cultural anthropologist can make a direct contribution involves the identification of stages in a person's life when he moves from one status or recognition point to another. Examples of this are the move from puberty to teen-age status, from teen-age status to adulthood, and from a single status to a married one. In addition, such events as confirmation in the church, the sixteenth birthday, high school graduation, entrance into college, and the twenty-first birthday hold significance. By identifying these turning points and determining their cultural significance the anthropologist can help the marketer capitalize on them in terms of specially adapted products and brand names, or special promotions. Also, they are important because they focus attention on specific market segments and the characteristics peculiar to them. The fast growing teen-age market is an example.

In concluding, several points deserve additional consideration. What has been cited herein undoubtedly does not constitute all of the possible contributions of anthropology to marketing, but represents those areas where the direct application of anthropological knowledge is possible. For the most part these are nonoverlapping in the sense that they concern those areas where only an anthropologist would normally have the needed information. There are, of course, additional areas which would overlap with the other behavioral sciences. Finally the most obvious contribution the cultural anthropologist can make is to help us sell in foreign markets. With the increasing need for market segmentation however, it is probable that the greatest benefits can be derived from what the anthropologist can tell us about subcultures. What is needed now is a greater degree of understanding and cooperation between marketers and anthropologists so that both may benefit from mutual exchange.

C. INTERNAL ASPECTS

The real fight now is to preserve, foster, and encourage a climate wherein marketing creativity can soar and leap and grow.

16

Marketing Snags and Fallacies

LEO BURNETT

By 1970 the United States can have an $800-billion economy; and by 1975 our economy can rise to one trillion dollars! This figure is so large and unprecedented in any economy that it cannot readily be grasped.

But in order to achieve this incredible rise in the economy, there will need to be at least one-third to one-half increase in consumer expenditures.[1] This means thousands of new products.

Our ability to produce the goods for this exploding economy is not the problem. What is really of concern is our capacity to ensure the consumption of them.

Our technology has been accelerating with a seemingly irrepressible momentum:

- Hundreds of millions of dollars are being spent today in a great variety of businesses on Research and Development, compared with a mere trickle of funds before 1950.
- In a single year du Pont scientists file as many as 800 patent applications.[2]
- The interval between discovery and application has been narrowing

Leo Burnett, reprinted from the *Journal of Marketing,* national quarterly publication of the American Marketing Association, Volume 30, No. 3 (July, 1966), pp. 1-5.

[1] Alvin Hansen, *Postwar American Economy* (New York: W. W. Norton & Co., Inc., 1964), pp. 34-35.

[2] *The Industry of Discovery* (Wilmington, Delaware: E. I. du Pont de Nemours & Company, 1965), p. 21.

rapidly: It took 65 years from the time it was invented for the electric motor to be applied . . . 33 years for the vacuum tube . . . and 18 years for the x-ray tube. But it took only 10 years for the nuclear reactor . . . only 5 years for radar . . . and less than 3 years for the transistor and the solar battery.

- The cost of atomic energy has been slashed—contrary to all forecasts—from 60 mills per kilowatt-hour in 1957 to less than 4 mills today. With energy soon to be available almost everywhere, the distinction between the haves and havenots could rapidly vanish, expanding the market to the optimum.[3]

The basic issue is whether we have the ability to develop the marketing power necessary to discover, shape, and particularly to *move* the goods that will best fulfill the consumer's needs within the framework of desirable social and moral goals.

For far too long have we continued to venerate mere productivity as a goal. Yet high productivity is meaningless if it outstrips consumption and is not matched by marketing power.

In this generation of accelerated marketing power, is our marketing perspective adequate? Are we plagued by "diseases of the marketing eye," tending to limit our vision of the future?

Here are two of the symptoms of this:

1. *Fear of the inexact*—the fear of playing the odds, and the rejection of imprecise data.

2. *Lack of real consumer orientation*—too much research on consumer *preferences* as compared with consumer *satisfactions*.[4]

Five Fallacies in Marketing

To be even more specific, we are suffering from at least five fallacies in the field of marketing.

FALLACY AS TO MARKETING FORESIGHT

The first fallacy is that the people already in the marketing field are the ones who understand it best and know what the potential customer wants.

Yet in actuality the only person who really knows what he wants is the customer himself. For example, if television producers *really* knew what the public wanted in entertainment, the mortality rate in programs would not be so wastefully high each new season.

In this connection, consider how many developments in any field of

---

[3] Mario G. Salvadori, "The Environment of Change" (Time, Inc., 1964), p. 18.
[4] Theodore Levitt, "Marketing Myopia," *Harvard Business Review,* Vol. 38 (July-August, 1960), pp. 45-46.

knowledge so often originate *outside* the ken of those specialists supposedly with the greatest insights:

- Three of the greatest discoveries of surgery, without which modern surgery would be impossible, are anesthesia, asepsis, and X-rays—and none of them was discovered by a surgeon!
- Of four important railroad devices, not one was invented by a railroad man. These were the air-brake, automatic coupling, the refrigerator car, and the streamlined train.
- It was not a physicist, but an anatomist, Galvani, who discovered current electricity.
- The development of tetraethyl lead came from outside the petroleum industry.
- The most successful innovation in inn-keeping, the motel, was not devised or developed by the traditional hotel-keepers, who looked with scorn upon this interloper until the success of motels forced the hotel corporations to enter the field.[5]
- The great movie-chains did not pioneer in that singular success, the drive-in movie, until long after newcomers had proved its viability. Everyone in the movie business "knew" that automobiles were to drive around in, not to watch a movie in.
- The break with traditional art and the rise of modern art forms was not encouraged by the museums and curators.
- Jazz was not developed within the halls of classical music.
- And the paperback books—one of the most successful revolutions in selling in our time—were not initiated by the giants of the book publishing business, who entered the field later and only when it was already thriving.

We continue to see some new products succeed and others fall by the wayside for the obvious reason that, although there seemed to be great need and promise for them and although they were heavily promoted, the consumer was less than enchanted. After all, the American purchaser is a "tough little baby" and does not have to be wrapped in cotton.

Given access to honest information, the consumer himself is the best judge of what he needs and wants, the form and the package it comes in, and the price he will pay. Moreover, he is most likely to get what he wants under a system in which thousands of business enterprises are competing fiercely but fairly for his favor.

Often he does not even know he wants a purple cow until he sees one.

David Belasco said that the secret of good showmanship is giving people what they want just before they know what they want. This also is one of the major challenges of marketing, whether achieved through better research, or more open-mindedeness to fresh ideas from any source, or a combination of both.

[5] John W. Gardner, *Self-Renewal* (New York: Harper & Row, 1963), p. 46.

FALLACY AS TO NEW MARKETS

The second fallacy is a limited definition of "competition," under which the chief marketing strategy is to attain the largest possible share of the existing market, rather than to create new markets and add to total consumption.

A few years ago the Brookings Institution completed a comprehensive study of successful and unsuccessful industries. The difference between success and failure hinged on a really simple thing—product leadership. Industries that failed to innovate and that failed to keep ahead of the market also failed to grow with the economy, and perished or were absorbed.

In the area of recent new product categories, consider the new "convenience" foods, which have had ten times the growth of foods in general over the last decade. Consider in this connection the "hi-fi" market of the last dozen years, bringing superbly recorded music to new and broader audiences. Consider also the record clubs by direct mail, which revitalized the whole record field—and which also flew in the face of conventional wisdom that "a person will not buy a record before he listens to it in a store."

We have had the recent boom in modified sports cars, with Ford's "Mustang" a tremendous success. And industry leaders invested some $200 million in developing color television without being sure whether people really wanted it or would demand it in large enough numbers to justify the investment.

It is true, of course, that many great companies are indeed bringing about innovation; and the overriding marketing strategy is to proliferate and diversify. Obviously, however, there is a tremendous need to *organize for change*—after all, the mere fact of corporate organization tends to conspire against it.

One way to lose money is to try to sell everyone on a given product. Many companies have learned this lesson just in time, and are now proliferating their marketing efforts to give the consumer what he wants rather than what the manufacturer thinks he ought to have.

FALLACY AS TO COMPETITION

The third fallacy in the marketing world is that competition is a closed system, and that our competitors are those making substantially the same products, or offering the same services, that we are.

In studying Nielsen share-of-market reports, do we sometimes know *too much* about our competitors? By putting such high priority on "me-too" products and competitive counter-moves, are there not serious dangers of standardization of products rather than market expansion?

Many an entrepreneur has made almost "seat-of-the-pants" decisions, then has plunged adventurously ahead—sometimes with failure, but often with brilliant success.

By no means does this imply any minimization of the value of the information available today. It does imply anxiety about our interpretations of it, and often our dogmatic reliance upon it.

It is a mistake to feel that the competition for a Cadillac is either a medium-priced car or another quality car such as a Lincoln or Imperial. The Cadillac is a prestige item. The true competitor of the luxury car is the swimming pool, or the summer place, or the private plane, or the winter vacation, and all the other prestige items dangled before people with large discretionary incomes.[6]

Likewise, the makers of bowling or billiard equipment are not competing so much with other makers of similar equipment as they are with other providers of "leisure-time" satisfactions—whether skiing or photography, or record-players, or ping-pong tables, or even adult-education courses.

All are competing for "disposable time" as much as for disposable income.

FALLACY AS TO INCOME BRACKETS

A fourth fallacy is the marketing theory of appealing mainly to present income brackets.

In the past, it was commonly believed, and it was generally true, that people bought "according to income." But today people increasingly are buying according to *expectations of future income.* Individual purchases have come to be more and more like company purchases—based on a projection into the next few years, and not necessarily on current income alone.[7]

The vast increase in credit purchases during the last dozen or so years, therefore, should not be viewed as mass imprudence (although undoubtedly in some cases families *are* imprudent), but as an expression of self-confidence and as a projection of a continuing upward curve in income.

People no longer buy solely what they "need," or even what they "want" for the present. They are anticipating new and future needs; and the industries that have grown most have been the ones catering to this sense of expectation.

Take, for example, the present booming "knowledge market." One of the important things about the expansion in knowledge is that its main appeal is not to the *affluent and educated,* but to the *aspiring and under-*

---

[6] Peter F. Drucker, *Managing for Results* (New York: Harper & Row, 1964), p. 95.
[7] *Ibid.*

educated. The encyclopedia field is a classic example: many families which buy encyclopedias perhaps cannot really "afford" them, in a practical dollars-and-sense way. Yet the growth of sales has been enormous precisely in this economic bracket, *because* these families have higher expectations for themselves, and most of all for their children.

All the demographic facts add up to a tremendous new market that is not based on the traditional concepts of "income" and "status" and "education" that have been our benchmarks in the past.

In addition, our cultural habits have changed enormously and are continuing to do so, and at a rapid rate. This also should make for a radical revision of our marketing concepts.

As one obvious example in the area of recreation alone, the game of golf used to be restricted very much to the so-called upper classes. Today it is an immensely popular recreation for all groups except the lowest economic fifth. Again, not so many years ago, skiing was considered a "class" sport. Each year, however, there are tens of thousands of new skiers drawn from a segment of the population which never would have been in the market a dozen years ago. They are taking up skiing as a part of their expectations, and not on the basis of present income.

In all this we have a dramatic example of *upward mobility*. The more prosperous we become, the higher do our expectations grow, and the more do new people become potential customers for markets that once seemed restricted.

Perhaps the most important marketing challenge of the decade ahead is properly to assess and satisfy the expectations and aspirations of this large group, rather than mapping out strategies on the basis of current income.

FALLACY AS TO DECISION-MAKING

The fifth fallacy is that because we are living in the age of the specialist, only qualified experts with specialized skills will be competent in the future to make basic decisions.

Actually, quite the reverse is happening. Our greatest need today is for the synthesizer, much more than for the specialist. He is not necessarily a computer programer; but he understands how computers work, and what they can do and cannot do.

In the field of advertising, he is not necessarily an accomplished copywriter or artist; but he has gone out of his way to understand what writing and artistry are about, as such acts are experienced by writers and artists.

He is not necessarily a laboratory technician; but he has absorbed enough science to understand and appreciate the scientific method.

After all the facts are in from the computers, research, and elsewhere, the "gut" decision finally must be made by a man, or by a very small group of men. And these men cannot afford not to know how their field relates to other fields, and how all of them interlock. The basic decisions in today's economy have much broader and deeper ramifications than ever before.

Information keeps on spewing from the computers; but there comes a time when somebody has to put his own value system on the block and to say go or no go. Computers merely print out numbers and letters on paper when fed an appropriate signal. This is not a decision.

In the search for a new breed of synthesizer or "generalist," business and industrial leaders are beginning to call for a different kind of graduate from the nation's schools of business; and the schools are responding rapidly.

The wheel has almost turned full circle. The industrialization that made men specialize has now given us automation as its final flower. And automation is going to drive many specialists into other fields.

What we need most in the immediate future are more truly educated men and women, that is, people who know one thing well, but many related things fairly well. And to be educated, in any useful sense of the word, means that you can differentiate between what you know and what you do not know, that you know where to go to find out what you need to know, and that you know how to use the information once you get it.[8]

So What?

What does all this mean to us as marketing men?

It means that change and the rate of change have been so rapid, and that the need for new marketing power is so great, that many a marketing man has been caught with his rusty calculus showing. He has not yet learned how to use the amazing new tools of cybernetics, electronic-data processing, and game theory, and is in fact scared silly by them, as he is by taking any kind of calculated risk.

Too many of us, I fear, who talk about "marketing" and the "Total Marketing Concept" still see it as a scientific, objective, statistical thing, which will be perfected as a mechanism, once we get sufficient information and data of a quantitative sort. Rather than regarding it as a *social* science, we are still trying desperately to emulate the physical sciences in precision, in calibration, in subtlety of analysis.[9]

We have research which describes the consumer in embarrassing detail

8 Alfred N. Whitehead, *The Aims of Education* (New York: Mentor Books, 1956), pp. 16-17.
9 John Madge, *Tools of Social Science* (New York: Anchor Books, Doubleday & Co., Inc., 1965), pp. 4-5.

—where she lives, what she wears, how many children she has borne, how much her husband earns, and how much education she has had. She stands before us, seemingly stripped of her every secret, clothed only in the mantle of our statistics; but in a majority of cases we still do not know exactly what gives her the urge to buy or to prefer one product over another.

New research insights now tell us clearly that people are not all of a piece. They are rational and cautious in some areas and at some times, but enjoy adventures in buying in other areas and at other times. Also there are some products which are best defined psychologically rather than demographically, such as jewelry, alcoholic beverages, small appliances, and automobiles.

The successful marketing man has developed strong points of view (as he should) about the ingredients of success in the marketplace. These points of view have evolved from his pragmatic interpretations of experience. He has done something, and it has seemed to work. Frequently he has worked with a mix—a marketing mix—that has produced desired results. He has not always known which factors in the mix were working and which were not, but nonetheless he has had to adopt points of view. Parts of these points of view undoubtedly are valid, and others possibly are pure mythology.

We are becoming more perceptive about marketing and the various factors that together make up marketing. But also we are now beginning to witness *the clash of the new insights and the old mythologies.*

Yes, it is healthy for a marketing man to demand that research establish the legitimacy of its new insights. But it is vital that he be receptive to these insights and seek to understand them, even those phenomena known as "inspiration" and "intuition."

The man who can assimilate the new, who can refurbish his arsenal of marketing weapons, and who can put them to use is the one most likely to "survive" and to contribute most to the new marketing power so urgently needed.

The real fight now is to preserve, foster, and encourage a climate wherein marketing creativity can soar and leap and grow. The marketing process is a fascinating adventure. But we shall have failed the future if we have not set up within our own business firms a climate where individual imagination can flower.

Nestled in the bosom of every person in the whole marketing chain are one or more great marketing ideas. Yet many of these will never see the light of day because nobody has had the sense or the patience to listen.

Obviously the things to be admired most in a marketing man are:

- an unwillingness to settle for the tried and true;
- a desire to seek the inherent promise in every product or service;

- a constant effort to put himself realistically into the shoes of the consumer;
- a belief that quality and thoroughness are significant in every detail of every job;
- a conviction that what is worth doing is worth doing as creatively as possible; and
- a dedication to providing the right climate for individual growth as the best climate for meeting the new challenges confidently.

As corporations have grown in size, executive problems have increased in complexity . . . the marketing group wants a long product line . . . the production people want long production runs . . . and the financial executives want to minimize capital investments in inventory and . . . production equipment.

17

What Kind of
Corporate Objectives?

HARPER W. BOYD, JR.

&

SIDNEY J. LEVY

AN OVERRIDING OBJECTIVE is critical to the successful functioning of a business enterprise.

Lack of specificity in objectives often causes management to fall back on vague, overgeneralized statements. When this happens, the decisions relating to such major strategies as product and product line, pricing, personal selling, advertising, channels, R & D, and plant location are poorly coordinated. Too often the decisions are made by merely following industry practice ("all companies have their own sales force"); by historical precedent ("we have always had exclusive dealers"); and by tradition, un-

Harper W. Boyd, Jr. and Sidney J. Levy, reprinted from the *Journal of Marketing,* national quarterly publication of the American Marketing Association, Volume 30, No. 4 (October, 1966), pp. 53-58.

certainty, and imitation, as well as by sound precedent and experienced insight.

As corporations have grown in size, executive problems have increased in complexity. Consider the desires of certain departments with respect to length of product line. The marketing group wants a long product line because it means a better position in the marketplace. But the production people want long production runs in order to minimize manufacturing costs. And the financial executives want to minimize capital investments in inventory and the extra production equipment needed to produce the longer line.

Reference to the firm's *overall objectives* is the only effective way of resolving such differences.[1]

Operations researchers long have been interested in the setting of objectives, both from the point of view of individual executives and the organization as a whole. Some have documented both the need and the difficulty of specifying objectives, and conclude that most organizations are unable to describe their specific goals satisfactorily.[2]

Multiple objectives can be stated in terms of departmental objectives or area responsibilities, such as those suggested by Peter F. Drucker—market standing, innovation, productivity, physical and financial resources, profitability, manager performance and development, worker performance and attitudes, and public responsibility.[3]

Such objectives, often conflicting, raise the question of *suboptimization.* A "best" solution to such a problem requires the assigning of relative weights to the objectives involved, and determining their substitutability.[4] Clearly the presence of a *governing objective* would increase greatly the efficiency of solutions to the problems of suboptimization. Thus, despite the conclusions drawn by some operation researchers, continuation of the search for some way to set forth an overriding objective is needed.

There have been a number of attempts to get at this problem. Typically the "procedures" center around the kind of businesses in which the firm should be engaged, what market niche the company should attempt to occupy, what product or products the company should produce, and where the company wants to be in the next five to ten years. All have one thing in common: lack of the precision necessary *if* the firm is to have a true rationale for existence.

[1] C. West Churchman, Russell L. Ackoff, and E. Leonard Arnoff, *Introduction to Operations Research* (New York: John Wiley & Sons, Inc., 1957), p. 5.

[2] David M. Miller and Martin K. Starr, *Executive Decisions and Operations Research* (Englewood Cliffs, New Jersey: Prentice-Hall, Inc., 1960), p. 44.

[3] Peter F. Drucker, *The Practice of Management* (New York: Harper & Brothers, 1965), p. 63: also Miller and Starr, same reference as footnote 2, at pp. 44-45.

[4] Russell L. Ackoff, *The Design of Social Research* (Chicago: The University of Chicago Press, 1953), pp. 375-376.

Categories of Objectives

Our purpose here is to discuss only the overriding or "broader" corporate objective, in contrast with the sub-objectives which would be used to accomplish the larger objective.[5]

Although there is no simple solution and no easy formula available by which to accomplish our task, it should be helpful to discuss those aims an enterprise might have—growing out of what it has to sell, the utilization of its products or services, and its relationships to its customers.

Study of more than 200 statements received from a research inquiry which pertained to corporate objectives, many discussions with corporate executives, and results from numerous research projects suggest different sources of objectives which have the potential of generating goals from which relatively specific plans can be developed. Here are six for consideration:

1. Focus on material resources
2. Concern with fabricated objects
3. Major interest in events and activities, requiring certain products or services
4. Emphasis on kind of person whose needs are to be met
5. Catering to specific physical parts of a person
6. Examination of wants and needs, and seeking to adapt to them

These categories are *not* mutually exclusive and do *not* include such nondifferentiating objectives as the making of profits, the generating of increased sales, the desire to perpetuate the firm, and other such management-centered aims.

Also, the discussion of the six categories centers largely around firms producing consumer goods, although the principles apply for the most part to industrial-goods firms.

1. Focus on Material Resources

Many modern companies owe their origin and continued existence to having owned or been granted rights to drill, mine, and hew. Still others were founded to process certain natural resources, including those derived from agriculture, for example, grain crops, meats, and milk. Earlier, the main problems were to get the raw materials and to overcome the transportation difficulties in bringing them to an expanding market.

[5] See Charles H. Granger, "The Hierarchy of Objectives," *Harvard Business Review*, Vol. 42 (May-June, 1964), pp. 63-74.

The companies that were founded to process agricultural products were the first to change, or else die. The very efficiency of the American farmer "choked" many to death. The growth of standardized processing methods, the development of substitute products via the laboratory, and the difficulty and cost of marketing also took their toll.

The milling and dairy industries are but two examples of the evolution that took place in the growth of large diversified companies. In natural fibers, the growth of the man-made synthetics altered substantially the viewpoints of those in the carpeting and clothing industries.

The metal, oil, and gas industries have not escaped the technological revolution. The competition among metals and between metals and plastics has been intense, with important effects on the management philosophies of the firms involved. The attention paid to the market and its needs by basic-plastics producers and by the aluminum companies has forced some of the old-line companies to accelerate their R & D efforts and do a better job of satisfying customer needs as an example, through the development of certain metal alloys.

The plastic companies rely on chemical research and recognize the inevitability of a product life-cycle, with the superseding of one plastic by another. In order to capitalize on innovations they engage heavily in market-development programs. Thus, to promote its polystyrene, the Dow Chemical Company established a product-evaluation program designed to evaluate end-products on the following basis: (1) General plastics application—should *any* plastic material be used? (2) Specific material application—should Dow styron be used, and if so, what formulation? (3) Product design, (4) Workmanship.

In recent years many producers of raw materials have devoted considerable effort to increasing demand by finding new and attractive uses for their products. Thus, the producers of raw asbestos fibers have expanded their market by producing asbestos woven sheets which will withstand extremely high temperatures and which can be used by a variety of industries. Such producers have been led from merely supplying industry to thinking about ultimate consumption. They often start with the need to sell byproducts of raw materials and as they think about how to foster consumption of their products, they may start to use and sell other products in conjunction with their own.

The fact that the oil companies typically sell certain chemical products as well as tires, batteries, accessories, mechanical repairs, soft drinks, travel items, and food, is a case in point.

Although raw-material oriented companies have come to be highly concerned about their markets, many tend to remain heavily preoccupied with the discovery of new supplies, new techniques for shipping, automated processing, negotiations with governments, geo-political problems of extracting minerals, large-scale effects of laws, fiscal policies, and economic patterns.

Thus, the attempt to be market-oriented centers mainly on helping the customer to sell, and the customer's customer to sell. Personal selling and the heavy use of consumer advertising are the means used. But while these activities may have a beneficial effect on market share, they rarely solve the long-range problems of finding new and better ways to satisfy the needs and wants of the ultimate consumer.

Individuals who manage "raw-materials" companies probably are more "tough-minded," more dedicated to a single-minded purpose, and more centered on inner-oriented activities of the company than those managers who, at the other extreme, are concerned with examining human wants and needs and seeking to adapt to them. The latter survive not by battling nature but by ingratiation and catering to whims. Compare, if you will, the food company to an oil company.

The danger of being materials-oriented in objectives is obvious. Given the fast pace of technological change, a company that concentrates narrowly on its materials power can easily be rendered obsolete. The management of such a company would find it difficult to change successfully the company's mission. The very attributes which make for a successful manager of a raw-materials company would serve as liabilities, given a set of objectives that are market-oriented.

2. Concern with Fabricated Objects

A significant center of energy and attention is the manufactured object. It has been and remains a major source of interest and dedication to many company executives.

The main objective of many companies is the production of a "thing" (or "things"). Attention focuses on what it is, what its characteristics are, how it gets made, its contents and specifications, and how it works. Questions dealing with who uses it, what is done with it, and why people might or might not want it may be left unanswered.

Clearly, product-orientation and concern with production problems are uppermost in the minds of such managements. This preoccupation with production restricts the horizons of company thinking. This means that the urge to perfect the product may be greater than the willingness to change it radically, or to make variations that might lead to a product line, or to develop alternatives to replace it.

As an example, the president of a large and well-known quality producer of men's suits reacted to synthetic fibers by indicating that they did not fit into his way of doing business. He said that his buyers were wool buyers, not synthetic buyers.

It is also likely that a company's interest in just *selling more* of a product can become the main goal of management, since the channeling of energy into production makes increased productivity the only apparent avenue to profits. Given a stable history and growing demand for the product, such a production-orientation is likely to build a strong feeling of security and confidence.

On the other hand, when market changes occur that affect the demand for the product, such managements are vulnerable. The area where they exert the greatest control—within the plant—is least helpful in modifying their relationship to the external environment. Many traditionally-minded small businessmen often find themselves in such difficult situations.

The focus on material resources and the concern with fabricated objects are basically oriented *away* from the consumer, or at least are not specifically aimed at him. He is largely taken for granted. The sources of objectives which follow tend to develop an awareness of the consumer; there is some more or less direct concern with meeting his needs and wants, and gratifying him or stimulating him.

3. Major Interest in Events and Activities

If the major interest of the management of a company is to sell products or services which fit into a consumer's life in a special way, then this will serve as a useful source of company vitality.

If a management perceives of its objective as that solely of producing a golf ball, then it is likely to be less flexible and responsive to change than a management which thinks of itself as making products which are to be used in golfing, or in sports activities, or in recreation. This larger definition which deals with what people are doing in the sporting world, or in the changing world of recreation, enlarges the scope of management's thinking about what the company should be trying to accomplish. Management will be more likely to search out new lines, and to anticipate or foster new trends.

Events and activities can be a useful way of segmenting the market. Emery Air Freight developed a unique service "to handle emergencies" through the use of a complex network of air carriers and delivery trucks. Emery even took into account the psychological aspects of an emergency by offering, at extra cost, a time of delivery service which informed the buyer exactly where his shipment was and when it would be delivered.

Events and activities which tie to style considerations tend to generate flexibility and sensitivity to change in the management of those companies

which cater to such objectives, for example, clothing for holidays or vacations. When the consumer's goals transcend the significance of the product
itself and management recognizes this fact, then the firm is also likely to
be more sensitive to the external environment and the opportunities inherent in the process of change.

In recent years the American public has taken up in increasing numbers
"new" sporting activities—including skiing, surfing, and skin-diving. Golf
is more popular than ever. These changes in our avocations have provided
many manufacturers with new and lucrative markets.

Another illustration has to do with high-school graduation. This used
to be an occasion celebrated with the gift of a watch. But today fewer
watches are given if only because the new graduate is likely already to
possess one.

4. Emphasis on Kind of Person

Through various historical circumstances, the management of some companies have come to think of themselves as serving the needs and wants
of a particular kind of person. They are focused on a certain market segment, rather than on supplying a product line to different kinds of people.

This makes a great difference in what policies are pursued. Gerber advertises "Babies Are Our Business—Our Only Business." If Gerber were
to extend this policy (and it has done so to some extent) it might end up
with a diversified line of clothing, furniture, and other articles—all designed solely for babies.

This "targeting" on a certain kind of person, depending on how the
"kind" is defined, can make a great deal of sense. Many small specialized
retailers or service establishments build business around such an objective
—for instance, a quality haberdasher. But if the objective centers on a
disappearing "kind" of person, then the firm will experience trouble. A
publisher who caters to the education and amusement of the wives of
blue-collar workers might, over the next decade or two, experience a substantial reduction in his potential market.

The ability to be successful in serving people, as contrasted with producing things for people, has merit, of course, since the executives of a
firm must understand what is different about "their kind of people" as
compared with other kinds. And a preoccupation with a type of person
may induce great sensitivity to any changes in such individuals, as retailers
who have catered successfully to college students over the past decade can
testify.

The behavioral sciences have provided some insightful information about
certain groups of individuals. For example, knowledge of how social classes

differ with respect to their life-style and buying behavior is helpful in the establishment of market segments.[6]

5. Catering to Specific Physical Parts of a Person

Consider the concern of companies as to eyes (Maybelline), teeth (Dr. West), feet (Florsheim), skin (Noxema), hair (Alberto Culver), beard (Gillette), and legs (Haynes).

However, the physical part of a person for which concern is expressed is merely part of a person's total *gestalt*. The use of lip rouge and hair dye and the colors involved are affected by cultural norms as well as by the life-style to which a woman aspires.

Still, the "parts" objective has considerable appeal. By focusing on a relatively small and specialized part of a person, a firm can build a relatively secure market. But it may be difficult to build up sufficient sales to compete against a larger and more diversified seller.

A related problem has been experienced in the channels of distribution. Companies producing products having to do with the feet and legs, that is, shoes and stockings, have had difficulty in obtaining specialty-type selling without setting up their own outlets or leased departments. Only the larger firms have been able to afford such expenditures.

6. Examination of Wants and Needs

To have real meaning, an objective must be specific—as to what wants and needs of what parts of the market are to be satisfied.

This objective can be accomplished with some probability of success if the management of a firm considers (1) what generic use is to be satisfied, and (2) what consumption systems are operating to satisfy these generic uses.

GENERIC USE

Too broad an affirmation of corporate intentions provides little guidance to planning. It makes considerable difference whether a company defines its goals as being primarily financial, and sets about acquiring divisions chosen for their tax advantages rather than for their product fit; whether it aims to cater to, say, the textbook market and develop academic contacts

[6] Pierre Martineau, "Social Classes and Spending Behavior," *Journal of Marketing,* Vol. 23 (October, 1958), pp. 121-130. For an example of another classification system, see Janet Fisher, "Family Life Cycle, Analysis in Research on Consumer Behavior," from Lincoln H. Clark, Editor, *Consumer Behavior: The Life Cycle and Consumer Behavior,* Vol. 2 (New York: New York University Press, 1955), pp. 28-35.

to attract authors; or whether it wants to provide a congenial environment for bright and inventive engineers.

One important aspect of defining need objectives has to do with a product's *generic use*. Companies not only sell their products, but the functions which these products can serve in satisfying customers' wants.

In this sense, companies sell transportation, nutrition, energy, comfort, self-expression, escape, intellectual development, and conformity—rather than cars, bread, gasoline, pillows, pens, novels, textbooks, and uniforms. Transportation can be served by objects other than cars, and bread serves other functions than nutrition, and so on.

This means that objectives can be phrased and interpreted in different ways by companies in the very same industry. A company that centers its objectives on helping people to express their individual styles of communication might do better with the market by creating a new, more malleable pen, rather than by devising a cigarette lighter just because it happens to have the equipment to turn out small gadgets.

A logical starting point in the setting of need objectives would be to state the end-uses to which the product applies, and the basic needs that the end-use is attempting to satisfy. For example, a manufacturer of wristwatches might state that the basic need for the product is to measure time. The human outlook here rests in compulsive attention to precision and accuracy. Less literally, there is the definition of the wearer as mature enough to control the organization of his timed activities, and to relate to other people in a "socially synchronized" way.

If precision and accuracy are to be the main factors, then the necessity for fineness and quality of workmanship follows. If control of timed activities is given precedence, the company may begin to develop activating mechanisms and miscellaneous automatic timing devices. If social relationships and synchronization are emphasized, the company may turn toward making watches for children, for cocktail wear, and for jewelry adornment.

The petroleum industry will take quite different courses—depending on whether company managers see themselves as providing power, automotive service, transportation, or as being a conveniently located channel of distribution for a variety of products.

Generic use refers to the satisfaction of fairly general consumer needs and wants. But how they are gratified can vary and change through time.

People need food, shelter, and sex if they and their kind are to survive; but overweight people, "high-rise" dwellers, and contraceptive-users have made some significant modifications in their diet, environmental control, and sensual gratifications. It is necessary to keep abreast of changing social, cultural, and psychological situations and what they imply for product variation and innovation.

CONSUMPTION SYSTEMS

It is useful to think of the consumer as a decision-maker who individually or in conjunction with others controls the operation of a system comprised of products, effort (labor), and machines.[7]

Every product is, therefore, by definition a part of some consumption system. The totality of the system exists to satisfy some basic need or want —that is, to solve a problem.

This "solving a problem"—or goal-directedness—is critical. A failure to understand the nature of the goals and the standards set by the consumer will inevitably result in difficulties. Typically, there are a "constellation" of goals; for example, the housewife cleans a floor to remove dirt, to show that she is a competent housewife, to demonstrate to her family that she loves them, and so on. The housewife uses many systems as she goes about her household tasks. Cleaning house, preparing food, washing clothes, caring for the baby, and getting ready to go out provide examples of consumption systems in operation.

Here the consumer is like an economic entity—engaged in buying, transporting, changing raw materials into finished products in a sequence of events that is more or less efficient, and more or less satisfying to the participants. A manufacturer wishing her business has to produce and sell a product that will "fit." He has to understand what she is doing behavioristically (her actions), as well as teleologically (her goals).

Knowledge of the consumption system, more fully and carefully dissected, can alert the manufacturer to the fact that the housewife is acting in an orderly or purposeful way, according to her likes and dislikes; that there is a series of interrelated steps which require decision-making based on knowledge, expectations, standards (as well as ignorance, surprise, and uncertainty), and that the product is used with other products with which it must be compatible.

When the manufacturer knows these systems in detail and keeps his knowledge current, then he is in a position to assess opportunities (perhaps he can meet the standards of a housewife better with a new or modified product) as well as threats (for example, the development of a new washing machine which cleans by vibration).

We can also assume that a knowledge of the more important systems will help him to innovate, or at least provide him with a better understanding of the opportunities to do so. Certainly he has a point of reference, since time as well as the actions of competitors no doubt will change the system, thereby providing him with new opportunities.

[7] See, for example, Churchman, Ackoff, and Arnoff, same reference as footnote 1, at pp. 8-9, 20-56, and 107-114.

A seller of industrial equipment or supplies should easily be able to perceive the usefulness of the systems approach to objectives. Manufacturing systems are more precise and logical in their operation than are consumer systems. They center around a "flow," so that a manufacturer can predict with a fair degree of accuracy what he must do to "plug into" a given system at a specific point.

The revolution in marketing management, along with the revolution in information technology, may very well portend a reversal of the trend to decentralization and a strong recentralization of major business functions in the corporations serving the markets of the sixties.

18

New Organization Patterns for Marketing

EDWARD G. KOCH

WHAT'S SO NEW about the "marketing concept"? The term has been discussed and written about so much that the uninitiated might be forgiven for assuming that the marketing concept is a dramatic and revolutionary theory that has recently burst upon the management scene; actually, of course, most of the ideas it embodies have been around for some time. What *is* new—at least for many companies—is the emphasis on making marketing a central part of the business philosophy of the company and elevating the marketing function to a pre-eminent position in the organization.

There was a time when most companies were production-oriented: First they produced the product, then they made a market for it. Selling was thus the important concept—and the difference between selling and marketing is more than a semantic exercise. Selling focuses on the needs of the seller, marketing on the needs of the purchaser. Selling means moving

Reprinted from *Management Review,* publication of American Management Association, Inc., Volume 52, No. 2, (February, 1962), pp. 4-12.

products; marketing means obtaining customers. In production-oriented companies, management tells the sales department, in effect, "You get rid of the products; we'll worry about the profits." In contrast, the marketing-minded company makes every effort to create goods that customers will want to buy at a reasonable profit to the company.

We have had marketing-minded companies with us for some time; such pioneer companies as Sears, Roebuck, John Wanamaker, J. C. Penney, and General Foods have understood and practiced the so-called marketing concept for many years. Today, however, more and more companies are adopting this point of view; management thinking is becoming more customer-oriented, and profitable selling is replacing sales volume as the primary objective of the marketing program.

A Mature Market

The reasons for this changing emphasis are not difficult to determine. During the past decade and a half, the United States market, although by no means saturated, has become mature. A great many U.S. consumers have satisfied their basic needs for products and goods. They have become more discerning buyers, and they can afford to pass up products that do not completely meet their desires and standards. Moreover, they are spending a larger proportion of their income on services than ever before. Thus, producers of consumer goods must compete not only with each other, but with the growing appeal of vacation trips, higher education, better medical care, and the wide array of services that are becoming part of the "good life" to the American consumer.

Focus on the Consumer

Faced with this situation, many companies are finding that they cannot afford a hit-or-miss approach to marketing problems. The consumer has become the pivot point about which the entire business must move. This shift in emphasis requires more research expenditures, greater product-development activities, and increased attention to the short- and long-term planning of marketing activities. Marketing plans have become the basis for the design and erection of total corporate planning. Future market plans and sales potentials, for example, serve as premises for the planning of advertising expenditures, sales and promotion efforts, plant expansion and location, financial requirements, and other short- and long-term business commitments.

At the same time, sheer sales volume is no longer considered the key to corporate profitability. As competition increases and profit margins shrink, many companies have found that their marketing plans, policies, and strategies must be designed chiefly for their contribution to profits, rather than predicated on sales-volume objectives alone. And marketing goals must be consistent with over-all company objectives in order to contribute most to the long-range benefit of the firm. This means that the marketing function must be more closely coordinated and integrated with the other activities of the company, and the marketing responsibility has been expanded and reorganized to interlock all functions of the company into greater effectiveness.

Organizational Changes

In short, the modern marketing concept demands that the activities of the entire business be directed toward the satisfaction of consumer needs at a profit, and to accomplish this goal it has often become necessary for a company to rearrange its organizational structure. Although the changes that have been made have varied widely from company to company, depending on the peculiar circumstances in which they may operate, enough experience has been logged to identify several basic types of organizational set-up that have been established by companies who have adopted this management philosophy.

Simple Product Line

In companies with a narrow product line, relatively simple problems of distribution, and a single channel of distribution, marketing and selling activities are often diffused among the various functions making up the business. Usually, the product-planning function reports to the production or engineering departments, the pricing function reports to the finance or accounting department, and sales and advertising are separate departments. Sales forecasting and budgeting are often under a separate department or report to the finance or accounting departments.

When such a company adopts the marketing-management concept, all these activities, which obviously bear on the consumer, are properly moved to the direction and control of a marketing director or manager. This executive is under the general supervision of top management and at the same level of delegated authority as production, engineering, and finance.

The specific arrangement of the marketing-management function will be determined by the particular needs and scope of the company's operations. In some companies, for example, some of the technical activities related to the product or product group—such as product development or product research—are not under the direct control of the marketing director but are a responsibility of the production or engineering organization. Other companies place technical product activities in his care, even, in some cases, locating the repair service work with him rather than with production or manufacturing. In all instances, however, the tendency has been toward a task-force approach to departmentalization, giving the marketing director full charge of such activities as market research, advertising, sales promotion, product planning and budgeting, and sales management.

The Marketing Director

This increased centralization of marketing functions requires a marketing executive who is more than the traditional sales manager. The marketing director must think in corporate terms, rather than confining himself to building up sales volume; he must define problems for research, analyze results, and develop the indicated policies, plans, and strategies. In doing this, he must integrate the activities of other functions into the over-all plans, working harmoniously with all members of top management and with the board of directors.

Such men are not always easy to find; in fact, the chief difficulty many companies experience in adopting the marketing-director form of management is obtaining the right executive for the job. Executive recruiters indicate that the specifications most frequently sought in a marketing manager are these:

1. Ability to plan and coordinate the entire marketing activity on a profit-minded, businesslike basis.
2. Working familiarity with both manufacturing and research.
3. Sufficient knowledge of finance and accounting to be able to judge merger and acquisition possibilities intelligently.
4. Ability to set up and carry out long-range plans for new markets.

Committee Systems

It is quite possible that a company lacking such executive talent but desiring to go ahead with a reorganization under the marketing concept might start with a committee system. Indeed, even companies with highly capable managers often prefer the committee approach, believing that it facilitates communication and coordination among the various functions of the business. In Dennison Manufacturing Company, for example, the president serves as chairman of a marketing committee composed of the marketing manager, the general merchandise manager and his assistant, the research and development director, and the controller. Meetings are held at least every other week to discuss profits, make concrete plans, and decide on courses of action. In other companies, marketing committees are composed of the top executives from sales, advertising, market research, finance, and production.

The advantage of the committee system is that it eliminates many obstacles to interdepartmental coordination. The problems of communication between activities are greatly lessened because each, through active participation, is constantly abreast of the problems, needs, and findings of the other activities represented on the committee. But many companies find committees unwieldly, and they prefer to pinpoint the marketing management responsibility under the line authority of a single corporate marketing director.

Diversified Companies

Although the reorganizations that implement the marketing concept are significant in functional-type companies, they are even more dramatic in corporations with decentralized operations, many of which have shown a decided movement away from the General Motors type of decentralization. This is not to say that all companies with this marketing approach have changed their organizational patterns; some, like General Electric, adhere to the decentralized structure of self-contained divisions. But more often than not there is a strong trend toward a "recentralized decentralization" under the modern marketing concept.

To see how this trend changes organizational patterns, we can examine the effect of adoption of the marketing-management concept in four types of decentralized companies: (1) those with a package of complementary products or services using the same channel of distribution; (2) those with similar products using separate channels of distribution; (3) those with dissimilar products using the same channels of distribution; and (4) those with dissimilar products using different channels of distribution.

Complementary Products—Same Channels

Companies with a package of complementary products using the same channels of distribution often centralize the marketing-management activity and geographically decentralize selling operations.

In these cases, the pure selling functions are decentralized under regional or territorial line managers for reasons of economy, selective selling, and expanded penetration. Top marketing management reports to the chief executive officer and operates on a staff basis, with "functional authority" over *all* marketing and selling activities. This pattern of organization is well suited to a company selling complementary products through common distribution channels because the company is often more concerned with marketing a "whole idea" rather than individual products.

It is not difficult to find examples of large corporations that have re-organized in this fashion. Among the companies that are now emphasizing centralized marketing are the following:

- Burroughs Corporation, after a three-year tryout of product-line decen-tralization in which each division was responsible for its own marketing, manufacturing, engineering, and the like, abandoned this structure and set up a single marketing activity at headquarters to oversee the marketing of almost everything the company produces.

- Illinois Tool Works also centralized its marketing management and decen-tralized its product groups, which are responsible for their own selling.

- Monsanto Chemical revamped its organization to centralize marketing at the top corporate level. This reorganization was designed to bring market-ing and production closer together and to get better-coordinated product planning.

- Humble Oil consolidated six operating affiliates into one, with centralized marketing management at the headquarters office and decentralized field selling operations in four regions across the country. Company manage-ment anticipates that over-all sales volume can be increased appreciably in the years ahead through the use of a single marketing organization and a company-wide trademark or symbol. The new organization will be able to make use of national advertising and promotion, to enter new market-ing areas where none of the separate affiliates operated before, and to ex-pand the network of marketing facilities in some areas where present representation is comparatively light.

Similar Products—Separate Channels

A second type of marketing organization in decentralized companies can be found in companies with similar products and separate channels of distribution. Under this kind of organization, production and marketing are centralized activities and selling is a responsibility of the divisions. Examples of this pattern are evident in the automobile industry, where Ford Motor Company and Chrysler Corporation—and, to some extent, General Motors Corporation—are moving toward this kind of "recen-tralized decentralization."

In 1955, Ford Motor Company planned to set up separate, self-contained car divisions to compete line by line with General Motors. Within four years, the company created four new divisions—Continental, Lincoln, Mercury, and Edsel—and dismantled them because sales volume was not robust enough to absorb the divisional overhead. In 1957 and 1958, Mer-cury, Edsel, and Lincoln were combined into one division. In 1959, Ford dropped the Edsel line and transferred the Lincoln-Mercury division's assembly, purchasing, and production to the Ford division, leaving Lincoln-

Mercury merely a sales organization. In 1960, the company took all assembly, purchasing, and production-engineering operations out of the Ford division and placed them in a new centralized automotive activity. This was the final step in centralizing all production, keeping market planning and strategy centralized at headquarters, disbanding self-contained profit centers, and assigning only selling responsibilities to the divisions.

Chrysler Corporation experienced a similar evolution in its organization structure. In 1950, Chrysler was structured on the simple lines of any manufacturing plant of an earlier generation, with a chief executive officer and vice-presidents for finance, engineering, and sales—all operating executives. Reorganizing was a gradual process that started with a program of divisionalization to get control of costs. In 1956, sales responsibilities were taken from the divisions and given to the central staff, evidently to obtain marketing information for headquarters. The system got another upheaval in 1958, when manufacturing operations were taken from the car divisions and put into centralized functional groupings, and the divisions were once more given responsibility for sales. As a result, Chrysler now has a strong policy, market-analysis, and planning staff at the top corporate level, and a centralized manufacturing activity to handle all production. The divisions have no other task than to sell automobiles.

General Motors is the least consolidated of the "Big Three." Each GM car division has its own engine, suspension, and assembly facilities, and Chevrolet and Buick have their own transmission operations. However, a dispersal of activities has started: Now Buick and Oldsmobile share an engine, Chevrolet makes transaxle and rear suspension parts for Pontiac, and Pontiac produces differential parts for Oldsmobile. It is conceivable that the future will see a changing pattern of "recentralized decentralization" in General Motors as it seeks to gain more of the advantages of the modern marketing concept and, along with them, the paring of burdensome divisional overhead costs.

At all three major automotive companies, responsibilities for breaching new markets, capitalizing on new-product diversification, and utilizing the modern marketing concept is lodged in a separate office—next door to the chief executive.

Different Products—Same Channels

A third type of recentralization occurs in companies with dissimilar products but common channels of distribution. In this structure, selling operations are centralized under a sales division, because selling methods are the same for all products, but marketing and production functions are delegated to various separate product divisions. Although these divisions are responsible for enterprising efforts and expanded profits on their respective lines, their activities are subject to stringent central-office control by the vice-president of marketing, who oversees marketing management throughout the organization. He approves all short- and long-term planning of the product divisions, including advertising appropriations, sales-promotional deals, pricing policy and strategy, and expense budgets. In addition, he is usually responsible for marketing research, advertising research, and broad consumer-research functions.

Companies with this type of organization—among them, General Foods Corporation, Pillsbury Company, H. J. Heinz Company, and Procter & Gamble Company—depend heavily on consumer and product research to guide them in producing products that meet consumer needs and desires, thus attuning the entire corporate effort to the consumer. Such companies are truly "marketing managed." They utilize research to define needs or desires that a product might be designed to fulfill. New-product ideas come from interpretation of consumer surveys or from astute anticipation of consumer needs. Product divisions, working with the central office of research and development, are responsible for initiating product ideas and improvements: pure research is left to the central R&D activity.

During a product's lifetime, the product division uses research to analyze the quality and value it represents to the consumer, so the company can predict or ward off competitive inroads. Should a product develop trouble, it is the job of the product division and central R&D to determine how much of the problem lies in the product and how much is created by outside pressures. Even when products are successful and trouble-free, product divisions continue to study them for opportunities to redesign or repackage them, or otherwise to improve their salability and expand their market penetration. The "marketing managed" companies are most sophisticated in the use of research and the marketing concept to satisfy today's mature consumer needs at an adequate return to the company.

Different Products—Different Channels

A fourth type of recentralization is found in companies with dissimilar products using different channels of distribution. Even though product responsibilities may be delegated separately—e.g., for consumer and industrial products—they are often controlled by a top management executive operating under the modern marketing concept, as is the case with Du Pont, Borden, and General Mills.

Companies with a wide variety of products, both consumer and industrial, must always be alert to the possibility that their profit position may be impaired even while their total sales are growing. Top-heavy selling and marketing activities can be a serious drain on company resources, sometimes to the point where it is actually more profitable to eliminate some lines than to have too many irons in the fire. It is interesting to note that Monsanto Chemical Co. developed an excellent consumer product in "All," a home-laundry detergent, but sold it outright because the product did not fit their line, used a different channel of distribution, and required a separate selling effort.

Recentralized Decentralization

All these organizational realignments, different as they are, have a common element: a marked tendency for strong central-office control over marketing and product planning, analysis, and strategy. This strict marketing direction from the top, which is akin to the rigid central-staff financial control found in the General Motors type of organization, is a feature of the organization of an increasing number of companies.

The revolution in marketing management, along with the revolution in information technology, may very well portend a reversal of the trend to decentralization and a strong recentralization of major business functions in the corporations serving the markets of the sixties.

. . . many companies have diligently pruned distribution costs
—in the warehouse and in inventory, in order processing and
in transportation—only to find
that these hard-earned savings
are somehow not translated into
improved profit margins.

19

The Total Cost Approach
to Distribution

RAYMOND LeKASHMAN

&

JOHN F. STOLLE

THE MORE MANAGEMENT focuses the company's efforts on cutting distribution costs, the less successful it is likely to be in reducing the real costs
of distribution. This apparent paradox is no abstract or armchair play on
phrases. It explains why so many companies have diligently pruned distribution costs—in the warehouse and in inventory, in order processing
and in transportation—only to find that these hard-earned savings are
somehow not translated into improved profit margins. They have been
watered down or actually washed out by increases in other costs scattered
throughout the company.

It is these "other costs," motley and miscellaneous as they first seem,
that turn out on closer analysis to be the *real* cost of distribution. They
never appear as distribution costs on any financial or operating report, but
show up unidentified and unexplained at different times and in assorted

Raymond LeKashman and John F. Stolle, "The Total Cost Approach to Distribution," *Business Horizons*, Volume 8, No. 4 (Winter, 1965), pp. 33-46.

places—in purchasing, in production, in paper-work processing—anywhere and everywhere in the business. When these gremlin-like costs are traced to their roots, however, one finds that they are, in fact, all intimately interrelated, linked together by one common bond. They all result from the way the company distributes its products.

It is this aggregation of distribution-related costs—rather than what managements usually mean when they complain about the cost of distribution—that represents the important and increasing drain of distribution on earnings. These are the costs—rather than those usually defined and dealt with as distribution costs—that have eluded even the most earnest cost-cutting drives. Because of its size and its elusiveness, this cost complex remains for many companies a promising profit-improvement potential.

The Total Cost Approach

WHEN TO USE IT

For earnings-minded managements, the dimensions of this profit potential, and a practical technique for tapping it, have now been tested and proved. A handful of companies have faced up to the across-the-board impact of distribution on costs and profits. They have accomplished this by applying an approach—we call it the "Total Cost Approach"—that is designed to convert these intangible and intricate cost interrelationships into tangible dollar-and-cents improvements in profit margins.

- A major food manufacturer, after applying effectively an assortment of rigid cost-cutting techniques, has found that this new approach is enabling the company to add 1.7 per cent to its margin on sales.

- A major merchandiser, already enjoying the benefits of advanced distribution techniques, found that this same new approach could cut from its corporate costs an additional $7.5 million—3 per cent of the sales value of its products—while at the same time significantly improving service to customers.

- At Du Pont, a company well known for its general management excellence, this same new approach underlies the announcement that programs recently instituted are expected to cut $30 million from its total cost, a 10 per cent reduction of the costs attributed to distribution.

These success stories shed some light on how distribution drains profits —and on what can be done about it:

The real impact of distribution on profits is much greater than most managements think. In companies in which distribution-connected costs have been studied, they turned out to be significantly greater than management estimated—as much as from a third to a half of the selling price of the product.

This untapped profit-improvement potential exists because these costs lie in a managerial no-man's land, where they can increase because they are outside the scope of responsibility or control of any operating executive. These distribution-related costs are not strictly the responsibility of the man in charge of distribution, because they are costs of purchasing, manufacturing, or some other function of the business. But they cannot be dealt with effectively by the executive in charge of these other functions because they are actually caused by distribution decisions, for which only the man in charge of distribution has any responsibility. They are the result of complex interrelationships involving all of the functions of the business. Distribution lies at the crossroad of these complex interactions, and that is what is so different about distribution. In no other function of the business can decisions made at the operating level look so right and be so wrong.

These costs will not respond to the usual cost-cutting approaches. Management has achieved near miracles in cutting costs in one function of the business after another, including costs within the distribution function, notably in warehousing, transportation, and order-filling. But conventional cost-cutting approaches are limited to costs that fall within any one operation of the business; for cutting these costs, management can hold some executive responsible. Distribution-related costs are organizational orphans, beyond the reach of even the most diligent, skillful cost-minded executives.

These costs will respond only to a high level across-the-board re-examination of how distribution affects the total costs and total profits of the business, and of what management action is necessary to tap this profit opportunity.

Thus the problem and the opportunity are deposited squarely on the desk of the chief executive. The pursuit of these added profits has to get its start, its support, and its sanctions at the top management level. With this high-level effort, even companies that have tightened and tidied their distribution operations can greatly increase earnings by a frontal attack on the basic framework of their distribution decisions and practices.

This broad, basic approach has a continuing payoff, for once the most profitable pattern of distribution has been defined for the present operations of the business, management has in its hands a yardstick for measuring the impact on total profits of any proposed management move. This makes it possible to define the impact on total profits of a new plant or a new product, or a cluster of new customers, and so makes it possible to determine what changes in distribution—if any—will ensure peak profits from these new ventures.

What is this total cost approach? What is new about it? Why have we not heard more about it?

THE APPROACH SIMPLY STATED

This approach sounds simple. *First,* analyze the distribution impact on each cost of the business, and select for more detailed study those activities the cost of which is significantly affected by distribution policies and practices. *Second,* develop the data necessary to measure the profit impact that alternative distribution decisions would have on each of these activities. *Finally,* determine which distribution decision will maximize profits.

Obviously, if it were as simple as it sounds, more companies would long ago have beaten a path to this better mousetrap. Three sets of facts explain why this has not been so:

1. The impact of distribution on costs is more difficult to unravel than is the effect of other business decisons. All functions of a business are somewhat interrelated, but distribution is more complexly intertwined with each. And it is these interrelationships—rather than the costs of the distribution functions per se—that are the cause of high distribution costs and the key to understanding and reducing these costs.
2. Because corporate accounting has historically been oriented to finance and production, rather than to marketing or distribution, the operating reports that guide managerial action do not tot up in any one place the full impact of distribution on costs. The real cost of distribution never stares management in the face.
3. Even where managements have become aware of these costs and their impacts on profits, there was until recently very little that anyone could do about the pervasive effects of distribution. Even a relatively simple problem in distribution system design can involve hundreds of bits of information that interact in thousands of ways. So there was no way of dealing with the distribution cost complex until techniques were developed to manipulate this mass of material as a single integrated entity.

This last is, in fact, the major reason why these distribution-related costs have continued to rise and to depress profit margins throughout our economy. And for that same reason the total cost concept remained until recently a topic for textbook discussion, theoretically provocative but of little practical use. But techniques have been developed to deal with information in these quantities and with interrelationships of such complexity. They have converted this sound but previously unworkable concept into a practical management approach.

The examples that follow are composites of a number of companies. The relevant facts and figures have thus been disguised without in any way changing the practical significance of the results. The first example traces the step-by-step process involved in the analysis of the factors that enter into the application of the total cost approach in a business engaged primarily in the retail distribution of a wide range of consumer products; the second shows how this complex array of information is analyzed and manipulated to provide management with profitable answers to some familiar distribution problems.

What Makes Distribution Different

Consider the problem facing the management of a large company whose business consists of a widely dispersed chain of retail stores and a few factories that produce some of the merchandise sold in these stores. This company has shipped directly from its suppliers and its factories to its stores, but wants to determine whether there would be any profit advantage in shifting to a national system of field warehouses.

> When this company looked at the combined cost of warehousing and of transportation that would result from introducing various combinations of field warehouses, it appeared, as shown in Figure 19.1, that the lowest cost system was one with six warehouses. But this would *increase* its distribution costs by $12.9 million. Thus, on the basis of apparent distribution costs alone, there was no profit advantage in any field warehouse system.
>
> However, when this study investigated how alternative distribution networks would affect other costs in the company, the answer was quite different. As shown in Figure 19.2, the most efficient warehouse system turned out to be one with five, rather than six, field warehouses. And this five-warehouse system would cut the total costs of the company by $7.7 million; an increase of 1.4 per cent on sales.

Looking at distribution from a standpoint of total costs, this company discovered an opportunity to increase its profits that it could not have identified or taken advantage of in any other way. What explains the difference? What legerdemain turned up this handsome profit potential that represented a 22.4 per cent return on the investment required to design and install this field warehouse system? The answer, in this case as in other similar corporate experiences, involves following through the various steps of the total cost approach—that is, to determine the total cost of the present operation and then compare it with the total costs that would follow from alternative distribution systems.

At its very inception, the total cost approach is different in a number of ways from the traditional functional approach to distribution management. In the first place, it deals with the impact of distribution decisions on business costs wherever these costs appear. Secondly, many important cost factors and many critical relationships between distribution and other parts of the business are not usually translatable to quantitative terms. Customer service is a classic example.

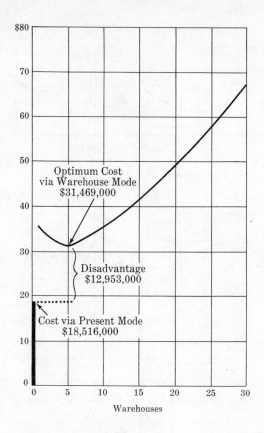

FIGURE 19.1

Distribution Cost Solution

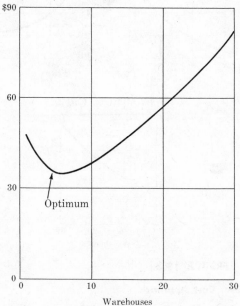

FIGURE 19.2

Total Cost Solution

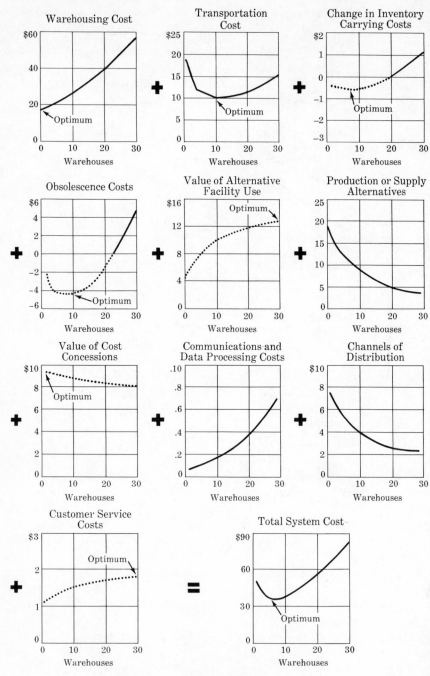

FIGURE 19.3

Total Cost Approach

212

The first step was to determine what distribution-related factors contribute significantly to total costs, trace the interrelationships of these factors, and then quantify both the factors and the interrelationships. This process has to be repeated anew for each company because of the important differences from industry to industry and even from one company to another in the same industry.

Then each of these have to be translated into a common denominator, so they can be measured and compared. If impact is measured in dollars, a unit that meets these requirements, it is possible to reduce all of the cost and profit considerations and all of these intricate interrelationships to one final total dollar cost for each alternative course of action.

The significance of this for management is seen in Figure 19.3; graphs show, for each major activity affected, the impact of different field warehouse systems (indicated by the numbers along the base of each graph) on the total cost of this operation. These graphs clearly show that for each factor of costs, a certain number of warehouses would yield the lowest costs and the maximum profit. Because each of these factors has its own built-in logic, each curve takes on its own configuration. The sum of all of these curves—each with its own optimum—is one final curve that defines the total cost. That in turn defines the optimum number of warehouses for this operation, when all considerations are taken into account. Except by chance coincidence, this point will differ from the optimum of each of the component curves. Obviously, a piecemeal approach to cost reduction will not yield the maximum profit impact achieved by this total cost approach.

These graphs show that even though one or several elements of distribution cost are cut to their lowest practical level, total costs may actually increase, and dealing with these costs one at a time will not produce the best result. They show the pitfalls of considering these various factors as single and static, instead of as interrelated and dynamic. The first and second graphs in the series make apparent the process whereby the consideration of distribution costs alone—the cost of warehouse plus the cost of transportation—led to the conclusion that no change in distribution could add to the profitability of the business. Only the final graph, summing up all of the interacting factors involved, demonstrates unmistakably that a shift to the five-warehouse system would be a very profitable move for this management.

Actually, in this case as in so many others, a reduction in warehouse and transportation could in fact lead to increases in other distribution-related costs, with the result that total costs would be increased and this significant profit opportunity missed. Only by increasing these distribution costs could total expenses be cut and total earnings increased in this company. By this kind of trade-off the total cost approach brings a company closer to achieving its maximum potential profit. The actual figures from this company's calculations for the five-warehouse system are shown in the accompanying table.

It is difficult to conceive of a distribution problem in a company of any substantial size that could not show near-term benefits from this kind of analytical approach; the approach does much more than offer a one-time solution to what is actually a perennial problem. Because this company distributes mostly through its own retail outlets, the channels of distribution are not currently an important variable. They involve only the small amount of its product that it makes in its own factories but sells to other customers. The availability of field warehouses, however, would make it possible to sell and ship more of the output of these plants direct to customers rather than through local jobbers. As it turned out, the $200,000 it added to profitability was just about what it cost to design and engineer this whole new distribution system.

In this case, the company had good reason for considering the significance of distribution channels. Looking ahead, it could see the possibility of integrating backwards, then becoming more heavily involved in manufacturing. In that case, alternative channels of distribution might become more important. The point is that in this kind of analytical exercise it is essential to consider all possible directions for company growth. Otherwise, a new distribution system, however profitable it may be under present conditions, might freeze the company into a set of cost factors that would preclude an otherwise profitable growth opportunity. The total cost approach offers management this built-in flexibility in assessing alternatives.

Every time management makes a decision of any magnitude, it ought to be in a position to get an answer to the question, "How will it affect distribution costs throughout the company?" The total cost approach puts the company in a position to make continuing gains by applying a rigid yardstick to any proposed corporate venture. Whenever manufacturing management designs a new plant, develops a new production process, or turns to a new source of raw materials, the pattern of distribution-related costs will be changed throughout the business. Similar far-flung changes will take place whenever marketing management adds a new product or a promising new group of customers. The total cost approach enables management to define how these changes will interact with distribution to affect the company's total cost and its total profits. It tells management what distribution decisions need to be made to avoid the loss of potential profits, or to add to them. So both short-term and long-term benefits result from management's recognition of these complex cost and profit relationships.

Profit Impact of Distribution—Gains (Losses)
(in millions of dollars)

Warehousing	(14.4)
Transportation	0.5
Total distribution costs	*(13.9)*
Inventory	
Carrying costs	1.4
Obsolescence costs	4.3
Value of alternative use of facilties	7.8
	13.5
Production and purchasing	
Production and raw materials costs	0.2
Reduced cost of purchased finished goods	6.7
	6.9
Data processing	*(0.2)*
Marketing	
Channels of distribution	0.2
Customer service	1.4
	1.6
Total profit impact of distribution-related items	*21.8*
Pretax Profit Increase	7.9

From Data to Decision

How these complex interrelationships and the mass of related data enable management to put a dollar value on alternative courses of action can be seen quite readily in the following case. The total cost approach was used by a division of a large manufacturing company. This division does an annual business of about $45 million, with over 3,000 customers located in every state. It has manufacturers and warehouses at five points across the country, shipping to customers via both rail and truck.

The profit problems this management posed have a familiar ring; some are long-range problems.

- Without any major investment, can we increase our profits by changing our distribution system?
- Can total costs be reduced by shifting some of our available equipment from one factory to another?
- Can we further reduce costs and increase profits by changing our marketing approach?
- Is there any profit advantage in changing the capacity of one or more of

our present plants, or perhaps building a new facility at another location?
- Could we further improve profitability by changing our warehouse capacities or locations?

An analysis of this company's business showed quite readily what factors
and what interactions determined the total profit of the product delivered
to the customer.

FINDING RELEVANT FACTS

Every distribution study has to start with a definition of where the customers are located and what requirements they impose on their suppliers.
In this case, some customers requested that they be shipped to by rail, and
others stipulated that they be served by truck. Some buy FOB, others at
a delivered price. Options, consolidation requirements, or other ingredients
of the customer service package are often relevant.

Different companies will have differing requirements for details. In this
case, it was important that the data be broken down by sales districts.
Therefore, it was determined for 160 sales districts what percentages of
sales came into each district by rail and by truck, and percentages were
found in each sales district for FOB and delivered prices.

The company then knew where the products were going and how they
were going to get there. Next, information was needed that would help
determine from which of the five plants and warehouses each sales district
should be supplied. This involved an in-depth analysis of the cost of production and warehousing per unit in each of the plants and warehouses
for various volume levels.

Figure 19.4 shows the total plant and warehouse cost for the Indiana
installation of this division, for amounts from zero to 2,100,000 hun-
dredweight. The total plant cost is built up by analyzing the cost for varying production volume of materials, inbound freight, direct labor, and plant
overhead. Each of these cost elements, will, of course, differ at each plant,
even within the same company. Total warehouse costs over this same
volume range were similarly analyzed. The same calculations were made
for each of the company's five facilities.

Figure 19.5 shows these total cost curves for all of the plants and warehouses. These costs are, of course, different for each facility at each point
on the curve. Not only does each curve start at a different point, reflecting
different overhead costs, but the rate of increase is also different, reflecting
different variable cost factors at increasing volumes for each installation.
These cost differences play an important role in the calculations. It then
became necessary to know the cost of shipping from each warehouse to
each sales district, by train and by truck. This information is readily available, though gathering it is often a time-consuming chore. Any other fac-

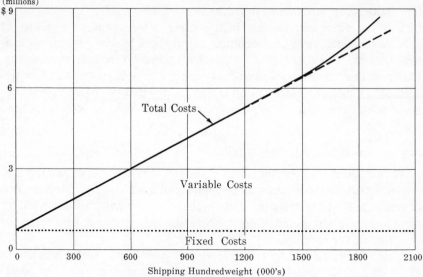

FIGURE 19.4

Total Plant and Warehousing Cost, Indiana Plant

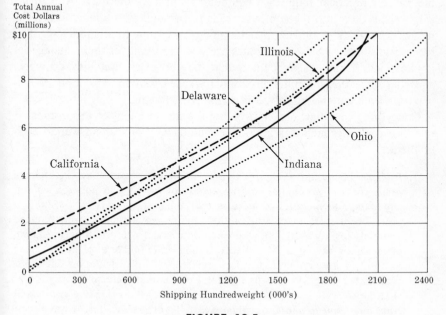

FIGURE 19.5

Total Plant and Warehousing Cost, Five Plants

217

tors influencing profitability have to be studied similarly, in relation to each of the other cost factors. In this case, management, as a matter of policy, eliminated from consideration any changes in data processing, customer service, and channels of distribution, so these were held as constants. Under other circumstances these factors might have been evaluated as significant variables. Similarly, in other company situations, other cost factors might have required analysis so that their impact could be introduced into the final decision.

MANIPULATING THE DATA

At this point, available information showed for each unit of product and for each customer the profit contribution under all possible combinations of production and distribution. The problem that remained was to put all these possibilities together into a single solution that will maximize the company's total earnings.

While this could be done by a series of pencil and paper calculations in which each combination of factors could be worked out and the profitability of each pattern determined, it would represent an enormous and costly chore. That, of course, is the reason why the total cost concept has not found its way into management thinking until recently. To make the process practical requires a computer to process the data. And to introduce this data into the computer calls for a range of mathematical techniques known as nonlinear programming and simulation modeling. The technical aspects of these techniques are not important for their managerial implications. What is significant is that they do exist, that they do work, and that once the computer program has been written, this kind of distribution problem can be solved in a matter of minutes.

Concerning the questions confronting the management of this company, the total cost approach was able to provide a very precise answer to each of them:

1. *By rearranging the company's distribution pattern and making appropriate shifts in production and warehousing loads, it was possible without any change in facilities to increase this company's profits by $492,000 a year.* The largest ingredient in this change would come from reduced materials cost at $126,000, with warehouse savings contributing $138,000, direct labor saving in the plants adding $57,000, and plant overhead $27,000. Transportation, so often overstressed in distribution decisions, contributed only $54,000 to this total profit improvement package.

2. *Additional savings of $180,000 could be effected by shifting equipment from one plant to another at minor cost.* To determine this, it was necessary to develop new production cost curves for alternative arrangements of equipment and run these through the computer, comparing them with the most profitable way of using the equipment as presently located.

3. *Further savings of $447,000 a year would result if about half of the customers could be persuaded to shift from truck to rail delivery.* These reduced costs could be added to earnings or passed on to the customer, thus giving the company a competitively significant price advantage.

4. *It was determined that there was no plant addition that would provide an acceptable return on investment.* Although building a new plant in Michigan would result in lower production and warehousing costs amounting to $225,000, the return on the investments would be only 2 per cent, and the "other costs" discussed above more than offset any possible gains, so that this investment would not be a wise one.

5. *On the other hand, an addition to the capacity of the warehouse at the Delaware plant would add $75,000 a year to profits and represent a sound investment.* This was determined by setting up new warehousing cost schedules and running them through the computer alongside the costs under existing conditions. The comparison showed that the investment in the added Delaware warehouse capacity would return almost 25 per cent a year.

The total addition to profits adds up to almost $750,000 a year, from changes in distribution and facilities, that were well within the company's capabilities. These would add 1.7 per cent to this company's margin on sales. The important point is this: these profits could not have been generated by decisions based on the insight or the experience of the most competent line executive. Only the total cost approach could have established, for example, that the earnings of this business could be increased by supplying its customers in the Dakotas from a plant in Ohio rather than from a much nearer facility in Illinois. Yet when total profits were calculated, this turned out to be an element in the most profitable use of the existing facilities of this company.

Similarly, only a total-cost calculation could provide the background for estimating the return on investment that could be expected from building a new facility in Michigan. Actually, that new plant would have reduced production and warehousing costs by an appreciable figure. However, other costs would be incurred in serving customers from this facility rather than from the present plant in Illinois; these other costs substantially reduced the potential savings and made the investment an unsound one. This ability to put precise price and profit tags on each pattern of alternatives makes the total cost approach a particularly effective management tool.

Making the Total Cost Approach Work

The successful applications of the total cost approach illustrated by these examples leave no doubt that this approach can, for many companies, uncover profit opportunities previously obscured by established ways of looking at distribution costs and by existing methods of managing distribution functions. But the experience of the successful companies also serves as a warning to those who are tempted to use the term "total cost" lightly. Understanding of many factors is required in order to undertake the kind of analysis required to define what all these costs are and what they really amount to, to develop a way to recover the profits they represent, and then to translate that solution into actual practice.

Though experience shows that the approach works out differently in every practical application, the sequence of steps that management has to take is always the same and it always involves the same inexorable logic:

To succeed, the total cost approach must have the active endorsement of top management. The total cost concept can be initiated at any place in the company, but unless it receives strong support from the top, it will not progress successfully, for the simple reason that only top management can insist that the real cost and profit impact of distribution be defined and measured, and at regular intervals. Only top management can see to it that there is a senior executive actively concerned with doing something about this impact of distribution on costs and on profitability. And only top management can assign to this executive the authority necessary to tackle this problem across organizational lines, in order to identify and take advantage of this profit opportunity.

Only a carefully conceived feasibility study can determine whether or not a restructuring of the distribution system is likely to be profitable. This thorough kind of study requires a wide range of technical and managerial skills. The team that can do such a study has to include transportation, production, and materials handling specialists, warehousing and logistics experts, as well as analysts with backgrounds in economics, mathematical decision-making and operations research.

Some companies have found it appropriate to assemble these skills within the company, while others have preferred to bring the necessary talent in from outside; this is a decision that management must make. But one fact cannot be avoided: this kind of study involves a much wider range of talents than is usually brought to bear on distribution problems, as well as a broad experience in the application of these capabilities to these total cost problems.

A more substantial and more time-consuming study is then required to determine in detail what changes are indicated, what profits can validly be expected from alternative ways of effecting these changes and what improvements in profits can be anticipated from the most practical solution.

To succeed in this effort the firm must develop quantitative information on the variables that affect each cost factor and the interrelationships among the various factors. Much of this information may be available in company records, and some of what is not available can usually be derived from existing reports. In most cases, it will be necessary to generate additional data.

Then, all of the significant interrelationships must be traced through the operation, the significant correlations defined and quantified, and all of this data subjected to mathematical analysis.

Next, the appropriate mathematical models must be constructed and then tested against past experience to validate their effectiveness. Then, alternative solutions to present and foreseeable problems have to be developed, and these studied by putting them through the model. This puts dollar values against each alternative and defines the optimum solution—the one that is most practical and most profitable.

Finally, the business implications of this solution need to be checked against organizational requirements, implications for competitive strategy, and ultimately for practicality in terms of timing and return on investment.

The final stage in the application of the total cost approach is the actual implementation of the solution. Initially, this involves putting into place the distribution system that matches the company's existing needs and its requirements for the short term future. Since the business itself and its external environment are both changing inevitably with the passage of time, with changes in product and in marketing policies and practices, as well as in response to changes in competitive forces and strategies, it is likely to prove profitable to rerun the problem at regular intervals. This process will redefine optimum distribution decisions and adjust plant loads and shipping schedules.

The companies that have been successful in using this approach have found that along with this restructuring of their distribution system, certain additional steps are likely to be critical. The assignment of responsibility for distribution has to be clarified. An information system has to be developed that will provide data on distribution costs and performance to whomever is responsible for controlling these activities. The company's data-gathering and data-processing system must be adapted so that it will pick up routinely the necessary informational input. Procedures must also be established to feed into the information system intelligence concerning conditions in the marketplace, and notably a continuing reassessment of prevailing customer service levels.

Thus the accumulated experience not only confirms the practicality and profitability of the total cost approach, but it also defines some clear-cut guidelines for managements who propose to put this approach to work. Experience in applying this approach suggests, too, that a number of additional considerations need to be clarified.

The fact that this substantial profit opportunity exists in a company is no implicit criticism of its operating management. No traffic manager or transportation specialist can be expected to deal with a problem the roots of which extend far beyond his sphere into manufacturing and marketing. Nor can the best warehouse manager be expected to come up with solutions to problems the causes and conditions of which extend from purchasing and supplier relationships at one extreme, to customer service considerations at the other. Even those companies that have centralized distribution responsibility in the hands of a single high-level executive rarely can provide this executive with the wide range of supporting capabilities and in-depth experience necessary to deal with this profit potential.

Nor does the fact that the necessary action requires top management support mean that the chief executive has to become an expert in the complexities of the mathematical tools involved, any more than he has to become knowledgeable in computer technology or the relative merits of the hardware and software. No one intends to suggest that management has to do or know anything specific or technical about distribution. What is required is management's insistence that something be done, by someone with the appropriate capabilities and experience.

In this sense, the challenge of the total cost approach has another interesting management meaning. The relentless and increasing impact of distribution on profits is one of a growing category of management problems that are not going to be solved satisfactorily within the framework of traditional organizational and decision-making approaches. The most effective solution to any company's distribution problem requires looking at the company as a whole and dealing with the profitability of the entity. More and more, management is being faced with problems requiring this kind of across-the-board attention.

At the same time new concepts, new techniques, and new technology are becoming available that are peculiarly able to cope with this very kind of problem. The more we learn about the computer and about such techniques as simulation, the more apparent it is that they are used to fullest advantage when they are used to deal with problems like these for which no other problem-solving technique is truly appropriate.

There is every reason to believe that with the increasing complexity of modern businesses and the mounting competitive pressures in their environment, the ability of companies to forge ahead and to grow profitably may have a direct relationship to the ability of management to put these new tools and their vast new capabilities to work. In the days ahead, competition between companies may in large measure reflect the skill with which competing managements take advantage of these new management tools.

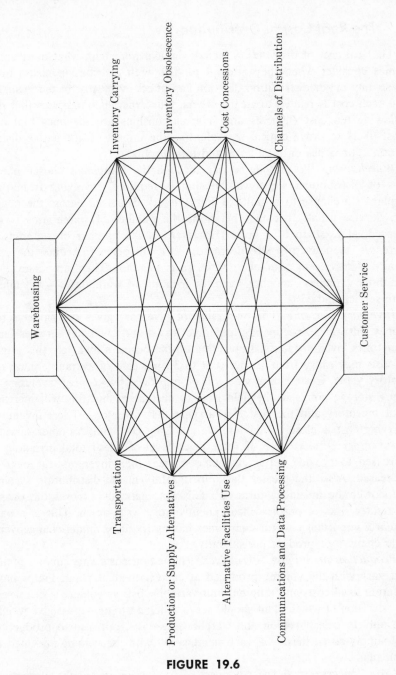

FIGURE 19.6

223

The Real Cost of Distribution

The real cost of distribution includes much more than what most companies consider when they attempt to deal with distribution costs. In a sense, any major distribution decision can affect every cost in the business and each cost is related to all the others. Our experience indicates that the following ten cost elements and interrelationships are the ones that are most likely to prove critical in evaluating the impact of alternative distribution approaches on total costs and total profits.

Warehousing. To provide service through the company's chosen channels of distribution, some warehousing is required, involving from one in-plant warehouse to a multiple-unit network dispersed across the country. Service usually becomes better as the number of warehouses is increased, at least up to a point. However, as the number of warehouses increases, their average size decreases; this will begin to reduce the efficiency of service to customers. Also, costs increase. Thus, any change in the three variables—number, type, or location of warehouses—will affect both service and costs.

Inventory Carrying. The ownership of inventory gives rise to costs for money, insurance, occupancy, pilferage losses and custodial services, and sometimes inventory taxes. Depending on the business involved, this group of costs may range from 10 per cent to 30 per cent of average annual inventory value. Customer service will be improved by keeping inventory at many storage points in the field near to customers, but this will increase total inventory and the cost for carrying that inventory. Thus, inventory carrying cost is closely linked to warehousing cost and customer service.

Inventory Obsolescence. If (at a given level of sales) total inventory is increased to provide better customer service, then inventory turnover is decreased. Also, the greater the "pipeline fill" in the distribution system, the slower the inventory turnover. This automatically exposes the owner to greater risks of obsolescence and inventory write-down. This is a particularly important cost for companies having frequent model changeovers, style changes or product perishability.

Production or Supply Alternatives. Production costs vary among plants and vary with the volume produced at each individual plant. Plants have different fixed costs and different unit variable costs as volume is increased. The decision of which plant should serve which customers must give weight not only to transportation and warehousing costs, but also to production and supply costs; these will vary significantly with the volume allocated to each plant.

Cost Concessions. A special aspect of production or supply alternatives arises from the fact that distribution decisions can affect costs otherwise incurred by suppliers or customers. For example, when a retailer creates his own warehouses, this may free suppliers from packing and shipping small quantities or from maintaining small local warehouses in the field. A retailer who establishes his own warehouse network may be able to recoup some of these costs by negotiation with the supplier.

Channels of Distribution. The choice of distribution channels profoundly affects the nature and costs of a company's sales organization, its selling price and gross margin structure, its commitment to physical distribution facilities. These in turn will affect production and supply costs.

Transportation. Changing the number or location of warehouses changes transportation costs, sometimes in unanticipated and complex ways. For example, an increase in the number of warehouses may initially reduce total transportation costs; but past some determinable point, the cost trend may reverse because of the decreasing ratio of carload to less-than-carload tonnage.

Communications and Data Processing. These costs vary with the complexity of the distribution system and with the level of service provided, including costs for order processing, inventory control, payables, receivables and shipping documents. These costs rise as more distribution points are added to the system. Additionally, as the cycle time or response time of the communications and data processing system is shortened, costs of this service are increased.

Alternative Facilities Use. Changes in inventory requirements or in other aspects of the distribution operation will change space requirements and utilization in a plant-warehouse facility or a retail store. Space used for distribution may be convertible to selling space which yields incremental sales and profits. In the case of retail business, this is actually a variation of the customer service factor since it increases the availability of goods with which to fill customer requirements.

Customer Service. Stock-outs, excess delivery time, or excess variability of delivery time all result in lost sales. Any change in the distribution system will influence these elements of customer service, and therefore must either gain or lose sales for the company. These effects, while difficult to measure, must be considered part of the real cost of distribution.

. . . as a marketing function
the credit operation may be
managed as a marketable service creating valuable utility in
the market.

20

Credit Management as a Marketing Function

ROBERT BARTELS

ALTHOUGH THE CONCEPT of functional integration has been widely adopted in both general management and marketing management, the employment of *credit* for the accomplishment of marketing objectives has not progressed as far as it might. There are several reasons for this, all of which stem from a limited concept of the role of credit in business.

Credit and Credit Service

For one thing, the essential nature of credit continues to be misunderstood. The idea persists that sellers "give credit." More accurately it should be said that they *perform a credit service.*

In selling on credit, sellers provide a service which must be regarded like any other service they perform. It is offered for the satisfaction of the market; for the differentiation of their market offering; and for additional income, either indirectly through the increased sale of products or directly through a charge made for the credit service.

Credit service must be marketed like any other service or product. The character of market demand for it must be ascertained. Operating costs

Robert Bartels, reprinted from the *Journal of Marketing,* national quarterly publication of the American Marketing Association, Volume 28, No. 3 (July, 1964), pp. 59-61.

are incurred in the performance, and these must be taken into consideration in setting price or in estimating profit.

The market for credit service arises from the utility which buyers attribute to it. Both sellers and buyers, however, have erred in their interpretation of credit, and this view has obscured the role of credit both in business and in the economy.

Sellers sometimes believe that in meeting credit competition they are forced to provide a "free" service. Thus, they may fail to allocate to this function all costs involved and neglect to program their credit service as part of their total product-service offering.

Buyers at times believe that they "get nothing" for the credit service charge or that they are charged more *for the goods bought* because of credit. As a result, they form attitudes antagonistic to those who provide credit service, tending to regard creditors as extortioners and themselves as defenseless customers.

Many legislators and public critics of credit also overlook the service inherent in credit operations, and tend to equate all credit business with the simple lending of money.

Credit and Possession Utility

Many of these misconceptions are traceable to conditions which antedated the present prominence of credit in business.

Prior to about 1920, in the effort to give theoretical justification to marketing activity, use was made of the economists' concept of "utilities." In marketing literature at that time it was claimed that marketing activity created time, place and possession utilities. By the latter was meant a value supposedly created in the transaction itself. Embracing a number of factors, possession utility never really received explicit definition but appeared to result from such activities as selling and merchandising. It was not related specifically to credit business.

So long as markets were essentially cash markets, that explanation sufficed; but with growth of the credit economy a new explanation of credit was needed. This is offered in the following interpretation of credit service as creating possession utility.

When a cash transaction is contemplated, buyers estimate the value or utility of a product to them *at that time,* and sellers calculate the cost and price of providing it then. If buyers must defer purchasing until cash is accumulated at a future time, immediate evaluation of the product's usefulness *now* may in the mind of the buyer exceed his appraisal of it if no delay in use were imminent. Thus, if through credit service he may acquire the product at once, the sum of utilities gained may include both that of the *product* and that of *using* the product prior to the time when it could otherwise be obtained through cash purchase.

Credit service, therefore, creates an identifiable value which might be called "possession utility." Such utility is not limited to the field of consumer buying, but is also involved in mercantile transactions and in lending.

Little Interest in Credit Work

The notions that "sellers give credit," that credit service is not distinct from the commodities to which it is applied, that credit service has no value, and that the offering of credit service is primarily a finance function —these are fallacies which have hindered the development of credit theory and practice.

For many years credit was regarded as an unproductive business activity, and the position of credit manager was at a much lower level than other marketing roles. Generally credit management has been assigned to the finance and bookkeeping departments and has been concerned mainly with allocation and utilization of working capital, turnover of receivables, sources of long-term and short-term funds for carrying receivables, credit loss ratios, cash discount tactics, economic indicators of the quality of receivables, and the like.

Although business use of credit was one of the functional fields of business first studied, the conceptual framework of credit management has remained essentially the same since the 1920s. A study of the location of the credit function in general organization structure was made by the National Association of Credit Management following World War II; but little progress has been made either among credit practitioners or among marketing theoreticians in developing a unified theory of the relation of credit to marketing. Only in recent years has credit management been regarded somewhat as a sales function, or more recently as a marketing function.

As a consequence of this narrow view, credit courses in business schools have specifically borne the adverse criticism made of specialization in the business curriculum. Furthermore, although employment in credit work is today at an all-time high, and although the importance of marketing has increased, relatively little interest in credit management is shown by college men preparing for business careers.

Marketing Perspective of Credit

In proper perspective, credit has very broad marketing significance. A credit operation is not merely the financing of an asset. It is the *financing of markets*—both ultimate and intermediate markets. It is the financing not merely of an *asset held* by the seller but of an *inventory sold* and in possession of buyers. It is the financing of the distributive channel, and of the processes involved in moving goods through channels. It is the providing of an auxiliary service essential to the marketing of goods and one which may also be income-bearing. It is a means whereby mere buying desires may be converted into effectual demands.

Credit service is a means of reaching new segments of a heterogeneous market. Credit terms increase market potentials by creating a new form of purchasing power. Credit classifications of customers serve as a basis for selective distribution policies.

Moreover, through the offering of credit service the following marketing objectives also may be achieved:

- Creation of a service "image" for the organization
- Addition of a marketable line of service
- Increase of revenue directly through the sale of credit service or indirectly through the increased credit sale of the commodities
- Profitable employment of available working capital
- Meeting of competition through terms of sale
- Extension of markets so as to utilize production capacity
- Counteraction of seasonal and cyclical trends through manipulation of credit sale terms

Organization for Credit Management

From the decisions implicit in the marketing objectives toward which credit policy may be directed, it is evident that credit management is not solely the function of the position traditionally designated as "credit manager." Rather, the credit function is involved in *marketing management;* and as a means for accomplishing broad corporate objectives credit management is a function for which *top management* should be responsible.

Recognition of this marketing character of credit operation has not always been evident in credit organization structure or in job specifications. As a rule, credit organizations have taken form in line, staff, and functional relationships. Usually line relationships have been established within the credit department itself, or among credit personnel, for the allocating of responsibility and duties. Within the broader organization structure of the firm, however, the credit group usually have occupied staff and functional positions. In staff capacity they have served to advise general management; and in functional roles they have worked collaterally with the sales organization, which has always performed as a line function.

This concept of credit organization has been altered somewhat in recent years, as the direct marketing contribution of credit work has been acknowledged. This has been evident even in the terminology by which credit management has been designated: at first, Credit Manager; and later, as Credit Sales Department and Manager of Credit Sales.

Not semantics but a new concept of credit is involved. Insofar as credit management initiates marketing policies and plans, participates in the formulation of overall corporate objectives and programs involving credit service, and works directly with customers (particularly in providing income-bearing credit service)—to this extent the credit organization presents the characteristics long regarded as line organization. Authority and responsibility commensurate with this concept are implied.

The division of credit responsibility among credit management, sales management, and top management is *not* a question of usurpation of rights or of subordination of operational activity. Rather, it is a division of responsibility for achievement of objectives for which different levels of management are responsible with respect to the offering of credit service.

Shifts in the Credit Function

As a means to the achievement of corporate, marketing, and credit operational objectives, the credit operation should be regarded only as a *means*.

Thus, the performance of this function must be appraised economically like any other function. In the absence of adequate data on the cost of performing credit service, such appraisal has not always been made. Consequently, credit policy often has been determined on the basis of custom, belief, and personal preference; but today credit performance increasingly is regarded as the offering of a service—a marketable service.

This means that business management has to consider and decide how *in their particular circumstances* they can best perform the three basic functions inherent in credit operation; investment of capital in receivables, bearing of credit risk, and performance of the routine of the credit operation.

In other areas of marketing, such considerations have at times resulted in shifting functions to specialists for the most effective, most efficient performance. Advertising agencies, manufacturers' and selling agents, brokers, warehouses, and common carriers are a few examples of functional specialists engaged by business. In credit operations, functions have not been so commonly shifted, although the opportunities to do so are increasing.

The use of factors by manufacturers' and selling agents is one example of the shifting of all of the credit functions; and economy and efficiency are presumed to result. Similarly, credit insurance companies and financing organizations accept part of the credit functions when circumstances warrant using them.

Also in the field of consumer credit such shifting of functions to specialists is occurring, with the rise of credit-card companies and of charge-account banks and companies.

Thus, as a marketing function the credit operation may be managed as a marketable service creating valuable utility in the market. It is a function for which several echelons of management are responsible. And it is a function which may be performed either by the business firm itself or shifted elsewhere, depending on business conditions.

INTEGRATED MARKETING
DECISIONS

THE IMPORTANCE OF VIEWING MARKETING as a total effort is reflected in the concept, "marketing mix." This concept suggests that there is an interdependent relationship among the many activities included in the field of marketing. In essence, a proposed decision or action in any one of these areas should be evaluated in terms of the firm's total marketing strategy. Such a total approach to marketing decisions often will permit serious and unnecessary mistakes to be avoided and will contribute to the total impact of the firm's new strategy.

The formulation and execution of a marketing strategy involves coordinating the product, marketing channels, promotion, and price in a manner designed to produce a total, integrated effort. The increasing competitiveness and complexities of business operations have made this coordination increasingly difficult to attain. As a consequence, greater attention is today being directed toward improving the basis upon which marketing decisions are made. Such improvement can take a variety of forms. Among those currently receiving prime attention are the following: organizing to facilitate the timely flow of useful information within the marketing organization; utilizing the computer to expand the flow and type of information made available; and simulating the firm's operations to depict possible outcomes and relationships. Each of these information-related activities can permit the executive to sharpen his perceptions of marketing and provide him with a basis for improving marketing decisions.

Although activities in each of the major areas of marketing can be evaluated separately, it is a primary responsibility of the marketing manager to relate decisions in each area to the total marketing program. The ultimate effectiveness of this program will depend upon attaining a coordinated effort which is focused upon the consumer, which is consistent with other aspects of the firm's operations, and which reflects the firm's marketing environment.

A. IMPROVING MARKETING DECISIONS

. . . companies now have it within their power to make substantial improvements in their marketing information system—and can ill afford to neglect them.

21

A Design for the Firm's Marketing Nerve Center

PHILIP KOTLER

AS COMPANY OPERATIONS EXPAND in size and complexity, company executives grow further removed from first-hand contact with the scenes of marketing action. They have to rely increasingly on second-hand information for their picture of what is happening in the marketplace, and, on the basis of highly fragmented and typically tenuous information, must make decisions that have profound consequences. The company's effectiveness in the marketplace is increasingly at the mercy of the executive's marketing information.

It is hard to find executives who are satisfied with the quality of their marketing information. Their complaints fall into a number of categories:

- There is too much marketing information of the wrong kind, and not enough of the right kind.
- Marketing information is so dispersed throughout the company that a great effort is usually necessary to locate simple facts.
- Important information is sometimes suppressed by other executives or subordinates, for personal reasons.

Philip Kotler, "A Design for the Firm's Marketing Nerve Center," *Business Horizons*, Volume 9, No. 3 (Fall, 1966), pp. 63-74.

- Important information often arrives too late to be useful.
- Information often arrives in a form that leaves no idea of its accuracy, and there is no one to turn to for confirmation.

Despite these serious complaints, few companies have taken the trouble to consider basic alternatives to their present marketing information arrangements. They are surprisingly slow to take advantage of new information-management concepts and technology. The typical attitude seems to be that important marketing information eventually flows to the right executives, that each executive can gather best the information he needs, and that a system of information management carries the danger of manipulation.

My work with companies convinces me that these premises are wrong. Key executives are often abysmally ignorant of important marketing developments; they do not always make optimal use of existing information; and they frequently distort information in passing it on. A systematic solution to these problems is absolutely necessary if executives are to make effective and swift marketing decisions in an age characterized by intensifying competition, frequent product change, and complex and shifting customer wants.

The literature on total management information systems is singularly uninformative on the specific subject of marketing, and, while a small handful of progressive companies are conducting their own experiments, these are either undisclosed or revealed in a form too fragmentary to provide concrete guidance. This article will present a coherent view of the major concepts and design steps in developing a modern marketing information system.

Present Inadequacies

The marketing information requirements of the modern executive have changed radically in the postwar period while the basic information arrangements have remained essentially the same.

On the one hand, the firm is involved in many more markets and products than ever before; the competitors are able to move more swiftly and deftly; and the environment of surrounding law, technology, economics, and culture is undergoing faster change.

On the other hand, executives must still hunt for their information from highly dispersed sources within and outside the company. The marketing research department typically supplies only a fraction of what is needed. The executive must also seek and receive information from the controller, the research and development department, the long-range corporate planning department, the legal department, the economic research department, and other parts of the company. He must supplement these findings by scanning hundreds of salesmen and dealer reports, and by reading half a dozen magazines and newspapers for possible items of significance. In short, he is on a perpetual information safari.

The marketing research department's primary obligations are to conduct special field studies, generate some routine reports and analyses of current sales, and send occasional clippings that might interest particular executives. On the other hand, it does not actively search for all sorts of marketing intelligence that might be needed by executives; it does not typically develop computer programs to aid in marketing analysis and decision making; and it generally does not render information evaluation, indexing, storage, and retrieval services, which would be the mark of a real information center. The marketing research department generally lacks—both in spirit and form—a conception of itself as the total information arm of the modern marketing executive.

One aspect of the insufficiency of information arrangements is dramatized in a planned experiment by Albaum. Albaum set out to study how well information flowed from the customers of a large decentralized company through company salesmen to company executives. He arranged with a sample of company customers to pass on six fabricated pieces of market information to company salesmen. The intelligence told of the changing requirements of customers, the building of a new factory by a competitor, the price being quoted by a competitor, the availability of a new material that might be used in making the product, and the development of a competitive product made from a new material. Clearly, all of these constitute useful marketing information in the right hands. Albaum wanted to discover how far, how fast, and how accurately this information would travel within the company.

Of the six pieces of market information, only two ever traveled beyond the company salesmen! For one reason or another, the majority of the salesmen chose not to pass on their intelligence to anyone in their company. Of the two reports that reached company executives, one arrived in three days but was seriously distorted; the other arrived in about ten days in fairly accurate form, although its usefulness could have been impaired by its tardiness.[1]

THREE INFORMATION PROBLEMS

Albaum's report suggests that at least three different problems arise in an unmanaged information system. They are information disappearance: the salesmen may forget to relay information, may not know who can use

---

[1] Gerald S. Albaum, "Horizontal Information Flow: An Exploratory Study," *Journal of the Academy of Management,* VII (March, 1964), pp. 21-33.

it, or may purposely suppress it for personal reasons; information delay: intelligence takes longer than necessary to travel from the original relay point to the decision center; information distortion: the message becomes distorted in the process of being encoded, transmitted and decoded many times. The likelihood of disappearance, delay, and distortion tends to increase with the number of relay points between the source and the final decision center.

ATTEMPTS AT CORRECTION

There are signs here and there that a few companies have recognized that these problems are sufficiently serious to warrant the development of new concepts and innovations. One such company is Du Pont:

> . . . Du Pont is moving toward marketing information centers. Basically, it means storing in a computer a great deal of information about specific markets, your position and your competitor's in those markets, the vehicles which cover the markets, etc. When the time comes to make a move, all this information is at your fingertips, so you're working on facts, not hunches.[2]

Monsanto is another company that is taking steps to put marketing information on a technologically advanced footing. Wherever feasible, the computer has been harnessed to supply rapid information and complex marketing analysis. Computer programs have been developed to help the executive select the best warehouse from which to ship an order, the best means of shipment, and the best allocation of customer sales effort. Computer programs also are available to generate sales forecasts, customer profitability studies, analyses of sales call effectiveness, and pricing proposals.[3]

In addition, United Air Lines recently commissioned the Univac Division of Sperry Rand Corporation to build a $56 million online computerized system designed to provide United with a totally integrated reservations, operations, and management information capability. Applications will range from passenger reservations, complete name record storage, crew and aircraft scheduling, and flight and meal-planning data to air freight and cargo loading information.

Retailing is also showing signs of innovation in the area of marketing information. The Chicago department store of Carson Pirie Scott & Company recently installed an in-store system that enables its retail personnel to check a customer's credit in a matter of seconds by dialing the customer's number on a phone. The computer returns a spoken answer,

[2] Malcolm McNiven, "An Interview with Malcolm McNiven," *Sales Management* (April 19, 1963), p. 42.

[3] William A. Clark, "Monsanto Chemical Company: A Total Systems Approach to Marketing," in Alan D. Meacham and Van B. Thompson, eds., *Total Systems* (Detroit: American Data Processing Inc., 1962), pp. 130-42.

either authorizing the sale or giving other instructions. Giant retailers are also experimenting with computerized inventory-ordering systems, direct computer lines to suppliers, and improved sales analysis systems.

Other companies, such as the Hotpoint Division of General Electric, the Mead Paper Company of Dayton, Ohio, and General Mills, are known to be developing a total systems approach to their marketing information needs. But these companies still number only a handful. Other companies are interested but lack a comprehensive understanding of the marketing information problem or how to proceed to solve it.

The Major Information Flows

Every company is involved in three distinct marketing information flows (see Figure 21.1a). The first, the marketing intelligence flow, is the flow of information from the environment to relay points within the firm. Information on dealers, competitors, customers, government actions bearing on marketing, prices, advertising effectiveness, and so forth would be considered marketing intelligence. The second, the internal marketing information flow, is the flow between relay points within the firm. This includes intelligence as it flows through the company and internally generated reports germane to marketing. The third, or marketing communications flow, is the flow of information from the firm outward to the environment. It consists of both straight information and product and company promotion. The importance of marketing communications cannot be overemphasized but, as an outward information flow, it will not concern us here.

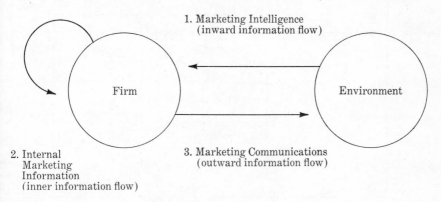

FIGURE 21.1a

Three Marketing Information Flows

THE MARKETING INTELLIGENCE FLOW

The flow of information known as marketing intelligence consists of salient facts about institutions and developments in the environment that affect the company's opportunities and performance. Figure 21.1b shows the nine major institutions in the environment that the firm monitors for marketing intelligence. It represents an elaboration of the marketing intelligence flow in Figure 21.1a.

Marketing intelligence is a broad term, embracing raw data, summary statistics, qualitative inferences, expert and lay opinions, impressions, and even rumors. Examples include figures showing that a certain important customer is beginning to divert some of his purchases to competitors; rumors that a competitor is developing a substantially improved product; and a survey indicating that many customers are dissatisfied with the service provided by the manufacturer's representative.

Each item constitutes marketing intelligence since it has potential action

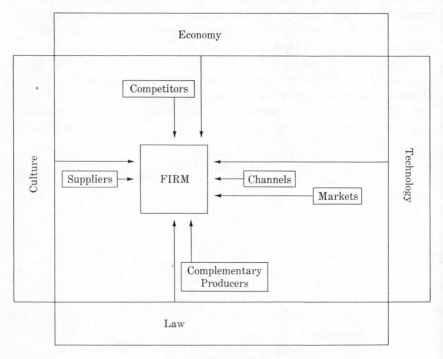

FIGURE 21.1b

Major Sources of Marketing Intelligence

implications for one or more marketing executives in the firm. Information about a wavering customer is useful intelligence to a district sales manager, although it would be trivial to the new product manager. Reports about a competitor's development of a new product would be useful to the new product manager, and information about customer dissatisfaction with the manufacturer's representative would be useful to the trade relations manager.

The idea of marketing intelligence comes from the military. The high level military decision maker is usually far removed from the battlefield and therefore totally dependent upon second-hand information in directing the battle. He requires continuous data on the current position of his troops, the occurrence and outcomes of skirmishes, and the plans of the enemy. He needs hunches and rumors as well as hard facts.

The marketing executive is in an analogous situation. He fights for terrain (markets) with allies (channels) against an enemy (competitors) for a prize (sales). Because he is remote from the battle scenes, he needs reports on the positions and effectiveness of his salesmen, on the resistances they are encountering, and on the activities of competitors. He needs current and accurate facts as well as some of the talk and gossip of the marketplace.

Marketing intelligence varies in its availability. Information about broad characteristics of the market—such as the number of buyers or their geographical dispersion—is the easiest to obtain. The information is public and often can be drawn routinely from secondary sources—government and trade associations. Information about present and potential customer preferences and attitudes is a little more difficult to acquire. Generally, it does not exist in published form, and, since it may have to be gathered as primary information, its value must be considered carefully in relation to its cost. Most difficult to collect is information related to the marketing expenditures and plans of competitors. Such facts are tightly controlled for security reasons. The firm that wants it may have to develop an industrial espionage unit within the marketing intelligence unit. This, however, raises fundamental issues in business ethics.

THE INTERNAL INFORMATION FLOW

A crucial point about marketing intelligence is that it must reach the right executive to be useful; the information must flow not only to the firm but through it. The internal flow is made up of downward, upward, and horizontal flows. The three are illustrated in Figure 21.1c where a pyramid form of organization is assumed. The downward flow consists of communications from higher company officials to subordinates. The upward flow consists of requisitioned as well as unsolicited information moving from

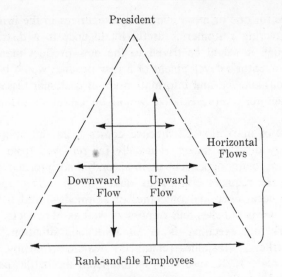

FIGURE 21.1c

Three Types of Internal Information Flows

lower to higher levels in the organization. The horizontal flow consists of information passing among company employees who occupy approximately the same levels.

In the typical company, these internal flows are left to take place in a natural unmediated way. It is assumed that employees generally will know where to find needed information within the company and will receive vital intelligence from others in the company as a matter of course. But these assumptions about the free flow of internal information in an unmanaged communications system are not justified, as Albaum's earlier cited study shows.

Examining Information Needs

At least three steps must be taken by the company that is serious about a total systems approach to marketing information. The first step is to appoint a responsible committee; the second is for this committee to develop studies of present information arrangements and needs. Third, the committee must design the new system on the basis of its studies and carry out its gradual implementation.

THE COMMITTEE

Responsibility for the quality of marketing information should rest ulti-

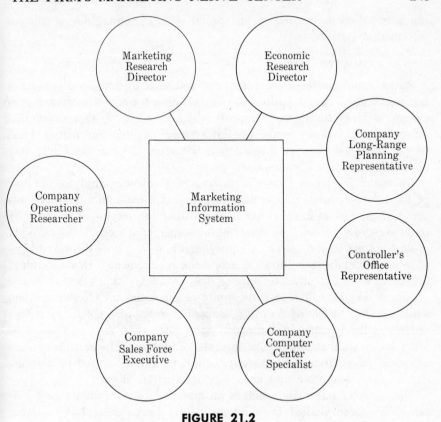

FIGURE 21.2

The Marketing Information Systems Committee

mately with the vice-president of marketing and his top ranking executives. This group must define the objectives that are to guide the supply of marketing information; it is also their responsibility to review the workings of the system and to institute desirable reforms.

These same men, however, are not equipped with either the time or training to play a first-hand role in studying, designing, or implementing the improved system. The actual work must be done by a special team usually consisting of the following personnel: the marketing research director, the economic research director, a company sales force executive, a representative from the long-range corporate planning office, a representative from the controller's office, a company computer center specialist, and a company operations researcher (see Figure 21.2). Each man is on this committee, either because of his special concern for the quality of marketing information or because of his special skills in helping design efficient information systems.

COMMITTEE STUDIES

At its initial meetings, the committee will want to develop a consensus on broad objectives regarding the marketing information system and a general strategy for improvement. It will find, however, that substantial information is lacking on the present system, and that information must be collected. Two studies in particular will loom large in the future recommendations of this committee.

Internal Information Flow Characteristics. Elementary study of the flow of basic information through the company often leads to substantial improvements. For example, what happens after the receipt of a customer purchase order? How long does the customer credit check take? What procedures are used to check inventory, and how long does this take? How soon does manufacturing hear of new stock requirements? How long does it take for sales executives to learn of daily or weekly total sales?

Ringer and Howell reported a study of one company's order routing, which resulted in cutting down the elapsed time between the receipt of an order and the issuance of the order to be filled from sixty-two hours to thirty hours without any change in costs.[4] Evans and Hague showed how advanced information flow charting techniques could be used to describe and improve interoffice and intraoffice information flows.[5]

The effect of information delays on marketing and manufacturing efficiency has been studied most intensively by Forrester at M.I.T. Using simulation techniques, Forrester is able to show how various delays in the processing and transmission of information lead to marketing decisions that often accentuate production fluctuations beyond those caused by forecasting errors and resource immobilities. His technique enables an estimate to be made of the cost-benefit effects of proposed alterations in the speed of information transmission through the organization.[6]

Executive Marketing Information Needs. The committee also will want direct feedback from executives on their satisfactions and dissatisfactions with current marketing information. Sampling of a small but representative group of executives from different levels and parts of the organization is adequate. The purpose is not to find out individual needs at this stage since information appetites and decision-making styles differ from execu-

4 Jurgen F. Ringer and Charles D. Howell, "The Industrial Engineer and Marketing," in Harold Bright Maynard, ed., *Industrial Engineering Handbook* (2d ed.; New York: McGraw-Hill Book Co., Inc., 1963), pp. 10, 102-3.

5 Marshall K. Evans and Lou R. Hague, "Master Plan for Information System," *Harvard Business Review* (January-February, 1962), pp. 92-104.

6 Jay W. Forrester, "Advertising—A Problem in Industrial Dynamics," *Harvard Business Review* (March-April, 1959), pp. 100-110.

Sample Questionnaire for Determining Marketing Information Needs

1. What types of decisions are you regularly called upon to make?
2. What types of information do you need to make these decisions?
3. What types of information do you regularly get?
4. What types of special studies do you periodically request?
5. What types of information would you like to get which you are not now getting?
6. What information would you want daily? weekly? monthly? yearly?
7. What magazines and trade reports would you like to see routed to you on a regular basis?
8. What specific topics would you like to be kept informed of?
9. What types of data analysis programs would you like to see made available?
10. What do you think would be the four most helpful improvements that could be made in the present marketing information system?

FIGURE 21.3

tive to executive. Rather, the purpose is to determine how the information needs of product managers, territorial sales managers, customer account executives, advertising managers, salesmen, and other types of executives differ from each other.

Executive attitudes can be surveyed in a number of ways, including interoffice mail or the telephone. The best technique, however, is through personal interviews. Figure 21.3 suggests the major types of executive responses sought. The questionnaire covers the executive's information sources, attitudes, needs, and suggestions. The questions are stated mainly in an open-end fashion to encourage more involvement and frankness on the part of executives. Results will be more difficult to tabulate, but open-end surveys lead to deeper insights into the problem being studied.

DEVELOPING A LONG-RANGE PLAN

The studies of the present information flows and executives' needs provide the basis for developing a long-range plan for improving the marketing information system. The committee will not accept all suggestions because the value of additional or faster information must always be measured against the costs of providing it. The committee's task is to rate the various information needs against their probable contributions to better

decision making and control. The resulting long-range plan would be submitted to the executive committee for comment and approval, and would
be implemented in a series of steps over a number of years.

The Marketing Information and Analysis Center

This section will describe a blueprint for an organizational unit that
promises to improve the accuracy, timeliness, and comprehensiveness of
executive marketing information services. This unit is a generalization of
the marketing research department into something infinitely more effective
known as the Marketing Information and Analysis Center (MIAC).
MIAC will function as the marketing nerve center for the company and
will not only provide instantaneous information to meet a variety of executive needs but also will develop all kinds of analytical and decision aids for
executives—ranging from computer forecasting programs to complex simu-
lations of the company's markets.

The concept of this center can be understood best if we view its functions as being completely user oriented. It is designed to meet the total
planning, implementational, and control needs of the modern marketing
executive. Figure 21.4 shows the flow of marketing information from ultimate sources to and through MIAC to those who use this information. The
ultimate sources consist of parties outside the firm, such as customers,
dealers, suppliers, and competitors (see Figure 21.1b), and parties inside
the firm, such as the accounting department, the economic and forecasting
department, and the field sales force. The ultimate users consist of company executives, such as product managers, sales force managers, advertising managers, traffic managers, and production scheduling personnel.
The MIAC stands between these two groups and performs over a dozen
different services to enhance and expedite the marketing information and
decision-making process. These information services break down into three
major types: gathering, processing, and utilization.

INFORMATION GATHERING

Gathering involves the effort to develop or locate information sought by
company executives or deemed to be relevant to their needs. This function
is made up of three constituent services.

The first is search, which is activated by requests for specific marketing
information. Search projects can range from quick "information please"
inquiries to large-scale field marketing studies. Marketing research departments traditionally spend a substantial portion of their time in search
activity.

The second information gathering service is scanning. This describes

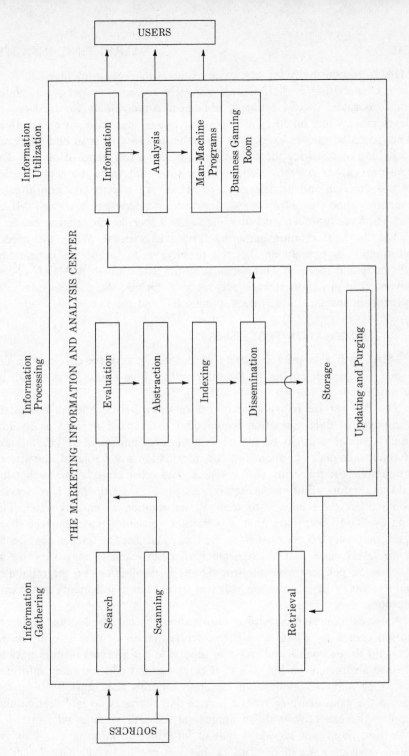

FIGURE 21.4

A Schematic Diagram of MIAC's Information Services

247

MIAC's responsibility for assembling general marketing intelligence. Intelligence specialists in MIAC will regularly scan newspapers, magazines, trade journals, special reports, and specific individuals to uncover any developments that might have import for one or more company executives. This partially relieves executives from the necessity to scan endless reams of written material for the sake of finding only a few items of interest. Because executives have overlapping information interests, the centralization of this function and its delegation to MIAC is likely to save considerable executive time. Its effectiveness, however, depends on how well MIAC personnel really understand the differing and specific information needs.

The third information gathering service is retrieval. When the needed information is already on file, the problem is to locate the information efficiently and speedily. This depends on the extent to which MIAC adopts advanced information storage and retrieval techniques, such as computer systems, microfilm devices, display consoles, and the like.

INFORMATION PROCESSING

MIAC will also offer a variety of processing services designed to enhance the over-all quality of the information. Five major services can be distinguished.

The first service is evaluation. One or more MIAC staffers trained in techniques of data validation would offer a technical opinion as to how much confidence might be placed in a piece of information. The amount of confidence depends upon how the information was gathered, the size of the sample, the reliability of the source, and other considerations that the data evaluator would immediately recognize as pertinent. This service would offset the tendency to treat all information as equally valid. The data evaluator may show that a particular consumer panel market share figure may vary 20 per cent from the true value (at the 95 per cent confidence level), and that a magazine readership estimate may vary by as much as 50 per cent from the true figure. These opinions on the reliability and credibility of information will temper executive judgments in making decisions.

A second important service is information abstraction. Marketing information comes to MIAC in highly discursive forms. Many executives do not want to read pages and pages of reports to get a kernel of information. Trained abstracters on MIAC's staff condense and edit incoming information; they may omit important material, but this risk must be balanced against the gains accruing from a service that sharpens up information and supplies the executive with an immediate sense of what is relevant.

A third important service is that of indexing the information. This involves devising a set of descriptors that will permit its efficient classification for storage and retrieval purposes, and a ready identification of which executives might be interested in it. For example, information about a proposed merger of two supermarket chains in California might be assigned the descriptors "supermarkets," "mergers," and "California," so that marketing executives interested in either supermarkets, mergers, or California would find this information readily. Developing a good indexing system is the key to the rapid dissemination of marketing information among the right parties and to its easy retrieval.

Dissemination is a fourth important information processing service. Dissemination involves getting information to the right people in the right form in the shortest feasible time. Among the devices used are periodic newsletters, telephone calls, teletype services, and interconnected company computers. Companies are experimenting with new and bolder dissemination procedures, as the following two examples show.

A large chemical company compiles during the week news of special interest to its salesmen, records the news on magnetic tapes, and sends the tapes to them. Each salesman's car is equipped with a tape recorder, and the salesmen pass many otherwise idle driving hours assimilating relevant marketing and company information.

A large supermarket chain is considering the idea of preparing up-to-the-minute reports of news affecting store operations, which its managers around the country can dial into.

MIAC's final information processing service is that of storage. Every company must find an efficient way to store and compress the mountains of information that come in yearly; otherwise, it is storage without utility. Executives should be able to put their fingers on past sales figures, costs, dealer data, and other information with minimum effort. The engineering of an efficient system is a problem for the technicians. Each company must determine the economically desirable life of different types of information so that it can be periodically updated and purged.

INFORMATION UTILIZATION

MIAC must offer more than information gathering and processing services if it is to add substantial leverage to the executive's planning and control capabilities. The executive basically needs three types of staff assistance.

His first need is for information itself. Under this heading fall periodic reports, special market studies, and general marketing intelligence. We have seen how MIAC represents an improved vehicle for these services over the traditional marketing research department.

The second major need is for assistance in analysis. In this connection, MIAC's staff would include research specialists in statistical analysis, econometric analysis, psychometric analysis, and operations research, as well as research generalists to gauge needs and interpret results. These analysts would assist the decision maker in formulating problems and developing models for a solution. They would be able to specify the data needed and analyze the gathered data for important relationships and parameters. In this way, complex marketing decisions such as dropping a price, revising sales territories, or increasing the advertising expenditure level can be preevaluated and post-evaluated through the scientific analysis of available data. These analysts would also help make periodic analyses of distribution costs, sales trends, expense records, and product and salesman performances.

The third major need of the executive is for computer programs, which will enhance his power to make decisions and to control operations. Future management gains in decision-making effectiveness will depend on the development of "man-computer" systems of decision making. Cohen and Miller have defined this type of system in the following way:

> . . . it makes use of mathematical models (processed by a computer) to arrive at many decisions, but requires management to monitor these decisions and make others that are less subject to programming. The computer not only relieves the firm of much clerical work in handling and compiling the data, but it permits the use of mathematical techniques for optimizing certain decisions which involve large quantities of data and numerous calculations. Where models are not available, the computer often can produce information, from data on hand, to permit more efficient decisions.[7]

The nature of this new and growing service area is best conveyed by several examples.

- A large paper company is developing a computer hookup among its plants and warehouses, which will permit salesmen to obtain quick answers to customers' questions concerning how soon they might receive the goods if they placed an order. The inquiry is entered at a console and transmitted to the central computer system where a determination is made as to whether the item is in stock. If it is in stock, the computer indicates how long it would take to schedule its production and ship it to the customer. The salesman can give the customer his answer in a number of minutes.

- At a large chemical company, an executive can have a statistical demand analysis made for any product or product item by entering its past sales into the console. The computer program selects the economic and other variables (from a set of 200), which are most highly correlated with the product's past sales and prints out the resulting demand equation.

---

[7] Kalman J. Cohen and Merton H. Miller, "Management Games, Information Processing, and Control," *Management International,* III (1963), p. 168.

- At a large packaged food company, sales executives get weekly reports on deliveries to retail trade with a red asterisk after those figures showing unusual variances from norms. The red asterisks alert the executives to look into these situations and determine if any special measures are needed.

- A large department store is experimenting with a computer program that can make ordering, pricing, and markdown decisions on some staple items and thus free buyers' time for the less routine decisions.

- A major advertising agency uses the computer to develop an initial media plan, which will optimize on the clients' objectives, given the available information and constraints. The computer's proposed plan is then refined by changing certain assumptions or information, or by modifying it according to more intangible considerations.

- A large chemical company uses a computer program to help evaluate each new product's promise at any point in its development. The executive enters the best information at his disposal regarding probable price, advertising, size of market, competitive strength, cost of development, and so forth, and the computer prints out possible rates of return and their respective probabilities.

- A major electrical manufacturer uses a large and complex computer model of the company's markets for one of its products to pretest the likely effects of alternative trade promotions on competitors, customers, and final sales.

All of these are contemporary examples of the possibilities that lie in the exploitation of the man-machine interface. The ultimate implication is the development of a business gaming room, as part of MIAC, where information comes in continuously on field operations, and is evaluated, indexed, abstracted, and disseminated; important developments lead to speedily arranged executive meetings to decide on marketing defensive or offensive actions. Information can be retrieved instantly as the meeting progresses, and the executives can pretest proposed moves on a simulation model of the relevant markets.

There is considerable evidence that executives are dissatisfied with the quality and quantity of their marketing information. Contemporary information systems are usually inadequate to supply the information and analysis needed by marketing and other company executives to respond rapidly and optimally to changing opportunities and challenges. Only a handful of companies are presently pioneering an assortment of innovations, which promise to synthesize one day into the outlines of a new and more effective marketing information system.

A look at the nature and types of information flows provides perspective on planning an improved system. The plan of attack for an organization serious about improving its system calls for the formation of a systems committee, studies of present information flows and executive information needs, and a long-range plan for progressive improvement of the information services. The nerve center of such a system, MIAC, carries out information gathering, processing, and utilization services, which go far beyond those observed in traditional marketing research departments.

The description of MIAC is more a blueprint for the future than a feasible system for the present. Marketing information systems cannot be overhauled overnight. Yet present systems can be guided to evolve in the direction of this blueprint. Difficult questions have to be answered concerning the proper relation between MIAC and other company information centers; the proper relation between MIAC and grass roots marketing research efforts by company personnel; the proper administrative arrangements within MIAC; the cost of MIAC; and so forth.

It must also be asked what the dangers may be in the centralized management of marketing information, and whether this system could make a fetish of information, causing more to be gathered than is economically justifiable. There are no general answers to these questions. They call for inventiveness and good judgment on the part of individual firms. The only judgment to be ventured here is that companies now have it within their power to make substantial improvements in their marketing information system—and can ill afford to neglect them.

> . . . by making more realistic
> systems of marketing variables
> amenable to analysis, simula-
> tion techniques allow market-
> ing people to move even closer
> to a practical theory of market-
> ing.

22

Simulation for Decision Making in Marketing

DOYLE L. WEISS

THE DEVELOPMENT of the modern computer and its problem-oriented languages has made simulation a feasible technique to apply to the complex problem situations faced by researchers and policy makers in marketing.

Problem-oriented languages allow researchers to instruct the computer with terms and symbols which are most meaningful to the problem being studied. The result is that the computer with its language systems provides researchers with a flexibility for model construction that has never before been available.

Before the arrival of the computer most marketing theories which attempted precisely to relate the decision variables, initial conditions, and parameters (constants specific to the problem being studied) to observations of actual business operations were restricted in form to linear models.[1] This restriction was necessary because large systems of nonlinear equa-

Doyle L. Weiss, reprinted from the *Journal of Marketing,* national quarterly publication of the American Marketing Association, Volume 28, No. 3 (July, 1964), pp. 45-50.

[1] A. T. Steele, "Why Daily Department Store Sales Fluctuate" in Robert Ferber and Hugh G. Wales, Editors, *Motivation and Market Behavior* (Homewood, Illinois: Richard D. Irwin, Inc., 1958), pp. 381-388.

tions representing a theory cannot for the most part be solved by standard analytic techniques to yield solutions for their decision variables.

The result of this constraint has been a failure by researchers in following up on the development of models with enough detail to describe adequately the phenomena being observed.[2] The extreme computation speed and programing flexibility of modern computers allows the researcher to build as complicated a theory as he desires, and still be confident that its overall implications may be computed for any given set of parameters and initial conditions.

However, optimal solutions are not guaranteed by computer simulation models, as they are when linear and quadratic programing or calculus can properly be applied to the problem being investigated. When linear or quadratic programing models can be used, the structure of rules for performing their calculations (or algorithms, as they are usually referred to) is such that optimal solutions *are guaranteed*. The test for using one of these techniques as an alternative to simulation, though, must be made in terms of the amount and kind of abstraction from the "real-world" situation made necessary by the rigid form of their structure.

Such difficulties are well illustrated by the researcher who encounters advertising-effectiveness problems after an initial exposure to statistical methods. His usual response to the problem is to build a simple regression model, relating sales to advertising expenditures. This he finds appealing because he knows he can apply standard statistical techniques and generate a correlation coefficient which will allow him to "predict" the sales response to a firm's advertising expenditures. The results of this model's predictions, however, will usually be poor enough to convince him that the model is much too simple (abstract) to handle his problem adequately.

If he persists in his search for an explanation of advertising phenomena, his next theory is likely to be expressed as a multiple regression model, with such additional independent variables as income levels, retail availability, and price considered along with advertising expenditures. Unfortunately the results are still unlikely to be satisfactory; and this model, as the first one, will lack sufficient predictive power.

The problem is that the variables in the system tend to influence each other *simultaneously;* and simple models are unlikely to predict or explain the underlying processes adequately.

For useful results to be achieved, this means that models rich in essential details must be constructed. Such detailed models are quite unlikely to fit the computational form demanded for analytic solution, and so must be studied by an application of simulation techniques.

[2] A good example of too much abstraction is Reilly's Law of Retail Gravitation. A version of this model may be found in C. H. McGregor, *Retail Management Problems* (Homewood, Illinois: Richard D. Irwin, Inc., 1962), p. 27.

Simulation Procedure

The role of the computer in simulation is as a computational device. Actually it does nothing more than could be done by a human being with a desk calculator, a pad of paper as a memory aid, and a *few years of spare time.*

The important aspect of both the computer and the human desk-calculator system is the quality of their operating instructions. Neither the computer nor simulation is a substitute for sound theory construction. This must precede *any* use of the computer, although the process of programing the model for the computer is a step-by-step logical process which may in fact aid in theory development by forcing every aspect of the model to be specified completely.[3]

What the computer does is to allow the model to be evaluated repeatedly when initial conditions, parameters, and current values for the variables have been supplied. Time paths for years of operation can be produced by a fast computer in only a few minutes!

One researcher has described a single evaluation of a simulation model as an experiment performed upon the model.[4] In the experiment the model has been operated for one cycle after all conditions affecting the outcome have been completely specified. By examining the results of many such experiments the response characteristics of the model can be discovered.

Such experimentation with the model may expose a time path which is completely at variance with the time path of the "real-world" system being simulated. Turning points may be overlooked; or perhaps the response characteristics of the model are unstable, with the result that the time path produced by the model is quite erratic. When this occurs, it may mean that the theory must be revised or even abandoned.

Only a small number of simulation studies have been attempted that are of interest to people in marketing. A few of these will be described.

Department Store Pricing Model

One of the earliest and more interesting of these was a simulation of a specific department of a major department store, in which the internal

---

[3] A description of how this process was conducted for one problem may be found in Alfred A. Kuehn and Ralph L. Day, "Simulation and Operational Gaming" in *Marketing and the Computer,* Wroe Alderson and Stanley J. Shapiro, Editors (Englewood Cliffs, N.J.: Prentice-Hall, 1963), pp. 234-247.

[4] Guy H. Orcutt, "Simulation of Economic Systems," *The American Economic Review,* Vol. 50 (December, 1960), pp. 893-907.

pricing and ordering decision rules of the department were modeled.[5] This model hypothesizes two general goals which serve as performance evaluation criteria. These are a sales goal and a markup goal. Decision making by the department takes place in response to problems associated with one or the other of these goals.

Nonfulfillment of these goals causes the department to search for methods of reducing the variance between the goal and the actual performance. Search takes place within the context of a well-defined list of alternatives, and continues until some means have been discovered for reducing the observed variance. Among the alternatives for variance reduction examined by the search procedure are markdown promotions directed toward stimulating sales, introduction of new merchandise to help sales or relieve pressure on markdowns, or even re-evaluations of the original goals.

Parts of the model were tested, and with encouraging results. In estimation of monthly sales, the model was able to predict 95% of such sales within 5%. The model was able to predict prices from a sample of invoices to the penny in 95.4% of the cases tried.

An interesting feature of this model is that it is not expressed mathematically, but consists mostly of fairly elaborate "switching rules" based on logical tests. Furthermore, the model is descriptive rather than normative in that it attempts to describe what is actually happening within the department rather than what should happen. Such a model affords a very good point of departure for any research aimed at improving the department's performance generally.

A Model for Retail Credit Applications

A credit-card application rejection rate considered to be high in relation to the industry's average rejection rate caused the Gulf Oil Corporation to develop a probability model which simulates the decision criteria of their human credit appraisers.[6]

The initial concern was to discover the importance imputed by credit appraisers to characteristics on application forms and credit reports (such as importance attached to age and occupation). As a means of finding which characteristics best classified the applicant as an acceptable or unacceptable credit risk, a sequential least squares analysis was used—ran-

[5] Richard M. Cyert, James G. March, and Chadwick G. Moore, "A Model of Retail Ordering and Pricing in a Department Store" in Ronald E. Frank, Alfred A. Kuehn, and William F. Massy, Editors, *Quantitative Techniques in Marketing Analysis* (Homewood, Illinois: Richard D. Irwin, Inc., 1962), pp. 502-522.

[6] Robert H. Nelson, Coordinator of Statistical Sampling, and Robert J. A. Pratt, Graduate School of Business, University of Pittsburgh and Consultant to Gulf Oil Corporation, "Problems in Retail Credit," internal publication by the Domestic Marketing Department, Gulf Oil Corporation.

dom samples of 500 accepted applicants and 500 applicants who were rejected were taken to develop the decision model.

The statistical procedure used sequentially adds the various characteristics to the least squares model, and tests them to see if they have added any significant predictive power to the model being constructed. The result of the analysis is a list of characteristics, and attendant weights, which allows the applicant to be labeled acceptable or unacceptable.

The resulting model was tested under two different conditions. It was used to process 191 applications in which the credit appraisers had decided that Credit Bureau reports were not necessary as additional information. Of the 191 applications, the model disagreed with the human appraiser on only 6 individuals. It rejected 4 applications that the appraiser had accepted, and it accepted 2 that he had rejected.

For 834 applications on which the additional information from Credit Bureau reports was used, the model did not do quite as well. It rejected 34 applications which were accepted by the human, and accepted 59 which the human had rejected. Its error rates, as compared with the human appraiser, were 3% and 11% respectively in the two tests.

The researchers then extended their model to a 2-stage process.

Stage I classified the applicants three ways: accepted, rejected, or Credit Bureau report needed before a classification can be determined.

Stage II then determined the final acceptance or rejection of the remaining applications, using the credit report as additional information. This 2-step model produced the results shown in the accompanying table:

Results From 2-Step Model
(1,474 applications)

Credit appraiser		Model decision (Stage I and II combined)	
Decision	Applicants	Acceptance	Rejections
Acceptance	968	887	81 [a]
Rejection	506	87 [a]	419
Total	1,474	974	500

[a] A total error rate of 11.4%.

A low acceptance criterion was established intentionally, in order to produce a bias toward accepting more of the human appraiser's rejections. By providing an objective criterion for acceptance, the model allows the proportion of acceptances to be raised or lowered by including the marginal applicant; that is, if expansion is desired, only the best of what would have been rejections are accepted. This bias was placed in the model to reduce what was considered to be a high rejection rate by the human appraisers.

Work with the model has led to solutions of several problems associated with retail credit applications. It is now possible to begin to relate the relative emphasis on certain characteristics (such as age) with the present value of an applicant's expected total revenue. Losses from bad accounts can also be investigated as a function of the sales expected to be lost as a result of an overall acceptance rate of only 63%. In addition, Stage I of the model has cut the use of Credit Bureau reports and resulted in immediate and direct cost savings. (The Credit Bureau report is used as an additional decision variable for 72% of the applications processed by the Credit Department.)

An extension of the model to include the process by which the Gulf Oil Corporation loses credit-card holders is being planned. The inclusion of this process will allow the simulation model to define the long-term distribution of credit-card holders (and the profits associated with such a distribution) for a number of different acceptance criteria. Comparisons among these distributions will allow the credit standards to be defined in terms of some long-run profit criteria.

A Model of the Detergent Market

The author is also experimenting with a simulation model of the detergent market.[7] The complicated nonlinear model attempts to consider most of the effects and interactions of the merchandising variables in the detergent industry controlled by competing detergent manufacturers.

CONSUMER CHOICE STRUCTURE

The consumer choice of brands in the model is based on the brand shifting model first developed by Alfred A. Kuehn.[8] In this model, sales for a brand are produced by two kinds of consumer purchasing behavior.

In the first of these, the consumer is treated as repurchasing the same brand he purchased last period because of habit. This demand, termed habitual demand, may be thought of as the core of a brand's sales, consisting of purchases by the brand's established customers. Although each

[7] Doyle L. Weiss, "Simulation of the Detergent Industry," in *Marketing Precision and Executive Action*, Charles H. Hindersman, Editor (Chicago: American Marketing Association, 1962), pp. 152-161.

[8] Alfred A. Kuehn, "A Model for Budgeting Advertising," in *Mathematical Models and Methods in Marketing*, Frank M. Bass, Mark R. Greene, Edgar A. Pessemier, Abraham Shuchman, Robert D. Buzzell, William Lazer, Donald L. Shawver, Chris A. Theodore, and George W. Wilson, Editors (Homewood, Illinois: Richard D. Irwin, Inc., 1960), pp. 315-348.

consumer has a unique probability of making this habitual buying response, determined by his recent purchase history and the length of time between purchases, the simulation model uses an average probability as a parameter representative of all the consumers in the market.

If the consumer is not making a habitual purchasing decision, he is a potential brand shifter for the current period. That is to say, the consumer considers all of the marketed brands as feasible alternatives. As a result, he is subject to competing influences from the marketing activities of all the available brands, although he may in fact repurchase the brand he purchased in the last period. The process underlying this kind of a decision to repurchase a brand is quite different from the one for habitual repurchases.

MARKET STRUCTURE

Because the model is dealing with products which retain brand identity and have distinct product characteristics, its demand function is unlike the market-clearing mechanism of pure competition.[9]

However, total industry demand is a function of several industry parameters, including price elasticity. For instance, total demand for the industry will expand (but not necessarily at the same rate) with an expansion of industry advertising and promotional expenditures. Industry demand in the model is also responsive to the price of the individual brands (actually an average price in which each brand's price is weighted by market share) and the level of consumer disposable income. A trend term is included in the industry demand function, to allow the effects of a growing, dying, or stable industry to be simulated and studied.

Marketers have long recognized that the end use for which a product is purchased will influence what the consumer prefers in terms of product characteristics. For example, the products of the detergent industry com-

---

[9] The actual industry demand function used in the model is the following:

$$Q_t = Q_o \cdot \left(\frac{p_t}{p_o} \right)^{\eta_p} \cdot \left(\frac{\overline{Et}}{Eo} \right)^{\eta_E} \cdot \left(\frac{Yt}{Yo} \right)^{\eta_Y} \cdot K^t$$

where: o   is a subscript implying a base or normal industry value for the subscripted value,

Q = demand in units

$\overline{p}$ = average industry price weighted by market share

$\overline{E}$ = total promotional expenditures by the industry

K = growth term for period to period trend effects

Y = disposable income (exogenous to this model)

η = elasticity constant determining the responsiveness of demand to changes in the variables

t = time period

peting in the dishwashing submarket (detergents for automatic dishwashing equipment are not considered) usually are promoted for their high-sudsing characteristics and their gentleness. By contrast, much of the promotional emphasis on products produced for the home laundry market seems to be on low sudsiness and a high washing power characteristic.

These differential effects of product characteristics on demand are handled in the simulation model as distinct submarkets. This does not mean that a consumer who is buying a detergent for dishwashing purposes cannot buy a brand generally thought to be more suitable for home laundry uses. It does mean, however, that a brand's physical product characteristics will have their greatest impact on those consumers making up the submarket for which it is most suitable.

INTERBRAND COMPETITIVE ASPECTS OF THE MODEL

Marketing researchers recognize more clearly than ever that the effects of the marketing variables such as price, advertising, retail availability, and the physical product characteristics interact together. In most cases they cannot effectively be "compartmentalized" and studied independently of each other.[10]

Each of these variables can be expected to influence both the sales position of the brands and the effectiveness of the other variables to such an extent that only poor predictions of the outcome of a promotion can be made in terms of the advertising budget and price alone.

Also, the timing of the sales force's efforts in providing shelf space and in-store promotional activities for the brand—along with advertising expenditures, pricing policy, and physical characteristics of the product— are important in sales outcome. It is in this complex area of interdependency that computer simulation models should make the greatest contribution to understanding the complete system of these interrelationships.

The model of the detergent industry attempts to explain how these interactions take place, and the effects they have on sales in a specific market. It relates the interdependent variables in what is believed to be a realistic and rational manner, so that the combined effects of the variables on sales may be observed and studied.

The manner in which the physical product characteristics are handled by the model provides a good example of its theoretical detail. The model considers three physical product characteristics: sudsiness, washing power, and gentleness. With washing power and gentleness, consumer reactions are fairly straightforward; that is, the more washing power and gentleness possessed by a brand, the more desirable that brand is for most consumers.

---

[10] Alfred A. Kuehn, "How Advertising Performance Depends on Other Marketing Factors," *Journal of Advertising Research,* Vol. 2 (March, 1962), pp. 2-10.

However, gentleness is relatively more important in the dishwashing sub-market, and washing power more important in the automatic-washer and general-purpose submarkets.

As to sudsing characteristics, though, this is not true. For certain uses such as dishwashing, suds are desired by the consumer, while for other purposes such as home laundry, an excess of suds may be thought of as interfering with the "cleaning action" and resulting in damage to the laundry equipment.

This means that we can consider consumer preferences to be distributed across a scale of sudsiness values, ranging from zero to some upper limit where demand is zero. Concentrations of demand will appear along the distribution as peaks occurring at values of the product characteristics most preferred for particular end uses. If other effects were equal, and if consumers were considered to purchase the brand nearest in sudsiness value to their preferences, then the relative effect of sudsiness for a brand would depend on its position on the sudsiness scale with respect to the position of competing brands, and the distribution of consumer preferences representing the various end uses.

The fact that consumers are not able to tell with perfect accuracy when the characteristics of the product they are considering represent their exact preferences was taken into consideration in developing the model. As the characteristics of the product being considered move farther away from the levels of the consumer's exact preferences, the probability of the consumer recognizing this difference is treated as increasing in a fashion which is consistent with empirical blind-product preference test data.[11]

In addition to the usual variables of price and advertising expenditures, inputs of sales-force size and a retail allowance are provided. The management may hire or fire salesmen and direct the allocation of their effort among brands; also, management may offer a retail allowance of $X per case of product sold. The computer model treats the allowance as if it were given to the retailer by the detergent manufacturer. The retailer passes on part of this price concession to the consumer in the form of a deal which serves to stimulate retail sales. If the manufacturer offers retail allowances too frequently, the promotional price effect is lost.

The interaction of a brand's advertising expenditure, retail allowance, allocation of sales-force effort, and market share determine the relative measure of a brand's retail availability. This measure attempts to simulate the effect of retail distribution, the allocation of shelf space, and in-store special display promotions on the brand's sales. Once these interaction mechanisms are tested and developed to the point where they are reason-

[11] Also see Alfred A. Kuehn and Ralph L. Day, "Strategy of Product Quality," *Harvard Business Review,* Vol. 40 (November-December, 1962), pp. 100-110.

ably correct determinants of sales effectiveness, guidance can be provided to marketing executives in proper allocation of resources to these variables.

RESEARCH WITH THE MODEL

The model is capable of simulating any number of firms which have one or more brands. In practice, the only limitations to the number of brands and firms that can be simulated are the speed and capacity of the computing system being utilized.

With minor changes in the parameters and structure, the model will simulate a wide range of market conditions, including those of imperfect markets as well as the less complex market structures of perfect competition, monopoly, and oligopoly.

Research is being undertaken to discover the relationships underlying the market variables of advertising, price, retail availability, and product characteristics at competitive equilibrium for a variety of market structures. In particular, the effects of variable costs, the number of brands in the market, and the distribution of brands among firms are being studied. By varying these values and then searching the model directly with the aid of a computer for the attendant equilibrium positions, the nature of the effects can be isolated.

This research is expected to yield answers to questions of market strategy for products whose characteristics are quite different from those of competing products. Problems connected with the allocation of resources among brands competing in different submarkets are expected to be partially solved. In addition, the question of how a new product should be introduced with respect to timing and the promotional variables controlled by the firm is being analyzed.

The model has also been programed in the form of a marketing game as well as a market simulation.[12] This allows experimentation with alternative strategies to be done in the "synthetic" market instead of the real one, and without danger of large sums of money being lost.

Provisions have been made in the game to enable the players to purchase research reports. These are estimates of various aspects of competitive marketing activities, such as price, advertising expenditures, market share, retail stockout, and distribution. There are additional provisions to permit the firms to develop and improve new products, to copy competitor's products, and to conduct blind-product paired-comparison preference tests.

The usual claims made for the educational value of business games can

---

[12] Alfred A. Kuehn and Doyle L. Weiss, "CIT Marketing Game," Research in Marketing Project Paper No. 4, Graduate School of Industrial Administration, Carnegie Institute of Technology.

be made for this one.[13] However, since it is a relatively realistic game, the participant not only gains experience in operating in a dynamic world of business, but also discovers some institutional facts about marketing interrelationships.

Implications

It would be both foolish and presumptuous to predict that simulation will solve completely all of marketing's problems. Indeed, if it is very successful it may even be instrumental in exposing new problems which are now unformulated, because the current state of theory is not well enough developed to recognize them.

However, by making more realistic systems of marketing variables amenable to analysis, simulation techniques allow marketing people to move even closer to a practical theory of marketing.

[13] William R. Dill, James R. Jackson, and James W. Sweeney, *Proceedings of the Conference on Business Games as Teaching Devices* (New Orleans: Tulane University), 1961.

> The computer is flashing with
> dazzling speed across the pan-
> orama of marketing—which
> takes in the entire relationship
> between the design of a prod-
> uct, the manufacturer, seller,
> buyer, and user.

23

Computers Begin to Solve
the Marketing Puzzle

ROUTINELY, EVERY EVENING at J. C. Penney stores across the country, a chain of events begins that reflects the changing nature not only of retailing but of every other marketing practice.

The small, punched tickets that have been taken off merchandise sold during the day are dispatched to either New York City or Los Angeles. There the tickets, coded to describe the merchandise to which they were attached until it was sold, are fed into machines that transfer the information to punched cards. From cards, the data can be put on magnetic tape or fed directly into electronic digital computers.

The computers have been programmed to know what each store should stock of so-called "staples"—men's shirts, socks, ladies' hose, lingerie, and similar goods.

Every two weeks, a computer will match a store's planned stock level against merchandise sold in that store; and, when a store needs merchandise, the computer will send out an order to buy, along with shipping instructions.

Theory into fact. A retail store doesn't have to be as large as Penney—1,700 stores and $2-billion annual sales—to use computers in this way to

Reprinted from the April 17, 1965, issue of *Business Week* by special permission. Copyrighted © 1965 by McGraw-Hill, Inc., pp. 114-115 ff.

control its stock level and ordering procedures. A score or so of stores around the country are using some variant of the system. In fact, some local chains, such as Woodward & Lothrop in Washington and Goldblatt Bros. in Chicago, use more complex and sophisticated systems to give them daily reports of stocks and sales.

In theory, it has always been true that a store's buyers could give management a daily report of stock conditions and what was sold the preceding day—just as in theory someone in almost any business gets the pertinent marketing figures every day. But as a matter of hard, cruel fact—as opposed to theory—this just hasn't been so.

The importance of what Penney and other companies are doing is simply this: They are turning the computer with its fantastic computational speed into a new marketing tool. It may be just a big adding machine, as is often said, but it adds at a speed that hardly gives a man a chance to have a second thought.

Legerdemain. A customer of Owens-Illinois Glass Co. had that brought home to him recently. He had ordered some containers from O-I's Libbey Products Div., changed his mind, and called to cancel the order. He couldn't cancel; the shipment was already at his plant.

This disconcerting legerdemain was possible because Owens-Illinois is one of the hundreds of U.S. companies that are managing production, finished inventory, and distribution with a mathematical system controlled by computers.

O-I's data processing headquarters in Toledo (10 computers and 100 people) is connected by wire to 100 different sales and manufacturing locations. An order comes in, the computer determines whether the product ordered is in stock, indicates where it is, and sends a release and shipping order to the warehouse, or orders to a plant to make it.

What the customer who couldn't cancel was relying on is an order-shipping-billing procedure that is passing from the industrial scene. Normally, weeks elapsed between the time a salesman took your order and you got the shipment and the invoice. At Owens-Illinois, says Thomas H. Browning, manager of data processing, electronic data processing cuts the time to no more than 35 hours.

Over the wire. Helping to reduce the order-shipping-billing time is a system tying the computer that manages inventory to a data transmission network employing any one of a group of devices known as a Data-Phone. It is an adaptation of a normal telephone, and is used with what the trade calls a "terminal" (the exact designation varies according to who makes it).

Together they transmit voice and numeric signals. Instead of a salesman dropping around to fill out an order pad, orders are filed by punched card or tape over wires direct to the supplier's receiving equipment, where they are put into form to go into the computer.

At Beals, McCarthy & Rogers, Inc., a large Buffalo industrial distributor, the combination of computer-managed inventory and Data-Phone ordering in the past four years has meant a reduction of inventory of $200,000 and a sales increase of more than $2-million, according to Frederick L. Davis, the company's marketing manager. When you can know faster, and fill quicker, what your customers are ordering, you can carry a smaller stock.

It works if you're the customer, too. When you can get faster delivery you can carry a smaller inventory. Davis reports it is common now for his customers to do without general stores and tool cribs entirely. Normally, placing an order costs $15 and up; a BM&R customer has reduced this by 17%.

Taking over. The computer is flashing with dazzling speed across the panorama of marketing—which takes in the entire relationship between the designer of a product, the manufacturer, seller, buyer, and user.

Electronic data processing not only is managing inventory in nationwide chains of retail stores; it is telling large department stores which customers are the best prospects for certain merchandise, is "advising" a food company when to offer special "deals," is giving rifle-accuracy to the calls of an apparel manufacturer's salesmen, is forecasting crop yields for a canner, giving greater precision to the selection of media by advertising agencies.

There are still plenty of skeptics. A computer guided by programmers unfamiliar with the specific industry so thoroughly fouled up one heavy equipment maker's replacement parts production that it took two years to untangle. Most retailers, particularly supermarkets, are loath to use computers as anything but bookkeepers.

Too late? Strictly marketing uses of EDP, going beyond inventory management, are still uncommon in U.S. business. But those who have sampled its magic are convinced the hour is late for the laggards. In a shockingly matter-of-fact way, a department store man in an Eastern metropolis says: "Our competition is finished; they can't compete with us any more. They started too late with their [EDP] systems and now we are getting so much of the business they'll never be able to afford the system to do the job."

His competition is about as old, as well-established, and as outwardly prosperous as his own store. But in the age of the computer, the hands on marketing's clock are at half-past eleven—30 minutes before the witching hour. The use of EDP is about to become routine in many marketing operations which until now have defied systemization.

Only a year ago, Richard F. Neuschel, a director of McKinsey & Co., wrote in *Marketing and the Computer:* "In none of the major functions of American business has the impact of the computer been so lightly felt as in marketing. Yet, in none of the major functions is its potential so great."

I. The Data Collectors Go to Work

The potential of EDP in marketing is great simply because of a pervading belief that there are not enough good, hard numbers in marketing to make a fair-sized computer work up a mild sweat.

In the book, *Decision Exercises in Marketing,* Dr. Arnold Corbin, professor of marketing at New York University, Dr. George Blagowidow, and Dr. Claire Corbin, write: "To many people, marketing . . . is regarded as a business function in which most decisions are highly qualitative in nature and strongly rooted in intangible factors. . . . Hence marketing decisions are often made on the basis of hunch, guess, or intuition, rather than on a rational analysis of the measurable relationships among the principal variables involved."

John F. Stolle, a Booz, Allen, & Hamilton vice-president and specialist in operations research, comments that "marketing is the most difficult area to get quantification in."

You hear that strain throughout business: EDP, to do any good, needs hard data, tons of them, needs them fast—and there is a lack of data all through the marketing stream.

The automobile industry is about the only one that really knows who buys each of its products, where the customers live, and other useful bits of information about them. In contrast, another consumer goods manufacturer refuses to advertise in Indianapolis because his records show no sales there; actually, his Chicago distributor serves Indianapolis retailers, but the manufacturer's own positive information about sales stops at the distributor level.

Bridging the gap. Yet it simply isn't true that data do not exist in marketing; they exist in probably greater quantities than in any other business function. Until now there has never been a means to collect the information or to analyze it fast enough for it to be useful.

With the "peripheral" equipment associated with the computer—input-output devices such as the Data-Phone, tape, ticket and card readers, and high-speed printers, for feeding information to the computer and getting it out—the vast gap between collection of information and its analysis has been bridged.

Archibald J. McGill, an industry manager for the Data Processing Div. of International Business Machines Corp., figures that only 5% of the solution of what he calls the distribution problem is the computer, and

95% is the system. "Input-output devices are of more significance in distribution than the computer itself," he says.

There are computers whirring and blinking throughout U.S. business—for the accounting department. Now, with the input and output devices, the marketing department also is finding ways to get information for the computer to work on.

THE MACHINE KNOWS WHAT'S IN STOCK

While the retailer is by no means in the van in the use of EDP, what's being done in stores around the country is exciting because it shows how much can be done.

You can see the future best, perhaps, at Woodward & Lothrop, Inc., in Washington, D.C. There, C. Robert McBrier, vice-president, finance, has installed what many authorities think is the most advanced EDP system in the country. Soon, Woodward & Lothrop executives every morning will get an 81-page report that, for each of the company's nine stores, will give the previous day's sales by store, by department, by dollar amounts, and a comparison with the previous year-to-date and the trend of sales. A record of sales for selected items will also be available.

The key to this astonishing flood of figures is a special cash register, for which McBrier designed the keyboard. There are eight keys across and nine from top to bottom, in addition to 13 control keys. The salesperson can punch in everything store management needs to know; every detail of every transaction is recorded on optical tape.

Each evening the information on the tape is read by an optical scanner and "exploded" into separate pieces for accounts receivable, accounts payable, inventory management, reordering and other store functions.

More and more. When additional equipment is received later this year and next, Woodward & Lothrop's system will include a direct connection from cash register to computer, a voice response from the computer when a clerk checks the credit standing of a customer, and even a daily report on the sales performance of each person on the selling floor.

Other big department store operations have many elements of what Woodward & Lothrop is doing; Joseph Horne Co., in Pittsburgh, is one step away from a voice response on credit authorization—the computer keeps up to date a list of accounts that, for one reason or another, should not be honored. Bullock's-Magnin Co. on the West Coast has its charge accounts so well organized they can be used for imaginative merchandising.

Goldblatt Bros., Inc., in Chicago, one of the most sophisticated EDP users in the country, even has a Data-Phone system to transmit daily sales reports of tapes from its 29 stores in the area to its State Street headquarters store.

Buyers' new role. Management's daily report of stock condition is already changing one hallowed role in department stores: the preeminence of the buyer. Since retailing began, buyers have been the leading figures, responsible for keeping their stores stocked with salable merchandise. But because of the enormous increase in the number of items a store now carries, the buyer has become too busy with a physical count of stock to try to know what the customer wants and when.

At EDP-equipped stores, management knows before the buyer does what's moving and what isn't. Some buyers find this disconcerting indeed. In the words of Jack Jacobson, Goldblatt's director of electronic data processing, they "don't trust computers and are not analytically inclined."

But others use the freedom EDP has given them to get out on the floor once more to see what customers are like. Jack Hanson, senior vice-president of Macy's New York, says buyers now have a chance to "get back into the market where they were 30 years ago, to get better prices and better merchandise."

Penney's merchandise planning and control manager, Emerson Tolle, sees another advantage to the end of physical stock-taking (Penney's counts stock only every quarter): "Instead of being under the counter counting stock, the sales clerk can be standing up taking care of customers."

Precise weapon. Putting accounts receivable—customer's charge account records—on the computer might seem to be only another accounting procedure. But it can be a merchandising weapon of profitable precision. Macy's has more than 1.3 million charge accounts on magnetic tape. Depending on what it is told to do, the computer will break up those accounts any way the store wants them—by alphabet, by house number, by size of average charge.

Not long ago Macy's had its computer print out a list of all charge customers of the Herald Square store who lived in four counties, and invite them to a special after-hours sale of furniture and furnishings.

The results can't be measured precisely because nothing like it had been done before; but compared with other special sales using radio and direct mail, the computer-based effort cost less and sold more.

SMALLER STOCK, BUT MORE STORES

In food retailing, the problems are different from those in a department store, and EDP has scarcely penetrated the retail end of food distribution.

For one thing, food retailing is about the most hidebound of all businesses dealing with the consumer. For another, a food store's after-tax profit is normally less than 2% on sales—so operators look at the cost of EDP and blanch. Yet, their low rate of return is in itself a reason to get involved with EDP; it offers opportunities for cutting costs and raising profits.

In food processing and warehousing, though, EDP has cut deep, mostly by use of an IBM-developed system known as Impact (Inventory Management Program and Control Technique). All major food manufacturers, as well as other companies that sell through supermarkets—Scott Paper Co. and Procter & Gamble Co., for example—have data links between sales offices, plants, distribution and shipping points, and are managing production, warehousing, and shipping by computer programmed economics.

Latest link. The newest trend is a data link between a manufacturer and a distributor for the automatic ordering of staple items.

This has barely started. Kellogg Co. warehouses are linked with warehouses of Safeway Stores, Inc., on the West Coast and of Wakefern Food Corp., a distributor for a group of New Jersey supermarkets. Pillsbury Co. has a similar hookup with Spartan Stores, Inc., a small chain in the Grand Rapids (Mich.) area—after having proved the procedure in experiments with Kroger Co. and Super Valu Stores, Inc.

Savings with this sort of system can be sensational; James Rude, Pillsbury director of information services and systems, quotes a Spartan official as saying the chain can save enough in lead time and storage to build another store.

There is no longer any question about the marketing power of a data link between supplier and customer. The clincher is what has happened in industrial selling.

SAVE CUSTOMERS AND PREPARE FOR SYSTEMS

The data link between supplier and customer originated on the West Coast with Ducommun, Inc., an industrial distributor, about three years ago [BW Jul.21'62p64]. It is now in use all over the country, but has reached perhaps its most influential and precedent-setting level in the Houston area.

"Ordermation"—a very well-suited term coined by Industrial Distribution, a McGraw-Hill magazine—was just beginning to be known in Houston when J. K. Bevel, purchasing agent at Hughes Tool Co., took a worry to Jack P. Cunningham, whose Cunningham Bearing Co. does an annual volume of about $1.5-million. Bevel wanted to cut down on the time his buyers were spending in placing repetitive orders, and thought an automatic ordering system would do it.

But he was aware of one danger: When you have a number of distributors in an area, each may use a different system; so a customer dealing with more than one distributor could wind up with a roomful of incompatible systems. Bevel warned Cunningham that, as a customer, he would use one data transmission system and expect his suppliers to conform. But that way, he pointed out, a single distributor could wind up with as many as 18 different systems.

Taking off. From this came the Houston Industrial Distributors Assn. With an IBM salesman coordinating the efforts—the IBM 1001 in conjunction with the Data-Phone is the common transmission device—the association now has 30 distributors "on line" to 10 customers. It will take 40 to 50 customers for the system to remain economically feasible. Cunningham hopes the idea "will really take off once the results begin coming in from the customers already participating."

Although the Houston operation is being studied by groups of industrial distributors in other parts of the country—and is bound to be a pattern— ordermation has not aroused universal enthusiasm. Distributors' reservations come mainly from unfamiliarity with EDP; some fear the system will make them lose contact with customers.

That fear is not shared by Owens-Illinois Glass Co.'s Thomas Browning. He asks: "How much does it mean, for example, if we can cut delivery time for a good customer from six days to one day? It may not mean much in one case; in another, it may mean that we have retained business that might have gone elsewhere. How do you measure that?"

Goal. The data link alone, of course, cannot make a radical cut in delivery time. It is an essential input, though, to a procedure that goes a long way toward the goal of building a "total information system." And that is the goal at Owens-Illinois, at General Mills, Scott Paper, Procter & Gamble, Hotpoint Div. of General Electric, and other long-time EDP users. Westinghouse Electric Corp. is one of the very few companies that already has a total system.

To such companies, inventory management, sales analysis, a rapid order-shipping-billing cycle, though rewarding in themselves, eventually become as routine as the coffee break. But they are a necessary preliminary to more complicated and challenging EDP work—getting the information to use in making the decisions that bring higher profits.

The ultimate question. There's an example of where this is heading in the Carborundum Co., which has been using computers for about 10 years and, says Group Vice-President Robert W. Lear, is "still experimenting." Carborundum, with more than 1,000 programs on computers, is ready for the next plateau, which is defined best by a series of questions Lear asked in a recent speech:

"Which of our districts, salesmen, distributors, customers, markets, and products are the real profit producers? How much does it cost to make a sales call? What does it cost to process an order item? If it's four bucks, can we afford to continue accepting five-buck or even twenty-five-buck orders without some kind of a surcharge or premium?

"What was the return on investment from our last promotion? Did we even try to calculate it? Which is more profitable—a direct sale, or one through a distributor? Did our last price adjustment take into consideration the distribution cost for each item, or did we just study our factory gross margins and assume an arbitrary average for everything below the line?"

Those questions get to the heart of the reason for using computers in marketing, for you can't answer them without getting data. Then, for the first time in marketing, management can ask the question: "What if . . . ?"

II. Marketing by Mathematics

Dr. Wendell R. Smith, president of the Marketing Science Institute, tells of a former business associate who constantly used computers to ask the question: "What if . . . ?" He explained to Smith: "I can ask the computer without starting a rumor. If I went to the controller and asked him what would happen to our profits if we dropped a certain product line, it would be all over the plant before lunch that we were getting ready to go out of that particular business."

Storage in a computer of mathematical models that simulate a market or that duplicate a marketing situation is perhaps the ultimate contribution EDP can make to marketing.

C. A. Swanson, manager of P&G's Data Processing Systems Dept., lists four things his company expects from EDP: savings of money, accuracy, speed, and "doing things not otherwise possible."

There is wide agreement that model-building and simulation is perhaps the most significant of those things not otherwise possible without a computer. As of now, an electronic digital computer is the only device that can handle variable on top of variable and give management a choice of alternatives while there's still time to make a decision.

Changing management. In a masterful little book, *Mathematical Models and Marketing Management,* published by the Harvard Business School last year, Prof. Robert D. Buzzell wrote: "The model-builder offers a general, systematic approach to the analysis of management problems. To the extent that this approach is accepted and implemented, fundamental changes may take place in the practice of marketing management."

The biggest change that model-building is bringing about in marketing management is almost defamatory to mention: It is forcing management to plan, and to define its goals. To John Stolle, of Booz, Allen & Hamilton, one of the things that has slowed down the use of EDP and model-building in marketing is simply the fact that "it exposes the non-planners."

As Buzzell brings out, few developments in marketing have churned up so much skepticism and downright suspicion among marketing executives as model-building and simulation. The man who rose through the ranks from salesman to vice-president for marketing usually has little sympathy for the "fellow who's never met a payroll"—and into that category fall most of the mathematicians who are skilled at model-building and simulation.

But already models are regulating some marketing programs.

IT'S BETTER THAN A CRYSTAL BALL

Just about a year ago, Chrysler Corp.'s top management asked its planners the sort of question with which all marketing efforts must begin, for it was about the future.

"Can you tell us what the market for heavy trucks will be in 1970?"

The market analysts broke out the significant components of the heavy truck market for every year back to World War II. They determined the relationship of truck sales, by weight class, to population, national income, industrial production, and so on.

In about a month, they had a mathematical model—a simulation—of the heavy truck market. They found that of 36 variables in the model only about a dozen had substantial significance. Applying these variables in different combinations, they plotted the range for heavy truck sales in 1970.

Shortly afterward, Chrysler made an effort to merge with Mack Trucks, Inc., but was restrained by the Justice Dept.

What's new? There was nothing new in the Chrysler people's approach to the problem. Examination of past relationships—multiple regression analysis—is a standard statistical technique, and mathematical models are ancient.

The new thing was the speed with which the analysts were able to process an enormous amount of data and in only a month or so give management the information needed for a decision. That speed was due to the electronic computer.

Light on lamps. General Electric Co. (one of its divisions was the very first to put the computer to work on business problems, in 1954) has at least two models routinely assisting marketing management. One is in the Photo Lamp Dept. This division has 2,000 distributors, who customarily order in September (Christmas is the peak selling time for photo lamps) and pay in January.

The model is constructed on the assumption that each distributor has an interest problem; it takes into account 25 different types of distributors and interest rates and arrangements. It is designed to give answers to the question: What will happen if we let distributors delay payment—will they order more lamps?

At one of GE's heavy apparatus operations, a model is producing results that you'd expect only from a ouija board. This division sells on a bid basis, and the computer model is programmed to propose bids on the likelihood of what competitive bids will be. Says a GE man: "They have been amazingly accurate."

Routine. Simulation with computer models also is routine at all of the big package goods companies such as P&G, Pillsbury, General Foods, Libby, McNeill & Libby, and General Mills. Usually, companies such as these test in models the presumed results of price changes and promotions and what the probabilities are of competitive responses.

Producers of consumer durables use models to forecast sales. International Minerals & Chemical Corp. has a model of its complete agricultural chemical business (65% of the company's total volume), which has a strange cycle: Its year begins in July, but no fertilizer sales are made until the following spring.

Surprised admen. Models were at the root of all the hoopla in advertising agency circles a year or so ago about using computers to select media. The intention was to simulate a market area, then test the exposure gained by differing combinations of media buys. The problem, to a large extent, was proper data. The agencies didn't have it. Now they are collecting it—and are finding some strange byproducts.

At Leo Burnett Co., Inc., accumulation of demographic and economic data for one account showed a wide open area for a new product. At another agency, the collection of data showed that the agency's principal client should have very high on its magazine schedule one of the "confession" books. The magazine has never made a presentation to the agency —and the client is not yet ready to concede that his customers have such reading tastes.

The agencies are still far from satisfied with the data that can be obtained. The biggest hole is pointed out by Seymour Banks, a vice-president at Burnett: "What happens when people are exposed to an ad?" The agencies, meanwhile, are doing the best they can with what they have.

The top agencies all have simulation models; Norman Sondak, data processing director at J. Walter Thompson Co., says: "We continue to build models closer and closer to reality." And at several agencies, work is beginning on models that simulate test markets.

BRINGING MARKETING INTO MANAGEMENT

Advertising practitioners have always presumed that what they do is more art than science. So it may seem strange that all of the larger agencies now have people practicing operations research, which is presumed to be a science—the science of management. In reality it is not strange at all, for part of operations research deals with the weighing of alternatives—and the advertising man may have more numeric alternatives to deal with than anybody.

A media man with one ad and 30 media where he can spot it can be confronted with more than one billion combinations. The computer—that big adding machine—is the only way to run quickly through those combinations and weed out the obviously worthless.

What combinations remain are subject to management decision. The example used is in advertising, but it could just as well be in other marketing functions. Throughout marketing these days you are finding the computer used to weed out the obviously worthless things to do, leaving management with only a few alternatives to consider—sometimes, even, alternatives leading to a go or no-go decision:

What would be the returns now, compared to 60 days from now, on a cents-off promotion? Would it be more efficient to ship to Point A from Plant 1, or build a new distribution location to serve Point A and a potential future Point B? Would it be more economic to double our order for fast-moving baby food and receive shipments every other week rather than every week, even though it ties up more capital? Would it be more profitable to kill immediately Old Product, the life cycle of which is ending, and use the resources to push New Product harder?

Total. Decisions such as these involve determining the proper allocation of a company's total resources—in other words, operations research. Only now are the numbers so necessary for operations research being assembled for the marketing function, for only now is there a way to work with them: the computer. The more EDP sophistication pervades marketing, the closer a company moves toward a total management information system, toward true operations research. Says John Stolle, the OR man at Booz, Allen & Hamilton: "When we add marketing to our collection of trophies, we will be able to build models of total business systems."

It will still be some years before marketing's scalp hangs from the belt of the OR man, but the way marketing data already are being used indicates some changes the future may bring.

III. Big Brother Will Always Watch

What's ahead for marketing because of EDP is summed up pithily by Michael H. Halbert, technical director of the Marketing Science Institute: "A man can no longer get away with the excuse 'We've thought about it, but we don't know how to get it.' "

Today, if "it" exists in numbers, or can be assigned numerical values, "it" can be used in an EDP system. What this means, explains Robert G. Dee, vice-president, marketing, at RCA Electronic Data Processing Div., is that in the future "marketing staffs are going to get a greater amount of direction, and get a better hit value for the money spent."

One of the first groups to feel the effects of this will be the salesmen— no matter what they sell.

Bobbie Brooks, Inc., Cleveland-based manufacturer of ladies' sportswear, presents a fairly common example of what is on the way. Each week, the salesman gets a report showing the current orders and past activity of the stores in his area. This tells him where he should be spending his time.

Bobbie Brooks also prints out a report of each salesman's results by style, color, and frequency of order. "By looking at the report," says Burton L. Kamberg, vice-president, "our supervisors can tell if a man has perhaps prejudged a garment and left it in his car rather than taking it into the stores." If he's taking Thursdays off, or avoiding certain stores, that shows up, too.

"The salesman gets used to living in a goldfish bowl," Kamberg says, "and we don't stress the Big Brother side of the computer, but the helpful side. It gives the salesman an excellent selling tool. He can, for example, tell his customers what styles are going best across the country, and help them in their purchasing."

DEATH OF A SALESMAN, BIRTH OF A CONSULTANT

The computer not only is changing the selling function; it is going to change the salesman. He will have to know far more about merchandising than he does now; he will have to know far more about his customer's business and how it fits into an EDP system—already, some food companies report that their salesmen have had to show distributors how to fit new products into the IBM Impact system, which began with food distributors. In short, the salesman will have to be more of a consultant than ever.

Salesman's week. Herbert M. Cleaves, senior vice-president of General Foods Corp., describes the week of a food salesman in the computer age —but it could just as well be any salesman:

Monday, the salesman calls on a major food chain, passes right by the buyer and goes to the chain's home economist to ask her support for a new recipe that will be used in a regional promotion. Next, he discusses details of the promotion's advertising program with the chain's advertising manager, and of store displays with the merchandising manager.

Tuesday, the salesman goes from store to store explaining the promotion to the managers and making suggestions for tie-ins and displays. Wednesday, he is in the chain's warehouse to learn how his company can pack a product differently to save the customer money.

Thursday, the salesman is back in the stores, to explain a new shelving arrangement his own company's market planners had worked out to solve a particular problem. The salesman spends all day Friday in his home office working with his district sales analyst on a presentation to a chain that does not carry his products.

The week has passed, Cleaves emphasizes, and the salesman "hasn't personally made a traditional sales pitch or taken an order." The orders have been transmitted electronically, "and his supervisor knows before he does how well his various marketing efforts are being translated into orders."

Eyes and ears. Data transmission devices cast a long shadow, blotting out the routine calls that salesmen have been accustomed to make. So in the future the salesman who now spends a good part of his time writing orders is going to have to spend more time digging out new accounts, and ideas for new products.

He will have one other, potentially enormously valuable function. He will be his company's eyes and ears, its intelligence agent, in his territory, compiling information on market growth and development, competitive efforts, and everything his company needs to know.

LOTS OF PRODUCTS AND PLANS FOR RETAILERS

In perhaps no area of marketing is EDP going to make as many changes as in retailing—which lags not only in use of EDP, but frequently in modern business thinking.

In a study of department store control systems, Douglas J. Dalrymple, assistant professor of business administration at the University of California at Los Angeles, found "that a small minority of the merchandising executives . . . believed that stock turnover was an important control factor, but to most executives it was only a vague concept of secondary importance." Yet, fast stock turnover was the weapon the discounters turned loose on department stores 15 years ago. The higher the turnover, the higher the profit on a constant amount of money used in the business.

But the computer is forcing retailers to become aware of the importance of stock turnover.

The EDP way. Stock turnover is usually about four times a year for general merchandise and about twenty times for dry groceries. There's a traditional way to turn it faster: Simply sell more without carrying a higher inventory. But it's a rare merchant who can do that.

The EDP way to get a higher turnover is by keeping such fresh data on sales that you know what's moving fast and what isn't, and by having a data hookup that will give you automatic replenishment of the fast-moving or high-profit items. In food retailing, one estimate is that a 24-

hour replenishment cycle will reduce inventory by 30%, without creating out-of-stock situations that hurt sales.

In general merchandising, Seymour Helfant, head of the Small Stores Div. of the National Retail Merchants Assn., says he has reports of stores using EDP that lower their inventory by 25% and increase profits by 25%. And a specialty store that formerly turned its stock six times a year has added one full turn.

Analysis of information handled by a store's EDP system can also guide store executives in when, what, and how to promote.

Big and small. The benefits of EDP are not reserved for the big stores and chains. "Any retailer, regardless of size, will be able to be on-line to a big processing center," says James Hotchkiss, assistant director of product planning of National Cash Register Co., which probably has more experience than any other computer manufacturer with the problems of small retailers. NCR, of course, has data processing centers throughout the country [BW Aug.8'64,p66], as do GE, IBM, and other computer manufacturers. NRMA is sponsoring a cooperative processing center for small retailers.

An example of what a data processing center can do for small retailers is found at Santoro Management Consultants, Inc., in Houston. Santoro has 60 clients—whose volumes range from $50,000 to $500,000—for whom it provides a full package: budgets, advertising, merchandising, sales analysis and projection, inventory records. Says Mrs. Daisy Strother, of Fort Worth: "The service took the butterflies out of my stomach. We know which department is making money . . . our buying is controlled, dead merchandise eliminated and we have reorder money."

At present, most of the small stores mail or deliver tapes to the processing centers. But when Hotchkiss says small stores can be "on-line," he means a direct data link to some establishment using a computer. Once such a link is created, it will drive right through a barrier that (excepting, again, only the automobile business) still separates a manufacturer from sure knowledge of what's happening on the retail level.

A few months ago, B. S. Durant, president of RCA Sales Corp., did a little dreaming for a group of marketing executives. RCA, in common with other consumer electronics producers, is always in doubt as to how much of its product is in distributors' warehouses and how much is moving out of retailers' doors.

Durant began by conceding that a small retailer will probably never be able to afford a computer, "but he could afford a low-cost transactor of some type. . . . Before the dealer goes home at night, he would put the transactor device on standby. Somewhere along about a quarter after two, a central computer would interrogate the transactor and take from it the data covering the dealer's daily business transactions." Durant offered a new, and provocative thought: The independent distributor might have that central computer and be the retailer's data processing center.

If the distributor's computer could interrogate the retailer's transactor, then each night the manufacturer's computer could interrogate the distributor's computer. The next morning, the manufacturer's executives would have—for the first time in their experience—actual records of their product sales at retail the day before.

Gleaming vistas. This opens vistas that gleam so brightly that any marketing man has to shield his eyes to avoid snow blindness. New product performance could be gauged day-by-day and promotion money deployed for maximum effectiveness. A product that isn't going to make it could be withdrawn from the market before it hurt either profits or reputation significantly. When you know precisely what is selling where, and when, you can identify your customers, plan future promotions intelligently, simulate all sorts of situations.

You would even know enough to advertise in Indianapolis.

B. PRODUCT DECISIONS

Success in planning marketing activities requires precise utilization of both product differentiation and market segmentation as components of marketing strategy.

24

Product Differentiation and Market Segmentation as Alternative Marketing Strategies

WENDELL R. SMITH

DURING THE DECADE OF THE 1930's, the work of Robinson and Chamberlin resulted in a revitalization of economic theory. While classical and neo-classical theory provided a useful framework for economic analysis, the theories of perfect competition and pure monopoly had become inadequate as explanations of the contemporary business scene. The theory of perfect competition assumes homogeneity among the components of both the demand and supply sides of the market, but diversity or heterogeneity had come to be the rule rather than the exception. This analysis reviews major marketing strategy alternatives that are available to planners and merchandisers of products in an environment characterized by imperfect competition.

Reprinted from the *Journal of Marketing*, national quarterly publication of the American Marketing Association, Volume 21, No. 1 (July, 1956), pp. 3-8.

Diversity in Supply

That there is a lack of homogeneity or close similarity among the items offered to the market by individual manufacturers of various products is obvious in any variety store, department store, or shopping center. In many cases the impact of this diversity is amplified by advertising and promotional activities. Today's advertising and promotion tends to emphasize appeals to *selective* rather than *primary* buying motives and to point out the distinctive or differentiating features of the advertiser's product or service offer.

The presence of differences in the sales offers made by competing suppliers produces a diversity in supply that is inconsistent with the assumptions of earlier theory. The reasons for the presence of diversity in specific markets are many and include the following:

1. Variations in the production equipment and methods or processes used by different manufacturers of products designed for the same or similar uses.
2. Specialized or superior resources enjoyed by favorably situated manufacturers.
3. Unequal progress among competitors in design, development, and improvement of products.
4. The inability of manufacturers in some industries to eliminate product variations even through the application of quality control techniques.
5. Variations in producers' estimates of the nature of market demand with reference to such matters as price sensitivity, color, material, or package size.

Because of these and other factors, both planned and uncontrollable differences exist in the products of an industry. As a result, sellers make different appeals in support of their marketing efforts.

Diversity or Variations in Consumer Demand

Under present-day conditions of imperfect competition, marketing managers are generally responsible for selecting the over-all marketing strategy or combination of strategies best suited to a firm's requirements at any particular point in time. The strategy selected may consist of a program designed to bring about the *convergence* of individual market demands for a variety of products upon a single or limited offering to the market. This is often accomplished by the achievement of product differentiation through advertising and promotion. In this way, variations in the demands of individual consumers are minimized or brought into line by means of effective use of appealing product claims designed to make a satisfactory volume of demand *converge* upon the product or product line being promoted. This strategy was once believed to be essential as the marketing counterpart to standardization and mass production in manufacturing because of the rigidities imposed by production cost considerations.

In some cases, however, the marketer may determine that it is better to accept *divergent* demand as a market characteristic and to adjust product lines and marketing strategy accordingly. This implies ability to merchandise to a heterogeneous market by emphasizing the precision with which a firm's products can satisfy the requirements of one or more distinguishable market segments. The strategy of product differentiation here gives way to marketing programs based upon measurement and definition of market differences.

Lack of homogeneity on the demand side may be based upon different customs, desire for variety, or desire for exclusiveness, or may arise from basic differences in user needs. Some divergence in demand is the result of shopping errors in the market. Not all consumers have the desire or the ability to shop in a sufficiently efficient or rational manner as to bring about selection of the most needed or most wanted goods or services.

Diversity on the demand side of the market is nothing new to sales management. It has always been accepted as a fact to be dealt with in industrial markets where production to order rather than for the market is common. Here, however, the loss of precision in the satisfying of customer requirements that would be necessitated by attempts to bring about convergence of demand is often impractical and, in some cases, impossible. However, even in industrial marketing, the strategy of product differentiation should be considered in cases where products are applicable to several industries and may have horizontal markets of substantial size.

Long-Term Implications

While contemporary economic theory deals with the nature of product differentiation and its effects upon the operation of the total economy, the alternative strategies of product differentiation and market segmentation have received less attention. Empirical analysis of contemporary marketing activity supports the hypothesis that, while product differentiation and market segmentation are closely related (perhaps even inseparable) concepts, attempts to distinguish between these approaches may be productive of clarity in theory as well as greater precision in the planning of marketing operations. Not only do strategies of differentiation and segmentation call for differing systems of action at any point in time, but the dynamics of markets and marketing underscore the importance of varying degrees of diversity *through time* and suggest that the rational selection of marketing strategies is a requirement for the achievement of maximum functional effectiveness in the economy as a whole.

If a rational selection of strategies is to be made, an integrated approach to the minimizing of total costs must take precedence over separate approaches to minimization of production costs on the one hand and marketing costs on the other. Strategy determination must be regarded as an overall management decision which will influence and require facilitating policies affecting both production and marketing activities.

Differences Between Strategies of Differentiation and Segmentation

Product differentiation and market segmentation are both consistent with the framework of imperfect competition.[1] In its simplest terms, *product differentiation* is concerned with the bending of demand to the will of supply. It is an attempt to shift or to change the slope of the demand curve for the market offering of an individual supplier. This strategy may also be employed by a group of suppliers such as a farm cooperative, the members of which have agreed to act together. It results from the desire to establish a kind of equilibrium in the market by bringing about adjustment of market demand to supply conditions favorable to the seller.

Segmentation is based upon developments on the demand side of the market and represents a rational and more precise adjustment of product and marketing effort to consumer or user requirements. In the language of the economist, segmentation is *disaggregative* in its effects and tends to bring about recognition of several demand schedules where only one was recognized before.

Attention has been drawn to this area of analysis by the increasing number of cases in which business problems have become soluble by doing something about marketing programs and product policies that overgeneralize both markets and marketing effort. These are situations where intensive promotion designed to differentiate the company's products was not accomplishing its objective—cases where failure to recognize the reality of market segments was resulting in loss of market position.

While successful product differentiation will result in giving the marketer a horizontal share of a broad and generalized market, equally successful application of the strategy of market segmentation tends to produce depth of market position in the segments that are effectively defined and pene-

---

[1] Imperfect competition assumes lack of uniformity in the size and influence of the firms or individuals that comprise the demand or supply sides of a market.

trated. The differentiator seeks to secure a layer of the market cake, whereas one who employs market segmentation strives to secure one or more wedge-shaped pieces.

Many examples of market segmentation can be cited; the cigarette and automobile industries are well-known illustrations. Similar developments exist in greater or lesser degree in almost all product areas. Recent introduction of a refrigerator with no storage compartment for frozen foods was in response to the distinguishable preferences of the segment of the refrigerator market made up of home freezer owners whose frozen food storage needs had already been met.

Strategies of segmentation and differentiation may be employed simultaneously, but more commonly they are applied in sequence in response to changing market conditions. In one sense, segmentation is a momentary or short-term phenomenon in that effective use of this strategy may lead to more formal recognition of the reality of market segments through redefinition of the segments as individual markets. Redefinition may result in a swing back to differentiation.

The literature of both economics and marketing abounds in formal definitions of product differentiation. *From a strategy viewpoint,* product differentiation is securing a measure of control over the demand for a product by advertising or promoting differences between a product and the products of competing sellers. It is basically the result of sellers' desires to establish firm market positions and/or to insulate their businesses against price competition. Differentiation tends to be characterized by heavy use of advertising and promotion and to result in prices that are somewhat above the equilibrium levels associated with perfectly competitive market conditions. It may be classified as a *promotional* strategy or approach to marketing.

Market segmentation, on the other hand, consists of viewing a heterogeneous market (one characterized by divergent demand) as a number of smaller homogeneous markets in response to differing product preferences among important market segments. It is attributable to the desires of consumers or users for more precise satisfaction of their varying wants. Like differentiation, segmentation often involves substantial use of advertising and promotion. This is to inform market segments of the availability of goods or services produced for or presented as meeting their needs with precision. Under these circumstances, prices tend to be somewhat closer to perfectly competitive equilibrium. Market segmentation is essentially a *merchandising* strategy, merchandising being used here in its technical sense as representing the adjustment of market offerings to consumer or user requirements.

The Emergence of the Segmentation Strategy

To a certain extent, market segmentation may be regarded as a force in the market that will not be denied. It may result from trial and error in the sense that generalized programs of product differentiation may turn out to be effective in some segments of the market and ineffective in others. Recognition of, and intelligent response to, such a situation necessarily involves a shift in emphasis. On the other hand, it may develop that products involved in marketing programs designed for particular market segments may achieve a broader acceptance than originally planned, thus revealing a basis for convergence of demand and a more generalized marketing approach. The challenge to planning arises from the importance of determining, preferably in advance, the level or degree of segmentation that can be exploited with profit.

There appear to be many reasons why formal recognition of market segmentation as a strategy is beginning to emerge. One of the most important of these is decrease in the size of the minimum efficient producing or manufacturing unit required in some product areas. American industry has also established the technical base for product diversity by gaining release from some of the rigidities imposed by earlier approaches to mass production. Hence, there is less need today for generalization of markets in response to the necessity for long production runs of identical items.

Present emphasis upon the minimizing of marketing costs through self-service and similar developments tends to impose a requirement for better adjustment of products to consumer demand. The retailing structure, in its efforts to achieve improved efficiency, is providing less and less sales push at point of sale. This increases the premium placed by retailers upon products that are presold by their producers and are readily recognized by consumers as meeting their requirements as measured by satisfactory rates of stock turnover.

It has been suggested that the present level of discretionary buying power is productive of sharper shopping comparisons, particularly for items that are above the need level. General prosperity also creates increased willingness "to pay a little more" to get "just what I wanted."

Attention to market segmentation has also been enhanced by the recent ascendancy of product competition to a position of great economic importance. An expanded array of goods and services is competing for the consumer's dollar. More specifically, advancing technology is creating competition between new and traditional materials with reference to metals, construction materials, textile products, and in many other areas. While such competition is confusing and difficult to analyze in its early stages, it tends to achieve a kind of balance as various competing materials find their markets of maximum potential as a result of recognition of differences in the requirements of market segments.

Many companies are reaching the stage in their development where attention to market segmentation may be regarded as a condition or cost of growth. Their *core* markets have already been developed on a generalized basis to the point where additional advertising and selling expenditures are yielding diminishing returns. Attention to smaller or *fringe* market segments, which may have small potentials individually but are of crucial importance in the aggregate, may be indicated.

Finally, some business firms are beginning to regard an increasing share of their total costs of operation as being fixed in character. The higher costs of maintaining market position in the channels of distribution illustrate this change. Total reliance upon a strategy of product differentiation under such circumstances is undesirable, since market share available as a result of such a promotion-oriented approach tends to be variable over time. Much may hinge, for example, upon week-to-week audience ratings of the television shows of competitors who seek to outdifferentiate each other. Exploitation of market segments, which provides for greater maximization of consumer or user satisfactions, tends to build a more secure market position and to lead to greater over-all stability. While traditionally, high fixed costs (regarded primarily from the production viewpoint) have created pressures for expanded sale of standardized items through differentiation, the possible shifting of certain marketing costs into the fixed area of the total cost structure tends to minimize this pressure.

Conclusion

Success in planning marketing activities requires precise utilization of both product differentiation and market segmentation as components of marketing strategy. It is fortunate that available techniques of marketing research make unplanned market exploration largely unnecessary. It is the obligation of those responsible for sales and marketing administration to keep the strategy mix in adjustment with market structure at any point in time and to produce in marketing strategy at least as much dynamism as is present in the market. The ability of business to plan in this way is dependent upon the maintenance of a flow of market information that can be provided by marketing research as well as the full utilization of available techniques of cost accounting and cost analysis.

Cost information is critical because the upper limit to which market segmentation can be carried is largely defined by production cost considerations. There is a limit to which diversity in market offerings can be carried without driving production costs beyond practical limits. Similarly, the employment of product differentiation as a strategy tends to be restricted by the achievement of levels of marketing cost that are untenable. These cost factors tend to define the limits of the zone within which the employment of marketing strategies or a strategy mix dictated by the nature of the market is permissive.

It should be emphasized that while we have here been concerned with the differences between product differentiation and market segmentation as marketing strategies, they are closely related concepts in the setting of an imperfectly competitive market. The differences have been highlighted in the interest of enhancing clarity in theory and precision in practice. The emergence of market segmentation as a strategy once again provides evidence of the consumer's pre-eminence in the contemporary American economy and the richness of the rewards that can result from the application of science to marketing problems.

The ease or difficulty of introduction and the characteristics of the successful marketing strategy depend basically on the nature of the "new" in the product—the new as the customer views the bundle of services he perceives in the newborn.

25

What Is "New" About a New Product?

CHESTER R. WASSON

CONSIDER the case of the soup-maker who, by freezing, was able to develop commercial production of soups which previously had to be fresh-prepared—an oyster stew among them. Estimating that the market potential might be approximated by the average relationship between frozen and canned foods, he tried his soups in a single test market. The oyster stew sold out so fast that he had to withdraw it from test until he could expand production facilities even for this one market.

Or take the case of the industrial manufacturer who developed a silo-like forage storer, capable of increasing livestock production profits substantially if properly used. Yet when put into distribution through experienced dealers in heavy farm equipment, it lay dormant for more than four years. In fact, no appreciable market headway was made until it was taken out of the hands of what had seemed to be a logical channel for any kind of farm equipment.

Then, consider the business executive with soap-and-cosmetic experience

Reprinted from the *Journal of Marketing,* national quarterly publication of the American Marketing Association, Volume 25, No. 1 (July, 1960), pp. 52-56.

who acquired rights to a promising soil improver. Trade checks indicated that consumers liked it very much, and an impartial laboratory test indicated technical properties of substance. Put into a few test garden stores with no more than nominal advertising, sales seemed satisfactory. Nevertheless, jobbers would not take it on, and when direct sales to a wider group of dealers was tried, none of the outlets developed any major volume. Even though both amateurs and professionals who have tried it like it, and come back for more, and in spite of the fact that the economics of its use is reasonable and that theoretical demand seems attractive, the executive is about to write it off after four years of trying.

The Difference Lies in What Is New

All three cases are simple examples of a too prevalent failure to analyze the "what's new?" in the new product . . . to make sure that marketing strategy, channels of distribution, and available resources are compatible with the elements of novelty in the new product. The ease or difficulty of introduction and the characteristics of the successful marketing strategy depend basically on the nature of the "new" in the new product—the new as the customer views the bundle of services he perceives in the newborn.

Take the oyster stew—what was really new, the stew itself? In "R" months, oyster stew has been traditional in homes and restaurants from Boston and San Francisco to What Cheer, Iowa . . . from the Waldorf-Astoria to Harry's Diner. Assuming adequate quality in the commercial product, oyster stew was an old and welcome dinner-table friend. Was the idea of commercial preparation new? For oyster stew, yes, of course, but not for soup. Just look at the facings in the gondolas of any supermarket, or at the empty cans in the trash of any restaurant.

Of course, the idea of a frozen soup was new, but not the concept of frozen prepared foods. Food-store freezer cases had indeed established the association of fresh-quality taste with freeze-processing. But to the consumer, the only "new" aspect about frozen oyster stew was the greater availability and convenience implied in "frozen." With this particular item, the probability of great development might have been anticipated and prepared for in advance.

The silo and the soil improver, by contrast, looked deceptively similar to known items. But actually both embodied, for the consumer, radically new ideas; and both required extreme changes in user habits and user ways of looking at familiar tasks.

The forage storer looked like the familiar silo from the outside, but really embodied a new principle of preservation whose major benefits would be realized only when livestock were taken off pasture and barn-fed harvested forage the year around. Adoption of the device meant, in effect, adoption of a radically new pattern of work organization, and even of farm buildings in some cases.

No matter how great the promised benefit, such a major turnabout of habits requires a great deal of personal selling to get even the more venturesome to try it. Traditional farm-equipment channels are not prepared to carry out the prolonged and intensive type of pioneering personal sales effort and demonstration required. A reasonable degree of success began to accrue only after the manufacturer realized these facts and made the necessary changes in his selling plan.

Likewise, the soil improver resembled other growth stimulants in that it was sold in large bags and had a granular appearance. But the method of use was entirely different from, and more difficult than, the methods of surface application common to most growth stimulants in garden use. It had to be dug in, to be physically intermixed with the soil. In addition, the benefit was an unfamiliar one, and perhaps not easily believable—simple soil aeration. True, in cultivation, all gardeners practice aeration; but they think of weed killing, not aeration, when they hoe their gardens.

With such a product, success can reasonably be expected only after a strong educational campaign based on intense advertising, wide publicity, and personal contacts with consumer groups such as garden clubs and women's clubs. The resources needed were far in excess of those available in a "bootstrap" operation.

THE TONI EXAMPLE

Determination of the novel aspects of a new product is no simple mechanical process. What is new depends on what the prospective consumer perceives, or can be brought to perceive, in the new product.

Determining such potential aspects requires a high order of imagination, and spectacular successes such as the Toni Home Permanent are due in no small part to the introducer's skill in pinpointing the nature of the novel aspects of the product, and devising the kind of marketing strategy needed to fit the various types of "new" elements in his product.

When the Harrises first introduced Toni, they clearly perceived that their key problem was to gain credibility for the idea of a safe and satisfactory "permanent wave" done in the home. Home curling of hair was an old custom, but the home-produced curl had always been very temporary. Permanent waves had been available, and proven, for nearly thirty years, but only at the hand of a skilled hairdresser, and in a specially equipped beauty parlor. With the perfection of the cold-wave lotion, a true home permanent became possible, using a technique not very different from those already in use for temporary home curling. The principal benefit was one for which the times of the middle and late 1940's were ripe—a major saving in cost as compared with the professional job.

The problem was to gain credibility for the safety and the effectiveness of the product claiming the benefit (Toni)—a problem requiring intense selling effort. The Harris strategy consisted of: persuading the girl behind every cosmetic counter in town to use a kit herself before it went on sale; making sure that every cosmetic counter had a stock before the day of introduction; working one town at a time, putting the maximum advertising effort behind the introduction; plowing back all income into further advertising until market saturation was accomplished; and then using funds from established markets to open new ones.

If, on hindsight, this solution seems to have been the obvious, it should be noted that Toni was not the first cold-wave home permanent—merely the first successful one. The forgotten competitor, who was really first, never appreciated the intensity of consumer education that would be needed, and had so little success that his product is remembered by few.

Ways a Product Can Be "New"

In how many ways can a product be new? Of course, each case should be analyzed on its own. Nevertheless, there are at least thirteen possibilities which should be considered:

A. Six novel attributes are positive, in the sense that they ease the job of introduction:

1. New cost—or, better yet, price—if lower.
2. New convenience in use—if greater.
3. New performance—if better, more dependable and in the range of experience of the prospect—if believable.
4. New availability, in place, or time, or both (including antiseasonality).
5. Conspicuous consumption (status symbol) possibilities.
6. Easy credibility of benefits.

B. At least four characteristics make the job more difficult, slow up market development, and usually make it costlier:

7. New methods of use (unless obviously simpler).
8. Unfamiliar patterns of use (any necessity for learning new habits in connection with performance of a task associated with the new product).
9. Unfamiliar benefit (in terms of the prospect's understanding).
10. Costliness, fancied or real, of a possible error in use.

C. Three others are ambivalent in their effect—that is, the effect on market development probably depends not only on their exact nature, but also on the cultural climate at the moment. However, extreme unfamiliarity would probably be negative in effect:

11. New appearance, or other sensed difference (style or texture, for example).
12. Different accompanying or implied services.
13. New market (including different channels of sale).

The oyster stew had four of the six positive characteristics (only lower cost and conspicuous consumption omitted), and no negative ones. The silo and the soil improver had all of the negative attributes listed, and only performance among the positive. Toni had cost and performance in its favor, and marketing strategy involved an overwhelming attack on the negative aspects (fear of error and credibility of results).

The ambivalence of style should be obvious to those who have followed automobile history. The turtle-shaped DeSoto of the 1930's was one of the most spectacular design failures of history. The design was "too radical" for the motorists of that era. Twenty years later, the very similar appearance of the Volkswagen "beetle" proved no deterrent to the initiation of a radical reorientation of the American automobile market. And while the Volkswagen brought into that market items of dependable performance, greater convenience in use, and a lower cost than had been available for some time, one element in its success was the recognition of the necessity for continuing the availability of an established implied service in the sale of the car—ready availability of parts and service. Volkswagen entered no area until it had made certain of a high-grade service network in that area.

A FOURTEENTH CHARACTERISTIC

Omission of a possible fourteenth characteristic—new construction or composition—is purposeful. This characteristic is neutral—that it, it has no consumer meaning except to the extent that it is identified with, or can be associated with, one or more of the consumer-oriented characteristics listed above.

All that is new in any product is the package of consumer-perceivable services embodied in it. The innovator leads himself astray who analyzes the novel in his newborn in terms of physical and engineering attributes.

AN EXAMPLE IN TELEVISION

The physical similarity of color TV to black-and-white TV probably led the electronic industry to expect, erroneously, that color-set introduction would parallel the "mushroom" market development experienced with black-and-white. Physically, the parallel was certainly there. Color adds a new dimension to the signal received, just as the picture added a new dimension to the radio signal. But black-and-white television was not, for the consumer, a simple extension of radio. To the family, and most especially to the children, it was a vastly more convenient theater—it was "movies in the parlor." In an era in which children were being granted almost everything they asked for, the pressure for ownership soon became overwhelming. And to add to that pressure, the black-and-white television set required an unmistakable and quite conspicuous symbol of possession—the distinctive aerial. Black-and-white television never had to be sold—it was bought.

Color television, however, to the consumer, *is* simply an extension of black-and-white, which he already owns, and to which he is thoroughly accustomed. The mere idea of an added color dimension has only potential interest to the adult, and probably little to the child. Programs, moreover, are fully compatible—the owner of the color TV set can talk about no program the black-and-white neighbor has not been able to see.

Color television's one positive characteristic is thus simply better performance—a degree of better performance which has not as yet acquired much value in the eyes of the consumer. Offsetting this are the factors of higher cost, questions as to perfection of color TV, and a benefit that is relatively unfamiliar, so far as the experience of most prospects is concerned.

If color television is to become dominant, it will have to gain acceptance the way most other home appliances have—by "hard" direct-to-customer personal selling, probably operating through selective retail distribution, backed up by strong advertising and shrewd publicity that will build up the latent added value of color reception into kinetic reality.

THE OLD CAN BE NEW

Even the well-established can be "new" so far as the buyer is concerned. The pharmaceutical industry is well aware that when its ethical formulations can be made available for over-the-counter sales, new sales vistas can be opened by a new sales effort. Ecko discovered that an invention of the 1890's could gain quick success when reintroduced to the modern market (the case of the one-hand egg-beater). And one of the most interesting research results the author ever had was the discovery that a minor product which a client had been making for over fifty years needed only a different kind of sales effort, including a new channel of sale, to turn it into a promising new major product in the industrial-component field.

Market Management of Innovation

Skilled management of the innovation phase of the enterprise is, increasingly, a prerequisite to business success. Today's fast-moving markets pay best profits to firms in the van of those with product improvements and new products. In some industries, even mere survival depends on constant, successful new-product introduction. New-product success follows only when the marketing plan is suited to the innovational characteristics of the individual product, as the customer views it, or can be brought to view it.

Really consistent success in the marketing of innovations requires an all too rare understanding that the extent and nature of the new is not measurable in terms of the physical specifications of the product nor in the logical blueprint of the service. The nature of the new is in what it does to and for the customer—to his habits, his tastes and his patterns of life.

Some aspects of the new product make familiar patterns of life easier, cheaper, more convenient, or otherwise more pleasant. These aspects aid speedy introduction and adoption. Other aspects of the innovation require new patterns of life, new habits, the understanding of new ideas or ways of looking at things, the acceptance of the difficult to believe, or the acquisition of new tastes. The latter require the maximum concentration of marketing energy, to add enough value to the strange service to counterbalance the pain of the new idea.

Finally, some characteristics can be positive, negative, or neutral, dependent on the trend of the cultural climate. The current valence of these must be carefully evaluated at the time of introduction, and the marketing plan, or even the product design, fitted to the value determined.

Skillful development of new-product marketing plans would thus seem to consist of three basic steps:

1. Careful analysis of the positive and negative aspects of the specific product.
2. Maximum exploitation of the improvements in the familiar embodied in the product, to gain added value necessary to overcome the negative aspects.
3. Application of the maximum promotional effort in countering the negative aspects and lending value to the new and unfamiliar.

The chief reason for the increasing pressures on management for product planning is universally recognized, namely the acceleration in recent decades in the shifting demands of consuming groups—both industrial and consumer buyers—in response to the increasing number of product offerings presented by an aggressive business community.

26

The Growing Problems of Product Line Planning

NEIL H. BORDEN

I THINK there will be consensus in this audience that among the many responsibilities of top managements of corporations the task of determining and fashioning the product lines to be offered the market stands at the top. Generally, no single functional area has so much bearing on the sales and profit opportunities, present and future, as that of having products that meet the desires of consumer groups and yield margins permitting a satisfactory profit.

The importance of the product line has always been recognized, but the pressures on top executives of determining the products to offer now and in future periods have been constantly increasing until today among dynamic corporations the planning and direction of the procedures to arrive at product lines which assure a profitable and healthy future are at or near the head of the list of the responsibilities of top executive teams.

Reprinted from the *Thirty-second Annual Boston Conference on Distribution*, October 17-18, 1960, pp. 27-30.

I am going to devote my brief time in this talk primarily to a presentation of some of the more important forces that have brought about these increased pressures in product planning. Then we may point out certain generalizations as to organization and procedures whereby managements have sought to meet the problems of product line planning which have developed.

The chief reason for the increasing pressures on management for product planning is universally recognized, namely the acceleration in recent decades in the shifting demands of consuming groups—both industrial and consumer buyers—in response to the increasing number of product offerings presented by an aggressive business community. Some 25 years ago W. H. Lough in his volume on "High Level Consumption" [1] gave a significant observation. Said he: "One plain characteristic of high-level, in contrast to low-level, consumption is its *fickleness*. Offerings to consumers, if they are to hold their markets, must be continually remodelled —always with a risk that the supposed improvement will fail to 'click.' Popular demands are apt to shift suddenly, undermining whole industries."

When Lough made this observation the fickleness of demand was well beyond that of the 'teens or 'twenties of this century and far beyond the relative certainties that held in a simpler economy. But the threats to existing products from consumer response to new offerings arise far more frequently now than when Lough spoke. The discretionary buying power of American families is far beyond what it was in 1935. The product choices on which to spend this income are far greater than then. The improvements in existing products come at a faster clip. Innovations, new products not previously on the market, are constantly appearing.

In order to develop processes that might give lower costs, to keep existing product lines up to or ahead of competition and to develop new products that promise profits, corporations have increased their budgets for industrial research until the R and D group is now far larger than it was in Lough's time. Where the efforts of the research people at Lough's writing were in considerable measure devoted to efforts to improve industrial processes, their efforts have been directed in ever larger measure in recent years to the improvement of the old and the development of new products. Moreover, these research people have had at their command an expanding technology which has permitted the development of product improvements and new products at a rate not dreamed of in earlier days. Accordingly, the threats against items in any existing product line have loomed ever larger and have called for a vigilance and an attention to future demand far beyond what was required of management in earlier times.

---

[1] W. H. Lough, *High Level Consumption,* New York, McGraw-Hill, 1935.

The acceleration in rate of new and improved product offerings has brought about the phenomenon of the "shortened life cycle" of branded products. In my work in the Harvard Advanced Management Program executives have increasingly testified to the shortened life cycle of their branded products, particularly among those producing mass package products. I have had similar testimony from executives outside this group.

The concept of the life cycle involves not merely the length of time during which a company's new product enjoys a rising and substantial volume of sales, but the relation of profit margins to the sales over this period. As has been pointed out by C. Wilson Randle [2] the cycle of profits from the new and differentiated products is usually shorter than the sales cycle. Profits tend to turn down before the sales curve turns down. After a period of good profits there may well follow a period of appreciable sales with declining profit margins. Such a phenomenon places upon management the burden of developing and introducing new and profit-promising products not merely with an eye to their probable sales growth but also, and more important, to their probable profit productivity over a period of time.

There are several reasons for the shortened life and profit cycles of product lines. First of all, with well managed companies universally carrying on programs of new product research a number of them often are working on the same new product ideas. In any case, unless there is an unusually strong patent position for the firm first in the field, the promising new idea, as has always been the case, quickly attracts competitors to the industry fold. In the next place, under present conditions of product research and development, the improvements offered consumers by one corporation are likely to be met and if possible exceeded by competitors in a relatively short period. If a competitor hits upon an improvement that is really better (perhaps based on an entirely new technology), and he markets it well, both sales and profits of the original product innovator may decline drastically.

But in many product fields what ensues is a game of leap frog with competitors all trying to introduce product advantages but tending to end in something of a draw so far as consumer preferences are concerned. Under such conditions price competition usually sets in on an increased scale or promotional costs may rise or both of these things may happen. And though industry sales may continue to increase, the net for the product line turns downward. If the industry develops excess capacity, as not infrequently happens, the phenomenon of "profitless sales" is likely to ensue.

Another development that has contributed to a shortened profit cycle for manufacturers' innovations has been the growth of private brand competition over the past few decades. The large scale retailers are not real

2 See C. Wilson Randle: "Selecting the Research Program" II, *California Management Review*, No. 2 (Winter, 1960).

innovators in the sense of developing and introducing products for which primary demand has to be built. Rather, they wait until a wide acceptance has been established for innovations before they seek a share of the established demand under their own brands. It is my observation, however, that entry into new product areas by private branders has tended to come sooner in many product lines than was previously the case. The tremendous volume of sales of some of the large scale retailers which stem from their widespread and important retail outlets makes it economic for them to seek private brand sources of supply for relatively new lines of merchandise for which they see enough demand established to justify offering their own brand. Generally they find sources willing to sell to them.

Moreover, we find some of these large retailing corporations once in a product field carrying on aggressive programs of product improvement. They seek to match or outdo the offerings sold under manufacturers' brands. Along with this product development work, which provides them with specifications for their manufacturing sources, they employ engineers and procedure specialists to help these sources attain costs which will permit their private brands to be sold with price as an important element of their selling strategy, the basis on which their businesses have grown.

The over-all effect of private brand competition is to keep price competition alive and to narrow profit margins. Here, then, is another significant force which drives profit-seeking managements to increased attention to the development of product lines that will yield profitable sales.

The threat of quick obsolescence or of declining profits in a corporation's existing product lines has brought about the widespread trend among corporate managements during the past decade of seeking diversification of product lines, either through new product development, through merger or through both means. Since any one product line lives under the threat of being made obsolescent or profitless through the offerings of competitors, stability in sales and profit outlook is sought by broadening the base of the corporation's offerings.

The broadening of the corporation's product lines, however, has imposed the need for a management to be vigilant in every product area in which it operates. Consequently, organization along product lines has been the order of the day. The product or brand manager type of organization has been adopted, or separate corporate product divisions have been established. Each product manager or divisional manager has been charged with responsibility for keeping his product line competitive. Divisions have been provided with research and development departments. Product managers are directed to initiate needed improvements and to indicate when impending threats may call for radical change in the product lines.

The placing of product line responsibility on product managers, however, fails to solve all difficulties. I have cases which indicate that these executives may fail to do a first-rate job of product planning because the pressures of meeting the everyday operating problems they face leaves too little time for the planning job. Or their breadth of understanding of impending technological developments and social trends makes them not fully suited for the job. Moreover, there must rest with chief executives the responsibility for searching for and appraising new product ideas being beyond the franchise of the product or the divisional managers. They are charged with determining the long range product objectives of the corporation and of setting in motion steps necessary to attain these objectives. This is product line planning in its larger sense. Each corporation is a small entity in a large, complex and fast changing cosmos. The task of each management is to keep its operations adjusted to the changes that are taking place and to try to foresee and plan for future change. As stated at the start, product line planning, whether it involves only product improvement, the development of new products or the planning of mergers must be a first consideration of top management. Realization of this need to adjust to ever changing markets should rest with every member of the top management team and cannot be left solely with marketing men in the organization. This requirement of looking to the market by every one on the management team is, I think, the core of the much-used term "the marketing concept."

Let us turn briefly to some of the problems of organization and procedure.

First of all, good management now calls for the clear assignment of responsibility for product line planning. As noted before, case evidence shows that the details of product line planning cannot be left to line operating executives. They have too many daily preoccupations in getting operating tasks cared for. Hence the growing practice of establishing product line planning departments on a staff basis.

More and more it is recognized that such staff departments should tie in at the top level of management. There are several outstanding reasons for this. First, while the top executives must finally decide what products are to be developed and the direction in which the company will go, they need a procedure that will insure that good product ideas are gathered and that the factual material needed for decision as to what to accept and what to reject is available to them. The kind of information which should come from such a department, if it really does its job, relative to the sales and profit potentials of new product ideas, to market trends, to impending technological developments and to social trends affecting demand for company products can be not only the material for specific decisions but also a basis for broadening the understanding of the management team for its most important assignment.

In the next place, the development of a new product and the planning for its entry to the market involves every department of a business. The new development must be guided through R&D; its sales and profit potential must be subject to continuing appraisal; the venture must be financed; the product must be produced; its marketing must be planned and tested; and finally it must be handed over to the marketing department with market entry already well on its way. During the developmental and planning stages the suggestions and criticism of knowledgeable people in the organization must be sought. In the end an organizational enthusiasm for the new product is to be desired. A good product planning program should set up an orderly procedure to see that all the steps necessary for appraising product ideas, selecting among them for research and development and for fully conducting the project to the point where it is turned over to the marketing department. But along the way, however well procedures are set up, disagreements and difficulties generally appear. Perusal of the tasks to be performed reveal that the product line planning manager should be a marvel in his human relations. But in case of need, and case material indicates such needs not infrequently arise, he should have the authority of a president or an executive vice president behind him to help avoid or to resolve difficulties.

What I have said would seem to indicate that the Product Line Planning Manager should be a know-all who should be the President of the corporation. Such is not the case. He might well be a relatively young man, but he should be quite a man in breadth of understanding and if possible, in experience. The appraisals and recommendations which he hands to the top management team require that he be broad gauge enough to give the essential fodder for top management decision as to whether to risk venture into a product area or not. He and his department associates need not have in themselves the knowledge and factual material that go to make up their reports and their recommendations but they should know where to turn within and without their organization to get the facts desired. Let us note just a few of the more important specifications for the head of such a department.

First of all, he should be "market oriented" in the fullest understanding of this phrase. He should have an awareness of the importance of technology for he must gather essential forecasts of the feasibility of technical development of a product idea. In addition, he should seek out and try to assess the likelihood and timing of technological developments that may threaten any existing or proposed products. He should have enough experience in production to deal intelligently with the production department. Similarly he should be equipped to deal with financial and control data along with market forecast data in order to arrive at reasonable estimates of return on investment on the ventures studied. Finally he should be equipped to work with the marketing department to assure good marketing plans, and if marketing testing is feasible his department should be allowed to supervise and appraise the tests.

The need for being a master hand at working with company associates above and below him in status has been mentioned. Yes, he should be quite a fellow. If the President or executive-Vice President spots a comer to groom for his job, truly this is an ideal spot to put him for training.

Few new-product programs are started without the intention of making money, yet for each new product that is introduced, there are 500 or more that never reach the market. And of those that do, surveys have shown that from 50 to more than 90 per cent are failures within the first two years.

27

Developing New Products for Profit

JAMES W. RUSSELL

FEW NEW-PRODUCT PROGRAMS are started without the intention of making money, yet for each new product that is introduced, there are 500 or more that never even reach the market. And of those that do, surveys have shown that from 50 to more than 90 per cent are failures within the first two years. For whatever purpose they are initiated, then, it's clear that a tremendous proportion of new-product programs aren't adding a penny to the profits of the companies that invested time and money in them.

Your company is an unusual one if it has not faced one or more of the following problems:

- *The illegitimate engineering "baby."* The sales department does not want it and refuses to have anything to do with it.
- *The "Lazarus" idea.* This type of idea rises from the dead regularly every few years.
- *The "me-too" product.* This is a so-called "new" product that isn't new and isn't better than competition.

Reprinted from *Management Review*, publication of American Management Association, Inc., Volume 47, No. 8 (August, 1958), pp. 9-13 ff.

- *The "wandering ghost" idea.* This idea floats from department to department. No one knows just what to do with it, and yet it is never fully laid to rest or developed.

- *The ninety-eleven dollar product.* This product is worth $100, but it cost so much to develop that it would have to sell for $500 to make any money.

- *The false-start project.* This is most pitiful of all—the new product development that has to be killed for nontechnical reasons that could and should have been foreseen before development was started.

In view of the problems involved, it is easy to agree with the old production man's lament, "New products are a damn nuisance!" And yet these problems have to be faced. Most companies need new products if they are to grow, and in many others they are essential to survival.

It is not uncommon for a company to have half of its present sales in products that were not in use a decade ago. This trend is increasing, with whole industries anticipating future growth at vastly increased rates—and primarily in new products.

The odds are high against converting the average "hot idea" into a profitable new product, but the odds can be beaten if we can control the factors involved. Any company that makes a realistic appraisal of its new-product needs, and plans a program to fulfill those needs, will be able to develop successful products specifically designed to increase profits.

What Is a New Product?

A product is some*thing* that is sold to some*body*. If it isn't going to a market, it may be an idea, an invention, or a device, but it isn't a product yet—and it obviously is not a business.

A product is new if it expands beyond your present business. It can be an addition to your product line, sold through your present distribution channels. It can even be one of your present products introduced and sold to a different field. To qualify as new, a product need not be new to the customer. The criterion of newness is newness to your company.

In thinking of new products, it helps to keep in mind the types of newness. These degrees can be expressed in four categories:

1. *Product Improvement.* The automotive people carry this to a profitable extreme by selling a new set of improvements every year.

2. *Product Obsolescence.* Improvements alone appeal to a portion of the customers. The rest must be reached by obsoleting present products with new ones. One example of this is women's fashions: New styles may not be an improvement, but they certainly render the old models obsolete.

3. *Product-Line Expansion.* This is the broadening of present lines or the addition of allied lines. AMF, for example, started with a tricycle line

and later expanded into the allied lines of sidewalk automobiles and baby strollers.

4. *Product Diversification.* This most far-reaching category of newness consists of developing a new product for a new field—one in which the company has no previous experience.

Every new-product endeavor, of whatever type of newness—product improvement, product obsolescence, product-line expansion or product diversification—should be a planned and coordinated program aimed at profits. With this in mind, how do we set the size and direction of a program that will be appropriate for our particular company?

Defining the Goals

The first necessity is a definition of the company's goals in such terms as size, areas of interest, and type of newness. We must distinguish between the *need* for new products to keep the company healthy and the *desire* for new products to force additional growth. Such a desire is legitimate, but it should be differentiated from need in spelling out company goals.

An analysis of the need or desire for new products, and the category of newness required, should start with an analysis of present products. These questions can serve as a basis for this analysis:

- How does my present product serve its user?
- What more could it do?
- What more would the user like it to do?
- What are its primary appeals?
- How can these appeals be increased?
- What are its present competitive advantages and disadvantages?

Analysis of this type should be directed toward a list of possible improvements in the product. Any important improvements that are feasible could lead to new models—thus obsoleting older models.

Approaching the next category of newness, product-line expansion, requires an additional analysis—the analysis of the organization. It becomes necessary to review such things as plant capacity, engineering capabilities, manufacturing capabilities, the distribution organization, and the breadth of distribution channels. We must also determine what other products could be produced or sold with the present organization—or with some degree of expansion of the present organization. An organization and distribution analysis such as this is aimed at determining what allied products could be handled with present capacities and capabilities, and what additional products could be handled with limited expansion of these capacities or capabilities.

Moving to the broadest category, product diversification, the analyses of product and organization should be supplemented with an over-all business analysis. This requires a major financial assessment of the company and its position in its industry, other industries, and the economy as a whole. It involves a review of such factors as where our industry is going, compared to the economy, and what outside fields may really be greener.

Internally, we must know management's goals, the size of program the company can afford, and any advantages the company has that would enable it to start a new business successfully. Such an analysis can be used to set the size and direction of a diversification program tailored to the particular company.

In essence, then, a new-product program should be started not by looking at possible new products but by looking at existing products—by determining where we stand and where we want to go. Knowing our advantages, limitations, and directions, we can set the goals of a new-product program that offers our company particular advantages and, consequently, has the seeds of success.

Stages of New-Product Development

Once a program is planned, it must be organized and directed. Before it becomes a commercial reality, any new-product idea must go through six basic stages, which we at AMF call selection, screening, business specification, development, testing, and commercialization.

In the *selection* stage, product ideas are sorted to see which ones could be of interest to the company. No detailed check of patents, markets, or technical feasibility need be made if the product does not fit the company's goals. The number of ideas eliminated at this point can vary tremendously, but too high a ratio of rejections at this stage should be suspect. A lack of imagination may be responsible if too many ideas are rejected because their possibilities are not evident at first glance. The goal at this stage is a preliminary review based primarily on broad criteria—company fit, apparent potential, etc.—to weed out the obvious misfits.

In the *screening* stage, selected ideas pertinent to the company and its goals are screened for those appearing to offer real promise. This stage may include an engineering review, preliminary market or patent studies, or other investigations necessary to check the idea for commercial values.

The relatively few ideas not found wanting in some major area during the screening stage are then approved for full investigation and *business specification*. Here the idea is really taken apart and put back together.

Engineering analysis and exploration studies are performed, a full patent study is made, and full-scale market study takes place. The results of these studies are then combined to spell out the details of the potential business.

Risks are assessed, estimates are made, and forecasts of sales, profits, and investment are completed during this stage.

In short, the business goals and possibilities of the product idea are spelled out in sufficient detail to determine whether the commitment of funds for the program is warranted. This stage is of primary importance if products are to be developed for profit.

The fourth stage, *development,* consists of the actual engineering design and development. Although the primary responsibility in this stage rests in the engineering area, other areas of the company are involved. Marketing, for example, is further reviewing the market—not only for the unit as originally specified, but also for product specifications that engineering may suggest as the development activity proceeds. Progress is measured against the goals and specifications set earlier, and the effect of any changes in the product or in the program is reviewed and measured.

The *testing* stage involves both final engineering testing and preliminary market testing. The final stage is the *commercialization* of the product. This involves releasing it for production and taking the final steps in the build-up of the sales program. At the conclusion of this stage, the product is on a profit-and-loss basis.

Narrowing the Field

The number of proposals reviewed decreases drastically at each stage of development. Of 1,000 proposed ideas, for example, probably less than 10 per cent will get through the screening stage and 1 per cent or less through the business specification stage. Meanwhile, the cost put into carrying proposals forward increases rapidly through at least the development stage.

The critical point occurs in the business specification stage. Before this stage we have been reviewing many proposals in a general way, but after this point the company will be investing sizeable funds in engineering development effort—money that will be lost if a profitable commercial product is not obtained.

At this important stage, then, the variety of facts, guesses, and estimates uncovered during the previous steps must be separated into two categories for final evaluation and decision. The first category involves the intangible risk factors. These are points of advantage and disadvantage that cannot be reduced to numerical terms. They include product fit with the present business, the possibilities of future growth in lines allied to the proposed product, the probable reactions of competition, and the general chances of success for the proposed program. These points include the guesses, the "feel," and the judgment factors.

Analyzing the Measurable Risks

The second category of factors to be assessed at this point involves risks that can be defined and measured in terms of dollars: engineering cost estimates, production cost estimates, market forecasts of sales volume at various price levels, and organizational costs of getting into business. These factors should be analyzed separately, since they are more tangible than the first group.

One means of performing this analysis is to use a table, such as the one designed and used by the new products subcommittee at AMF (see page 235). The purpose of this table is to aid in the listing and analysis of the tangible factors obtained in the business specification studies. The goal is to arrive at a single figure that can be weighed against the intangible risks previously mentioned.

The first seventeen lines of the table constitute a pro forma profit-and-loss statement of the operation by year. Costs and expenses through line 7 are restricted to "normal" items, resulting in the "normal" profit of line 8.

The second section (lines 9 through 14) covers the nonrecurring expenses that are required to get the enterprise started. Production and marketing start-up expenses are included, as well as product development and tooling. These one-time costs are separated from the "normal" costs to facilitate analysis as well as later changes in the forecast.

The after-tax cumulative profit and loss is shown in line 18 to indicate the flow of speculative funds required for the program. At this point, the estimated working capital requirements are also shown (line 19), so that we can calculate the actual funds tied up at any point in the program. The speculative funds are not combined with working capital on this sheet, however, since working capital involves a relatively low order of risk and should not be confused with risk capital in evaluating the program.

The fact that working capital will be tied up is recognized, however, by levying an artificial working capital charge against the enterprise (line 20). This charge is deducted from the profit after taxes to give a "criteria" investment, which is used to calculate the discounted rate of return on the speculative investment.

Using the Table

The example shown outlines a business based on a hypothetical new machine with a potential market of 2,500 units and an attainable market of 80 per cent, or 2,000 units, within ten years. The rate of sales build-up and decline of this particular unit is forecast at a selling price of $10,000.

TABLE 27-1

Financial Projection and Analysis for a Proposed New Product

(All figures in thousands of dollars except unit sales)	Basis	1st Year	2nd Year	3rd Year	4th Year	5th Year	6th Year	7th Year	8th Year	9th Year	10th Year	Totals
1. Unit Sales — Penetration:	80%					50	300	450	500	400	300	2,000
2. Sales at $10,000 per unit	100%					500	2,000	4,500	5,000	4,000	3,000	20,000
3. Normal Mfg. Cost at $5,500 per unit	55%					275	1,650	2,475	2,750	2,200	1,650	11,000
4. Normal Mfg. Profit	45%					225	1,350	2,025	2,250	1,800	1,350	9,000
5. Normal Marketing Expenses	15%					75	450	675	750	600	450	3,000
6. Normal Product Engineering	1%					5	30	45	50	40	30	200
7. Normal G. & A.	4%					20	120	180	200	160	120	800
8. Normal Profit	25%					125	750	1,125	1,250	1,000	750	5,000
9. Production Start-up Expense					40	100						140
10. Marketing Start-up Expense				10	50	150						210
11. Product Development		80	110	120	40							350
12. Tooling					150							150
13. Misc. & Contingencies (30% of Dev. & Tooling)		20	30	40	50	10						150
14. Total Non-Recurring Expenses		100	140	170	330	260						1,000
15. Pretax Profit (Loss)		(100)	(140)	(170)	(330)	(135)	750	1,125	1,250	1,000	750	4,000
16. Income Tax Provision	50%	(50)	(70)	(85)	(165)	(67.5)	375	562.5	625	500	375	2,000
17. Profit After Taxes (Line 15—Line 16)		(50)	(70)	(85)	(165)	(67.5)	375	562.5	625	500	375	2,000
18. Cumulative Cash Flow		(50)	(120)	(205)	(370)	(437.5)	(62.5)	500	1,125	1,625	2,000	—
19. Working Capital Requirements	50% of Sales					250	1,500	2,250	2,500	2,000	1,500	—
20. Working Capital Charge	5%					12.5	75	112.5	125	100	75	500
21. "Criteria" Investment (Line 17—Line 20)		(50)	(70)	(85)	(165)	(80)	300	450	500	400	300	500 Discounted Rate of Return 31.5%

308

Estimates of all expenses necessary to build up and maintain a marketing organization are made and entered in the table.

Engineering development cost estimates and manufacturing, tooling, start-up, and production costs are also developed and entered, together with normal product engineering and appropriate general and administrative expenses. In this particular case, the product development and tooling expenses are burdened with a 30 per cent miscellaneous and contingency allowance.

The working capital requirements are forecast at 50 per cent of annual gross sales, and the charges on use of working capital are assessed at 5 per cent after taxes.

Thus, the business estimated for the proposed machine amounts to $20 million gross sales over a six-year sales period. Preceding this is a four-year engineering development, testing, and tooling-up period which, together with initial marketing expense, will cost $1 million. Most of this money must be committed before any return can be anticipated.

In order to compare this investment with other investment possibilities, the "criteria" investment is obtained and the discounted rate of return on investment is found to be 31.5 per cent. The discounted rate of return represents the rate at which compound interest would have to be earned by the outstanding investment in order for the interest plus the principal to provide sufficient funds to pay the cash flow-backs anticipated at the times predicted. This one figure can serve as a realistic measure of the desirability of the venture, and it is an important criterion in evaluating the proposal as a favorable or unfavorable company move.

The All-Important Profit Motive

The table as a whole can also serve as a measuring device during each succeeding stage of the product's evolution. As the development, testing, and commercialization stages proceed, the effect of changes or further refinements in each of the estimates and forecasts can be readily seen. The rechecking and re-evaluation necessary throughout a new-product program is thus focused on the ultimate effect of each change on the over-all business picture. Decisions made can be based on their net effect on the profit goals.

Particular care must be taken to be as realistic as possible in each of the estimates and forecasts. Overestimating the costs or underestimating the market for the sake of conservatism can quickly reduce the forecast rate of return to an uninteresting level. The converse, of course, is equally true: Underestimating costs could lead to heavy losses before the realities become evident.

Of course, a table such as this can never be the sole criterion in deciding for or against a program. Patent position, potential competition, product fit, growth potential of allied lines—these and many other factors must be considered in judging whether the project's goals are both attainable and worthy of the company's efforts.

Properly used, however, this type of financial analysis is a valuable tool in putting the pieces of the project into perspective and yielding a rate-of-return figure for comparison with the risks involved.

In developing new products, hot ideas, internal company analysis, and planned new-product programs are all important, but the profit goal must be the primary consideration at each step. We believe this type of analysis to be a key tool in developing profitable new products.

Just as a crust of barnacles on the hold of a ship retards the vessel's movement, so do a number of worn-out items in a company's product mix affect the company's progress.

28

The Death and Burial of "Sick" Products

R. S. ALEXANDER

EUTHANASIA APPLIED TO HUMAN BEINGS is criminal; but aging products enjoy or suffer no such legal protection. This is a sad fact of business life.

The word "product" is used here not in its broad economic sense of anything produced—such as wheat, coal, a car, or a chair—but in its narrower meaning of an article made to distinct specifications and intended for sale under a separate brand or catalogue number. In the broader sense of the word, certain products may last as long as industrial civilization endures; in the narrow sense, most of them are playthings of change.

Much has been written about managing the development and marketing of new products, but business literature is largely devoid of material on product deletion.

This is not surprising. New products have glamor. Their management is fraught with great risks. Their successful introduction promises growth in sales and profits that may be fantastic.

But putting products to death—or letting them die—is a drab business, and often engenders much of the sadness of a final parting with old and

R. S. Alexander, reprinted from the *Journal of Marketing,* national quarterly publication of the American Marketing Association, Volume 28, No. 2 (April, 1964), pp. 1-7.

tried friends. "The portable 6-sided, pretzel polisher was the first product The Company ever made. Our line will no longer be our line without it."

But while deletion is an uninspiring and depressing process, in a changing market it is almost as vital as the addition of new products. The old product that is a "football" of competition or has lost much of its market appeal is likely to generate more than its share of small unprofitable orders; to make necessary short, costly production runs; to demand an exorbitant amount of executive attention; and to tie up capital that could be used more profitably in other ventures.

Just as a crust of barnacles on the hold of a ship retards the vessel's movement, so do a number of worn-out items in a company's product mix affect the company's progress.

Most of the costs that result from the lack of an effective deletion system are hidden and become apparent only after careful analysis. As a result, management often overlooks them. The need for examining the product line to discover outworn members, and for analysis to arrive at intelligent decisions to discard or to keep them, very rarely assumes the urgency of a crisis. Too often, management thinks of this as something that should be done but that can wait until tomorrow.

This is why a definite procedure for deletion of products should be set up, and why the authority and responsibility for the various activities involved should be clearly and definitely assigned. This is especially important because this work usually requires the cooperation of several functional groups within the business firm, including at least marketing, production, finance, and sometimes personnel.

Definite responsibility should be assigned for at least the following activities involved in the process: (1) selecting products which are candidates for elimination; (2) gathering information about them and analyzing the information; (3) making decisions about elimination; and (4) if necessary, removing the doomed products from the line.

Selection of Products for Possible Elimination

As a first step, we are not seeking the factors on which the final decision to delete or to retain turns, but merely those which indicate that the product's continuation in the product mix should be considered carefully with elimination as a possibility. Although removal from the product line may seem to be the prime aim, the result is not inevitably deletion from the line; instead, careful analysis may lead to changes in the product itself or in the methods of making or marketing it.

Sales Trend. If the trend of a product's sales is downward over a time period that is significant in relation to the normal life of others like it, its continuation in the mix deserves careful examination. There may be many reasons for such a decline that in no way point toward deletion; but when decline continues over a period of time the situation needs to be studied.

Price Trend. A downward trend in the price of a new product may be expected if the firm introducing it pursues a skimming-price policy, or if all firms making it realize substantial cost savings as a result of volume production and increased processing know-how. But when the price of an established product whose competitive pattern has been relatively stabilized shows a downward trend over a significant period of time, the future of that product should receive attention.

Profit Trend. A declining profit either in dollars or as a per cent of sales or investment should raise questions about a product's continued place in the product line. Such a trend usually is the result of a price-factory cost squeeze, although it may be the outcome of a loss in market appeal or a change in the method of customer purchase which forces higher marketing expenditures.

Substitute Products. When a substitute article appears on the market, especially if it represents an improvement over an old product, management must face the question of whether to retain or discard the old product. This is true regardless of who introduces the substitute. The problem is especially difficult when the new product serves the same general purpose as the old one but is not an exact substitute for it.

Product Effectiveness. Certain products may lose some of their effectiveness for the purposes they serve. For example, disease germs may develop strains that are resistant to a certain antibiotic. When this happens, the question of whether to keep or delete the drug involves issues not only of the interests of the firm but of the public welfare.

Executive Time. A possible tipoff as to the location of "illness" in a product mix lies in a study of the amount of executive time and attention devoted to each of the items in the product line. Sick products, like sick people, demand a lot of care; but one must be careful to distinguish the "growing pains" of a new product from the more serious disorders of one that has matured and is now declining.

The six indicators mentioned do not of themselves provide evidence justifying deletion. But they can help management to single out from a line of products those upon which it can profitably spend time and money in analyzing them, with elimination from the line as a *possibility*.

Analysis and Decision Making About "Sick" Products

Although the work of analyzing a sick or decrepit product is usually done by people other than the management executives who decide what to do about it, the two processes are interdependent. Unless the right factors are chosen for analysis and unless the work is properly done, the decision is not likely to be an intelligent one. Accordingly, these two factors will be discussed together.

What information does a decision-maker need about a product, and what sort of analysis of it should he have in order to render a sound verdict as to its future? The deletion decision should not turn on the sole issue of profitability. Profit is the most important objective of a business; but individual firms often seek to achieve both long-run and short-run objectives other than profit.

So, in any individual case the critical factors and the weights assigned them in making a decision must be chosen in the light of the situation of the firm and the management objectives.

PROFITS

Profit management in a firm with a multi-product line (the usual situation in our economy) is not the simple operation generally contemplated in economic theory. Such a firm usually has in its product mix (1) items in various stages of introduction and development, some of which may be fantastically profitable and others deep "in the red"; (2) items which are mature but not "superannuated," whose profit rate is likely to be satisfactory; and (3) declining items which may yield a net profit somewhat less than adequate or may show heavy losses.

The task is to manage the whole line or mix so that it will show a satisfactory profit for the company. In this process, two questions are vital; What is a profit? How much profit is satisfactory?

Operating-statement accounting makes it possible to determine with reasonable accuracy the total amount of net profit a company earns on an overall basis. But when the management of a multi-product firm seeks to determine how much of this total is generated by its activities in making and marketing each product in its mix, the process is almost incredibly complex; and the results are almost certain to be conditioned on a tissue of assumptions which are so debatable that no management can feel entirely comfortable in basing decisions on them.

This is because such a large portion of the costs of the average multi-product firm are or behave like overhead or joint expense. Almost inevitably several of the items in the product mix are made of common materials, with the same equipment, and by manpower which is interchangeable. Most of the company's marketing efforts and expenses are devoted to selling and distributing the mix or a line within the mix, rather than individual items.

In general, the more varied the product mix of a firm, the greater is the portion of its total expense that must be classified as joint or overhead. In such a company, many types of cost which ordinarily can be considered direct tend to behave like overhead or joint expenses. This is particularly true of marketing costs such as advertising that does not feature specific items; personal selling; order handling; and delivery.

This means that a large part of a company's costs must be assigned to products on some arbitrary basis and that however logical this basis may be, it is subject to considerable reasonable doubt in specific cases. It also means that if one product is removed from the mix, many of these costs remain to be reassigned to the items that stay in the line. As a result, any attempt to "prune" the product mix entirely on the basis of the profit contribution, or lack of it, of specific items is almost certain to be disappointing and in some cases disastrous.

But if a multi-product firm could allocate costs to individual items in the mix on some basis recognized as sound and thus compute product-profit accurately, what standard of profit should be set up, the failure to meet which would justify deletion?

Probably most managements either formally or unconsciously set overall company profit targets. Such targets may be expressed in terms of dollars, although to be most useful in product management they usually must be translated into percentages on investment, or money used. As an example, a company may have as its profit target 15% on investment before taxes.

Certainly *every* product in the mix should not be required to achieve the target, which really amounts to an average. To do so would be to deny the inevitable variations in profit potential among products.

Probably a practical minimum standard can be worked out, below which a product should be eliminated unless other considerations demand its retention. Such a standard can be derived from a balancing out of the profit rates among products in the mix, so as to arrive at the overall company target as an average. The minimum standard then represents a figure that would tip the balance enough to endanger the overall target.

What role, then, should considerations of product-profit play in managerial decisions as to deletion or retention?

1. Management probably will be wise to recognize an overall company target profit in dollars or rate on investment, and to set in relation to it a minimum below which the profit on an individual product should not fall without marking that item for deletion (unless other special considerations demand its retention).

2. Management should cast a "bilious eye" on all arguments that a questionable product be kept in the mix because it helps to defray overhead and joint costs. Down that road, at the end of a series of decisions to retain such products, lies a mix entirely or largely composed of items

each busily "sopping up" overhead, but few or none contributing anything to net profit.

3. This does not mean that management should ignore the effect of a product deletion on overhead or joint costs. Decision-makers must be keenly aware of the fact that the total of such costs borne by a sick product must, after it is deleted, be reallocated to other products, and with the result that they may become of doubtful profitability. A detailed examination of the joint or overhead costs charged against an ailing product may indicate that some of them can be eliminated in whole or in part if it is eliminated. Such costs are notoriously "sticky" and difficult to get rid of; but every pretext should be used to try to find ways to reduce them.

4. If a deletion decision involves a product or a group of products responsible for a significant portion of a firm's total sales volume, decision-makers can assess the effects of overhead and joint costs on the problem, by compiling an estimated company operating statement after the deletion and comparing it with the current one. Such a forecasted statement should include expected net income from the use of the capital and facilities released by deletion if an opportunity for their use is ready to hand. Surviving joint and overhead expenses can even be reallocated to the remaining products, in order to arrive at an estimate of the effect that deletion might have, not only on the total company net income but on the profitability of each of the remaining products as well. Obviously such a cost analysis is likely to be expensive, and so is not justified unless the sales volume stakes are high.

FINANCIAL CONSIDERATIONS

Deletion is likely not only to affect the profit performance of a firm but to modify its financial structure as well.

To make and sell a product, a company must invest some of its capital. In considering its deletion, the decision-makers must estimate what will happen to the capital funds presently used in making and marketing it.

When a product is dropped from the mix, most or all of the circulating capital invested in it—such as inventories of materials, goods in process, and finished goods and accounts receivable—should drain back into the cash account; and if carried out in an orderly fashion, deletion will not disturb this part of the capital structure except to increase the ratio of cash to other assets.

This will be true, unless the deletion decision is deferred until product deterioration has gone so far that the decision assumes the aspects of a crisis and its execution that of a catastrophe.

The funds invested in the equipment and other facilities needed to make and market the "sick" product are a different matter. If the equipment is versatile and standard, it may be diverted to other uses. If the firm has no need of it and if the equipment has been properly depreciated, management may find a market for it at a price approaching or even exceeding its book value.

In either case, the capital structure of the company is not disturbed except by a shift from equipment to cash in the case of sale. In such a case management would be wise, before making a deletion decision, to determine how much cash this action promises to release as well as the chances for its reinvestment.

If the equipment is suited for only one purpose, it is highly unlikely that management can either find another use for it or sell it on favorable terms. If it is old and almost completely depreciated, it can probably be scrapped and its remaining value "written off" without serious impairment of the firm's capital structure.

But if it is only partly depreciated, the decision-makers must weigh the relative desirability of two possible courses of action: (1) to delete immediately, hoping that the ensuing improvement in the firm's operating results will more than offset the impairment in capital structure that deletion will cause; or (2) to seek to recapture as much as possible of its value, by continuing to make and market the product as long as its price is enough to cover out-of-pocket costs and leave something over to apply to depreciation.

This choice depends largely on two things: the relation between the amount of fixed and circulating capital that is involved; and the opportunities available to use the funds, executive abilities, manpower, and transferable facilities released by deletion for making profits in other ventures.

This matter of opportunity costs is a factor in every deletion decision. The dropping of a product is almost certain to release some capital, facilities, manpower skills, and executive abilities. If opportunities can be found in which these assets can be invested without undue risk and with promise of attractive profits, it may be good management to absorb considerable immediate loss in deleting a sick product.

If no such opportunities can be found, it is probably wise to retain the product so long as the cash inflow from its sales covers out-of-pocket costs and contributes something to depreciation and other overhead expenses. In such a case, however, it is the part of good management to seek actively for new ventures which promise satisfactory profits, and to be ready to delete promptly when such an opportunity is found.

EMPLOYEE RELATIONS

The effect which product elimination may have on the employees of a firm is often an important factor in decisions either to drop or to retain products.

This is not likely to be a deciding factor if new product projects are under development to which the people employed in making and marketing the doubtful product can be transferred, unless such transfer would deprive them of the earning power of special skills. But when deletion of a product means discharging or transferring unionized employees, the decision-makers must give careful thought to the effect their action is likely to have on company-union relations.

Even in the absence of union pressure, management usually feels a strong sense of responsibility for the people in its employ. Just how far management can go in conserving specific jobs at the expense of deferring or foregoing necessary deletions before it endangers the livelihood of all the employees of the firm is a nice question of balance.

MARKETING FACTORS

Many multi-product firms retain in their marketing mixes one or more items which, on the basis of profits and the company financial structure, should be deleted. To continue to make and market a losing product is no managerial crime. It is reprehensible only when management does not know the product is a losing one or, knowing the facts, does not have sound reasons for retaining it. Such reasons are very likely to lie in the marketing area.

Deletions of products are often deferred or neglected because of management's desire to carry a "full line," whatever that means. This desire may be grounded on sound reasons of consumer patronage or on a dubious yearning for the "prestige" that a full line is supposed to engender. But there is no magic about a full line or the prestige that is supposed to flow from it. Both should be evaluated on the basis of their effects on the firm's sales volume, profits, and capacity to survive and grow.

Products are often associated in the marketing process. The sale of one is helped by the presence of another in the product mix.

When elimination of a product forces a customer who buys all or a large part of his requirements of a group of profitable items from the firm to turn to another supplier for his needs of the dropped product, he might shift some or all of his other patronage as well. Accordingly, it is sometimes wise for management to retain in its mix a no-profit item, in order to hold sales volume of highly profitable products. But this should not be done blindly without analysis.

Rarely can management tell ahead of time exactly how much other business will be lost by deleting a product, or in what proportions the losses will fall among the remaining items. But in many cases the amount of sales volume can be computed that will be *hazarded* by such action; what other products will be subject to that hazard; and what portion of their volume will be involved. When this marketing interdependence exists in a deletion problem, the decision-makers should seek to discover the customers who buy the sick product; what other items in the mix they buy; in what quantities; and how much profit they contribute.

The firm using direct marketing channels can do this with precision and at relatively little cost. The firm marketing through indirect channels will find it more difficult, and the information will be less exact; but it still may be worth-while. If the stakes are high enough, marketing research may be conducted to discover the extent to which the customer purchases of profitable items actually are associated with that of the sick product. Although the results may not be precise, they may supply an order-of-magnitude idea of the interlocking patronage situation.

Product interrelationships in marketing constitute a significant factor in making deletion decisions, but should never be accepted as the deciding factor without careful study to disclose at least the extent of the hazards they involve.

OTHER POSSIBILITIES

The fact that a product's market is declining or that its profit performance is substandard does not mean that deletion is the *only* remedy.

Profits can be made in a shrinking market. There are things other than elimination of a product that can be done about deteriorating profit performance. They tend to fall into four categories.

1. *Costs*. A careful study may uncover ways of reducing factory costs. This may result from improved processes that either eliminate manpower or equipment time or else increase yield; or from the elimination of forms or features that once were necessary or worth-while but are no longer needed. The natural first recourse of allocating joint and overhead costs on a basis that is "kinder" to the doubtful product is not to be viewed with enthusiasm. After reallocation, these costs still remain in the business; and the general profit picture has not been improved in the least.

2. *Marketing*. Before deleting a product, management will be wise to examine the methods of marketing it, to see if they can be changed to improve its profit picture.

Can advertising and sales effort be reduced without serious loss of volume? A holding operation requires much less effort and money than a promotional one.

Are services being given that the product no longer needs?

Can savings be made in order handling and delivery, even at some loss of customer satisfaction? For example, customers may be buying the product in small orders that are expensive to handle.

On the other hand, by spending more marketing effort, can volume be increased so as to bring about a reduction in factory cost greater than the added marketing expense? In this attempt, an unexpected "assist" may come from competitors who delete the product and leave more of the field to the firm.

By remodeling the product, "dressing it up," and using a new marketing approach, can it be brought back to a state of health and profit? Here the decision-makers must be careful not to use funds and facilities that could be more profitably invested in developing and marketing new products.

3. *Price.* It is natural to assume that the price of a failing product cannot be raised. At least in part, its plight is probably due to the fact that it is "kicked around" by competition, and thus that competition will not allow any increases.

But competitors may be tired of the game, too. One company that tried increasing prices found that wholesalers and retailers did not resent a larger cost-of-goods-sold base on which to apply their customary gross profit rates, and that consumers continued to buy and competitors soon followed suit.

Although a price rise will not usually add to the sum total of user happiness, it may not subtract materially from total purchases. The decision-makers should not ignore the possibility of using a price reduction to gain enough physical volume to bring about a more-than-offsetting decline in unit costs, although at this stage the success of such a gambit is not likely.

4. *Cross Production.* In the materials field, when small production runs make costs prohibitive, arrangements may sometimes be made for Firm A to make the *entire* supply of Product X for itself and Competitor B. Then B reciprocates with another similar product. Such "trades," for instance, are to be found in the chemical business.

SUMMATION FOR DECISION

In solving deletion problems, the decision-makers must draw together into a single pattern the results of the analysis of all the factors bearing on the matter. Although this is probably most often done on an intangible, subjective basis, some firms have experimented with the formula method.

For example, a manufacturer of electric motors included in its formula the following factors:

- Probability
- Position on growth curve
- Product leadership
- Market position
- Marketing dependence of other products

Each factor was assigned a weight in terms of possible "counts" against the product. For instance, if the doubtful item promised no profits for the next three years, it had a count of 50 points against it, while more promising prospects were assigned lesser counts. A critical total for all factors was set in advance which would automatically doom a product. Such a system can include other factors—such as recapturability of invested capital, alternate available uses of facilities, effects on labor force, or other variables peculiar to the individual case.

The use of a formula lends an aura of precision to the act of decision-making and assures a degree of uniformity in it. But obviously the weights assigned to different factors cannot be the same in all cases. For example, if the deletion of a doubtful product endangers a large volume of sales of other highly profitable items, that alone should probably decide the matter.

The same thing is true if deletion will force so heavy a writeoff of invested funds as to impair the firm's capital structure. Certainly this will be true if all or most of the investment can be recaptured by the depreciation route if the product stays in the mix.

This kind of decision requires that the factors be weighted differently in each case. But when managers are given a formula, they may tend to quit thinking and do too much "weighing."

The Deletion of a Product

Once the decision to eliminate a product is made, plans must be drawn for its death and burial with the least disturbance of customer relations and of the other operations of the firm.

Such plans must deal with a variety of detailed problems. Probably the most important fall into four categories: timing; parts and replacements; stocks; and holdover demand.

Timing. It is desirable that deletion be timed so as to dovetail with the financial, manpower, and facilities needs for new products. As manpower and facilities are released from the dying product and as the capital devoted to it flows back into the cash account, it is ideal if these can be immediately used in a new venture. Although this can never be completely achieved, it may be approximated.

The death of a product should be timed so as to cause the least disturbance to customers. They should be informed about the elimination of the product far enough in advance so they can make arrangements for replacement, if any are available, but not so far in advance that they will switch to new suppliers before the deleting firm's inventories of the product are sold. Deletion at the beginning of a selling season or in the middle of it probably will create maximum customer inconvenience, whereas at the end of the season it will be the least disturbing.

Parts and Replacements. If the product to be killed off is a durable one, probably the deleting firm will find it necessary to maintain stocks of repair parts for about the expected life of the units most recently sold. The firm that leaves a trail of uncared-for "orphan" products cannot expect to engender much good will from dealers or users. Provision for the care and maintenance of the orphan is a necessary cost of deletion.

This problem is much more widespread than is commonly understood. The woman who buys a set of china or silverware and finds that she cannot replace broken or lost pieces does not entertain an affectionate regard for the maker. The same sort of thing is true if she installs draperies and later, when one of them is damaged, finds that the pattern is no longer available.

Stocks. The deletion plan should provide for clearing out the stocks of the dying product and materials used in its production, so as to recover the maximum amount of the working capital invested in it. This is very largely a matter of timing—the tapering off of purchase, production, and selling activities. However, this objective may conflict with those of minimizing inconvenience to customers and servicing the orphan units in use after deletion.

Holdover Demand. However much the demand for a product may decline, it probably will retain some following of devoted users. They are bound to be disturbed by its deletion and are likely to be vocal about it; and usually there is little that management can do to mitigate this situation.

Sometimes a firm can avoid all these difficulties by finding another firm to purchase the product. This should usually be tried before any other deletion steps are taken. A product with a volume too small for a big firm to handle profitably may be a money-maker for a smaller one with less overhead and more flexibility.

Neglect or Action?

The process of product deletion is important. The more dynamic the business, the more important it is.

But it is something that most company executives prefer not to do; and therefore it will not get done unless management establishes definite, clearcut policies to guide it, sets up carefully articulated procedures for doing it, and makes a positive and unmistakable assignment of authority and responsibility for it.

Exactly what these policies should be, what form these procedures should take, and to whom the job should be assigned are matters that must vary with the structure and operating methods of the firm and with its position in the industry and the market.

In any case, though, the need for managerial attention, planning, and supervision of the deletion function cannot be overemphasized. Many business firms are paying dearly for their neglect of this problem, but unfortunately do not realize how much this is costing them.

... the choice of a product's package, no less than the choice of the total selling effort brought to bear on the product, has to represent a reconciliation of a variety of functions, each of which has potential merit in furthering the sale of the product, but all of which are, in part at least, mutually exclusive.

29

A Theory of Packaging in the Marketing Mix

WILLIAM R. MASON

IT IS AXIOMATIC that the job of packaging is to sell. But after that banality has been voiced, what guides to management judgment—what theories, if you will—influence the choice of a package?

This article is not a check list of features that should be built into a package, but a rough guide to basic judgments management must bring to bear in its choice of packaging before the particulars of type face, combination of colors, package count, or printing method are up for decision.

The critical judgments that must be made on the packaging choice concern the "mix" of packaging attributes best able to perform, in different degrees, the particular functions of the package that are believed to be important to sales. The basic judgment in choice of packaging is "What jobs should the package do, and how completely should it do each?" The answers to the lesser decisions can fall into place once the "mix" of desirable packaging attributes has been determined, once the assignment of

Reprinted from *Business Horizons,* Volume 1, No. 3 (Summer, 1958), pp. 91-95. Copyright, 1958, by the Foundation for Economic and Business Studies, Indiana University.

basic functions desired of the packages has been made. Frequently, too much effort and time are devoted to making lesser decisions, usually on questions of graphic art, rather than this basic judgment.

The packager may accept as a guide, when making basic decisions on product "mix," that: *"The major purpose of any package is to influence or control the location of product storage within the marketing channel."* "Storage," as I am using the term, means the holding of goods for future use at any level along the marketing channel, *including the level of the ultimate consumer.* Even at the ultimate consumer level, the product may be stored in several places—sugar, for example, may be stored on a shelf or on the table. The packager is interested in getting the bulk of his product's storage as near as possible to the point of ultimate use.

The functions of the product's package are:

- Protecting the product
- Adapting to production line speeds
- Promoting the product
- Increasing product density [1]
- Facilitating the use of the product
- Having re-use value for the consumer

The performance of a package in the first two of these basic functions is relatively easy to measure through physical testing procedures. And, because it is comparatively easy to evaluate the degrees to which these functions are fulfilled by any package under consideration, such measurement is very common. Today, it must be a rare package that reaches its market without being rated objectively on its degrees of protection and production line adaptability. However, these ratings seem to be applied too often without consideration of the package's ability to fulfill its other possible functions.

There are four other major jobs that the package can do at least partially; these should be assigned priority by company management, but often they seem to be neglected.

All packages have the opportunity to perform, at least partially, each of these functions. But it is an unusual package that performs each to the same degree. That the package gives a superior performance of one function does not necessarily mean that it will give a superior performance of another. Because he needs to choose a package, the packager, whether he recognizes it or not, must assign priorities to the value of each of these functions to further his product's sale and use.

To illustrate, it is usually easy to create a package that has uniquely promotable features quite aside from graphic arts; that is, a package that

[1] That is, increasing the ratio of product volume to package volume.

could eminently perform the promotional function. But something else has to give. Using such a package may require sacrificing a good job in one of the other areas, for example in adaptability to production line speeds or in failure to increase package density. In like fashion, it is frequently possible to build a feature facilitating product use into a package—but not always without sacrificing some measure of product protection.

After all, when a package is criticized as a poor sales- or use-builder, it can be criticized fairly only when its performance of *each* of the basic functions is evaluated. A product may seem "overpackaged" simply because the packager's assignment of priorities differs from the critic's.

Interrelationships

Let's examine in a little more detail the way each function impinges on the others:

PROTECTING THE PRODUCT

Beyond the requirements imposed by various governmental, carrier, and trade practice rulings, there usually are a substantial number of alternatives open to management with regard to product protection—even during the period when the product is in its distribution channel. To illustrate, even though a carrier ruling may require the product's 24-count carton to have a minimum corrugated fiberboard strength of, say, a 100-pound test, a company's management may choose board that meets more severe tests in order to permit higher stacking or use of mechanized materials-handling equipment by certain important handlers at various levels in the product's distribution channel. Accordingly, in such a situation, an opportunity to tailor the product's package to its product-protection job alone is relinquished because of a desire to better the package's performance of its density-increasing and promotional jobs.

But perhaps a more important range of product-protection considerations occurs at the time of product use—especially when the product is partially used. How much protection should the bread wrapper give a partially used loaf of bread? Will incorporating the use-facilitating features of a pouring spout or a tear tape opening require yielding too much product protection?

ADAPTING TO PRODUCTION LINE SPEEDS

Sometimes the operating speeds of packaging equipment do not match the speeds of other equipment in the production line. Until recently, for instance, the normal operating speeds of wrapping machinery that would handle polyethylene film did not match the normal production line speeds for many products. Two or more wrapping machines were often required in a production line, and the results were poor space utilization, greater capital investment, and sometimes greater labor costs. As an alternative to these wastes, the packager "made do" with other types of film that could be handled by high-speed wrapping equipment but lacked some of polyethylene's protective attributes. New types of wrapping machines have largely corrected this situation. But the point is that the freedom of the packagers to better their packages' protective attributes was limited.

The question of a package's adaptability to production line speeds, however, usually crops up before the package is actually used. The packager's advertising agency or his sales department suggests a new package with striking promise of being able to fulfill the promotional or use-facilitating function better than current packaging; but, upon analysis, the suggested new package is found to require either slow-downs in production line speeds or investment in new packaging equipment. The company's management is then obliged to judge whether or not the suggested package's better performance of the promotional or use-facilitating functions justifies the slower line speed or the different packaging equipment.

PROMOTING THE PRODUCT

Features may be built into a package which are promotable to consumers, to customers, and to intermediaries in its product's distribution channel. But sometimes a feature desirable for promotion to one of the three is not desirable for one of the others. Features that minimize a retailer's loss or pilferage are, presumably, important to him; but they are not necessarily of any interest to consumers. Features that minimize a consumer's embarrassment at purchase can increase a retailer's stacking or display difficulties and make inventory control more trying.

Even granting a package feature that is promotable regardless of level in its product's distribution or use, incorporation of the feature into the package frequently requires sacrificing some good package performance of one of the other basic package functions. For example, a gift-wrapped set-up box complete with nosegay of artificial flowers is a highly promotable candy package, as is a rigid plastic, reusable package for razors that is large enough to hold a fishing lure. But both packages sacrifice density for better promotion.

INCREASING PRODUCT DENSITY

This seems to be the area where the packager's sales department on the one hand, and his purchasing and production departments on the other, are most often in disagreement about the choice of packaging. Except on those occasions when the sales department recommends yielding a package's higher density in order to improve its promotional value, the sales department is usually advocating increased package density. It improves relations with carriers; it permits better utilization of space throughout the distribution channel, thus encouraging fuller inventory stocks in the pipeline; and it permits more units to be displayed per assigned running foot of self-service display space. But it frequently slows production line speeds and increases per-unit packaging cost.

Usually this issue turns on package shape. The cylinder, for instance, is an efficient package shape for liquids; a given measure of liquid can be packaged cylindrically with less material than is necessary for any rectangular container holding the same amount of liquid. But the normal 12-count (3×4 put-up) layer of a 24-count carton will occupy significantly less shelf space if it holds rectangular packages rather than the same number of cylindrical packages with the same amount of liquid.

But bettering a package's performance of its density-increasing function can inhibit good performance in other areas too. The density of many candy packages, for instance, could be improved significantly, but not without loss of their value as items specifically tailored for re-use as sewing baskets or cookie tins. Increasing density could also lessen the package's value as a promotional vehicle or as a promotable item in itself. Package designers seem better able to build points of brand differentiation into a 12-ounce beer bottle than into the higher-density 12-ounce beer can.

FACILITATING THE USE OF THE PRODUCT

Excluding changes in the graphic art of packages, most package changes in recent years have been in facilitating the product's use. All the changes to tear tapes, pouring spouts, squeeze bottles, aerosol cans, and so forth would have to be included here. And, as is obvious to anyone exposed to the mass advertising media, bettering the package's fulfillment of this function has proved to be a means of bettering the package's performance in promotion.

In many cases, however, where the use-facilitating function of a package has been improved, a case can be built that some degree of product protection has been sacrificed. And, bettering the package's use-facilitating job sometimes means relinquishing some package value as a re-use container for the consumer. The flow of a viscous liquid perhaps can be directed a little more accurately or easily from the mouth of a narrow-necked glass jar than from a tin can, but packaging the liquid in the glass jar means sacrificing the protection against impact provided by the tin can. The tear tape makes a corrugated carton easier to open but, for many purposes, lessens its value as a re-usable container. Some shaker openings make cleanser or spice packages easy to use but, once used, leave the product exposed.

HAVING RE-USE VALUE FOR THE CONSUMER

Perhaps the competition of the various functions of the package for recognition by company managements is most apparent in this area. In recent years, according much recognition to this function of the package seems not to have been in vogue. Typically, designing a package to do its other jobs well has meant slighting its re-use value—the previous illustrations of candy and razors notwithstanding. A package's re-use value generally has suffered with successive changes unless its re-usability has been very promotable.

The Principle, The Corollary, and Recent Trends

How does management know whether it is better to sacrifice a measure of product protection for a more promotable package or to build a use-facilitating attribute into the package instead of a density-increasing attribute?

Assuming that two "mixes" are in conflict or partial conflict, management may find the answer by deciding which will be more likely to push product storage as far from the packager as possible. This is, of course, another way of saying that the basic purpose of a product's package should be as much as possible to maximize product inventory near the point of use or possible use. If neither "mix" holds promise of increasing product inventory at the point of use, does either hold promise of increasing product storage at the next level back from the point of use? If neither "mix" aids in getting the product stored on the dining-room table, does either help in getting more of the product inventoried on the kitchen shelves? If neither helps there, which encourages the greater amount of well-placed open display at retail? If it is a tie between the two package "mixes" at this level, which of the two has promise of encouraging the greater retailer inventory—regardless whether in open display or not?

It follows, then, that the most successful package changes are those whose impact is greatest at a level in the product's marketing one step forward from the level currently storing the channel's largest share of the product.

Most recent packaging changes can be understood a little better if viewed against the backdrop of these generalizations. Interestingly, they explain current trends in package design that, on the surface, seem to be running in opposite directions. For instance, recently some company managements have been increasing package size or package count. Other managements have unit-packaged, lessened package size, or reduced package count. But both apparently contradictory approaches have the same purpose—*to maximize product inventory as close to a point of use as possible.*

Let's examine a few recent package changes in light of these generalizations (I am referring to those changes that typically affect more than just the package's graphic art):

CHANGES INVOLVING PACKAGE SIZE OR COUNT

Proprietary medicine, soap powder or detergent, beverages, and toilet tissue are among those widely distributed consumer products whose recent package changes have included addition of "king" or "giant economy" size packages to their lines. Table salt, facial tissue, crackers, and cereal on the other hand are among the items, distributed in large part through the same marketing channel, which have added smaller-size packages or "unitized" packages to their lines. In each case, promotion turning on "convenience" to the user frequently has accompanied the introduction of the new package size. Where the move has been to increase the package size, packagers are trying to encourage the consumer to maintain inventories of their particular brands far in excess of the consumer's normal needs for the product during any reasonable time span between shopping trips. In effect, the packagers are trying to move a greater share of their channel's total storage function closer to the point of use—from retailer to consumer in this particular illustration. Where the move has been to lessen package size, it is apparent that the packagers are trying to move storage location further forward: to get facial tissues into purses as well as on the vanity; to get brand-identified salt on the dining-room, breakfast, TV, or barbecue table as well as on the pantry shelf; to get half a dozen varieties of cereal in the home rather than in the store in anticipation of a family's vacillating demands. Again, the packagers are trying to move a greater share of the channel's total storage closer to the point of use.

CHANGES INVOLVING PACKAGE SHAPE

Ice cream and milk, in both powdered and liquid forms, are examples of items that have been undergoing changes from cylindrical to space-saving rectangular packages. In part, at least, the change has been precipitated by increased recognition of the marketing channel's limited capacity to store items under refrigeration and of its eagerness to husband its shelf space. In effect, the change permits a greater share of the inventory to be moved forward.

CHANGES INVOLVING PACKAGING MATERIALS

This is the area where packagers' desires to push storage forward probably have been most apparent. And, incidentally, it is in this area that the lie is put to the belief that a package's prime job is protection of the product. If product protection were the prevailing consideration, few if any of certain kinds of change in packaging materials would ever have taken place. For example:

   a. *Changes from Opaque to Transparent Materials* usually have been represented as irrefutable evidence of the packager's good faith in allowing his customers to see his product. Understandably, the suppliers of transparent packaging materials have done what they could to further this impression. But conversion from opaque to transparent packaging typically has meant something else as well; *It has been a means of obtaining favorable open display shelf space at retail,* where the product could be seen by the consumers. In effect, it has meant moving part of the storage function forward in the channel from concealed storage or low-traffic locations to prominent, high-traffic locations. Small wonder that such a premium has come to be placed on transparency—even for products not especially attractive to the eye.

   b. *Changes from Rigid to Flexible Materials* have almost always meant relinquishing some measure of product protection—and the recent changes from rigid to semirigid or flexible packaging are legion. The changes, while requiring some loss of product-protection value, typically have given the product an especially promotable package, one with conspicuous promise of moving product storage closer to a point of use.

CHANGES INVOLVING ADDITION OF "EASE-OF-OPENING" OR "EASE-OF-USE" ATTRIBUTES

   I believe that, where they have been successful, package changes incorporating this kind of feature have tended to move product storage increasingly closer—however slightly—to the point of use. Typically, the movement of storage effected by such "ease-of-opening" package changes has not been at the consumer level in the product's marketing channel; it has been at the retail level. Perhaps it could be argued that the extremely successful rigid flip-top cigarette package has helped move the smoker's storage of his cigarettes a little closer to the point of their use, but the main value of the package with regard to its movement of product storage has been at the retail level. The package, again, was a means of obtaining a good, high-traffic position in open display for the particular brands of cigarette that pioneered this packaging change. It was something distinctively new that could be promoted to the marketing channel itself—quite aside from its being amenable to use in effective promotion to smokers—for brands not having so extensive or complete retail inventories as those enjoyed by more popular brands.

   In summary, the choice of a product's package, no less than the choice of the total selling effort brought to bear on the product, has to represent a reconciliation of a variety of functions, each of which has potential merit in furthering the sale of the product, but all of which are, in part at least, mutually exclusive.

The most successful reconciliation will be the one that, to return to our original axiom, produces the most sales. It will emphasize that function which pushes the bulk of product storage one step farther along the marketing channel and one step closer to the ultimate consumer.

It is clear . . . that the competitive struggle between manufacturers and private brands will continue. Private brands have some strong advantages, but manufacturers will also be keen and quick to exploit their own brand positions.

30

Factors Motivating Consumer Choice of Private Brands

ROBERT S. HANCOCK

FOR THE PURPOSES of our discussion this afternoon, it is preferred to use the term "private brand(s)" as indicated in your program. In so doing, private brands are regarded as synonymous with "distributor brands," "controlled brands," "wholesaler-retailer brands" and other similar terms. Each of these terms seems to have identical meanings as they all denote the ownership of a brand by a wholesaler or retailer, and the marketing institution having ownership control assumes, 'if not the total merchandising task, a major portion of it.

The contents of this paper rely on certain phases of a recently completed research project by the marketing faculty of the University of Minnesota. This project was sponsored by an *anonymous* manufacturer. In other words the sponsoring company manufactures private brands exclusively for distribution to large scale wholesalers and retailers. It manufactures nothing under its own name. This particular company sells its products to regional and national distributors in the United States and Canada, and it has franchised manufacturing plants in several foreign countries. A number of its products are among the well known private brand names.

Reprinted from Richard M. Hill (ed.), *Marketing Concepts in Changing Times*, Proceedings From the Winter Conference of the American Marketing Association, December, 1959, pp. 66-74.

Much of the data for this project was gathered by means of personal interviews with the managements of 21 large-scale merchandising firms located in the United States and Canada. The sample comprised general merchandising and mail order houses, food retailers, automotive and hardware chains, department stores and their buying groups. Secondary sources of information were helpful in detecting general patterns and trends of private brands and also in adding confirmation and strength, here and there, to our primary data.

Growth Patterns of Private Brands

The growth of private brands is a counterpart of large-scale retailing. When or where private brands originated is not known, but a number of our present day corporate chains commenced buying by specification before the turn of the century. A rather strong and definite pattern of private brand growth was apparent in the 1920's and this continued until World War II. Setbacks in the development of private brands occurred during World War II and the immediate post-war years, when materials were scarce and production rates could not be maintained for private brands. There has, however, been a very strong resurgence of private brands during the past decade and this growth has every indication of continuing. It is this recent resurgence that has generated the concern of leaders in the retailing *industry* as well as attracted the attention of academic people. Hence, for manufacturers and distributors affected by private brands, and also to improve the academic persons' concepts and understanding of a marketing phenomenon, it is both timely and desirable to inquire into the marketing strategy that has been successful in motivating consumers toward private brands.

Before inquiring into this marketing strategy let us clarify the fact that private brand growth is a counterpart to large-scale retailing. Most of our retailing developments center on the vast size to which some retail organizations have grown. We all know that relatively few of the nation's retailers account for the bulk of the annual retail volume. Furthermore, only about 3.5 per cent of the retailers reach an annual sales volume in excess of one-half million dollars. Few of these, though, have the sales volume, and executive talent to enter the private brand field. There has, however, been the startling growth during the last few decades of a few hundred retail firms whose sales volumes now fall into the "multimillion dollar class" and six corporate chains whose sales volumes now fall into the "more than a billion dollar" category. During this same period, the corporate chain, voluntary chain, and retailer-cooperative have made their mark. Mass merchandising developments as spearheaded by these organizations have created many of the conditions which have tended to make private brands a logical course of action. These same retail firms have the financial strength and know-how to undertake the expensive demand-creating operations necessary to build private brand acceptance on a grand scale.

Associated with these developments has been horizontal integration, i.e., the expansion into many retail outlets. This has contributed the assurance of a high and sustained sales volume which is as essential to the success of a private brand as it is to a manufacturer's brand. Vertical integration is another condition contributing to the development of private brands. Retailers with sizeable sales volumes have found it advantageous to assume some manufacturing and wholesaling functions or to specify clearly their own requirements for their brands.

These developments, then, have contributed to the fundamental conditions which were necessary before a retailer could embark on a widespread private brand program, or before he could successfully exploit the advantages of private brands.

Factors Which Favor the Use and Acceptance of Private Brands

Without exception, the study by the Minnesota marketing faculty, found that a successful private brand hinges on the existence of either customer need, or the fact that customer good will and confidence in the retailer is so strong that consumer acceptance of the private brand is assured. Of course retailers are in a much better position than manufacturers when it comes to recognizing customer need and in building his confidence in the store and merchandise lines. There is no doubt that a number of our largest retailers have done just that. In other words, it is contended that consumers strongly associate the fulfillment of their needs with a retailer, and not (as commonly held by some) with a manufacturer who most often is at a distant place from the consumer-retailer community.

Recognizing the above basic considerations, large-scale retailers have found that in order to maximize their efforts to meet consumer need, satisfaction and service, it is necessary to have a marked degree of control over the products they sell. In doing this, private brands are recognized as an integral part of a well-rounded and effective merchandising policy, for without them either gaps, or marked deficiencies in their merchandising policies, or both, would occur. The firms involved in our study recognized three important merchandising gaps, and a like number of marked merchandising deficiencies, all of which could be wholly or partially overcome with their own brands. The merchandising gaps are:

1. *Price and quality gap*—A product of equal or higher quality at a lower price is needed to satisfy consumer demand.

2. *Ensemble and family of products gap*—A complete ensemble, or a family of products cannot be obtained economically by buying manufacturers' brands, and to have coordination of quality, style (or design) and price in order to create a uniform appeal, private brands are necessary.
3. *Prestige gap*—No appeal to the prestige market can be made with a manufacturers brand.

The marked deficiencies in merchandising effectiveness are:

1. A product or merchandise line is unstable because the line is sold by discount retailers, the price is unstable and subject to price cutting; or the line may be fair traded and this depresses the merchandising possibilities for the firm.
2. A manufacturer's brand either is not available or is weak in public acceptance; or if available, it has spotty distribution.
3. The cost of distribution of the manufacturer's line is too high or the distribution policies of the manufacturer do not coincide with those of the retailer, and hence greater distribution efficiency in the form of lower costs may be had by developing the private brand.

Some of the above factors are obviously stronger than others in motivating consumers. Certainly consumers are very likely to be more influenced by the product values they can feel and observe, rather than the "hidden values." It is quite clear that the three "gaps" and the closing of them by retailers are strong factors in motivating consumers. On the other hand, the latter group of factors are really merchandising policy matters and as such are not usually discernible by consumers. One thing seems certain—it is the entire complex of factors, rather than any single one, that has made possible the adoption of private brands by large-scale retailers. In turn, these same factors have had an important role in the widespread acceptance of these brands by consumers.

Private Brand Pricing

Because price and other factors of appeal account for much of the success in the acceptance of private brands, these factors are worthy of additional elaboration. The pricing of a private brand at a price lower than a manufacturer's brand of comparable quality is a typical example of the strategy employed. When customers are able to compare the merchandiser's brand and price with a manufacturer's brand and price, there is the obvious tendency for the price conscious customer to select the lower-priced product. But, great care must be taken so as not to price the item too low. For example, one general merchandising company reported having purchased a large quantity of men's sweaters which retailed at $12.95 in competing stores. This firm replaced the label with its own and featured the sweaters as a $12.95 value for only $4.98. They failed to sell these sweaters in great quantity until such time as they moved the price up to $7.98 and then featured them as a $12.95 value. Such experiences as this indicate to retailers that the price of a private brand cannot be set so low as to cheapen it in the consumer's mind.

For the most part, we found that it is typical for private-brand merchandise to sell for less, particularly when a comparable manufacturer's brand is also displayed. Frequently, the private brand is shown to its best advantage when the retailer is able to display it prominently along with manufacturers' brands. This, in fact, is a very common practice and is used for such diverse products as appliances, grocery products, cold cream, and aspirin.

So expansion is good.

If, however, price is set at the same level as the manufacturer's brand, additional accessories or quality features are promoted heavily so that, relatively, the private brand is lower priced. An example of this technique was found in one department store which featured private brand shirts at the same or higher prices than manufacturers' brands. In this instance the higher count broadcloth, stronger buttons and better workmanship were features which attracted the customer from the manufacturers' brands to the store brand. Prestige lines which have experienced considerable growth and acceptance usually have no comparable manufacturer's brand to compete against. Therefore, their reputation and value are usually supported by a prestige price. This is the exception to the more common policy of relatively low price. Many department stores have such lines.

Appeal is not on price alone, however, but also on value. Value is a function of both price and quality. If the customer accepts the stated policy of many private branders, e.g., "We have private brands only if we can offer the customer the same quality at a lower price or a higher quality at the same price," the greater value appeal is stronger than price or quality alone.

While price remains one of the strongest appeals, pricing has other advantages for the merchandiser. Price lining, for example, is easier to accomplish when products are tailored to specifications which are in accord with customer needs. To the customer, general price lining is an inducement to shop at the store which has definite price lines—price lines at levels which are acceptable to him.

Some retailers have found that vacuums existed at both the high and low ends of their price lines, with manufacturers' brands occupying a strong position in between. By filling these gaps with their own brands, a broader product and price appeal can be made. Such a broadening of the line exploits more completely the needs of the consumer. Women's shoes, house furnishings, and coffee are examples of products for which stores may have multiple private brands. Department stores frequently have separate brands for the Basement Store.

Pricing is closely allied to some other aspects of successful merchandising, namely fair trade and the need to control price. Fair trade which helped to foster the development of private brands, also fostered price competition as the historical margins on many lines became unrealistic and eventually broke down. This brought with it an expansion of discount selling and other aggressive competitive practices.

Without control over price the retailer may find himself selling at prices which do not afford a margin high enough to cover operating expenses. This was found to be one of the problems faced by department stores in the sale of major appliances. To compete with discount houses, department stores may be forced to sell appliances at a very small mark-up. A private brand retailer confronted with this problem may have a much wider margin on his own brand. He can stabilize his price at a lower level and still have sufficient margin to undertake aggressive merchandising profitably. When retailers merchandise on a price basis, control over price is essential to their success. Without control over price, they may be faced with an intolerable margin squeeze.

Creating Product and Store Distinctiveness

Finally, one very important hidden advantage results from the closing of the gaps just outlined. This advantage is *product* and *store* distinctiveness. Distinctiveness is a product of private brands not usually recognized by the casual observer. Large scale retailers clearly recognize that any retailer is at a competitive disadvantage unless he can create an image of distinctiveness for his products and his establishment. The merchandising of manufacturers' brands by large-scale retailers in all likelihood stimulates the demand for the brand in other stores as well. "Why should we advertise manufacturers' brands heavily and increase sales of those brands in other stores, when we can promote our private brands and our store's exclusively?" and "We feature our own brands so as to offer products that are distinctive—products that are different—from manufacturers' or competitors' brands," are the typical views of large-scale merchandisers. These retailers have clearly recognized the value of distinctiveness and this is one of the reasons they have developed private brands. But, more importantly this has given them a "captive" customer.

While distinctiveness may at first seem incongruous to private brands, this is an important success factor in retailing. To create distinctiveness, private branders fill the gaps at the high and low ends of the price lines, or develop brands in direct competition with moderately-priced manufacturers' brands. In this way stores refrain from becoming so similar to their competitors that they have little or nothing different to offer their customers. What then, is the force that attracts trade? Most of the really successful merchandisers have created a distinctiveness which has built their large volume of trade. Private brands enable merchants to create distinctiveness of product and store which is not possible through location, interior design and layout, promotion, or the use of commonly-handled manufacturers' brands.

The distinctive private brand can be a promotional aid which will help to attract customers away from competitors. This may be a price difference or quality difference, or it may be store loyalty built upon a succession of purchases of private-brand merchandise. The mixing of both manufacturers' brands and private brands has given some retailers a maximum appeal. Even those units with 90 or 95 per cent of their volume in private brands recognize the advantage of the mix, if for no other purpose than objective comparison by the consumer.

The Outlook for Private Brands

All signs point to the conclusion that private brands are in the ascendancy. Among these signs are the continuing growth of large-scale retailing and the steadily growing use of private brands. The same is true of department store groups and many centrally-owned chains. Voluntary chains, retailers-cooperatives and consumer cooperatives are today even more deeply engaged in private brand development.

The ever-present consumer interest in price favors the expansion of private brand business and the extension of private brands into comparatively new areas. Among these are house furnishings and even such products as clocks and watches, jewelry, silverware, and photographic equipment. Private brand developments in these lines are in the infancy stages.

Our study amply demonstrates that private brands can be sold on a high-price prestige basis as well as in competition with manufacturers' lower-priced brands. Retailers, therefore, have an opportunity in many lines to use several private brands at different price levels.

Leading private brand users have developed a high degree of customer loyalty and trust in their brands, and this good will in turn can carry them to new heights in the use of private brands. Product distinctiveness of this type is an asset as unique as it is valuable, and retailers are certain to capitalize on it.

As long as private brand users exercise care in the selection of their lines, supervise closely the quality of their products, and price their brands intelligently, consumer interest in private brands will perhaps remain high.

The exact growth pattern is difficult to predict. Where private brands are deeply entrenched, the rate of growth may be comparatively slow, but even this is uncertain because of the interrelationships between private and manufacturers' brands in such respects as quality, price, service policies, and sales promotion. It is conceivable that private brands may reach a plateau as lines most suitable for private brands are filled out. However, such a plateau, if there is to be one, is certainly not in sight, as the way toward further expansion seems wide open.

There is no prospect that private brands will in any sense drive out manufacturers' brands, however. Both types of lines are certain to increase in dollar volume with our expanding economy. Department stores, chain stores, and even the mail order houses will not be able, and in fact may have no desire, to cut off manufacturers' brands. Some consumers for various reasons will always prefer manufacturers' brands in certain fields. Good merchandisers will meet their customers' needs, whatever they may be, and many customers will continue to call for manufacturers' brands. In fact, if manufacturers become increasingly disturbed about the growth of private brands they will attempt to strengthen the competitive position of their own brands.

It is clear, therefore, that the competitive struggle between manufacturers' and private brands will continue. Private brands have some strong advantages, but manufacturers will also be keen and quick to exploit their own brand positions.

C. MARKETING CHANNELS DECISIONS

. . . channel activities must be thought of as only one aspect of the total marketing mix and one that must be coordinated with other ingredients, as these contribute to the objective of reaching a defined market.

31

Channels of Distribution — One Aspect of Marketing Strategy

WILLIAM R. DAVIDSON

IN RECENT YEARS, increasing emphasis has been placed upon modern concepts of "customer-oriented marketing management"; it has become more and more common to administer marketing activities with reference to some defined marketing strategy.

The formulation of a marketing strategy [1] consists of two steps:

1. Identification of a market target: the selection of an objective stated in terms of the segment of the market (group of consumers or industrial users) to which the company wishes to appeal.

Reprinted from *Business Horizons* (Special Issue—First International Seminar on Marketing Management), February, 1961, pp. 84-90. Copyright, 1961 by the Foundation for Economic and Business Studies, Indiana University.

[1] For further discussion, see Alfred R. Oxenfeldt, "The Formulation of a Market Strategy," in Eugené J. Kelley and William Lazar, *Managerial Marketing: Perspectives and Viewpoints* (Homewood, Ill., Richard D. Irwin, Inc., 1958), pp. 264 ff.

2. Development of a marketing mix: the choice of the relative emphasis to
   be accorded to different aspects of the total marketing effort, in order to
   best attain the objective of reaching the identified market.

While the number of separate, identifiable aspects of the total marketing
effort will vary from one company to another, it may be helpful to enumer-
ate some rather common ingredients. These are: marketing research,
product planning, channels of distribution, physical availability of product,
advertising and sales promotion, personal selling, and pricing.

Decisions concerning the relative emphasis to be placed upon each aspect
involve alternative uses of marketing man power and capital resources.
Within a particular company at a given time, it is not possible to increase
greatly the relative emphasis upon one aspect without decreasing the
relative importance of other ingredients of the marketing mix. Hence,
decisions that enlarge or reduce the importance of one item in the mix
can be made intelligently only by considering the potential effects of changing the relative importance of others, and by evaluating the total impact
of such changes upon the firm's ability to reach the market identified in the
first step of formulating a marketing strategy.

These introductory remarks set the stage for viewing channels of distribution as one aspect of marketing strategy. While such channels can
be singled out for special attention and discussion, managerial decisions
concerning the selection of trade channels and maintenance of relationships
with agencies in these channels should be made in the light of their relationship to an over-all strategy of marketing.

This discussion will deal primarily with the marketing of consumer goods
within the domestic market. This restriction offers some advantages. First,
channels are usually lengthier and more complex in consumer goods
marketing than in the industrial goods field, even though important
generalizations apply equally under similar conditions. Furthermore, discussion of channel problems in industrial marketing tends to be more difficult, because of different vocabulary and operating conditions among industries; in consumer goods marketing, on the other hand, all of us have
the perspective and experience of consumers, and hence can more readily
grasp the implications of examples and generalizations.

Channels Defined

The term "channel of distribution" is part of the working vocabulary
of every business executive, yet many would be hard pressed to define
its meaning precisely. This is not surprising because a wide variety of interpretations are available in the literature on the subject.

For example, the channel has been defined by one author as "the pipe-

line through which a product flows on its way to the consumer. The manufacturer puts his product into the pipeline, or marketing channel, and various marketing people move it along to the consumer at the other end of
the channel." [2]

Another authority states, "Marketing channels are the combination of
agencies through which the seller, who is often, though not necessarily,
the manufacturer, markets his product to the ultimate user." [3]

A third scholar views marketing channels as consisting of "intermediary
sellers who intervene between the original source of supply and the
ultimate consumer." In his view, the number and character of such intermediaries "are determined primarily by the requirements of sorting and
by the opportunity to effect economies by suitable sorting arrangements." [4]
On another occasion, the same writer described a marketing channel as a
group of firms that "constitute a loose coalition engaged in exploiting a
joint opportunity in the market." [5]

Another well-known source states that "the trade channel is made up
of the middlemen who move goods from producers to consumers" and that
"we usually think of the channel as being made up of those merchants who
own the goods and of those agent middlemen who effect sales." [6]

This variety of viewpoint leads to lack of clarity on several points. Does
the channel have to do primarily with the change of ownership of goods
or with the physical movement of product? Is the nature of a given channel
determined by the manufacturer, acting as a seller, or by middlemen and
consumers, carrying out their role as buyers? Is the channel made up only
of middlemen or intervening intermediaries, or does it include the manufacturer at one end and the consumer at the other?

Given some product to be marketed, several jobs must be done. First,
there is the question of arrangements for bringing about changes in ownership by performance of the functions of exchange, buying, and selling.
Second, there is the matter of availability of physical supply, which involves
the functions of transportation and storage, and related activities such as
physical handling and control of inventories. Third, there is the necessity
of various facilitating or auxiliary functions, such as the collection and

[2] Richard M. Clewett, *Checking Your Marketing Channels* (No. 120; Washington,
U.S. Small Business Administration, Management Aids for Small Manufacturers,
January, 1961).

[3] John A. Howard, *Marketing Managements: Analysis and Decision* (Homewood,
Ill., Richard D. Irwin, Inc., 1957), p. 179.

[4] Wroe Alderson, *Marketing Behavior and Executive Action* (Homewood, Ill.,
Richard D. Irwin, 1957), p. 211.

[5] Wroe Alderson, "The Development of Marketing Channels," in Richard M.
Clewett, ed., *Marketing Channels for Manufactured Goods* (Homewood, Ill., Richard
D. Irwin, 1954), p. 30.

[6] Paul D. Converse, Harvey W. Huegy, and Robert V. Mitchell, *Elements of
Marketing* (Englewood Cliffs, Prentice-Hall, 1958), p. 119.

dissemination of marketing information, management of market risks, financing of marketing activities, and standardization and grading.

Generally speaking, the functions of exchange may be considered as paramount because planning for physical supply and performance of facilitating functions do not become relevant in the typical marketing organization unless there is profitable opportunity for transfers of ownership.

It appears, therefore, most realistic to define the channel of distribution as consisting of "the course taken in the transfer of title to a commodity." [7] It is the route taken in transferring the title of a product from its first owner (usually a manufacturer) to its last owner, the business user or ultimate consumer. Such a route necessarily includes both the origin and the destination; hence, it should be viewed as including the manufacturer and the ultimate consumer, as well as any intervening middlemen, inasmuch as all three are originators and performers of much marketing activity. Middlemen in the channel include both merchants, who assume title and resell on their own account, and various kinds of agents or brokers, who do not take title but are nonetheless instrumental along the route taken to effect transfers of ownership. Broadly speaking, the channel also includes marketing establishment owned by vertically integrated companies, that is, those performing marketing functions on more than one plane or level of distribution. Examples are chain-store distribution warehouses and manufacturers' branch sales offices. There is no legal transfer of title between a factory and a sales branch operated by the same company nor between a chain-store warehouse and the retail units it serves; however, there are intracompany transactions that have the nature of sales or shipments, and which are comparable in nature to the transactions made by alternative suppliers or distributors performing similar functions on the same plane of distribution.

Physical Distribution

The general tendency is for the physical flow of merchandise to accompany the route of exchange. This is not, however, universally the case, and there are indications that separate structural arrangements for physical distribution are increasingly important. A few examples will illustrate a variety of arrangements for providing physical supply apart from the channel of distribution.

In the field of *industrial marketing* and in many lines of consumer goods, manufacturers' agents are used in lieu of manufacturers' sales branches. In combining the product lines of several manufacturers, the manufacturers'

[7] Theodore N. Beckman, Harold H. Maynard, and William R. Davidson, *Principles of Marketing* (New York, Ronald, 1957), p. 39.

agent provides economical sales coverage of a given area, and often reaches certain customers who would be difficult to contact by other means. While such agents are links in the channel used to effect transfers of title, they do not ordinarily carry stocks. The physical flow of goods is another arrangement, one that is usually direct from the factory to the customer of the agent.

In the *wholesale paper trade* (as in many other lines of wholesaling), most transactions are handled from warehouse stocks owned and stored by the merchant. A large proportion of the total dollar and physical volume of sales consists, however, of so-called "direct" sales. On individual orders of large size, the wholesale merchant buys from the manufacturer and takes title at the point where merchandise is loaded on cars, but the merchandise itself flows directly from factory to customer as a drop shipment, never coming near the establishment where the sale was negotiated.

Several retail *mail-order companies* have worked out arrangements to establish catalogue order departments in retail establishments operated by supermarket chains. While the facilities of another retailing organization are used as part of the route through which sales contact is made with the consuming public, the merchandise is shipped directly from the mail-order establishment.

In the field of *food-product manufacturing,* several companies with factories located in various parts of the country and wide product lines have recently established gigantic regional food distribution warehouses. Such warehouses consolidate in each region, a reservoir of all products in the line, permitting fast delivery of mixed cars at low freight rates to wholesalers and chain warehouses. This form of physical distribution tends to be separate from organizational responsibility for sales handled through branch offices or through food brokers, and the geographic flow of merchandise does not correspond to the location of establishments responsible for making sales contacts with customers.

In the *appliance industry,* some wide-line manufacturers have concentrated a physical supply of various items in the line, either by centralizing all manufacturing facilities or by providing for distribution warehouses. The wholesale distributor remains as the institution making sales contact with the retailer and assumes responsibility for developing the desired share of available market potential in the area of his operation. Many types of dealers at the retail level are able to purchase full cars containing a mixture of various items in the manufacturers' assortment, with the flow of goods direct from factory or manufacturers' warehouse. The retailer still has contact with the wholesaler as the next link in the distribution channel but, in many instances, this is related to transfer of title, financing arrangements, and sales promotion assistance, and has little to do with the physical flow of merchandise.

The last two examples, in particular, reflect a growing tendency to streamline physical distribution by setting it apart from the complex of channel links used for obtaining sales. In some companies, a new department of physical distribution combines a number of previously scattered activities, including finished goods inventory control, transportation and traffic warehousing, order processing, container design, and sometimes even manufacturing scheduling.[8]

As this practice becomes more widespread, there will be an increasing tendency to consider institutional arrangements in the channel used for effecting changes in ownership to be an element in the marketing mix, distinct from the arrangements for the availability of physical supply. In the majority of instances, however, both ownership changes and physical flow may continue along all or a major part of the same route.

Channel "Commanders"

In many discussions of the subject, the manufacturer is cast in the role of "commander" of the channnel situation. When introducing a new product or when making a major change in distribution policies, he examines a wide range of possible alternatives with respect to kinds and numbers of wholesale and retail outlets, weighs a number of factors that have a bearing upon sales volume, costs, and profitability, and selects the arrangements that best serve his purpose.

The types of decisions to be made by a manufacturer in choosing a channel may be divided into two classes: vertical considerations, which relate to the number of different levels or stages in the route used to effect transfers of title; and horizontal considerations, which pertain to the density or selectivity of distribution and the classes and number of outlets on a given plane (for example, wholesale or retail level).[9]

Vertical choices may be illustrated by alternatives of the following kind that might be available to a manufacturer of home furnishings. He could choose (1) to sell direct to the consumer without use of any middlemen, perhaps by means of catalogues; (2) to sell to retail furniture stores by means of a manufacturer-employed sales organization; (3) to sell to furniture stores through wholesale merchants; (4) to sell to wholesale merchants by means of manufacturers' agents who also sell other related

---

[8] "New-Fangled Routes Deliver the Goods—Faster and Cheaper," *Business Week* (Nov. 14, 1959), pp. 108 ff.; John F. Magee, "The Logistics of Distribution," *Harvard Business Review,* XXXVIII (July-Aug., 1960), 89 ff.; Edward W. Smykay, Donald J. Bowersox, and Frank H. Mossman, *Physical Distribution Management* (New York, Macmillan, 1961).

[9] For more comprehensive treatment, see *Principles of Marketing,* pp. 39 ff.

lines; (5) to use manufacturers' agents who call directly upon retailers; or (6) to use some combination of the above channels in order to reach different geographic markets or various classes of stores, perhaps differentiated on the basis of sales volume.

Horizontal choices may be illustrated by listing the channels open to a manufacturer of home furnishings who has his own sales organization calling directly upon the retail furniture trade. He must decide whether to (1) continue confining his distribution to retail furniture stores; (2) sell also to furniture departments in regular department stores; (3) offer his merchandise also to variety-department stores operated by certain variety chains who are expanding their merchandise offerings of this general type of merchandise; or (4) sell to various forms of discount houses.

Conventional discussions of channel problems have tended to devote more emphasis to questions of the vertical kind by stressing the factors that determine whether or when it is feasible for the manufacturer to move forward in the channel, assuming within his own organization the functions normally performed by various types of middlemen. He thereby carries his own marketing effort as close as possible to the final user. Among the various factors generally believed to contribute to the feasibility of short channels are a high unit value of product, a wide line of items marketed together, geographically concentrated markets, and financial strength and marketing know-how in the manufacturing company's organization.

In recent years, several factors have tended to make decisions of the horizontal type appear as matters of greater decision-making significance. For one thing, various types of retail outlets have greatly diversified their merchandise offerings, thereby invading what was once considered the private province of establishments in other categories. As a consequence, there is a wider range of alternatives at the retail level, and each class has unique operating problems, buying procedures, and operating philosophies. Second, choices at the horizontal level are more likely to cause frictions and tensions in channel relationship. For example, antagonism among regular household appliance stores and a possible withdrawal of sales support by them may occur when a manufacturer decides to aggressively solicit business from various types of discount houses. Similar frictions exist at the wholesale level when distributors in one line of trade find that new outlets in another trade classification are selling identical products formerly distributed in a more confined way. Third, decisions to use particular types of outlets at the retail level—a horizontal choice—may often dictate the kind of channel to be used in a vertical sense, since the retailer customarily uses certain sources of supply and a traditional outlook on buying arrangements.

THE MIDDLEMAN

In numerous situations, the manufacturer can realistically be regarded as the channel commander, at least in the short run. It is rather common for the manufacturer to call the plays when he is large and powerful, when he has developed high public status by his demand creation activities, when he finds it feasible to use a limited number of distribution outlets, and when distribution outlets operate under the terms of a franchise and would be seriously handicapped by the withdrawal of it. This tends to be the case with automobiles, major household appliances, and automotive petroleum products sold through gasoline service stations.

In many other instances, the manufacturer is channel commander not in any basic way but only in a derivative sense, owing to the strong position of middlemen in the channel. This circumstance stems from the two-fold role of middlemen as distributors of manufacturers' goods and as suppliers of the purchasing requirements of their customers. When the middleman carries a variety of items drawn from many original sources, he tends to be more strongly oriented to the latter role than to the former.

Briefly, it may be noted that the manufacturers' freedom to select among conceptually available alternatives is practically limited by conditions and attitudes prevailing among middlemen. Many circumstances limit the potentialities for distribution in certain types of channel situations, whether the choice be of a vertical or horizontal nature. Examples of these circumstances follow:

> The manufacturer finds that the most desirable types of outlets have already been pre-empted by strongly entrenched competitive organizations.
>
> The middleman, already using his space and capital resources to the maximum, is reluctant to add additional items to his line, since such proliferation poses serious logistics problems, particularly in terms of available display space, warehousing space, catalogue or stock control listings, capital required for inventory investment, and so forth.
>
> The pricing or discount structure on the item is not sufficiently attractive to induce middlemen to devote promotional effort adequate to ensure movement to the consumer.
>
> The manufacturer mishandles consumer packaging or shipping containers so that neither is acceptable under the conditions of selling or merchandise handling typical in a particular line of trade.
>
> The manufacturer has created tensions or frictions in trade channels, either by using distribution techniques that place him in direct competition with some possible outlets or by distributing through various outlets in different lines of trade with varying margin and sales supporting requirements. He thereby generates antagonism, which makes his products unacceptable or, at best, only marginally acceptable to certain types of potential outlets.

When the manufacturer encounters conditions of such a nature, he often learns that the middleman, in his role as a buyer and selector of sources of supply, really determines the nature of the channel of distribution.

THE CONSUMER

· Even when middlemen, whether they be wholesale distributors or retailers, are more strongly entrenched than manufacturers as channel commanders, their role too is more derivative than basic, owing to their need to adjust to constant changes. In a private enterprise economy characterized by high levels of buying income per family, the consumer has a wide range of choices when it comes to satisfying those wants that can be met in the market place. The consumer can, for example, decide whether to use more of his purchasing power to eat better, to travel more, to buy more clothes, or to purchase new appliances for his home. If the choice is for appliances, he can satisfy his needs at a department store, an appliance store, a mail-order company, a furniture store, a discount house, an automobile accessories store or, in some areas, a supermarket or consumers' cooperative organization. His choice will ordinarily be the outlet that has best harmonized its marketing mix with the buying interests of the group of consumers of which the individual purchaser is a member.

In the long run, therefore, the buying decisions of consumers determine the adjustments that occur in the relative importance of different kinds of channels of distribution. As adjustments occur at the retail level, they naturally have their impact in a vertical sense, by modifying the relative positions of various kinds of channel links between the manufacturer and the retailer.

Channel Choice

The discussion thus far indicates why certain manufacturers have found it necessary to modify their concept of factors that determine the choice of channels. In the company that follows a program of modern, consumer-oriented marketing management, considerations relating to consumer requirements are elevated to paramount status, and factors relating to company situation are subordinated, at least in the sense that the latter must be adjusted to the former. This means that the manufacturer must look beyond his own circumstances and beyond the situation of intermediaries in the channel, so that he is attuned to the wants and interests of the consumers in the market segment he is trying to reach.

EVALUATING CHANNEL RELATIONSHIPS

Too often, channel relationships do not receive due attention since they involve matters that are "outside" the company and, hence, are more easily taken for granted than other activities such as marketing research, advertising, or personal selling. These "internal" functions come up for more frequent review or appraisal since responsibility for them tends to be fixed on the organizational chart or in job descriptions, and the cost of them is conspicuously identified on accounting statements.

In manufacturing companies, opportunities for more frequent and more realistic appraisal of channel problems and relationships might be provided by new approaches to charting the organization of marketing activities. A new version of an organization chart might well show not only the various departments within the marketing division of the company, but also all of the vertical links in the channel used to effect transfers of title to eventual users, and, moreover, the different types of outlets on each horizontal plane or stage of distribution.

A related possibility is to prepare operating statements that reveal sales performance and cost situations through the channels used. At the top of such a statement would be sales, stated in terms of prices paid by the ultimate user, and showing as expenses the costs of marketing through the various channels in use.

In any event, manufacturers will have made progress in solving channel of distribution problems when they recognize two considerations. *First,* channel activities must be thought of as only one aspect of the total market-ing mix and one that must be coordinated with other ingredients, as these contribute to the objective of reaching a defined market; *second,* in the long run, the nature of channels is determined from "the bottom up" rather than from "the top down."

The institutions discussed here
—the modern supermarket selling non-foods, the discount
house and the controlled centers
—illustrate what the author believes is the essence of Schumpeter's innovating institutions:
institutions that force imitation
and adaptation.

32

Schumpeter, the "Big" Disturbance and Retailing

PERRY BLISS

SOME RETAIL ORGANIZATIONS operate in such a manner that their influence on retailing in general goes far beyond what could be conveyed by a simple listing of their number, or their sales volume, or their total employment— the three measures typically used to indicate size and influence in the retail field. The institutions we have reference to have the characteristics of innovators in whose wake come imitators and whose presence so colors the competitive picture that they require special analysis. Such organizations create what Schumpeter called a "big" disturbance because they ". . . disrupt the existing system and enforce a distinct process of adaptation."[1]

For Schumpeter the usual method of competition, in which *familiar* types of organization compete for the patronage of a given market by *familiar* methods, it is not the competition that counts. Rather, if there is to be "competition that matters," new institutions must enter the market place with new ways of organizing things, new sales-cost relationships, new methods of selling. Concerning competition in the retail trades, Schumpeter

Reprinted from *Social Forces*, Volume 39, No. 1 (October, 1960), pp. 72-76. Copyright ©, 1960, University of North Carolina Press. Reprinted by permission.

[1] Joseph Schumpeter, *Business Cycles* (1st ed.; New York: McGraw-Hill Book Company, 1939), I, p. 101 (italics Schumpeter's).

said: "In the case of retail trade the competition that matters arises not from additional shops of the same type, but from the department stores, the chain store, the mail order house and the supermarket. . . ." [2]

In the early part of the present century, the period which Schumpeter very likely had in mind, the department stores such as Macy's and Wanamaker's, the mail order houses such as Sears' and Ward's, the supermarkets of King Kullen and Big Bear, and chain store organizations such as F. W. Woolworth and the A & P, furnished the "competition that matters"; they indeed caused a "big" disturbance and compelled a "process of adaptation." It is the point of this paper that today we also have in the retail market place institutions that offer competition that matters and that are a source of a big disturbance.

The present day supermarkets by their disruptive effect on the service structure of *non-food* retailers, the discount houses by their impact on the retail price structure (especially consumer durables), and the planned regional shopping centers by their destructive effect on the location values of older retailers are innovating institutions in the Schumpeterian sense given above; they enter the market place with new types of organization, new cost-price relationships, and they compel imitation and/or adaptation on the part of the older forms of retail institutions.

Supermarkets and the Service Structure

The revolutionary effect supermarkets have had the last decade or two on the *food* industry has been nothing short of phenomenal. And their force is still being felt. Today they do something over 60 percent of all food business, and the overwhelming number of new food outlets being established are of the supermarket type. While supermarkets are apparently still increasing their share of the food dollar, the food industry has more or less learned to live with them; and so the supermarket revolution in the food field, as important as it was for Schumpeter, is not our present concern. Rather our interest here is centered on what the supermarket industry is doing to *non-food* stores such as department stores, variety and drug stores, retail lumber yards, clothing stores and hardware stores, to name a few.

While the method of operation of supermarkets has a tendency to bring

[2] Joseph Schumpeter, *Capitalism, Socialism and Democracy* (2nd ed.; New York, Harper, 1947), p. 85. This paper is concerned chiefly with Schumpeter's notion of a "big" disturbance and the imitation and adaptation which follow. Schumpeter was also greatly concerned with a larger system of analysis in which much weight was given the fact that innovating institutions were started by new men in the field, with new money and new organizations. Although it is beyond this paper, the retail institutions we will be discussing were initiated by new men, in new firms with new capital. Especially is this true in the case of discount houses and shopping centers; it is less the case in supermarkets.

a downward pressure on the price and margin structure of any non-food merchandise it handles, and we will comment on this again, it is the super-markets' part in forcing a reduction in the *service mix* of stores which traditionally were *full service* outlets that is being emphasized here. The apparent willingness or even eagerness of consumers to purchase a long list of non-food items (toys, beauty aids and drugs, small hardware items, women's hosiery, women's and children's soft goods, paper products, books, magazines, housewares, and so on) without the aid of salespeople and without the services and amenities of the traditional outlets has caused the older stores selling these categories of goods to adopt all, or part, of the supermarket technique of self-service, open display, check out stations, and cash and carry policies.

Just how far supermarkets will go in stocking non-food lines is difficult to say. Supermarket operators differ among themselves. Lansing P. Shield, president of the Grand Union Company, had this to say when asked about the trend toward operating a wider variety in supermarkets:

> . . . I'd say it probably will increase. Food stores now rival drug stores in the sale of many non-prescription medicines. For example, 37.9 percent of total aspirin sales are made through supermarkets. Also more than 31 per-cent of shaving products move through supermarkets.
>
> This year, Grand Union will open nine so-called "super general stores," with up to 90,000 square feet of selling space and as many as 25,000 non-food items. These stores will offer refrigerators, TV sets and wearing apparel for the entire family. In the near future, a considerable number of centrally located supermarkets will really be complete shopping centers in themselves.[3]

All supermarket operators, however, are not this enthusiastic. Safeway Stores and A & P, among others, have not adopted non-food items to such an extent.[4] And undoubtedly there are limits to the addition of non-food items to food store inventories. Presently it is felt that, in order to qualify readily for supermarket acceptance, goods must have such characteristics as high turnover, low price per unit, routine reordering procedures, ade-quate margins, quick identification, and high sales per square foot.[5] Over time these requirements may change.[6]

[3] *U. S. News & World Report,* June 20, 1958, p. 56.

[4] The Chairman of the Board of Safeway Stores, Inc., looks at the matter this way: "The trend to huge markets of 50,000 or 100,000 square feet has slowed down. Our present and future plans for Safeway Stores, with only a few exceptions, are under 23,000 square feet with most of our new stores around 14,000 square feet. The huge markets tend to get into completely new fields and nearly complete lines of mer-chandise: soft goods, furniture, etc. That's not for us. It's a question if you are in the food business or running a department store."

[5] Milton Alexander, "Where We Stand in Non-Food Merchandising," *Progressive Grocer,* October 1952, pp. 197 ff.

[6] The large volume of sales of non-food items through food stores has caused a revision in the estimates of expenditures for food. See Marguerite C. Burk, "Revised Estimates of Food Expenditures," *Journal of Marketing,* July 1949, pp. 31-35.

The pressure of food store competition is not the sole reason for less service in retailing. There are other pressures of a general economic nature, such as increasing costs of labor and the difficulty of attracting sales help from the apparently more attractive factory, clerical, governmental and other jobs, which also force the retailer to the economies of self-service where feasible. Nonetheless, supermarkets have thus far been sufficiently successful in selling a wide enough variety of non-food lines to bring about a significant change in the service mix of a broad area of non-food retailing and have forced competition *to imitate the supermarket type of selling by omitting many of the services which had previously been the operating strength of these outlets.* The important thing about this is that the removal of services, and hence the removal of the costs incident to these services, should have the effect of bringing about, over time, a downward trend in the price structure of the goods handled. The extent and depth of the price reductions in the future will depend on the degree of competition present. Inasmuch as supermarkets traditionally are highly promotional, low margin institutions, pressures to reduce margins in non-food outlets will be present to a much greater degree than had the supermarkets not decided to enter the non-food area.

Discount Houses and the Price Structure

The growth and popularity of those retail firms which operate their stores in such a manner that expense margins are at about 14-20 percent level on consumers' durables (and some soft lines) which traditionally called for 30-40 percent margins, and cut prices accordingly, have been among the really revolutionary forces in modern retailing.

It is not easy to define a discount house even though most people are familiar with both the term and the institution. Many retailers "sell at a discount," yet are not thought of as a discount house. Perhaps it is best to think of them in terms of the way they operate their business. They are characterized by ". . . a large selection of merchandise, emphasis on fast-turning national brands, price as the main sales appeal, inexpensive build-ings, a minimum of stock, limited customer services, low rent locations, extensive advertising, inexpensive and limited fixtures, far less use of merchandising and accounting controls than exist in the typical chain, or de-partment store, and frequently a willingness to bargain on price." [7]

There are several reasons why these low-margin, low-price discounters now loom so large. For one thing the capacity of manufacturers of con-

[7] Delbert J. Duncan and Charles F. Phillips, *Retailing: Principles and Methods* (Homewood, Illinois, Richard D. Irwin, 1959), pp. 446-447. A full discussion of both discount houses and discount selling is given in S. C. Hollander, "The One-Price System—Fact or Fiction," *Journal of Retailing,* Fall, 1955, pp. 127-144.

sumer durable goods has increased greatly since World War II and these manufacturers are apparently capable of producing larger quantities of merchandise than traditional channels can dispose of at current prices. This pressure of capacity has made many suppliers, especially of highly promoted national brands, eager to utilize these new price cutting outlets which can move their products in large quantities, even though the result is antagonism of the older retailers.

This need of suppliers for high volume outlets is not, however, sufficient cause alone to account for the tremendous success of the discount houses. There are also other reasons such as ". . . manufacturer preselling of brand merchandise, the umbrella hoisted by fair-trading retailers, the heightened interest of consumers in stretching their dollars, and the possibilities of cutting many cost corners in the handling of big-ticket hard goods." [8]

The success of the discount type of retailing has been rather dramatic. Polk Bros. of Chicago had sales in 1955 in the neighborhood of $40,000,-000, carried an inventory of some $2,500,000, allocated $1,500,000 for advertising, and utilized over 450 salesmen.[9] Korvette, Inc., of New York, in 1956 claimed sales of over $70,000,000 with an inventory mix composed of 60 percent hard goods and 40 percent soft.[10]

While these are admittedly giants of the field, the impact of the total array of discount houses in the retail system has been strong enough to bring readjustments from many types of competitors. The greatest readjustment is occurring in those outlets selling consumer durables such as appliance stores, hardware stores, sporting goods outlets, furniture stores, and in the sections of department and variety stores selling appliances and "big ticket" items. Soft lines are currently being affected as the discount houses add apparel items to their inventories.

The adaptation of the older retailers has taken several forms. Some stores, such as Marshall Field and Carson Pirie Scott, have inaugurated "warehouse sales." [11] In such instances goods are retailed from the organization's warehouse at cut prices and with very limited services offered. (Even Sears has adopted these warehouse special events.) Other stores, especially department stores, have dropped those appliance, radio and TV lines that are subject to discount house promotion; still others have con-

[8] Malcolm P. McNair, "Significant Trends and Developments in the Postwar Period," *Competitive Distribution in a Free High-Level Economy and Its Implications for the University*, ed. by Albert B. Smith (Pittsburgh, University of Pittsburgh Press, 1958), p. 13.

[9] Daniel Seligman, "Chicago's Red Hot Merchandiser," *Fortune* (September, 1955), p. 130 ff.

[10] For an interesting account of Korvette's history see "The Spectacular Rise of E. J. Korvette," *Fortune*, November, 1956, p. 122 ff.

[11] Charles Silberman, "Retailing: It's a New Ball Game," *Fortune*, August, 1955, p. 80. This article contains many instances of the devices used to combat discounters.

tinued the lines but lowered their prices appreciably and continued to handle the merchandise with their traditional services and/or charged extra for credit, guarantees, etc.

What is significant for those who wish to analyze retailing is that discount houses compelled a re-examination not only of the pricing policies and practices of manufacturers and distribution but *compelled a very broad range of retailers to lower their margins and adjust prices downward to adapt to this new type of competition.*[12]

Shopping Centers and the Location Structure

The third retail institution which has been selected as one of the innovating forces in retailing today is the shopping center—specifically, the *controlled centers.* Not a retail establishment, but rather a clustering of establishments, the controlled center of today is one that is in important ways (store selection, architectural design, etc.) planned, operated, and promoted as *a unit.* And the public tends to look upon these centers as units, as single places to shop. For example, Northland Center in Detroit or the Cross Country Center in Yonkers, to name just two, have a much greater market impact than a mere cluster of similar stores would have. The centers themselves are as well known as the big stores that happen to dominate these centers.

The presence in the centers of such giants of retailing as Penny's, Woolworth, A & P, Macy's, Marshall Field, Sears, Bullocks, etc., results in a "pull" of such a volume of consumer traffic that many smaller local independent hardware, drug, men's and women's wear stores, bakery shops, sporting goods and auto appliance outlets are drawn to the centers or to locations on their fringes.[13] Those that remain in the older neighborhood shopping areas have been forced to band together into "main street" associations to act *as a unit* to offset the draw of these new centers. And the downtown merchants are "fighting back" in a similar way—by promoting "downtown days" and by replanning the city center to imitate the "mall" idea of many of the new controlled shopping centers.[14]

[12] It's interesting to see the spread of the discount idea. "Paris Says Oui Oui to Discount Houses," *Business Week,* February 2, 1957, pp. 47-48. Also, discount houses are "upgrading" themselves. See Claire M. Gross, "Services Offered by Discount Houses in Metropolitan New York," *Journal of Retailing,* Spring, 1956, p. 1 ff. Malcolm McNair has an interesting thesis that in retailing market forces compel innovating institutions to upgrade themselves. McNair, *op. cit.*

[13] The impact on location choice of shopping centers is well illustrated by these figures: "Most new stores being opened today are in shopping centers. They account for 50 percent of the new grocery stores, 77 percent of the drug stores and 85 percent of shoe stores." *U. S. News and World Report,* June 20, 1959, p. 56.

[14] See Catherine Bauer, "First Job: Control New-City Sprawl," *Architectural Forum,* September, 1956, pp. 105-112; Victor Gruen, "How to Handle This Chaos of Congestion, this Anarchy of Scatteration." *Ibid.*

This does not mean that the older neighborhood clusters of stores, the string street outlets or the center-of-town locations are obsolete. Far from it. Just as the supermarkets do not by any means take all non-food business, nor the discount houses force price reductions on all other retailers, so the shopping centers, controlled and otherwise, do not make all other locations second class.[15] Nonetheless, shopping centers are a strong enough innovat-

---

[15] Apparently, for the big retailers there is not as much freedom as for small retailers. Earl Puckett, head of Allied Stores, states that if you attempt to "go it alone" others will follow and cluster around you. Hence, the choice is to go into a planned center or become the center of an unplanned one. See Earl Puckett, "Planned Growth for Retailers," *Stores,* January, 1956, p. 9 ff.

ing force to bring about basic changes in older location values; they have compelled large numbers of retailers *to "join them" or adopt the planning and coordinating techniques of these new controlled centers.*

The institutions discussed here—the modern supermarket selling non-foods, the discount house and the controlled centers—illustrate what the author believes is the essence of Schumpeter's innovating institutions: institutions that force imitation and adaptation. The competitive situation is never the same after such institutions enter the market place; they are institutions which seem to differ not only in degree, but in kind.

Retailing is undergoing a revolution, and there is little agreement about the causes or the probable outcome. . . . This article attempts to sift out the seeds of the revolution and to see wherein the new regime derives its strength and whether it promises anything new.

33

The Retailing Revolution: Why and Whither?

ALFRED R. OXENFELDT

THESE ARE TROUBLESOME TIMES in retailing, despite the nation's unprecedented prosperity. Vacant retail shops and bankruptcy sales are more common than they have been for almost two decades. Retailing is undergoing a revolution, and there is little agreement about the causes or the probable outcome. The discount houses are accused of being the leaders of the revolution; they will overthrow the small retailer, it is said, and undercut the influence of the department store and many other conventional forms of retailing.

This article attempts to sift out the seeds of revolution and to see wherein the new regime derives its strength and whether it promises anything new. It also tries to forecast the changes that will come about as a result of the revolution and its aftermath. In particular, it considers the plight of the small retailer who apparently is quite vulnerable to overthrow.

The discount house [1] skyrocketed in a short time largely because of the

Reprinted from the *Journal of Retailing,* publication of New York University, Volume 36, No. 3 (Fall, 1960), pp. 157-162. Reprinted with special permission.
[1] The discount house represents a wide variety of dissimilar types of business. It is therefore dangerous to treat them as essentially homogeneous, as space limitations in this article necessitate.

ostrichlike behavior of the department stores and many specialty chains. They allowed themselves to be "undersold" by very large amounts, probably because the market for goods was extremely strong during the early postwar years. During this period, the discount houses earned the reputation of offering substantial bargains, and they acquired great good will as a result. This good will has carried over, in somewhat diminished degree, to the present, even though the price benefit to be obtained from buying at discount houses has declined considerably.

Following the ostrich period, many stores adopted a "half-way" policy. They lowered their prices, but not enough to match the offerings of the discount house. They hoped to reduce the price advantage to be gained from patronizing the discount house just to the point where few customers would leave them for the discount house.

Discount House in Transition

At present, some large retailers—large department stores among them —have actually begun to outdo the discount houses, even in the matter of value. Specifically, they match the discount houses' prices and offer more service, wider assortments, and more convenient locations than do the discount houses. This third policy is only in its infancy, and it is too early to know whether stores that adopt this policy will be able to retain it and whether discount houses will be able to counter it successfully.

Discount houses are in a transitional stage for other reasons. First, they have not lived through an extensive shakedown period. Even during the minor postwar recessions, their business grew. A shakedown is almost certain to come at some time. One must expect substantial revision and sharpening of their operating methods and concepts to ensue. Second, the vast majority of discount houses are managed by their original owner-managers. Consequently, they include an unusually large proportion of industrious, imaginative, and daring businessmen who probably would have been highly successful even if they had conducted traditional types of retail operation. One must anticipate, therefore, some change in discount-house performance when the first-generation managements cease to be active.

Discount-House Innovations

No effort will be made to seek out historical "firsts" that may be credited to the discount house; an effort is made to isolate those of its features which are markedly different from conventional types of retailing. The main purposes of this undertaking are to determine which of the discount houses' innovations are uniquely exploitable by the discount house, which ones can be imitated—indeed, possibly put to better use—by competitive forms of retailing.

REDUCTION OF SERVICE

It is difficult to generalize about the kinds of services that discount houses have cut. Some provide return privileges, attractive facilities, wide assortments, gift wrapping, and credit. Some employ salesmen who are of higher quality than one finds in the average department store. In a large majority of cases, however, the discount house has reduced assortments, offered little salesmen's service, and required customers to wait for a long time when making purchases. Also, many frequently require long waits for delivery because merchandise is out of stock.

LOW-COST OPERATION

There is no question that most discount houses incur much lower costs of operation, figured as a percentage of sales, than the average department store. There is, however, serious question about the reasons for their lower costs. The obvious sources of economy probably are the least important. The savings discount houses achieve due to low occupancy cost, inexpensive fixtures and equipment, failure to keep extensive records, etc., rarely are major sources of saving. One might consider five per cent of sales to be a practical maximum of savings achieved by such economies. As will be explained, the discount house enjoys low costs of operation primarily because of its very large sales volume per foot of selling space and per dollar of investment, and per salesman—rather than because of economies of operation.

This point is crucial and deserves elaboration. Consider, by way of illustration, what would happen to the expense ratios of discount houses if their sales were cut in half (or, what would happen to the expense ratios of department stores if, somehow, they were able to double sales). If, as is to be expected, discount houses now in operation will be compelled to share their business with other stores, their expense ratios are likely to climb—without any addition of services or fancy frills.

INTERNAL OPERATING METHODS

Some people credit the discount house with applying self-service and self-selection to new kinds of goods and on a much broader scale. Whether this is the case or not, the discount house has no unique ability to exploit self-service; indeed, many other types of retailers use self-service.

More characteristic of discount houses than self-service is their going without traditional types of retailing procedures and record-keeping arrangements. Most large discount houses do not employ the record-keeping methods and other controls used by department stores. They boast of their very small ratio of non-sales personnel, which they achieve by giving up the management tools conventionally used by progressive businessmen. Two serious questions are raised by their difference. First, how much of a saving results from these methods? Second, do they improve or weaken the effectiveness of the discount house? Although evidence is lacking to permit a competent judgment on these questions, it seems quite possible that the *direct* savings achieved would be on the order of one to two per cent of sales; the consequence might be to expose the store to quite serious losses. One must recognize that department stores, specialty chains, and independent retailers could also go without the controls and records that most discount houses are doing without; they use them because, generally from bitter experience, they have learned that these controls were worth much more than they cost.

Thus the peculiar innovation of the discount house does not lie in the way it conducts its business internally. Its essentially distinctive feature is its pricing policy and its very large sales volume relative to space, personnel, and financial investment.

Large Sales Volume

In sales, the salient feature of the discount house is its outstanding ability to attract a large number of customers, relative to its facilities. In other words, it is able to build large sales volume without sizable outlays for sales promotion. Why is this so, and how did it come about?

The very rapid growth of discount houses must be attributed largely to the peculiar circumstances which made price appeals effective during their period of growth, since 1946. These circumstances include: the development of powerful brand names, the assumption by many manufacturers of quality guarantees (and often the provision of repair service), heavy sales promotion by manufacturers, and perhaps most important of all, the spread of list-price selling, resulting partly from widespread reliance on fair trade by manufacturers. Combined with these developments, the discount houses found a large accumulated demand for durables (items which customarily carry large margins) even while heavy savings were being accumulated with which consumers could purchase them. During this period, the traditional retailers were able to permit the discount house to enjoy great growth, for they were able to maintain their own total sales and profits. As a result, the discount house did not get much of a fight from traditional types of retailer until they had already won great loyalty from many customers on the basis of a strong "price appeal."

In other words, it is difficult to see in the discount house a dramatically new form of distribtuion or one that possesses peculiar advantages. The discount house is largely a low-price operator, like many other types before it. It was able to capitalize upon a favorable combination of circumstances that existed in the post-World War II period. The discount house does nothing that other businesses, including small ones, cannot imitate without unusual expense or added skills.

Through their pricing policies, the discount houses have—perhaps permanently—reduced the margins on a wide variety of merchandise. They have been able to do this primarily because of the sales volume engendered by their spectacular price appeals.

Discount houses have affected retailing in other ways also. For one thing, they have offered customers the alternative of sacrificing service for price saving. Some retailers have met this challenge by offering the consumer a combination of price appeal and some continuation of services. Second, and somewhat related, discount houses have spurred conventional retailers to have consumers pay for each service they use but not pay for others. Third, discount houses have provoked traditional retailers into soul-searching and self-examination that was long overdue, resulting in substantial improvements.

Future of Discounting

It should not be difficult to list several retailing developments that are almost certain to take place in the near future. In the first place, discount houses will meet the competition of more discount houses—as well as greater competition from other types of retailing. For this reason, one can confidently forecast a decline in sales per square foot of store space, per salesperson, and per dollar of investment. As a consequence, the costs of discount houses are almost certain to rise—even if they resist the temptation to acquire central locations, to install lavish facilities, and to indulge in advertising.

Accordingly, the average discount house will be pressed by competition from many sources. In the struggle to survive, probably very intensive sales promotion efforts will be made in order to gain volume, or at least to prevent further loss of volume. It is unlikely that the battle will take the form of further price reductions, for there really is little room for enough of a price cut to have much effect on consumers. Small traditional retailers will no doubt be hurt in this struggle, however, for even though discount houses will be mainly fighting other discount houses and department stores and specialty chains, small retailers who attempt to conduct their businesses in the traditional manner will suffer from the price war. One must expect failures among small retailers to grow, if anything, as a result of being caught in the middle of the battle for survival which awaits the average discount house.

Of course, it is impossible for anyone to predict the probable division of retail sales among the many forms of retailing; even the direction of change-over during the next ten years is unclear. It does appear that discount houses will obtain a somewhat larger share of the business than they enjoy at present, for they will spread to many communities where they are barely known today; the department-store and specialty-store chains are likely to hold their own or even gain ground; the increased profits of these groups will come largely at the expense of the small traditional retailer.

As one looks to the future of discount houses, he must recognize that the political hazards confronting them have not yet passed. Any substantial recession will revive efforts to eliminate price-cutting, which is the foundation on which the appeal of the discount house rests. The threat that *mandatory* enforcement of the Fair Trade laws will spread to fields outside the liquor industry cannot be ignored.

Less clear than the foregoing, but perhaps more important, is the probable future change in consumer reaction to price appeals. In the first place, increases in consumer income will foster consumer willingness to pay for broad selections of merchandise, competent sales assistance, wrapping, delivery service, etc. To the extent that the discount house relies upon price appeals only, it is not in tune with long-term trends, which are toward a more prosperous economy and one in which a larger proportion of the national income is devoted to services.

It is possible to view the existing popularity of the discount house, especially among prosperous groups, as part of a national fad. One might say that the discount house created a new game whose object is to obtain the maximum saving below list price. Customer satisfaction from effecting a saving would seem to have been far greater in most cases than the size of the saving would seem to justify. It is unlikely that this type of thinking and behavior will endure for a long time once the novelty has disappeared.

It is acknowledged that most low-income families must, and will, as a group, suffer inconvenience to effect savings. However, the low-income buyer has not been the primary patron of the discount house. In particular, many poor consumers are tied to traditional and more personal forms of retailing because they depend upon credit.

Effect of Discount House on Small Business

Clearly, the small businessman in many fields will be compelled to operate on a lower margin than he was able to obtain before World War II. Consequently, the discount house will, even as already is the case, force relatively inefficient small retailers out of business. Unfortunately, not only the inefficient merchant will perish in the process. For sometimes, simply because of greater financial resources to withstand a period of price competition, a *large* discount house will drive an efficient but small conventional retailer to the wall.

Consequently, retailing will be less of a haven for the untrained person seeking to be his own boss than it was during an earlier period of this nation's history. With the death of traditional markups, greater skill will be required to survive in retailing.

It should, however, be emphasized that the discount house and the changes it has induced in other types of retailing have not ended the opportunities for success in retailing for small firms. The retailer who acts as a conscientious purchasing agent for his customers, who is able to give skilled guidance to his customers on the selection among alternative brands, who can provide instruction in the operation and repair of what he sells, who possesses a high sense of style and can be relied upon for impartial advice in matters involving taste, will always be sought out by customers—and paid a premium for his talents. As national income rises, such retailers will be in even greater demand.

The real question that must be faced is whether it is possible for a small retailer to provide the kinds of services listed above and still take care of the many details of running a retail store. Retailers generally sell hundreds, if not thousands, of items. They face extremely complicated problems in keeping track of stock and in deciding what to order—without becoming experts on the relative merits of different brands and taking account of the particular needs and desires of individual customers. Perhaps it is not possible for many small retailers to do the many things that will be required to survive in the face of narrower retail margins. Certainly it will be harder to do so—with one possible exception; that is, if the small retailer elects to "join 'em rather than fight 'em."

The small retailer may be well suited to discount-house methods of operation, which call for limited assortments, limited service, no credit, and limited concern for record keeping and operating controls. Very possibly, the small retailer will become the typical discount house of the future, and will win a secure place for himself by providing goods at a low cost. In many ways, this alternative seems more feasible than attempting to offer greater service, better understanding of products and customers, greater skills in internal management, and the like. The latter course also would call for a period of self-education and considerable native ability. Unfortunately, not many retailers who possess these qualities would be able to survive long enough to make the change. And, of course, some small retailers would not make the change even if they had a long time in which to do so.

In conclusion, then, it seems that small retailers, like all others, will be compelled to do business on a smaller gross margin of profit. Under this pressure, they must either imitate the discount-house practices—which would not be difficult for them to do—or become a much more skilled type of retailer. The one thing they cannot do is continue to charge conventional markups and offer the mediocre quality of service which many of them render at present. The future of the small retailer is certain to be troubled, but he is not necessarily doomed.

> Whereas the retailer thinks of
> himself as a merchant concerned
> with value and quality, there is
> a wide range of intangibles
> which also play a critical role
> in the success or failure of his
> store.

34

The Personality
of the Retail Store

PIERRE MARTINEAU

- One of the leading retail grocery chains in Chicago has been exceptionally successful in the newer communities and particularly in the suburbs. In one neighborhood after another, stores of this chain far outsell competing stores offering the same services, the same merchandise, the same prices, the same parking capacity, the same amount of advertising. Why such an overwhelming preference?

- One midwestern dealer has become a leading seller of foreign sports cars without advertising either special "deals" or the engineering superiority of his cars. How does he manage to do it?

- One Chicago quality department store has tremendous customer draw for the middle-class Negro, far more than all the other department stores put together. Some actual research on the underlying causes of this consumer behavior stresses the absence of any classical price considerations or functional factors. Again, why the preference?

WHAT IS IT THAT DRAWS THE SHOPPER to one store or agency rather than another? Clearly there is a force operative in the determination of a store's customer body besides the obvious functional factors of location, price

Reprinted from the *Harvard Business Review*, Volume 36, No. 1 (January-February, 1958), pp. 47-55.

ranges, and merchandise offerings. I shall show that this force is the store personality or image—the way in which the store is defined in the shopper's mind, partly by its functional qualities and partly by an aura of psychological attributes. Whereas the retailer thinks of himself as a merchant concerned with value and quality, there is a wide range of intangibles which also play a critical role in the success or failure of his store.

Power of the Image

What kinds of intangibles are important? What is the effect of a retail store's personality? For answers, let us turn to the customers themselves—and, to make it specific, to the customers of the three retailers cited at the beginning of the article.

In the case of the grocery chain, for instance, one new unit developed over twice the sales of a new competing store of the same size and description. Research showed that the women of the community characterize the store as "clean and white," "the store where you see your friends," "the store with helpful personnel." This chain unit conveys a pleasant feeling of independence to the shopper. The aisles are spacious and not cluttered. In short, shopping in this store is a pleasure experience instead of a routine duty. It is significant that not once did any of the shoppers interviewed mention lower prices, better bargains, or greater savings.

The tip-off to the automobile dealer's success is in the agency personality he has created:

> This dealer is a former yacht captain, so that he developed outside the rituals and mythology of automobile retailing. Instead of belaboring "deals" and carburetors, economics and functions, he has imbued his establishment with the symbolic appeal of the foreign sports car.
>
> All the salesmen are British—no matter what they know about car mechanics, as long as they are recognizably British. Reinforcing their accents, they wear linen slacks and blazers with "Sports Car Club of America" emblems.
>
> Also, the dealer energetically promotes sports car clubs for different age groups, and he writes a column on sports cars in the classified advertising. In short, he has built and is constantly reinforcing a symbolic image congenial to a particular customer group.

In the example of the department store, the consumer group ascribe their preference to an atmosphere of acceptance for them. "I get a warm feeling of acceptance," "It makes you feel good to go shopping there," "I like it because it seems to have a warm atmosphere," and similar comments typified most of the customers' explanations. By contrast, Negroes dislike other stores in the neighborhood because of the feelings of rejection they have—even though the managements have been trying to serve them.

RETAILERS *VS.* SHOPPERS

Despite all of this, the typical retailer's promotions and advertising proclaim price cuts and huge savings to the shopper, as if that were the only consideration in a buying decision. Tire store advertising, liquor store advertising, furniture advertising, appliance advertising—all have the same monotonous chant. Chain drugstore advertising is typically a bargain potpourri of nondrug items such as alarm clocks, salad bowls, TV tables, flashlight batteries. A grocer builds a beautiful store in a modern shopping center and promptly plasters his windows with gaudy signs giving it a fire-sale atmosphere.

Yet research indicates that women do not believe there is any substantial difference between the pricing of various supermarkets. They are all competitive in price, customers think, and it is impossible to make any material savings by shopping at one chain instead of another. A woman's primary reason for reading a particular advertisement is "this is my store." If she glances at other advertising, it is largely to reassure herself that her favorite store *is* competitive in price. Instead of comparing prices, she evaluates the supermarket from a different set of criteria: variety of goods, orderliness of the store, services and nonservices, personnel, other shoppers, and goals of the owner or manager.

When our researchers talk to women about department stores, their comments invariably cover a wide range of elements which bear on whether they will or will not shop in a particular store. They are quite vocal about the physical plant itself, the elevator banks, the washrooms, the location; about the attitudes of the clerks and the other people in the store; about service facilities such as credit policies and returns; about whether the styling is extreme, conservative, smart, ageless, or in poor taste; about the displays and windows; about such intangibles as odors and colors—all these in addition to price considerations.

PERSONALITY IDENTIFICATION

When the shopper looks at a store's particular advertising, she unconsciously asks herself these questions:

- "What is the status of the store? Is it high-class or low-class or what?"
- "What can I expect of it in over-all atmosphere, product quality, and personal treatment?"
- "How interestingly does it fulfill its role?"
- "How does this image match my own desires and expectations?"

Of course, she is not oblivious to price; in fact, she may be proud of what she *thinks* is price-consciousness in order to justify her choice of a store. But plumb her mind—go beneath any pat answers—and you will find that she is not the "economic woman" that American businessmen have so long and glibly assumed.

THE TYPOLOGICAL APPROACH

The shopper seeks the store whose image is most congruent with the image she has of herself. Some stores may intimidate her; others may seem beneath her. A store may be acceptable for one type of goods and not for others. A shopper may go to one department store for bargains, children's clothes, or housewares, and to another one for gifts or personal items. Thus:

When the question was asked in a city-wide study about the preferred store for an everyday dress, two mass-appeal department stores were overwhelmingly chosen by the wage earners' wives. But when asked where they would buy a good dress, most of the women selected different stores. In fact, one store clearly stood out as the luxury store for the lower-income families.

Economic factors will always be important. But unless the store image is acceptable to the shopper, price announcements are meaningless. The upper-status woman cannot conceive of herself shopping in the subway store of a large department store. Regardless of bargains, she is repelled by the thought of odors, milling crowds, poorly educated clerks. Conversely, the wage earner's wife is not going to expose herself to the possibility of humiliation by shopping in the quality store, whether it be Bonwit Teller or Nieman Marcus or Lord and Taylor—even if she has the money to buy something there. In other words, regardless of ability to pay, all shoppers seek stores whose total image is acceptable and appealing to them individually.

This concept of the store image goes hand-in-glove with a growing realization that retailing generally must take a typological approach to marketing. As Virgil Martin, general manager of Carson, Pirie, Scott, has stated:

"It is high time we retailers recognize that we cannot be all things to all people. When we try to do that, we end up with no particular appeal for anybody. Each of us has his own individual niche in the market place. It is up to us to determine where we fit, who comprises our customer body, and then to fulfill as completely and satisfactorily as possible the expectations of our particular group and our logical market." [1]

ILLUSION OF MASS APPEAL

As a researcher with some crude tools for describing customer groups along both sociological and psychological dimensions, I am continually

[1] From a speech, "The Dynamics of the Present," 1957 National Conference, American Marketing Association.

confronted with amazing disparities between the retailer's concept of his customer draw and the actuality. For example:

- One Chicago retailer believes that his store does the largest volume in its product category in the market. When we discussed his marketing philosophy and future goals, I asked him about the character of his customer body. He did not hesitate to state that the entire market was his oyster—people from all income brackets, all surrounding areas, and all social groups.

  But an analysis of his sales tickets reveals that nothing could be further from reality. An extremely disproportionate share of his customers is concentrated in the lowest economic third. Although his store is located in the Chicago central shopping district and should attract traffic flow from all parts of the area, his customers are coming in a statistically significant ratio from the south part of the city and the southern suburbs.

- In making a social class analysis of the customers of Chicago retail organizations, we asked this question: "If you were going to buy new living-room furniture for your home, at which store would you be most likely to find what you want?" EXHIBIT I summarizes the answers in profile form for two leading stores. If the customer body of each store had been truly representative of the social classes in the metropolitan area—or, more precisely, if it had corresponded with the chance expectancy of choice based on the numbers of people in these classes—the result would have shown up as the horizontal broken line opposite the figure 100. But in neither case did it turn out this way, as the thick lines show. Store A appealed strongly to people in the upper and middle classes, and Store B appealed strongly to shoppers from the lower social classes.

  Yet the advertising director of Store A, a leading department store with a broad range of price lines and a basement store, was astonished to learn that not every person read his store's advertising. And the executive vice president of Store B, one of a chain of retail furniture stores, was on record as saying: "We sell everybody. We have stores throughout the area, we advertise in all the mass media, we have furniture in all price ranges."

  Not by any stretch of the imagination do these stores have universal appeal, Each organization is successful, yet each is attracting out of the market a distinctive customer group.

STORES OF DISTINCTION

The foregoing examples are not unusual ones. A lengthy list of customer profiles in many categories and along several dimensions makes it perfectly clear there is no such thing as a store image with equal appeal for all income groups, all social classes, all ages, all types. The store that is successful in the new communities and suburbs has competitive difficulties in the mill districts and the lower economic areas, and vice versa. The

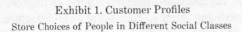

Exhibit 1. Customer Profiles
Store Choices of People in Different Social Classes

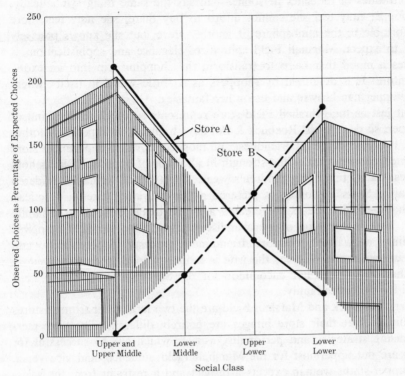

FIGURE 34-1

competitive pricing structure may be the same, but the elements of the store image which are so attractive to one group of shoppers are not attractive to another group.

It has to be this way. Different classes and different types of shoppers have different psychological outlooks on the world and different ways of life. Each segment of the market looks for a different emphasis. In general, the lower-status shopper looks at goods in a functional sense; she wants the store image to reflect her values of concreteness, practicality, and economy. She is concerned with quality of the merchandise and dependability of the store. The upper-status shopper, by contrast, is interested in whether the symbolic meaning of the store reflects her status and her style of life.

Take, for instance, the Marshall Field store in Chicago. It is much admired by perceptive competitors because all of the organization's activities are consistent and reinforce its strong symbolic character. The advertising, windows, merchandising events, restaurants, architecture, store policies, and attitudes of the sales personnel—all say the same thing symbolically. A shopper may feel she cannot afford to buy there, she may feel more comfortable in the atmosphere of another store, but she knows precisely what to expect. Marshall Field epitomizes elegance and sophistication. It creates a mood that helps to transform the shopping trip into an exotic adventure. It is described by shoppers as a "little world in itself" where the shopper can browse and enjoy her fantasies.

But just as the Marshall Field store represents so much to one kind of shopper, so does Sears, Roebuck & Co. have tremendous appeal to another kind. It is considered the friendliest and most comfortable department store in Chicago, with outstanding strength in all kinds of appliances, household staples, paint, tires, and children's wear. The type of woman considered typical of Sears' customers is pictured as hardworking, careful, practical, and home-minded. Sears has created a public image of itself as a family store, both in the type of merchandise it carries and in such intangible meanings as warmth, comfort, friendliness, honesty, dependability, and even unselfishness. Whereas the wife is more apt to go shopping alone at Marshall Field, it is not uncommon for the Sears shopping trip to be a safari for the entire family.

Sears, Roebuck and Marshall Field are the two largest department stores in Chicago, yet their store images are entirely different. The very merchandising strategies and personality aspects which are so successful for Sears are not uppermost for the Marshall Field audience, and vice versa. The upper-status woman expects a respect and a restraint from the sales-clerk that would be interpreted by the wage earner's wife as formal and forbidding. On the other hand, the family atmosphere and the great emphasis on savings which attract the Sears customer are distasteful to the Marshall Field shopper.

THE DULL PERSONALITY

What happens to the retail store that lacks a sharp character, that does not stand for something special to any class of shoppers? It ends up as an alternative store in the customer's mind. The shopper does not head for such a store as the primary place to find what she wants. Without certain outstanding departments and lines of merchandise, without a clear-cut attraction for some group, it is like a dull person.

When we asked Chicago women to characterize a department store on a range of qualities, the one attribute most applied to the alternative store was, "You don't hear much about it." It may spend many millions annually for advertising and promotion events, yet many, many shoppers will characterize it this way. Here is an interesting story of what happened to a store that lost its personality and then regained it:

A leading southern department store originally possessed a distinctive image emphasizing the traditionalist values of its city. The lighting and the fixtures were old-fashioned, and the total store atmosphere was congruent with the city-wide interest in antiques, old families, old homes, old restaurants, and historical monuments.

Then the women's apparel merchandiser modernized his department. He introduced new fixtures and lighting, more high-fashion styling, and a promotional flavor similar to any aggressive chain store in this field. The fortunes of the store declined in definite progression—first women's apparel, then children's, then men's, and finally all the hard-line departments.

A management consultant determined that the store had dissipated the strongest component in its image, the key to which lay in the women's apparel department. It had become indistinguishable from any other store. On his advice, the store set about restoring its traditionalist, distinctively period personality. The old-fashioned lights and fixtures and the ultra-conservative styling were brought back. As management reformulated the symbolic meaning which had given the store distinction and character, its fortunes changed sharply for the better in the same progression as they had declined—first women's apparel and ultimately the hard lines.

Personality Factors

What makes up a store's image in the minds of customers? There are many elements—architecture, color schemes, advertising, salespeople, and others. Let us look at the most important ones.

LAYOUT & ARCHITECTURE

The layout and architecture of the store itself invariably come in for comment. Women in modest-income suburbs are likely to describe changes in department stores over the years in terms of the modernization of the physical plant itself:

- "Modernization in the better stores is the big item nowadays."
- "They are all modernized inside now and are much better than they were ten years ago—in appearance and comfort for the customer."

Sometimes when elevators and escalators are set too deep in the store, women experience a panicky feeling of being lost. A shopper in such a store complained, "One day I thought I never would find my way out." Some shoppers are overwhelmed by counters and displays which are built too high. "They build up the display way over eye level so that things are staring at you and it bears down on you," they may comment; or, "On entering that store, the whole place gives you the feeling of crushing you."

Especially when comparing the advantages and disadvantages of the department store with those of the specialty shop, a very sizable proportion of women express feelings of confusion, of being overwhelmed by the crowds and size of the department store. Very possibly, the same reaction may be created by huge supermarkets.

The fixtures of a store add in a subtle but potent way to the general décor and atmosphere management wants to create—or subtract from it. They affect the success of promotions and can be used to transmit any elegant, exotic, or unusual emphasis in store policy. Thus:

- J. L. Hudson's new Eastland Center in Detroit, while located in a higher-income area than the same firm's fabulously successful Northland Center, is designed to be more colorful and lively while still reflecting highest quality. The entire décor of the first floor presents a subdued effect of dark woods, cherry showcases in center islands, but with a greater use of color on wall panels and in various metal displays running from floor to ceiling. Hardware finish is bronze, of the richest type of finish available. Besides the effect of various woods and colors to create personality, the type of fixture is significant. A quality store such as this uses a large number of showcases and center islands which lend a rich feeling to the store, as compared to a table-top presentation.

- T. A. Chapman's new Capitol Court in Milwaukee uses bronze profusely throughout, including bronze displays, plus many species of wood, to express a modern but high-fashion character.

- Julius Garfinkel's, which is an outstanding carriage trade department store in Washington, made two fixture changes in its new lower-level store in Fairfax County, Virginia, in deference to the modern age. While the design is similar to the fixtures in the downtown Washington store that express conservatism and fashion, the new store uses a light ash wood plus more open selling to create greater accessibility of merchandise.

- Harvey's, in Nashville, created a lively Victorian personality by buying an old carousel and placing the animals throughout the store and on the marquee. The store restaurant is in the form of a carousel, and the cashier's booth resembles a ticket seller's booth.

SYMBOLS & COLORS

In a psychological study which was conducted for us on gasoline brands and companies,[2] by far the most distinctions and meanings were created

[2] William E. Henry, *Gasoline, Gasoline Companies and Their Symbols* (Chicago, *The Tribune*, 1957).

by the emblems and the color schemes used on the retail stations, rather than by any product differences or verbalized claims of the companies. Sometimes these meanings were positive, sometimes negative. But whereas the differences between individual companies and brands were mostly blurred in the motorist's mind, rich meanings were conveyed to him by the symbols and colors.

A similar study, conducted by a New York industrial designer,[3] took the symbols of mid-western gasoline companies to eastern motorists who presumably were not familiar with them. Their evaluations of the companies were based therefore entirely on the shape and color of the symbols. Wherever this study examined the same symbols as our study did, the respondents' evaluations were in almost complete agreement. For example, the company using an oval-shaped symbol and a red, white, and blue color scheme was accorded by far the most positive evaluations. The company using a triangle was rated lowest on every scale. A dark color scheme used by another company cast an aura of dirtiness over its stations. Still another design and color created a company image that was "old-fashioned" and "inadequate" in motorists' minds.

What applies to gasoline stations applies with equal force to many other types of retailers. In the customer's mind color schemes and designs have an intrinsic meaning. They tell him something about the company as surely as the architecture, fixtures, and other visual factors. The association may not be logical, but it is real.

ADVERTISING

The retailer's advertising is an especially important factor in expressing the character of the store. But while the retailer thinks mostly of the factual *content* of his advertising—item, price, timeliness, quality of merchandise —the shopper is impressed by the physical appearance, general tone, and style of the advertising as well as by the words. Just as we instinctively make judgments about another person from his clothing and his mannerisms, so does the shopper believe she can abstract symbolic cues from the advertisement. To illustrate:

> This year, in a study of retail grocery advertising, we took characteristic advertisements of several Chicago chains to different parts of the country where the shoppers were totally unfamiliar with the stores. When the judgments of women who knew nothing whatever about the stores were compared with the opinions of Chicago women familiar with the stores, they were in remarkably close agreement.

Retail advertising has become a language unto itself. It accurately conveys to the shopper whether the store is exotic and high-style, a dependable

[3] *A Study of Consumer Response to Oil Company Gas Station Signs* (New York, Lippincott & Margulies, 1957).

family store, or a promotion store hammering at bargains and pennies saved. She decides which atmosphere is most appealing and where she fits. Certain elements of the advertising lend themselves by logical extension to the store itself and to the goals of the owner. High-style art and restraint of tone and typography convey that the store is expensive and formal. The advertisements which are overly black and filled with typographical tricks indicate that the store is disorderly, with ,cluttered aisles and a strictly volume-turnover philosophy.

Obviously, there is no one advertising style which is best for all stores because each is trying—or should be trying—to convey different meanings about itself. The promotion store and the predominantly mass-appeal store would be mistaken to run the beautiful advertising of the exclusive shop and the quality department store; for a grocery in one neighborhood it might be mandatory to promote trading stamps, but for a grocery in another section of town, very unwise; and so on. In other words, the symbolic meaning of the advertising has to be consistent with the character of the store itself.

SALES PERSONNEL

Perhaps the biggest single factor in the store image is the character of the sales personnel, in spite of the fact that so much discussion of retailing in recent years has virtually disposed of the salesclerk. The success of the supermarket and the extension of self-service into other fields has led some to assume that personnel will someday disappear from the retailing scene. We talk about robot retailing and the necessity for pre-selling; we say the store clerk performs only a wrap-up function in the typical store; we detail how the automobile salesman is now only a sharp-pencil operator instead of an aggressive outside salesman.

Moreover, many department-store executives to whom I have talked appear resigned to a steady downgrading in the quality of their sales help. They feel they cannot compete in the labor market with other industries and are therefore forced to take whatever is available.

Yet the fact remains that shoppers almost invariably evaluate the personnel in discussion of specific stores. Even in the grocery chains that have no salesclerks, women will talk about the checkers and the stock boys, whether they are friendly or indifferent, cooperative or brusque. As the shopper tries to imagine how her family would like some new dish or some unfamiliar brand, she naturally is anxious for support and information from some source. She is unhappy when the stock boys are so engrossed in their tasks of refilling shelves that she feels her questions would interrupt them and be resented.

In the case of department stores, clerks are mentioned more often than any other image-creating factor. Here are typical comments:

- "A salesperson's personality makes the store."
- "If the clerks are courteous and friendly and act as if they enjoy their work and their merchandise, I enjoy shopping."
- "The employees make you feel at home or uncomfortable in a store by their attitude when they wait on you. Sometimes if you decide not to buy, they can make you feel like you'll never go back."
- "I was just browsing in the millinery department of the store when a snippy saleswoman asked me not to handle the merchandise. That was enough for me. I would never return there again."

In contrast to the impersonality of the downtown-store salesperson, the relationship between clerk and customer in the outlying center can be more personalized. The fact that both usually live in the same community or general area makes the clerk more perceptive to the shopper's attitudes and wants. As one shopper said:

- "You get to know the same salespeople in the local stores, and they know just what size and style and price you want."

I believe that the courtesy and adequacy of sales personnel is one of the decisive factors in the growth of the outlying and suburban store. In the words of another woman:

- "Why shop downtown when the local stores are so much friendlier?"

It is ironical that at the very time when a better educated and discriminating shopper expects more from the store and the clerk, management is dragging its feet in upgrading salespeople. The stores are more beautiful and interesting; they have escalators, air conditioning, and improved fixtures; they have buyers ranging far and wide to offer the broadest merchandising selection. But what about the salespeople?

Trends in Behavior

Perhaps a great many retailers will consider this concept of the store image as vague and inexact. While they may find it pleasant to know that there is such a thing, they are far too much concerned with the operational problems of being good merchants to devote any mental energy to it. But I believe that somebody in top management should think about these intangibles of store reputation and public attitudes. Somebody high up should ponder whether the over-all store image is positive and appealing or negative and dull, and whether it is in tune with what shoppers want today. The image plays an increasingly vital part in the fortunes of business.

Some of the reasons for this are economic—for instance, the increase in discretionary spending power, or the rise of new types of competition. Such trends make the subjective element of choice more important at the same time that the consumer is presented with more alternative ways of spending his money. But there are other reasons why top management should give more attention to the company image—reasons that are not so obvious. Some of them apply with particular force to department stores; some are of interest primarily to other types of retailers. Let us see what they are.

SUBURBAN SHOPPING

Today with the customer flow in most great cities moving outward toward the periphery and the beautiful new shopping centers, with so much of the population moving away from the heart of the city, the retail executive is concerned with placing stores in various strategic outlying locations. Just as the manufacturer is weighing the risks of product diversification, so is the retailer studying the uncertainties of geographical diversification. In the central shopping district of the past, he did not have to concern himself with store personality so much because all roads figuratively led to Rome. All shoppers found their way to the downtown area.

Now the situation is quite different. The executive has to take his store image into fairly stratified communities whose shopping expectations and style of life may be totally out of keeping with the traditional image of his store. In one instance, when a promotional bargain store was located in a community of ambitious, mobile, well-educated young families, these people took the store as almost an insult to their set of values. In another situation, a high-status and a low-status store both entered a middle-class community, and both were rejected because shoppers said, in effect, "I don't trust them."

The problem is far more difficult than merely locating a store where there are population concentrations and doing research to learn what kind of a personality to give the new store so that it will "fit in." The branch store and the suburban store partake of the personality and character of the big downtown store. Even though management may build very attractive branch stores which in themselves would be congruent with the new community, these stores cannot dissociate themselves from the core meanings of the main store image, which are deeply etched into the shopper's consciousness. If, for example, merchandising techniques and promotional approaches have made the downtown store successful with lower-income families, a branch will operate under a cloud in a smart new suburb. And, conversely, when the high-status store locates a branch in a fairly prosperous mill district, the advertising which is building an image of sophisticated modernity for the main store's customers is also visible to shoppers in the mill district, who shy away from such a store image.

The spectacular growth of the outlying shopping center has created another problem. Very often this center has included whatever stores the real estate promoter could interest, quite without regard to how their images fitted together. As a result, the stores in many centers are pulling against each other. The smart high-fashion department stores and apparel stores find themselves in centers with drugstores, grocery stores, and a miscellaneous assortment of small shops negating their image, so that the center becomes a hodgepodge to the shopper.

If the opposite is true—if most of the store images *do* reinforce each other—a "shopping-center mood" will result that will make these stores more successful than they could have been operating by themselves. But any stores that are out of character with the over-all image will have a harder time than they would otherwise. As an illustration, one grocery chain is having difficulty in a very successful center which is dominated by stores that create a mood of elegance, ornateness, formality, and sheer luxury throughout. The shopper coming to this center is dressed for the occasion and not likely to be attracted to a routine grocery store.

Earlier I stated that the question of the image was one for top management. It should now be easy to see why this is so whenever store location is the issue. It makes no sense to ask a group of executives to operate a branch in a new location until careful attention is first given to the store personality they will be working with. It can bless their efforts or plague them! Either way it is a factor of tremendous importance.

THE NEW CUSTOMER

In a study of the new community shopper, based on four rising communities which I felt were typical of different social classes and income groups, I noticed two large-scale trends:

- A new set of family values is developing. There has been a shift from the philosophy of security and saving to a philosophy of spending and immediate satisfaction, to rise of the child-centered family, more self-indulgent spending, a tendency to equate standard of living with possession of material goods, and great emphasis upon community values.

- The influence of the store image is increasing. People place great stress upon their interaction with other people—talking and socializing with others. How do they react to the growing impersonality of metropolitan life? Cutting all her ties with friends and family to move to a new city or new suburb, shopping in stores where she cannot know the owner or the clerks or where there may be no clerks, the shopper compensates for less personal contact by personalizing the store. She behaves in considerable measure toward this inanimate object as if it were a person. It becomes a symbol to which she can form deep attachments or dislikes. A department store, like a person, is characterized as "modern, practical, casual, and exciting." A grocery chain is characterized as "young, progressive, growing, friendly." Another store is called "dull," and still another is described as if it were somebody she did not like.

The National Association of Retail Grocers has conducted seminars for its member stores whose sole theme was the importance of developing an appealing and distinctive store personality. Throughout the country there are countless instances of imaginative independents successfully competing with the chains because they have created their own character in many and diverse ways. One Chicago grocer recently opened a "kiddy theater" which adults cannot enter without crawling on hands and knees. The youngsters sit entranced on benches watching cartoons while mother enjoys her shopping.

BRAND PRODUCTS

Much of what applies to stores also applies to products and packages. Package designers startle our moral sense when they say that today's consumer is more interested in the package than in what is inside; she takes the contents for granted. Styling and décor are the key to the automobile sales picture today, not engineering. Refrigerators present the "sheer look." Today even the most prosaic products are offered in a choice of many colors.

All of these are externals which have nothing to do with economics or function, yet which are demonstrably important in the sales fortunes of the brand.

SERVICE ORGANIZATIONS

Company image and personality are also important to the success of service organizations. Here the primary differences between competing companies are generally not matters of price and service so much as they are stereotyped attitudes in the public mind. Whether true or not, they exercise tremendous influence upon buyer choice. For example:

Airlines offer the same rates and much the same services. Yet a Chicago *Tribune* study of the airlines serving Chicago shows very wide differences in their company images. In fact, no two of the seven airlines studied have anything like the same profile.

United Airlines is accredited with a broad range of rich meanings: safe, up-to-date, good for traveling with children, efficient stewardesses, extremely dependable, excellent food, comfortable, excellent personal attention, luxurious service, and attractive interiors in the planes.

Capital Airlines has a very different image, stemming largely from its use of Viscounts: fast, quiet, smooth, good views, comfortable seats, an ultramodern, progressive line.

Interestingly enough, the same feelings were expressed by those who had flown in Viscounts and those who had only heard about them. This confirms findings of other studies that the attitudes toward a company image are not necessarily formed from experience. Rather, they may be shared ideas relayed by word of mouth.

A Point of View

Management is accustomed to look at shopping in an atomistic way—in terms of how many items were bought in what stores and at what prices. It should and must analyze retailing in this way. But it must not forget that statistics on sales provide only a partial basis for intelligent decision making. It must not be so captivated by the logic of figures that it overlooks the nonlogical basis of shopping behavior. Whether the customer is buying airline tickets, gasoline, hardware goods, or department store merchandise, his actions defy analysis in terms of after-the-sale statistics alone. To understand "why," management must look for deeper insights on customer behavior.[4]

I have focused much of this article on department store customers not because they are different (they are, after all, the same people who buy automobiles, life insurance, and so on), but because studies of them offer some of the most dramatic evidence to support my points. We have found that the customer generally thinks of shopping as a total experience which runs through a number of departments in a number of stores and ends when she (or he) returns home. This is particularly true when she shops downtown or in a major shopping center requiring some travel and time. She faces many extraneous problems: How does she get there? If she drives, where does she park? Which store does she go to first? Is it the store where she plans to buy, or will it be the comparison point? If she expects to be gone for long, what about the restroom and restaurant facilities?

Curiously, the lowest-income shoppers mentioned the holiday aspects of such a trip more than any other group, probably because their routine lives are closer to humdrum practicality.

The shopping situation must therefore include many things not directly associated with specific items but closely connected with various patterns of consumer behavior. As the shopper fits the stores into her planning, she manipulates store images in her mind—not images of this counter or that department but impressions or pictures of entire stores. In large part, where she goes and what she buys depends on the subjective attributes that are part of these store images—atmosphere, status, personnel, other customers. Consciously or unconsciously, they sway her expectations and direct her steps.

4 For an explanation of the contribution of the behavioral sciences to this problem, see Pierre Martineau, *Motivation in Advertising* (New York, McGraw-Hill, 1957), Chapter XV; and Joseph W. Newman, "New Insight, New Progress, for Marketing," HBR November-December 1957, p. 95.

Today's wholesaler is no longer
the passive order-taker for producers or the simple purchasing
agent for retailers. He is a vital
element in the distributive chain
which is so necessary to the
orderly marketing of the huge
output of our vast industrial,
agricultural, and mining organizations.

35

The Modern Wholesaler
and His Adjustment to
a Changing Economy

HERMAN C. NOLEN

NEW AND EXCITING THINGS are taking place in our present economy, not
the least of which is the emergence of the wholesaler as a dynamic force
in our business and cultural progress. Today's wholesaler is no longer the
passive order-taker for producers or the simple purchasing agent for retailers. He is a vital element in the distributive chain which is so necessary
to the orderly marketing of the huge output of our vast industrial, agricultural, and mining organizations. The wholesaler is deserving of great
credit for his contributions to our economic progress but unfortunately he
so seldom receives that credit.

Many of us think of wholesalers as outmoded middlemen who have
been and are cluttering up the pathways of economic expansion. We think

Reprinted from W. David Robbins (ed.), *Successful Marketing At Home and
Abroad*, Proceedings of the 40th National Conference of the American Marketing
Association, June, 1958, pp. 409-415.

of them at times as institutions which are adding to the growing costs of getting merchandise from producer to consumer without contributing worthwhile services in return. In the next few minutes I hope to demonstrate to you that today's wholesaler is keeping pace with the rapidly changing developments in our economy and, in many ways, is actually showing the way to other units. Do not underestimate the ability, the influence, and the power of today's wholesaler. He may not have surrounded himself with a battery of publicity agents who are singing his praises to the multitude, but he is silently, steadily, and effectively doing his part to enable our economy to grow and bring prosperity and higher living standards to our people.

Who is this wholesaler who is doing so much to broaden the market for the huge quantities of new products which are flowing out of our vast productive empire? He is a specialist, a specialist in distribution, and this is an age of specialization. And we must remember that the benefits of specialization are not confined to our industrial operations. These benefits are equally applicable to the field of distribution. And today's wholesaler is proving himself to be a most efficient factor in our marketing mechanism.

The mere fact that buyers and sellers are constantly attempting to undertake to do the wholesaling job themselves keeps wholesalers efficient. Whenever a buyer or seller feels that he can perform wholesaling services more efficiently, cheaper, or better than the wholesaler, he is very likely to assume those services. The result is that the wholesaler is constantly under pressure to do his job effectively. He also is more responsive to changes in our economy than other agencies as he cannot afford to lag behind modern developments or he finds himself no longer being used. He must adapt himself quickly and continually to changes.

Before reviewing the changes which are taking place in wholesaling today, and the factors responsible for them, let us just briefly mention some of the functions which wholesalers are performing. For his customers, the wholesaler:

1. anticipates customer requirements,
2. assembles goods from a multitude of sources,
3. buys in economical quantities,
4. maintains a reservoir of goods,
5. delivers promptly,
6. grants credit,
7. provides informational and advisory services.

And for manufacturers, the wholesaler:

1. establishes connections with the whole field of retail outlets,
2. furnishes advice as a distribution specialist,
3. reduces costs of physical distribution,
4. reduces manufacturer's capital requirements,
5. simplifies accounting and credit problems.

Not all wholesalers perform all these services; full-line, full-service wholesalers do, others render one or more of the services mentioned. Retailers and producers will find it possible today to utilize from wholesalers just the services they desire to use. In the wholesale field there are many types of specialized distributors available and the list of wholesaler types seems to be growing larger all the time.

Before discussing in detail the various types of adjustments wholesalers have made and are making to meet the constantly changing factors in our modern economy, let us review some of the more important economic changes which are affecting the operation of wholesalers.

Most of the changes in our economy which are vitally affecting wholesalers today center around three basic elements: advertising, distribution costs, and mass distribution.

All of us are aware of the growing importance of advertising in our economy, not only in terms of money spent and media used, but in influence on producers, consumers, and particularly on distributors. No single agency is more affected by the growth in advertising than is the wholesaler. How is advertising influencing wholesaling?

First of all, wholesalers are feeling the influence of advertising on consumers. Consumers have become brand conscious. Wholesalers find it difficult to find a market for unbranded or unknown merchandise brands, and that is especially true of goods marketing through self-service. Advertising, too, is making consumers much more intelligent purchasers and vastly more style conscious.

Another advertising factor affecting wholesalers is that of its high cost and the necessity for manufacturers to make huge initial outlays for advertising. This is particularly true of television advertising today. The fact that a manufacturer may have to commit himself for expenditures running into millions of dollars for a comparatively short TV schedule forces him to utilize wholesalers to get maximum distribution for him prior to the appearance of his commercials. Not many manufacturers have selling organizations capable of assuming this responsibility, and you cannot finance TV network programs with gradually expanding or spotty distribution. The job must be done prior to the appearance of the ads or much of the advertising value may be dissipated.

The fact that distribution costs both absolutely and relatively appear to be rising is affecting wholesalers as well as other marketers. Producers and distributors are checking their costs more carefully than formerly. Labor and transportation costs particularly are rising. The demand for more services on the part of buyers is causing distribution costs to inch upward. The shorter work week with expanding fringe benefits is squeezing profit margins in the field of distribution.

Another important economic factor affecting wholesale distribution is the continued growth of large-scale retail outlets. The supermarket, the chain store, and more recently the shopping center developments are changing our distribution patterns. Meeting the requirements for capital for expansion is a real problem for the newer and less well-established operators. Inventory turnover is assuming added meaning for these people. Large-scale retailing has brought with it widespread unionization in retail outlets.

The postwar retailing phenomenon, the discount house, is altering merchandising patterns. So is the continued expansion of self-service, self-selection, and open display of merchandise.

In the past few months the recession has brought with it intense competition and, in markets hard hit by labor layoffs, savage price competition. Detroit, Pittsburgh, Seattle, and other such centers have been particularly hard hit by this movement.

The economic changes I have mentioned are not the only ones which are affecting wholesaling in the United States today but I believe they are the most important. The growing influence of advertising, the continued upward trend of costs, the growing importance of large-scale distributors, and the development of suburban shopping areas are causing wholesalers to readapt their methods, their policies, their plans, and their practices to these new conditions.

How the wholesaler is adjusting himself to changing economic conditions is a credit to him and also to American business know-how. He is adapting himself most promptly and continually to the constant flood of changes in our economy. His close margin of profit makes it necessary for him to be most responsive to even minor variations in the economic climate in which he works.

Let's first discuss his adjustment to the growing importance of advertising —to manufacturers, to retailers, to consumers—and the need for speed in attaining that adjustment. Wholesalers today are concentrating on the well advertised national brands and particularly on those which move rapidly over the retailers' counters. In many instances they are providing for automatic distribution for manufacturers. In many fields wholesalers accept automatic distribution from manufacturers and, in turn, provide retailers with automatic distribution of products in advance of advertising programs. This is enabling advertisers to secure a much better return on their advertising dollars. They are encouraging retailers to recognize brand ratios in their merchandising and to provide display areas in proportion to sales.

In many instances wholesalers today are providing display services including window, in-store, counter, and bin display services for advertised goods. Manufacturers today can engage in advertising activities with confidence that the merchandise they promote will be available for sale and properly displayed in retail outlets. Wholesalers today are offering cooperative advertising assistance to groups of retailers. They are assisting the manufacturer in merchandising his advertising to the retailers and in that way greatly increasing its effectiveness. Few manufacturers today can get full return from their investment in advertising without the assistance of wholesalers, particularly if the goods are sold in a large number of outlets.

The wholesaler's adjustment to rising costs in distribution is less dramatic but, I believe, even more effective. Like all businessmen, wholesalers have a constant battle to keep their costs in line and I think they are doing a good job in pursuing the majority of the conventional methods of keeping down expenses, such as increasing merchandise turnover, eliminating waste, and the like. However, there are certain areas in cost cutting in which the wholesalers have made great progress in the last few years. One has been in the simplification of warehouse and office jobs. Wholesalers, as experts in distribution, have done an outstanding job in eliminating wasted motion and effort. For example, if you will pardon the reference to my own company, in the past three years we are handling one-third more tonnage with 9% fewer people in our offices and warehouses. In my opinion, that is quite an achievement in an industry that is not highly mechanized. That increase in production has been achieved largely by getting people to do their jobs better and not by the introduction of labor-saving machinery.

A very large percentage of wholesalers are now using labor-saving devices in their accounting and general office departments. Recently, a wholesale druggist on the West Coast has developed and installed a mechanical warehouse machine for storing, picking, and packing merchandise. This revolutionary idea is still in the development stage but it may provide an entry for the introduction of mechanization to our basic distribution problems. Tabulating cards are fed into the machine at one end and thousands of individual items are picked by the machine and fed through a belt to the shipping platform. The fact that this machine was developed by a wholesaler and by the cooperative efforts of a number of wholesalers I believe is indicative of the kind of thinking which is present today in many of our wholesale establishments.

Another program for cutting costs, which wholesalers are following aggressively, is selectivity, and especially selective selling and selective servicing of customers. Wholesalers have learned that not all customers are entitled to all services; only those customers who will concentrate their purchases with a wholesaler are entitled to his red carpet services. Selective selling and servicing of customers are being practiced by practically every wholesaler in the country.

Wholesalers also are concentrating on increasing order size, on high line extension, and on promoting fast-selling merchandise. These practices bring down costs.

Earlier, I stated that one of our problems has been increased transportation and delivery costs. Wholesalers have been quick to adjust their operations to these increased costs by making use of the delivery services not normally used for servicing their customers. Many wholesalers are giving rapid service to their customers through the use of newspaper trucks, especially those returning after delivering newspapers. They are using buses extensively. They are having florists and milk delivery companies work for them. In our business we have made extensive use of Western Union delivery service. For example, in the city of Portland, Oregon, we can provide our downtown customers with 11 deliveries a day. In the city of Detroit we are providing five deliveries a day to our customers and at a cost which, percentagewise, is no greater than our cost of 15 years ago when we offered one delivery every three days to our customers.

In those industries where it is necessary to provide merchandise to customers at the very lowest cost possible, some wholesalers make available the basic service at a minimum cost. An example is the grocery field where the basic cost of servicing a store may be provided to a customer at $3\frac{1}{2}\%$ or 4%. If the customer desires additional services, such as display help in a store, advertising assistance, store design, etc., he pays extra for those services. In any event, he can get merchandise from the wholesale warehouse to his establishment at a cost which is phenomenally low. It might interest you to know that in one large city in the United States there is a single wholesale establishment that does over $300 million annually in that one area on that basis. That is a volume of business I believe that is unmatched in any field in so small an area.

One area of cost which is proving very stubborn to reduction is that of selling. Selling costs have not been so susceptible to expense control as have other costs in wholesale establishments. It has been very difficult to increase greatly the productivity of salesmen. Every wholesale establishment, probably more so than other business firms, has used telephone and mail services extensively. They are also using sales contracts and group-selling techniques to cut costs in this area. Progress is being made, but it is slow. And wholesale sales managers are very much aware of the value of their salesmen's time.

A third major area of adjustment for wholesalers to changing economic conditions has been in the field of customer relations. I feel that wholesalers, more than any other sellers, realize how important it is to keep their customers strong; fortunately they are doing just that. Wholesalers have long realized that a prosperous business cannot be built on weak customers, so wholesalers today are making every effort to keep their customers strong.

Let me go over some of the means by which wholesalers are assisting their customers, the retailers. Today most any individual retailer can go to his wholesaler for assistance on location analysis. Wholesalers have developed programs and means for evaluating the amount of business that can be done in an area. They know about the growth trends in cities and suburbs and their judgment in this regard is widely sought by individual retailers.

A second service which is being widely utilized is that of store design and modernization. If you will pardon further reference to an individual company to illustrate a point, our company has helped modernize one out of every five drug stores in this country in the past five years. We have provided store design service, traffic flow analysis, and, in most instances, we have actually provided the store fixtures. If the retailer needs assistance in financing that modernization program he is planning he can get help through his wholesaler. Depending upon his credit standing, he may be able to buy the fixtures and pay for them over a period of years, with or without a down payment, and in many instances the fixtures can be leased through the wholesaler.

Many retailers are finding today that taking a new location presents certain problems with the lease, which did not confront him a few years back. In shopping centers and other large-scale developments, the leases are pretty complicated arrangements and many wholesalers today provide legal assistance on new leases and adjustments in old leases for their customers. This is something which a wholesaler can provide better than anyone else because of his intimate knowledge of the business and its problems, which is not possessed by financial institutions or manufacturers.

Most wholesalers today provide store opening services. I have known of instances where retailers have opened a new store and the opening was handled completely by the wholesaler. He selected merchandise for the store; he put it on the shelves, he priced it; he prepared the advertisements; he made arrangements with local newspapers, radio, and TV stations; he trained the help; he provided all the gimmicks for the gala store opening; and then he turned over to the retailer a thriving retail business.

Sales training and merchandising assistance have been widely provided by wholesalers. Large chain organizations may be able to do their own training of personnel and may provide merchandising assistance, but the smaller retailer looks to his wholesaler for that service and he is being provided a service which is on a par with that which is available to the chains.

Advertising services are being provided to retailers; cooperative advertising, monthly mat services, and special event advertising are available to retailers in most fields through their wholesalers.

Store management counseling is available to retailers; not only are manuals and courses in management provided, but experts from the wholesale establishments can be called upon for assistance on individual problems. Accounting systems are commonly made available as well as income and other tax advice.

Some wholesalers are providing many special services to retailers. For example, rack jobbers will select, price-mark, shelve, inventory, and advertise merchandise for their retail customers. They will even provide fixtures; all the retailer has to do is provide space, collect the money, pay for the merchandise that disappears—the rest is all done by the wholesaler.

Whenever customers need special service, wholesalers in most cases will provide the service required. Wholesalers are constantly studying the need for new types of service required by their customers.

In order to keep the smaller retailers competitive with the large mercantile groups, wholesalers today will provide merchandising leaders and specials. In many instances these specials are provided at prices well below those which the chain stores have obtained.

The instances I have cited are not the only adjustments which wholesalers are making to the ever-changing economic patterns in this country, but they are some which I thought would be of interest to you and they are the types of adaptations that are proving extremely helpful to consumers, to retailers, and to manufacturers. Today's wholesalers are not old-fashioned, outmoded, antique operators. They are moving just as rapidly as our other business institutions and, I believe, they are adjusting themselves to changing conditions with greater speed than most others. In my opinion, there is no doubt that the wholesaler is making his full contribution to better living in this country through making available to our people the merchandise they need at the lowest possible cost. To accomplish this the wholesaler is extremely sensitive to those changes, and his adjustment to those changes is being made continually.

The fact that the wholesaler's relative position in our economy is about the same as it was 20 or 30 years ago shows that he has done a successful job of adjusting his operations to changing conditions. Of course, it is true that some types of wholesalers are not so important, yet on the other hand other types are considerably more so today. Wholesalers follow pretty much the same course as other institutions; some do a careful, skillful job, others slip because of certain inadequacies. Those who have learned to roll with the punches and counter aggressively are enjoying success. Those that do not, find that the parade has passed them by. Fortunately, wholesaling has attracted to its arena its share of good men. As a result, we can come to only one sound conclusion: The wholesaler will continue to occupy his niche in our American economy and continue to expand in service, in value, in prosperity, along with the other essential elements, the producers and the retailers, to bring better living to American consumers.

D. PROMOTION DECISIONS

The influence of culture and of private sensations modify and intermingle with the stimuli of advertising to achieve the final pattern of relationship between the seller's product (or ideas and services) and the consumer. What perceptions can advertising influence, and what can it not?

36

The Functions of Advertising in Our Culture

IRVING S. WHITE

THE FUNCTION OF ADVERTISING in our culture may be characterized in two theoretical ways.

First, there are those who state the theory within the framework of economic laws, asserting that advertising affects knowledge about and demand for a product.

This article attempts to develop a second orientation. It is that the function of advertising is to help to organize and modify the *basic perceptual processes* of the consumer, so that he is guided toward *seeing* and *feeling* a product in a given predictable way.

ADVERTISING AS A PERCEPTUAL PROCESS

With the recently formed partnership between the social scientist and the marketing professional, some foundation has been laid for a general

Reprinted from the *Journal of Marketing,* national quarterly publication of the American Marketing Association, Volume 24, No. 1 (July, 1959), pp. 8-14.

reorientation toward understanding this influence as a dynamic process between communicators and perceivers. David Ogilvy and other advertising practitioners have formally incorporated terms such as "brand image" as applied to various advertised products. Journalists such as Martin Mayer have come to see advertising as affecting the "values" of a product.[1]

Yet "images" and "values" have no meaning outside of the experience and outlook of the consumer as a personality and the consumer-market as a social group. Gardner and Levy, influenced by the social psychology of George Herbert Mead, have shown how consumers are swayed toward or against a product because of the way a brand image is perceived.[2] And Martineau's *Motivation in Advertising* is a practical and lucid application of that proposition.[3]

It is a truism that the function of advertising is to inform and sell. But the more basic theoretical question is, how does advertising perform this function?

THE VARIABLES OF CONSUMER EXPERIENCE

Most advertisers would agree that advertising should orient the consumer toward a consistent, and usually pleasurable, relationship with their products. Consistency implies a rather stable organization of meanings and values centering around a product as an "object" in one's life. It is this consistency which gives what is often called "character" to a product or service. Cadillacs, for example, have traditionally meant specific mechanical, aesthetic, and social experiences to their adherents, Buying a Cadillac has often meant success and power to the purchaser, and the conviction that in several years from the time of purchase his car would still connote the same qualities. Pleasure merely means that the consumer derives gratifications out of this object-relationship that motivate him toward repeating and reinforcing the experience.

To structure the experience of the potential consumer along lines of consistent and predictable satisfactions requires an understanding of the total source of meanings, the *whole* interaction between the consumer and the product. For any advertiser, there is a certain amount of realistic humility inherent in the knowledge that advertising is only one of the several sources of stimulation that a product contains for the individual in society. The influences of culture and of private sensations modify and intermingle with the stimuli of advertising to achieve the final pattern of relationship between the seller's product (or ideas and services) and the consumer. What perceptions can advertising influence, and what can it not?

[1] Martin Mayer, *Madison Avenue, U.S.A.* (New York: Harper and Brother, 1958).
[2] Burleigh B. Gardner and Sidney J. Levy, "The Product and the Brand," *Harvard Business Review,* Vol. 33-No. 2 (March-April, 1955), pp. 33-39.
[3] Pierre Martineau, *Motivation in Advertising* (New York: McGraw-Hill Book Company, Inc., 1957).

Even to begin to answer this question means an investigation of the structure of the product as an "object" in relationship with the individual. After interviewing hundreds of consumers, utilizing techniques of different levels of penetration, getting at "unconscious" and "conscious" attitudes and needs, three sources of meaning about a product have been isolated.

The first source is the set of meanings stemming from the *cultural definition* of the product. The second source of meaning comes from the consumer's organized set of notions about the brand, that is, the *brand image*. The third source of meaning is from direct *experience with the product*.

Cultural Definition of the Product

Social psychology and anthropology have dealt with the problem of objects in culture. That is, how do people come to understand and relate in a socially consistent manner to artifacts that are with them from time of birth?

The concept of "object" implies more than just a unidirectional flow of activity from the manipulator to the manipulated. It also implies a set of stimulations and communications in the reverse direction that guide the actions of the user. This means a dynamic relationship between the artifact and the user, wherein the latter perceives and acts upon the former according to the organized meanings that the culture and its subcultures have formulated for it.

The fact that few objects are naturally and intrinsically what they seem to be has been clearly indicated by such thinkers as George Herbert Mead, Jean Piaget, and Heinz Werner. A child growing up within a society begins by viewing an object in an idiosyncratic, self-centered way, and gradually redefines his relationship to it in terms of the broader, adult society. The acculturated individual internalizes the way the general society view the artifact, and sees the product in a setting of needs and values that control his action and attitudes about it. For example, there is nothing intrinsic in a baseball bat to account for its relationship to its user; a member of a primitive society could easily mistake it for a weapon.

It is perhaps more accurate to think of culture as involving a "climate of valuations" rather than being a thing apart from people. "Climate" implies the possibility for shift, and "valuations" suggests that the climate is made up of ideas, beliefs, feelings, and actions expressed by people. Yet the word "culture" as an abstraction also implies that the whole is greater than the sum of its parts, and that people learn from and conform to the patterns of people as a whole.

Elvis Presley in his early exposure on television and in popular music was responded to by a host of individual teen-agers who reacted to him with their own private senses. As Presley grew as an ideal, teen-agers were no longer free to accept him or reject him simply as individuals. They had to cope with a new level of values—that of the teen-age *society*.

Sometimes the important patterns of behavior and perception are learned from smaller reference groups, as adolescents, for example, respond to popular records. Sometimes learning is funneled through the larger, common culture, as in the singing of "The Star Spangled Banner." Although adults live in the same culture, they do not see a popular hit in the same light as teen-agers. Nor do non-Americans respond to the national anthem in the same way as Americans. An object or an idea differentiates itself along lines of the implied *membership* behind it.

Culture places the product in a social context and imbues it with meanings that set the broadest limitations on how it is experienced. A commercial product becomes culturally defined by the broad history of interaction with its market. In particular, the definition is determined by the social, biological, and psychic needs the product fulfills for its user. Thus, when a product achieves a niche in its cultural context, it is an object which denotes *consistent* (*not* unalterable) and *predictable* behavior within the social structure.

The ballpoint pen, for example, is intrinsically nothing but a complex set of tactile and visual sensations. These sensations are selected and modified by its user, according to the cultural definition of a ballpoint pen, and purposively placed in a social setting. That is, the object becomes perceived by the consumer. The result is that the user experiences a handy, easy-to-use, and relatively inexpensive tool for communicating his thoughts.

ADVERTISING AND CULTURE

Cultural influence is obvious when one thinks of how a cigarette in the mouth of a woman may be perceived today as compared to how it was perceived thirty or forty years ago. The above-the-ankle skirt might have indicated many qualities about its wearer during the last century that would be fallacious today.

Advertising must take account of the current values and product-definitions of the society (or subsociety) in which it intends to operate. In other words, advertisers must be aware of the role of the object in the life of the consumer. Likewise, advertisers must understand the limits of these broader cultural definitions before trying to amplify the product into a brand image.

For example, the social values implied by the concept "perfume" are such that its users are necessarily considered feminine. Any attempt by advertising to contradict the strong mores inherent in such a cultural definition might backfire as a commercial enterprise. Advertisers of male cosmetics and other self-indulgent items have discovered that they must carefully conceal the femininity and narcissism involved in colognes.

Culturally, then, the function of advertising is to understand, to reflect, and in most instances to accept the value-structure of society before it can go about its creative task of helping to organize in a consistent, gratifying manner the numerous stimulations a product contains for the potential consumer. Advertising can help to select and reinforce certain values and needs inherent in the role of the product. It can operate within the limits of culture to create new expectations for the consumer.

Occasionally an entire society may entertain negative or distorted notions about a product that may be a result of an unfortunate long-standing history between object and consumer. The potential for a limited, positive redefinition on a societal or subsocietal scale may exist in the case of such products.

The reader may think of numerous examples of products and services, the mere mention of which sends a wave of disdain, fear, disgust, discomfort, and other negative reactions through him. Spinach, dentists, hypodermic needles, and long underwear are examples of "objects" with a positive function subordinated to the unfavorable experiences behind them.

In these cases, advertising can embark on the Herculean task of pointing up new avenues of more pleasurable interaction between the product and the consumer, and reformulate aspects of the cultural definitions of a product class. Of course, true reformulation lies in the response by the consumer society to the communicator's message. If the message is consistent with the society's experiences, an advertising-success story may indeed occur in a social movement toward a product. In such instances, reformulation is based on a pleasure-pain principle that promises to take the consumer from an unsatisfying relationship to a gratifying one.

For example, dental care in the mind of the average American is fraught with annoyance and discomfort, on the one hand, or with special precaution, compulsiveness, and concern on the other. Dental care and dentists are too often associated with a conception of teeth as a set of nuisances which nature ordained shall be in one's mouth. The American Dental Association is trying to reorient the client toward conceiving of his teeth and their care in the positive light of self-grooming and social reward in much the manner of the cosmetic industries.[4]

And when the Tea Bureau suggested that tea is the "hefty, hale, and hearty" drink for the average man, it was attempting to counter the stereotyped notions of effeteness, femininity, and snobbishness culturally attributed to the drink.

---

[4] "A Motivational Study of Dental Care: A Pilot Investigation," prepared for the American Dental Association by Social Research, Inc., in the *Journal of the American Dental Association,* serialized in Vol. 56 (March, April, May, and June, 1958).

If the program of redefinition dramatically and effectively brings a product closer to the experience of the consumer, a new cognitive orientation toward the product will take place. Success in changing a popular concept depends upon how intense and stable, how true to experience, is the cultural tradition concerning products, ideas, or services.

Although advertising can help to reorganize some of the social interaction between a consumer and a product, it must be sensitive enough to these patterns to recognize their intensity and stability. An extremely exotic product, perhaps suitable for a small elite group, cannot be converted into a mundane, mass product *merely* by advertising.

The Brand Image as a Source of Meaning

The cultural definition of a product is too broad and generalized to allow a consumer to select a brand. It helps to create the initial set of expectations about the product which is then qualified by the second variable in product-consumer interaction, the brand image.

The brand image, as a source of meaning, helps the consumer further to select and organize the stimulations of the product, display, and other communications directed to him. Mead's social psychology suggests that an "image" guides one's actions and attitudes toward the object.[5]

It has been further suggested that the *meaning* of any message is the "change which it produces in the (already existing) image" that an individual harbors about the object in question.[6] This means that the message value of a television commercial, for example, lies in the degree and direction of change in a brand image previously held by the viewer. (Reinforcement of an already existing image implies a change in degree.)

Differences among brand images represent much more than literal product differences. A whole different set of notions and actions are inherent in the name "Lincoln" as compared with the name "Jaguar," despite the fact that each make has at least one or two models that are functionally comparable. It is somewhat difficult to imagine the typical Lincoln owner sitting behind the wheel of the typical Jaguar. The difference in the two images is, therefore, more intricate than the simple differences between the two lines of cars.

Tests of consumer reactions to various products and their advertisements indicate that the brand image may undergo change more quickly than the basic cultural definition of the product. Perception of the brand

[5] George Herbert Mead, *Mind, Self, and Society,* edited by Charles W. Morris (Chicago, University of Chicago Press, 1934).
[6] Kenneth E. Boulding, *The Image* (Ann Arbor: University of Michigan Press, 1956), p. 7.

image is more capable of being influenced than is the perception of the general class of the product. This is logical, as the image is formulated within the limits of a culture.

The changes which took place in the brand images of certain filter cigarettes, for example, were fairly swift once the underlying cultural attitudes about filter cigarettes were modified by broader social influences affecting their definition, such as science, medicine, group hysteria. Marlboro could become a *manly* cigarette rather quickly once society relaxed its notions about who might smoke such a cigarette.

The image of the brand appears to be a relatively stable organization of percepts about a product. Once established, a brand image lends the consistency and predictability in the consumer's relationship with the product which allow him to select and experience those aspects of the product he values. Schweppes quinine water must indeed be a different experience to those who have responded to its image than is that of several other brands. The senses become attuned differently, and the social values inherent in the product-consumer interaction are different from brand to brand.

ADVERTISING AND THE BRAND IMAGE

The major influence of advertising appears to be felt in the area of consumer perception of the brand. The brand image is the major organizing concept through which the consumer is guided toward perceiving unified patterns of stimulation. This imagery provides the emotional and sensual qualities which distinguish a brand from the general product-class and help the consumer discriminate from brand to brand.

Jello is not just a gelatin dessert, nor are Jello and Royal simply two products united by their common class. For the purchaser of a brand, there is usually a feeling that one has purchased a product distinctly different from another brand. This is probably most obvious in the case of beer and cigarettes.

This is the clue to what is often termed the "irrational" motive of the consumer in purchasing products. Skeptics, classic economists, and behaviorists in market research might demonstrate by blindfold tests how suggestible the average consumer is. They point out that the average consumer cannot distinguish between a Camel or a Philip Morris, or between Schlitz and Miller.

What such a literal understanding of the product-consumer relationship fails to consider is that *the value of a brand and its over-all symbolic effects on the consumer cannot be teased apart by tests oriented toward seeing the product in its barest, utilitarian terms.*

Another way of saying this is that the consumer purchases the brand and its cluster of meanings as much as he purchases the literal product.

What Vance Packard calls "hidden persuasion" is probably the reference-group and other symbolic values implied in most social communications.[7]

The function of advertising is to create strong sub-categories of values and needs within the social structure, and to associate these with the product. Consumers may then select those brands whose sets of implied experiences fit into the sub-group with which he identifies.

The *Chicago Tribune* study on cigarettes and smokers clearly indicated that it is as reasonable to talk about the man who smokes Camels, for example, as having a "Camel personality" as it is to say that the brand itself has a personality.[8] It is reasonable because the two are correlates of each other. To the extent that the consumer perceives the brand image in this stable, predictable (and pleasurable) manner, the brand becomes a need-satisfying monopoly rather than a competitor with other brands. The power of the monopoly is dependent on the degree to which the brand is differentiated from other brands and is pleasurable at the same time.

If this aspect of the function of advertising is recognized, much of the arrogant and sanctimonious tone in some advertising can be relieved and a positive program of distinctive image development put in its place.

This relationship between the consumer and the brand must be understood by the advertiser in the earliest stages of planning if some measure of control and predictability in one's message is to be realized. If it is believed that facial tissue "A" can appeal to an important part of the market not adequately tapped by facial tissue "B," its advertisers must understand both the expectancies of this market and how advertising might serve to fit in with, reinforce, and organize these sets into a satisfying perceptual whole.

Direct Experience with the Product as a Source of Meaning

The third perceptual area is that of direct experience, the *use* which classical theory states determines the *utility* of the product and ultimately its demand. By direct experience with a product, a consumer finally gets his "feedback" in terms of social gratifications and primary sensory experiences that the brand image and cultural definitions have set up for him.

In a sense, the consumer is not fully open to his experiences and is not likely to perceive all the stimuli of a product. His own needs, in conjunction with the social conceptions reinforced by the imagery surrounding the

[7] Vance Packard, *The Hidden Persuaders* (New York, McKay, 1957).

[8] *Cigarettes: Their Role and Function, A Study for the Chicago Tribune,* prepared by Social Research, Inc., Chicago, 1953.

product, emphasize certain aspects of direct experience and weed out others.

In some research on the ballpoint pen, for example, consumers were asked to describe their *writing* experiences with three brands of pens. One of these pens is a brand which stresses efficiency and predictability. The second brand emphasizes a general quality of competence, including prestige and status. The third brand focuses on inexpensiveness and dispensability.

Consumers described their experiences with the pens in terms of the generalized brand image, giving evidence of an awareness of how they were oriented toward the product. It is fairly evident that technical product improvements alone, unless they are highly dramatic or extreme, do not radically alter the consumer's previous ideas about the product. Some outside agent must serve to create a new expectation about the product that will allow the consumer to perceive the difference.

ADVERTISING AND DIRECT EXPERIENCE WITH THE PRODUCT

The function of advertising in this third area of consumer perception is to supply the *terms* in which the product is valued. In some ways advertising sets up a "self-fulfilling prophecy." [9] Most researchers are aware that a consumer's reaction to use is channeled in an important way by what he expects to experience. The terms in which the consumer responds to use are, in good part, supplied by advertising. The facets of experience beyond the scope of advertising are the concrete physiological sensations of the consumer.

Nor can broad organizing concepts, such as a cultural definition or a brand image, account for the unpredicted idiosyncrasies of either the consumer or the product. However, by the time the consumer has selected and organized all the communications of the product, he will evaluate the use experience in a fairly patterned manner.

Too often, the advertiser is so close to competitive aspects of his product that he has personally defined it in a manner that is not of optimum value to the consumer. Competition often causes advertisers to "hop on the current bandwagon" of advertising claims and to shout loudly about values that have little positive meaning to the consumer. In the automobile industry, a complex language of power dynamics has been foisted upon the consumer. Is this the optimum language of use available for him? In filter cigarettes, the language of use among certain competitive brands has been the number of filter-traps contained in the cigarette. Is the filter-cigarette

---

[9] Robert K. Merton, "The Self-Fulfilling Prophecy," in Robert K. Merton, *Social Theory and Social Structure* (Glencoe, Ill., Free Press, 1949).

smoker aided in getting gratification out of a cigarette by a terminology that concentrates upon the negatives of smoking?

The advertiser might improve his relationship with the consumer if he realized that his characterization of the consumer's use-experience helps the latter selectively perceive out of the product's numerous stimulations. Direct experience with a product is patterned by the communicable language of the product which has been created or reinforced by advertising.

In American business, commercial propaganda is part and parcel of the mass-production process. Our present American business could no more operate without advertising than it could without the automatic machine or the assembly line.

37

The Propaganda Function in Marketing

EDMUND D. McGARRY

THE MOST CONTROVERSIAL ASPECT OF marketing is advertising. Ever since advertising began to appear, moralists and critics have complained that it distorted people's natural desires, misinformed them as to the products they needed, played upon their emotions, and led to waste of resources.

Proponents of advertising, on the other hand, have argued that it is an economical method of distributing goods, that it provides entertainment, and actually adds to the value of the goods advertised. The purpose here is not to discuss these issues directly, but rather to place the advertising process in its proper perspective as a function of marketing.

Advertising as used today is primarily a type of propaganda. The essence of propaganda is that it conditions people to act in a way favorable to or desired by the propagandist. It deliberately attempts to influence, persuade, and convince people to act in a way that they would not otherwise act. Propaganda had its birth in the attempt of the church to propagate the faith. It is used by leaders who seek a following in politics, in religion, and in all affairs which require action by large bodies of people.

Reprinted from the *Journal of Marketing,* national quarterly publication of the American Marketing Association, Volume 23, No. 2 (October, 1958), pp. 131-139.

In business it is used primarily by sellers to obtain a market by conditioning people in the market to accept the particular products offered. The growth of new techniques of communication has greatly extended the range of propaganda penetration, has expanded the number of products advertised, and has increased the total amount of propaganda disseminated; but the aim of the messages carried is essentially unchanged since the beginning of civilization.

In fact, the use of force of argument instead of physical force marked the change from savagery to civilized living. "The creation of the world," said Plato, "is the victory of persuasion over force."

The use of persuasion is part of man's apparatus to adapt his way of life to change. Without some stimulus to action, man tends to be indifferent and apathetic to change, and unwilling to exert the effort which change necessitates. He prefers to follow his preconditioned routines rather than direct his effort in some different way. There must be some extra stimulus to action; and this stimulus is afforded either by compulsion of force or the threat of force, or by persuasion in the form of the written or spoken word.

Propaganda versus Education

Propaganda differs from education in that education presumably is oriented toward the dissemination of "truth"—dispassionate, objective, and unbiased. Pure education takes an impartial non-partisan point of view. It is not prejudiced; it has no slant. Yet all of us know that education must persuade to get students to study; it must propagandize to get funds.

Propaganda, on the other hand, by definition is biased, partial, and one-sided. It has an axe to grind; therefore, it is always controversial. But unlike education, in which there is no sponsor, the sponsor of propaganda, particularly advertising propaganda, is known. And everyone knows what the sponsor is trying to do, what his motives are, and how he would like others to act. The sponsor of commercial propaganda must identify himself and the product he advertises, and he must take the responsibility for it; otherwise, his propaganda cannot be directed to his purpose.

Every advertisement is designed to predispose its readers to a favorable consideration of its sponsor and his product. It is deliberately planned to make its readers and listeners take sides—to affiliate and ally themselves under its banner and to ignore all others.

Advertising is the obtrusive display of the conflict of interests in the market place. It represents a parade of the contestants in the battle for market supremacy, each imploring the audience to follow him. By its very nature advertising must be prejudiced in order to be potent.

The Barrage Effect of Propaganda

Commercial propaganda is a social phenomenon, and its analysis must necessarily be in a social framework. It is, in fact, a part of our culture and at the same time exercises a considerable influence on that culture. Professor David M. Potter speaks of it "as an instrument of social control comparable to the school and the church in the extent of its influence upon society." [1]

Like other types of propaganda, advertising has a barrage effect. Although it is designed primarily to induce people who have the money and the need to buy the product, its effect cannot usually be confined to these. It creates a pattern of thought in a much larger population. Its results are diffuse and pervasive rather than selective. Because of this diffusion, many who are not in a position to buy, read, or listen to the advertisement, and many others who do not see or hear the message directly, learn of it from others by word of mouth.

Moreover, the pattern of thought created by advertising is likely to last for an indefinite period. If consecutive appeals are used, the effect tends to be cumulative both because of the widening group which sees it and because of the intensification of the impression it makes. This cumulative effect continues to a point of diminishing returns which is reached either through saturation of the market, through the counteracting influence of competing messages, or through the saturation of receptivity.

There is another sense in which there is a spill-over of advertising effectiveness. This is what might be called the cross-product influence. It is said, for instance, that when vacuum cleaners were first advertised the demand for brooms increased; the inference is that the promotion of cleanliness in the home leads to the increased sales of any product that enhances cleanliness.

Still another type of spill-over effect is seen in the case of the firm selling a family of products in which the advertising of any one will increase to some extent the sales of other products in the same group. It seems probable also that the advertising of a particular brand influences the sales of all other products in the same use-class, even if they are marketed by competitors.

It would seem logical to assume that, when two competing advertisers attempt to promote their individual brands for a particular use, the impact will be greater than if only one is advertised; and, if the market can be expanded, the advertising of each will have a complementary effect on that of the other. If this is true, then there is a cumulative effect of ad-

[1] David M. Potter, *People of Plenty* (Chicago, University of Chicago Press, 1954), p. 168.

vertising generally in the sense that, as more advertising is published, there is developed a greater propensity to purchase advertised goods of all kinds. The increase may be at the expense of non-advertised goods, it may be at the expense of savings, or it may result in greater effort on the part of consumers to secure more income.

ADVERTISING *VERSUS* PERSONAL SELLING

Advertising today has to take a large part of the responsibility for making sales. To a great extent salesmen, particularly at the retail level, have become anonymous persons—unknown either to the selling firm or to the buyer—who merely facilitate the sale by formally presenting the product and accepting payment. The real job of adjusting the consumer to the product is done by the mass propaganda called advertising.

In taking over the task formerly performed by the salesman, advertising must substitute symbolic language for the personal appeal of man-to-man at a point where the merchandise is itself present and the transaction takes place. The task of persuading the customer is pushed back in time to a point where it can be planned and partly executed months before the product reaches the market. It is removed in space from the point of sale to the business office, where the entire selling technique is planned and developed without benefit of the presence of the buyer. The sale must thus consist of an impersonalized message to thousands of unidentified potential customers, who have no way of communicating their impressions.

Modern advertising has many tasks to perform, which do not arise when selling is done face-to-face at the point of sale:

1. It must create or point out a need by identifying the circumstances under which it arises.
2. It must link the need to the possibility of fulfilling it with a general product, so that when the need arises the respondent will think of the product that will fulfill it.
3. It must differentiate the particular brand and its sponsor from other products which might satisfy the need approximately as well.
4. It must connect the particular branded product with the place and the conditions under which it can be obtained.
5. It must show that the need is urgent and that the task of buying is easy.
6. It must give a rational basis for action, for people do not like to buy goods which they cannot justify to their own consciences.
7. It must stimulate the respondent to make a firm decision on which he will act at a later time.

In accomplishing these tasks, advertising acts under the klieglights of publicity. Unlike personal selling, where the promotion is carried on in private between two or more people, the messages publicized in advertising are conspicuous and cannot escape observation. This is one of the reasons why advertising comes in for a great deal of criticism that is equally relevant to selling on a personal basis. The so-called abuses which are concealed and disguised in the personal sales transaction are flaunted in the face of the public when they are published on the printed page or appear on the television screen. There is little doubt that there is more misrepresentation, deceit, and fraud in person-to-person sales relationships than in advertising.

THE PURPOSE OF ADVERTISING

Commercial propaganda or advertising had its genesis in the need of the mass producer to sell goods in large quantities, and competition of other goods forced him to resort to an anonymous market: an aggregation of people scattered geographically, and unknown and unidentified as individuals. These conditions, and the growing separation of the locus of production in time and space from the locus of consumption, necessitated some means of making an individual manufacturer's product known and thus assuring it a continuous market.

Through the use of propaganda it was possible to create markets that were more stable than their component parts; for, although individual consumers are notoriously whimsical in changing their minds, their reactions in the market as a whole tend to cancel each other out.[2]

In order to accomplish these results the advertiser must use all the tools at his disposal. He must have an intimate understanding of the product advertised and be able to sense these characteristics whether inherent or inferred, which will fulfill the hopes and expectations of the potential owner and user. He must envisage the product in its use-setting. He must comprehend and appreciate the nature of human behavior. And he must be able to use the tricks of his trade—often the same as, and always closely akin to, those used on the rostrum and in the pulpit.

If the propaganda which the advertiser writes is to be effective, it must be expressed in terms in which the consumer thinks, with the same overtones and exaggerations of the product that the well-disposed consumer will attribute to it. It must recognize that the consumer to whom it appeals is but imperfectly rational, that he hates the labor of rational thinking, and that he is sometimes more impressed by what seems to others to be superficial than by the real merits of the product.

[2] Compare Neil H. Borden, *The Economic Effects of Advertising* (Chicago, Richard D. Irwin, 1942).

Rational versus *Emotional* Appeals

In a broad, general sense advertising appeals either to man's reason or to his emotion or to both. It is difficult, of course, to differentiate in any precise way between these; but generally speaking rational appeals seem more effective in deciding alternative means to ends rather than the ends themselves. Emotion, on the other hand, is usually the trigger to action, particularly when the actions mean a change of attitude on the part of the person.

There are many road-blocks to actions based on rational appeals; for rational arguments tend to raise questions rather than to answer them. Emotional appeals, on the other hand, attempt to stimulate the individual to carry through impulses which he already has. Assuming that this is true, the rational appeal is likely to be more lasting and its secondary effect to be stronger, because people are more likely to repeat rationalizations than they are to communicate their emotional feelings.

Advertising is highly concentrated on marginal products, things that one can do without, things that can be purchased with free income after the more austere basic needs such as necessary food, housing, clothing, etc., are taken care of.[3] It is these marginal products that give the real satisfactions in life. Even in the case of basic products, it is the exotic, the unusual elements—the fringe benefits—that set one off from his fellow creatures and thus claim the attention of consumers.

THE MOST COMMON MOTIVES

Some years ago Victor Schwab suggested that there were ten leading motives or desires of the average consumer to which advertising must appeal in order to be effective: [4]

1. *Money and a better job.* "There must always be some kind of short-cut to getting ahead faster."
2. *Security in old age.* "When I get along in years, I want to be able to take it easy."
3. *Popularity.* "It's fun to be asked out all the time, to be wanted by everybody."
4. *Praise from others.* "Praise from others is a nice thing to get and I like to get it when I deserve it, and I often do."
5. *More comfort.* "A lot of people who are not as industrious or as capable as I am seem to have more comforts, so why shouldn't I spread myself once in a while?"

[3] F. P. Bishop, *The Ethics of Advertising* (London: Robert Hale, 1949), p. 48.
[4] Victor Schwab, "Ten Copy Appeals," *Printers' Ink,* December 17, 1943, pp. 17 ff.

6. *Social advancement.* "Where would a person be if he never tried to better himself and to meet and associate with better people?"

7. *Improved appearance.* "It is awfully nice to have people tell you how attractive and well-dressed you are. If I had the time and money some people spend on themselves, I would show them."

8. *Personal prestige.* "I am going to see to it that my children can prove that they have parents they need never be ashamed of."

9. *Better health.* "I don't feel any older than I did years ago, it's just that I don't seem to have the drive and energy I used to have."

10. *Increased enjoyment.* "I work hard, I do the best I can about things so why shouldn't I get as much enjoyment as I can?"

Advertisers have found by trial and error that these types of appeals are effective. It is evident that each appeal contains a bit of rationality with a large dose of sentimentality. The fact that these appeals are effective simply indicates that "the average human mind is a montage of hasty impressions, fuzzy generalities, bromidic wall-motto sentiments, self-justifications and sentimentalities." [5] It is out of this "jumble of ideas and feelings" that the advertiser must find a background for his appeals.

MORE AND BETTER WANTS

"The chief thing which the common-sense individual actually wants," wrote Professor Frank H. Knight, "is not satisfactions for the wants which he has, but more and better wants. There is always really present and operative, though in the background of consciousness, the idea of, and desire for a new want to be striven for when the present objective is out of the way." [6] Advertising attempts to present goods which are new or additional in the consumers' inventory of wants, and to indicate how they can be realized. In doing this, it both creates a want and the means of satisfying it.

The fact that advertising concentrates its efforts on changing people's customary wants has given rise to the contention that it corrupts people's desires and stimulates so-called "artificial" consuming habits. But this argument is beside the point for, as Professor Knight has indicated, "there is no issue as between natural and artificial wants. All human wants are more artificial than natural, and the expression 'natural wants,' if it has any meaning, can only refer to those of beasts. By the same token, human wants are more sentimental than real." [7]

Most people have always lived rather drab and unimaginative lives. The so-called golden ages of history were golden only to the few. The great masses lived by drudgery, and thought in terms of only the elemental emo-

---

[5] *Ibid.*, p. 17.
[6] Frank H. Knight, *The Ethics of Competition* (New York, Harper, 1935), p. 22.
[7] *Ibid.*, p. 103.

tions such as hunger and comfort. The so-called "democratic way of life" rests simply on the idea that our present economy is oriented to change the thinking of these masses. Propaganda, if it is to be effective, must appeal to the masses in the terms of their own mental processes.

It is sometimes alleged also that, through advertising, businessmen foist on people goods they do not want. This, of course, is sheer nonsense. There are, in fact, few acts necessarily more deliberate than that of the consumer's action in response to advertising.

Picture the consumer in his living room reading a magazine advertisement. He has had to choose the particular magazine, and pay for it; he has had to select from among the hundreds of pages those he wishes to read, and he can either accept or reject the arguments presented. Assuming that he accepts them and resolves to make the purchase, he must still wait hours or even days before an opportune time arises to make the purchase. During the interval between the time he reads the advertisement and the time he undertakes the overt act of buying, he is entirely outside the influence of the message and may deliberate and search his soul to his heart's content either in private or in consultation with his friends. There is not even mass psychology to influence him. He is a free agent and there is no possibility of coercion, duress, or constraint of any kind.

But the impossibility of advertising to force consumers to buy what they do not want should not be confused with the fact that advertisers sometime overstep the bounds of propriety to make claims for their products which cannot be justified. In some product areas effective protection has been provided by law, but in general the chief defense of the consumer lies in his own discrimination of whom he will patronize or refuse to patronize.

The Larger System of Beliefs

In discussing propaganda generally, psychologists Krech and Crutchfield state that "suggestions which are accepted as a consequence of propaganda tend to be in harmony with some larger system of beliefs or some already existing predisposition, and therefore presumably with the major needs and interests of the subject." [8]

To put this another way, at any given time the subject of propaganda has many prejudices, beliefs, and attitudes of different intensities. Some are deeply entrenched, while others are at a superficial level. The more deeply entrenched these predispositions are, the more difficult it will be to change them, and some seem to be entrenched so deeply that they cannot be changed by propaganda at all.

[8] D. K. Krech and R. S. Crutchfield, *Theory and Problems of Social Psychology* (New York, McGraw-Hill, 1948), p. 347.

Since it is easier and less expensive to modify existing predispositions than to oppose them, propagandists find it expedient to fit their messages into the current pattern of thinking rather than oppose it head on. It is for this reason that most changes in attitudes and wants achieved by advertising are almost imperceptible, and can be objectively observed only over a period of time.

Both in the selection of the characteristics of the product to promote and in the framing of appeals, the advertiser must give attention to consumers' preconceived ideas of what they want. He develops his product and its appeals to fit into these ideas and to project them further. If his advertising is successful in selling his product, competitors will find it necessary to discover other new products or new characteristics of old products, likewise in line with consumers' ideas, as a basis for their counter-propaganda. Thus, competition in advertising tends to develop a constantly increasing improvement of the product to fit consumers' wants, while at the same time it raises the standards of wants in the consumers' minds.

DISCOUNTING THE MESSAGE

The very mass of advertising and the great amount that comes to the attention of consumers is often open to criticism. Critics ask, for instance, "Is there no limit to the increasing din of the market place?" "Will it continue until all businesses are wasting their substance and crying their wares?" "Are there no antidotes for this infectious disease?" We suspect there are.

The editor of *Harper's Magazine,* puts it this way: "Perhaps, however, we will in the long run have reason to be grateful to the copywriters and press agents, even the worst of them. It may turn out that thanks to advertising and public relations, the American people will become the first people in history to be impervious to propaganda. Maybe it isn't such a bad thing that the advertisers and other word-manipulators have got us to the point that we never take words quite at their face value. In all events, it is hard to imagine that the people inured to American advertising would wholeheartedly believe the kind of promises and assurances, whereby Hitler and Stalin have enslaved two great nations in our time." [9]

When two advertisers say approximately the same things about their product, the message of one tends to neutralize that of the other, and the public learns to discount what is said by both. In a free world the right to persuade and be persuaded is one of the essential freedoms. We assume that each of us has the mentality and the fortitude to choose—to accept or reject what he hears or what he reads.

Each has the right to act or to refuse to act on the basis of all the propa-

[9] Robert Amory, Jr., "Personal and Otherwise," *Harper's Magazine,* September, 1948, p. 6.

ganda he absorbs, whether it is in the form of advertising or word-of-mouth gossip. That he often rejects propaganda is a matter of record. But we assume that, whether a person acts wisely or foolishly, he will take the responsibility for the act and that he himself will reap the benefits or the penalties of his action. For this reason he will eventually learn to listen more discriminatingly and act more wisely in the light of all the information available.

Effect on Media Content

It is sometimes alleged that advertising, because it pays most of the cost of magazines and newspapers, dominates and controls the information in these media. It is said that, since the advertiser pays the piper, he must call the tune.

Actually this is seldom true because the medium that publishes biased or slanted news tends to lose its circulation when its bias becomes known, and in this way it ceases to be an effective means of communication. Even the most severe critics of advertising admit that this type of direct and overt influence is pretty well eliminated by the intense competition among media themselves.

The effect of advertising on news content and editorial opinion is far more indirect and subtle. Editors themselves are human and they live in the same environment as the rest of us. They, too, are subject to the propaganda which all of us read; and it would be too much to expect that they are not influenced in a general way by what they read. As a part of the total environment it tends to set a point of view which is not unfavorable to advertising.

THE FUNCTION OF MEDIA

From the advertiser's point of view, the function of the newspaper, the magazine, the broadcasting station, or any other medium of publication is to gather a crowd or furnish an audience.[10] Once the crowd has gathered, it must be entertained, amused, or at least interested enough to hold together while the advertiser's message is being delivered. The need for holding the audience arises from the fact that advertising is selective, in the sense that a specific message is likely to have an appeal only to a scattered few among the many in the crowd. As for the many others who have no need or interest in the particular product, they become bored and resentful that their attention has been disrupted.

The fact that advertising is selective in its expectations, though not in its aims, means that its impact on those to whom the message does not

[10] See G. B. Hotchkiss, *Milestones of Marketing* (New York, Macmillan, 1938), p. 10.

apply or who do not care to listen ranges from irritation to exasperation. From the listener's point of view, it is an unwarranted intrusion on their privacy, by some "jerk" who wants to sell something.

Therefore, the advertiser must use every art he can contrive to make his message palatable, even to those who do not want to listen; and at the same time he searches for a vehicle which will capture and hold his audience while he gives them "the works." In rare cases he is able to convert his message into news which is interesting and entertaining in itself; but often there is a trail of resentment left in the listener's mind, and he deliberately tries to develop some means of shutting out the message from his consciousness. The result is that a great deal of advertising never passes the threshold of the reader's or the listener's consciousness.

Although there is danger of exaggerating the importance of advertising in causing certain changes in our culture, it would be erroneous to conclude that its influence is negligible. Advertising is so prevalent, so pervasive, so extensive, and so conspicuous that it would be absurd to argue that it does not affect our attitudes.

On the other hand, the fact that advertising, in order to be successful and economical, "must be in harmony with some larger system of beliefs or some already existing predisposition" indicates that its influence is tangential rather than direct, that it tends to fit in with and supplement other motivational influences rather than act as an independent force.

Effect on Consumer Standards

Advertising, both for individual products and in the aggregate, appeals to the anticipatory aspirations of the group.[11] It offers goals of attainment that would not otherwise be thought of. It sets up ideals to be sought after. Its appeals are designed to stimulate action which will result in a more comfortable, congenial, and satisfying life.

Thus, in the aggregate it creates an ever-expanding series of aspirations for the future. In doing this, it shapes the standards of living for the future; and, since man lives largely in a world of anticipation, it lays the basis for much of his enjoyment.

In American business, commercial propaganda is part and parcel of the mass-production process. Our present American business could no more operate without advertising than it could without the automatic machine or the assembly line. By means of this propaganda, the millions of people coming from many nations and races and diverse backgrounds are conditioned to want sufficient amounts of a given standardized product to make

[11] See Wroe Alderson, *Marketing Behavior and Executive Action* (Homewood, Ill., Richard D. Irwin, 1957), p. 276 ff.

it possible to produce that product at a fraction of the cost which would otherwise be necessary.

If left without such propaganda as is found in advertising, people would not choose the same products they do choose. Whether they would choose the same product at a later date is purely a matter of conjecture, but it seems unlikely. If it is assumed that without advertising they would choose something different, then no producer would be able to secure sufficient production to provide these diverse things at prices people could afford to pay. This is another way of saying that standardization of wants through advertising is in part the basis for the economies which come through mass production.

In spite of the necessity that people's wants be so standardized as to secure mass production, the enormous market and the high-level purchasing power available in America have enabled firms to proliferate these standards and to offer a wider variety of goods for sale than would be possible even under a handicraft system where goods are presumably made to fit the consumer's specifications.

Incidentally, the assumption sometimes made, that people would make wiser choices if there were no advertising, ignores the fact that preconceived notions of what they want have themselves been formed by other types of propaganda and other influences no less biased and no more rational than the propaganda used by sellers.

As people get more income, and as competition becomes stronger among sellers for a share of this income, adjustment of goods to the consumer becomes finer. More attention is given to the marginal aspects of goods. New quality standards are developed in terms of their psychological rather than their utilitarian values. For instance, people in buying shoes are often more interested in style and how they look to others than in comfort and durability, which are likely to be taken for granted.

These types of desires are often hidden and so subtle that sellers are faced with a continuously changing market, difficult to interpret and almost impossible to predict. They are thus forced to offer their products with infinite variations in characteristics and appeals. To the consumer, the opportunity to choose from this vast variety of products is itself a major element in his standard of living.

Most business investments are not made in ignorance of their probable impacts, whereas, many of the outlays for persuasion now are.

38

Does Advertising Belong in the Capital Budget?

JOEL DEAN

SHOULD ADVERTISING BE BUDGETED *as an expense or as an investment?* Advertising is now book-kept and budgeted as though its benefits were used up immediately, like purchased electricity. Management thinks about advertising as it is book-kept, as a current expense. The decision as to how much a corporation should spend on persuasion is made by the same criteria as for materials used up in the factory—impact upon the current P&L. The advertising budget is part of the *operating* budget.

So far as is known, no corporation puts advertising in its capital budget. But maybe it belongs there. Several disinterested parties say so:

- The stock market says it belong there. It says the benefits derived from promotional outlays are just as capitalizable as the tangible assets that the bookkeeper does capitalize. It says this when Bristol Myers sells at ten times its book value.
- Corporation presidents occasionally say it belongs there, especially when they evoke *investment* in advertising to justify poor current profits.
- New entrants into an industry say advertising belongs in the capital budget. They say it by including the promotional outlays required to build brand-

Joel Dean, reprinted from the *Journal of Marketing,* national quarterly publication of the American Marketing Association, Volume 30, No. 4 (October, 1966), pp. 15-21.

acceptance as an integral part of the total investment required to break into the business.

- Antitrust economists say advertising belongs in the capital budget. They say it by viewing brand-acceptance, which is built up by promotion, as just as substantial a barrier to entry as the investment required in buildings and machinery.
- It is just possible that the bookkeeper's guide to top-management thinking about advertising is wrong.

The Approach

The plan of this article is, first, to find whether promotion is an investment; second, to consider how to optimize it if it is an investment; and third, to speculate on the probabilities that this novel approach, even if theoretically valid, will do any good.

The approach here to the problem of how much to invest in advertising is formal and objective, rather than intuitive. The premise is that the overriding goal of the corporation is to maximize profits. The viewpoint is that of an economist concerned with managerial finance.

This article is confined to the conceptual framework for deciding how much to invest in promotion. Measurement problems are not examined, nor the mechanics of application. The analysis is presented in terms of advertising, but is equally applicable to all forms of persuasion. Advertising is used as an example simply because it is the purest and most indisputable form of selling cost, and for many firms also the largest.

My thesis is as follows. Most advertising is, in economic essence, an investment. How much to spend on advertising is, therefore, a problem of investment economics. A new approach is required—economic and financial analysis of futurities. This approach focuses on future after-tax cash flows and centers on the profit-productivity of capital.

Is Promotion an Investment?

To determine whether, as a matter of economics, outlays for advertising and other forms of promotion constitute an investment, rather than a current expense, is our first task.

So we must bravely face three basic questions concerning the economics of investment in corporate persuasion:

- *A.* Precisely what is a business investment; how is it distinguished from a current expense?
- *B.* Just what are promotional costs; how should they be distinguished from production costs?

C. What are the distinctive characteristics of promotional outlays; do they disqualify promotion for investment treatment?

A. CONCEPT OF INVESTMENT

What distinguishes a business investment from a current expense?

An investment is an outlay made today to achieve benefits in the future. A current expense is an outlay whose benefits are immediate. The question is not how the outlay is treated in conventional accounting, how it is taxed, or whether the asset is tangible or intangible. The hallmark of an investment is futurity.

B. CONCEPT OF PROMOTIONAL COSTS

Precisely what are promotional costs? How do they differ from production costs?

Promotional costs are outlays to augment the demand for the product—that is, to shift its price-quantity demand schedule upward, so that more will be sold at a given price. In contrast, production costs are all outlays required to meet this demand.

This different dividing line means that some costs which are conventionally classified as marketing costs, for example, physical distribution, are here viewed as part of production costs. It means also that some costs usually viewed as production costs, for example, inspection, are here viewed as promotional costs, even though they are incurred in the factory.

This is the cost-dichotomy needed for clear thinking about promotional investments. A clear idea of the purpose of an outlay is indispensable for a useful estimate of its effectiveness. Moreover, the criterion for optimization is quite different for production costs than for promotional costs. For production, it is sheer cost-minimization; for promotion, it is not cost-minimization but something much more intricate, as we shall see.

C. DISTINCTIVE TRAITS OF PROMOTIONAL OUTLAYS

Do promotional investments differ from unimpeachable corporate investments in ways that make it impractical to manage them like true investments?

Promotional investments *are* different from traditional corporate investments—for example, capital tied up in machinery. The question is whether these differences call for a different intellectual apparatus for measuring productivity and rationing the firm's capital.

- Promotional investments *are book-kept differently.* They are not capitalized and not depreciated. But this does not keep them from being investments. They tie up capital with equal inflexibility and do so with similar expectation of future benefits.

- Promotional investments *are taxed differently*. Unlike acknowledged investments, they are deductible against income fully at the time of outlay, regardless of the delay of benefits. The fact that the tax collector is oblivious to promotional investments increases their productivity. Immediate tax writeoff of the entire outlay halves the investment after tax and steps up its true rate of return.

- Promotional investments *are generally spread out over time* and usually can be adjusted in amount in relatively small steps. However, this is irrelevant in determining whether or not they are true investments.

- Most promotional investments *have an indeterminate economic life*. Brand-acceptance "planted in the head" of a teenager by television may influence his purchases for 50 minutes or 50 years. But uncertainty of duration of the benefits does not make the promotional outlay any less an investment. The obsolescence-life of a computer is also quite uncertain.

- Promotional investments *have multiple benefits* which can be reaped in optional ways. The profitability of augmented demand may be taken out either in higher prices or in larger volume. But this is not unique to promotional investments. Usually factory modernization not only saves labor, but also increases capacity and improves product-quality and employee morale.

- Promotional investments *usually have irregular and diverse time-shapes in their benefit-streams*. But this is a common characteristic of many tangible investments. Some oil wells, for example, come in as gushers, have an unexpected midlife rejuvenation from repressuring, and live out a tranquil old age as pumpers.

- Promotional investments *have a benefit-stream which is difficult to measure and to predict*. But they share this characteristic with many forms of outlay conventionally classified as capital expenditures. Obsolescence of chemical-processing equipment, for example, is hard to predict, yet vitally affects its rate of return.

- Promotional investments *are provocative;* they may induce rivals to retaliate. This adds to the difficulty of measuring and predicting benefits. Tangible investments, however, can also provoke competitors' reactions in ways that erode their profitability (for example, retail store modernization).

All this adds up to the fact that promotional investments *do* have unusual characteristics, different from many other investments that now fight for funds in the capital budget. However, these traits either are not distinctive, or if they are, do not destroy the essential investment-character of the promotional outlays.

All promotional outlays are now conventionally viewed exclusively as current expenses. Some are, if the time lag of benefits is sufficiently short; but others are instead true investments, because the delay in their benefits is substantial. Most promotion is a *mixture,* and the richness of the investment-mix varies over a wide range.

How to Optimize Investment in Promotion

Granted that much advertising is largely an investment in economic reality, how should a corporation determine how much it should invest in promotion? To solve this problem, we need answers to the following questions:

a. Does a satisfactory solution for the problem already exist?
b. Why has such an important problem remained unsolved?
c. To what corporate goal should the solution be geared?
d. How does promotion tie into other ways of getting business?
e. What are the determinants of the productivity of capital invested in promotion?
f. What concepts of measurement are needed to calibrate productivity of capital?
g. What is the most appropriate yardstick of capital productivity for promotional investments?
h. How would rate-of-return rationing work for investments in corporate persuasion?

A. PROBLEM UNSOLVED

Has the problem of how much a corporation should spend on advertising and other forms of persuasion been already satisfactorily solved?

The problem is important. The answer is crucial to the competitive success of many firms, and may involve vast expenditures.

In the future, it is likely to be even more vital. Depersonalized distribution, increased urbanization, rising consumer affluence, revolutionary advances in technology, and bigger economies of scale in some promotional media are dynamic forces which will make the decision as to how much to invest in promotion a jugular issue for many corporations in the next decade.

Surprisingly, this crucial problem is not yet solved. Despite yards of computer print-outs and millions of dollars spent on advertising research, most corporations do not really know whether their promotional outlays should be half or twice as large as they now are.

B. REASONS FOR FAILURE

Why has such an important problem remained unsolved? There are three main causes.

The first cause is *failure to acknowledge the importance of futurity.* The full impact of most promotional outlays upon demand is delayed with associated uncertainty. Hence, the conceptual framework of analysis that management needs for solving this problem is the kind that is used in modern, sophisticated management of conventional corporate capital appropriations.

A second cause is *lack of a conceptual apparatus whose orientation is economic*. The problem of optimizing promotional investment is basically a matter of managerial economics, that is, balancing incremental promotional investment against predicted benefits, so as to augment sales most profitably.

The third cause of failure is *the difficulty of measuring the effectiveness of promotional outlays*. Their impacts on demand are diffused, delayed, and intricately interwoven with other forces. To make the kind of investment approach needed to produce practical benefits will require an open mind, fresh concepts, substantial research spending, and great patience.

C. OVERRIDING CORPORATE GOAL

What is the corporate goal to which the solution of optimum investment in promotion should be geared?

Promotional outlays, like other expenditures, should be judged in terms of their contribution to attainment of the corporation's objectives. Most companies have several goals, some of which conflict; but the solution for the problem of how much to invest in promotion should be geared primarily to the goal of profitability.

The master goal of the modern corporation should be maximum profits in the long run. More explicitly, it should be to maximize the present worth at the corporation's cost of capital of the future stream of benefits to the stockholder.

All other objectives—such as growth or market-share or eternal life—should be either intermediate or subsidiary to this overriding corporate objective.

D. BUSINESS-GETTERS

How does promotion relate to other ways of getting business?

A company has three ways to augment its sales: by cutting price, by spending more on promotion, and by bettering its product. The three members of the business-getting threesome pull together. But being alternatives, they are at the margin rivalrous substitutes.

The three reinforce each other in a complex symbiotic relationship. For a product that is superior to rivals in wanted ways, promotional outlays will be more effective than for an inferior product. A given amount and quality of promotion will produce more sales of a product priced in correct economic relationship to buyers' alternatives than for an overpriced product.

Each of the three business-getters can have delayed impacts and hence be a business investment. Their delayed and intertwining effects on sales, now and in the future, increase the problem of measuring the effects of promotional investment.

E. DETERMINANTS OF CAPITAL PRODUCTIVITY

What are the determinants of the productivity of capital invested in promotion?

These need to be identified to find out whether capital tied up in advertising will yield enough profits to earn its keep. Its yield must pay for the cost of this capital in the marketplace, or its opportunity costs in benefits passed up by not investing the money somewhere else.

The productivity of an investment in promotion is the relation of its earnings to the amount of capital tied up. This relationship requires explicit recognition of four economic determinants to be measured: (1) the amount and timing of *added investment;* (2) the amount and timing of *added earnings;* (3) the *duration of the earnings;* and (4) the *risks and imponderable benefits* associated with the project.

1. *Added Investment.* The appropriate investment base for calculating rate of return is the added outlay which will be occasioned by the adoption of a promotion project as opposed to its rejection.

The investment should include the entire amount of the original added outlay, regardless of how it is classified on the accounts. Any additional outlay for point-of-purchase displays or for distribution of samples to consumers should be included in the investment amount, as should future research expenses caused by the proposal.

The timing of these added investments has an important effect upon true profitability and should, therefore, be reflected in the rate-of-return computation.

2. *Added Earnings.* Concern with capital productivity implies, of course, that the company's goal is profits.

The productivity of the capital tied up is determined by the increase in earnings or savings, that is, net cash receipts, caused by making the investment as opposed to not making it. These earnings should be measured in terms of their after-tax cash or cash equivalents.

Only costs and revenues that will be different as a result of the adoption of the proposal should be included. The concept of earnings should be broad enough to encompass intangible and often unquantifiable benefits. When these have to be omitted from the formal earnings-estimates, they should be noted for subsequent appraisal of the project.

3. *Durability of Earnings*. The duration of the benefits from a promotional investment has a vital effect on its rate of return.

Economic life of promotion depends (a) on frequency of purchase; (b) on loyalty-life-expectancy, that is, longevity of customers; (c) on gestation period of the purchase decision; and (d) on erosion by the promotional efforts of rivals.

For advertising investments, durability is often the most difficult dimension of project value to quantify. But the problem cannot be avoided. Some estimate is better than none; and estimates can be improved by well-directed research.

4. *Risks and Imponderable Benefits*. Appraising the risks and uncertainties associated with a project requires a high order of judgment. It is only disparities in risk among projects which need to be allowed for, since the company's cost of capital reflects the overall risks. Although measurement of this sort of dispersion is difficult, some headway can sometimes be made by a necessarily arbitrary risk-ranking of candidate projects or categories of projects.

Most projects have some added benefits over and above the measurable ones. If excessive weight is given to these imponderables, then there is danger that rate-of-return rationing will occur. When a low rate-of-return project is preferred to a high one on the grounds of imponderable benefits, the burden of proof clearly should rest on the imponderables.

F. CONCEPTS OF MEASUREMENT

For calibrating these four determinants of return on investment, what concepts of measurement are needed? Four are particularly useful:

1. *Alternatives*. The proper benchmark for measuring added investment and the corresponding added earnings is the best alternative way to do it.
2. *Futurity*. Future earnings and future outlays of the project are all that matter.
3. *Increments*. Added earnings and added investment of the project alone are material.
4. *Cash flows*. After-tax cash flows (or their equivalents) alone are significant for measuring capital productivity.

1. *Alternatives*. There is always an alternative to the proposed capital expenditure.

The alternative may be so catastrophic that refined measurement is unnecessary to reject it; but in any case, the proper benchmark for the proposal is the next profitable alternative way of doing it.

2. *Futurity*. The value of a proposed capital project depends on its future earnings.

The past is irrelevant, except as a benchmark for forecasting the future.

Consequently, earnings estimates need to be based on the best available projections. The outlays and earnings need to be estimated year by year over the economic life of the proposed promotion, and their time shape needs to be taken into account explicitly.

3. *Increments.* A correct estimate of both earnings and investment must be based on the simple principle that the earnings from the promotional proposal are measured by the total *added* earnings by making the investment, as opposed to *not* making it . . . and that the same is true for the investment amount.

Project costs should be unaffected by allocation of existing overheads, but should reflect the changes in total overhead and other costs likely to result from the project. No costs or revenues which will be the same, regardless of whether the proposal is accepted or rejected, should be included and the same goes for investment.

4. *Cash flows.* To be economically realistic, attention should be directed exclusively at the after-tax flows of cash or cash equivalents which will result from making the promotional investment.

Book costs are confusing and immaterial. But taxes do matter, because advertising investments are favored over depreciable investments in after-tax rate of return.

G. YARDSTICK OF FINANCIAL WORTH

The productivity of capital in a business investment is the relationship between its earnings and the amount of capital tied up. To measure this productivity for promotional investments, we not only must have a correct conceptual framework of measurements, but also must choose the most appropriate yardstick of investment worth.

The concept of advertising as an investment already has some limited acceptance in new-product introduction. The measure of productivity of capital often used is the payout period—a crude yardstick. The cutoff criterion is also set rather arbitrarily to get the original outlay back in two years or three years. Such standards have no objective justification as compared with corporate cost of capital.

What is the best yardstick of economic worth for investments in persuasion? Clearly, the yardstick that is economically appropriate for investments in promotion is true profitability as measured by discounted-cash-flow analysis.

1. *Discounted-Cash-Flow Analysis.* The discounted-cash-flow (DCF) method is a new approach to measuring the productivity of capital and measuring the cost of capital.

The application is new, not the principle. Discounting has long been used in the financial community, where precision and realism are indispensable. The essential contributions of discounted-cash-flow analysis to management thinking about investment in promotion are three:

    a. An explicit recognition that time has economic value—and hence, that near money is more valuable than distant money.

    b. A recognition that cash flows are what matter—and hence, that book costs are irrelevant for capital-decisions except as they affect taxes.

    c. A recognition that income taxes have such an important effect upon cash flows that they must be explicitly figured into project worth.

The discounted-cash-flow method has two computational variants.

The first is a rate-of-return computation, which consists essentially of finding the interest rate that discounts gross future after-tax cash earnings of a project down to a present value equal to the project cost. This interest rate is the rate of return on that particular investment.

The second variant is a present-value computation which discounts gross future after-tax cash earnings of all projects at the same rate of interest. This rate of interest is the company's minimum acceptable rate of return. This should be based on the company's cost of capital. Special risk should be reflected either by deflating project earnings or by adjusting the cutoff rate for projects of different categories of risk. The resulting present value is then compared with the project cost investment. If the present value exceeds it, the project is acceptable. If it falls below, it is rejected.

In addition, projects can by this variant be ranked by various kinds of profitability indexes which reflect the amount or ratios of excess of present value over project cost.

Both variants of the discounted-cash-flow approach require a timetable of after-tax cash flows of investment and of gross earnings which cover the entire economic life of the project.

In practice, the timetable can be simplified by grouping years in blocks. For projects for which investment is substantially instantaneous and gross earnings are level, simple computational charts and tables can be used to estimate the discounted-cash-flow rate of return directly from estimated economic life and after-tax payback. For projects with rising or declining earnings streams, this conversion is more complex.

2. *Superiorities of DCF.* The discounted-cash-flow method of analysis is particularly needed for measuring the profitability of promotional investments, for two reasons.

First, the outlays are usually spread out. Second, benefits, mainly incremental profits from added sales in the future, are always spread out and usually have a non-level time-shape.

The superiorities of discounted-cash-flow analysis over rival yardsticks for measuring the productivity of capital in promotional investments are imposing:

a. It is economically realistic in confining the analysis to cash-flows and forgetting about book-allocations.

b. It forces guided thinking about the whole life of the project, and concentration on the lifetime earnings.

c. It weights the time-pattern of the investment outlay and the cash earnings, so as to reflect real and important differences in the value of near and distant cash-flows.

d. It reflects accurately and without ambiguity the timing of tax-savings.

e. It permits simple allowances for risks and uncertainties, and can be adapted readily to increasing the risk allowance over time.

f. It is strictly comparable to cost-of-capital, correctly measured, so that decisions can be made quickly and safely by comparing rate of return and the value of money to the firm.

H. RATE-OF-RETURN RATIONING

How should rationing of capital work for persuasion-investments?

Rate-of-return "battling" among capital proposals is the essence of capital rationing. The standard of minimum acceptable profitability should (after proper allowance for special risks and for imponderables) be the same for all, namely, the company's market cost-of-capital or its opportunity cost-of-capital, whichever is higher.

Market cost-of-capital is what the company probably will pay for equity and debt funds, on the average, over the future. For a large publicly-held company, this cost can be measured with adequate precision for rationing purposes. There is no better cutoff criterion.

Opportunity cost-of-capital is the sacrificed profit-yield from alternative investments. Only when a company refuses to go to market for funds can its opportunity costs stay long above market cost-of-capital.

Practical Values

Will putting advertising in the capital budget do any good?

Granted that as a matter of economic principle much advertising and other forms of promotional spending are investments . . . and granted also that conceptually correct and pragmatically proved techniques for optimizing investment outlays are available for promotional investment . . . the question is whether this sophisticated and powerful mechanism, applied to promotional investments, will have any practical value.

Most business investments are not made in ignorance of their probable impacts, whereas, many of the outlays for persuasion now are. Characteristically, the amount and timing of the effects of advertising are unknown. The duration of their impact on economic life is unknown, and the probabilities of effectiveness are also unknown. Quite possibly, attempting to estimate these unknowns cannot improve overall results.

The problem of how much to invest in promotion can be solved either by intuitive and perhaps artistic processes, or through a more formal and more systematic study of objective evidence. Quite possibly men of experience and good judgment can determine how much the corporation should invest in promotion by subjective judgment, regardless of whether advertising is formally put in the capital budget. This article is nevertheless confined to a consideration of ways in which sophisticated economic models and systematic quantitative study can help to find the appropriate size of the appropriation for corporate persuasion.

In Summary

1. Much advertising (and other corporate persuasion) is in economic reality partly an investment. The investment-mix varies over a wide spectrum.

2. Investments in promotion are different from conventional capital expenditures; but these distinctive characteristics do not disqualify promotion for investment treatment.

3. Profitability must be the basic measurement of the productivity of capital invested in promotion. Despite the multiplicity of conflicting corporate goals, the overriding objective for decisions or investment of corporate capital should be to make money.

4. The main determinants of profitability of an advertising investment that need to be estimated are the amount and timing of added investment and of added earnings, the duration of advertising effects and risks.

5. The measurement concepts of capital productivity that must be estimated are future, time-spotted, incremental, after-tax cash flows of investment outlays and of added profits from added sales.

6. Discounted-Cash-Flow (DCF) analysis supplies the financial yardstick most appropriate for promotional investments. By comparison, payback period, although widely used, has no merit.

7. Advertising belongs in the capital budget. Promotional investments should be made to compete for funds on the basis of profitability, that is, DCF rate of return.

8. The criterion for rationing scarce capital among competing investment proposals should be DCF rate of return. The criterion of the minimum acceptable return should be the corporation's cost of capital—outside market-cost or internal opportunity-cost, whichever is higher.

9. Putting advertising into the capital budget will not perform a miracle. Judgment cannot be displaced by DCF analysis and computers. But judgment can be economized and improved. The most that it can do is to open the way for a research approach which is oriented to the kind of estimates

that are relevant and that will permit advertising investment in promotion to fight for funds on the basis of financial merit rather than on the basis of personal persuasiveness of their sponsor.

10. An investment approach to produce practical benefits will require fresh concepts, substantial research-spending, and great patience.

The old-time drummer has been replaced by a new kind of salesman. He doesn't sell the product; he sells service.

39

The Salesman Isn't Dead —He's Different

CARL RIESER

THERE IS NO MORE ABUSED figure in American life than the salesman. One group of critics scorns him for certain qualities that another group sneers at him for losing. To many novelists, playwrights, sociologists, college students, and many others, he is aggressively forcing on people goods that they don't want. He is the drummer, with a dubious set of social values— Willy Loman in the Arthur Miller play. The second group of critics, which includes the Secretary of Commerce and many business executives all over the U.S., charges the salesman with lacking good, old-fashioned, hard-hitting salesmanship. He was spoiled by the postwar days when competition was easy. If only he would get up off his duff, and get out and *sell,* the goods would move and business would be in fine shape.

Both sets of critics are swatting at a target that doesn't matter much any more. The plain fact is that, as one Boston sales executive recently said, "The old drummer type of salesman has gone by the board." Nor are his talents especially needed in today's economy. To be sure, there are plenty of aggressive, hard-hitting salesmen still around, and there will always be a place for their brand of selling. But this kind of man is no longer the archetype.

From bits and pieces of evidence in all sectors of U.S. business, it is now possible to discern the emergence of a new dominant type, a man

Reprinted from the November, 1962 issue of *Fortune* Magazine by special permission; © 1962 Time Inc., pp. 124 ff.

with a softer touch and greater breadth, a new kind of man to do a new—much more significant—kind of job. Whereas the old-time salesman devoted himself primarily to pushing a product, or a line of products, the new-era salesman is involved with the whole distribution pipeline, beginning with the tailoring of products to the customer's desire and extending through their promotion and advertising to final delivery to the ultimate consumer.

The salesman has been cast in his new role by "the marketing concept," a term that originated at General Electric around 1950 and has gained wide currency recently. It means essentially that companies are orienting their organization and effort toward the market, toward the ever changing needs of the customer, and the ever shifting calculations of their own production costs and opportunities. The emphasis is less concentrated on the isolated point-of-sale; it is spread forward, into the buyer's operations, and backward into the seller's operations. The profound consequences of this trend have been suggested by Orm Henning, marketing manager of industrial products at Texas Instruments:

"One should remind oneself that selling is only part of marketing—particularly in the scientific-industrial world. Marketing is communicating back to your factory your individual customer's needs and particular problems. When you realize and practice this, you open an entirely new vista in the area of sales. You cannot afford to sell a product, a static product—not in our business."

And what's true today in the electronics business—and many others—is going to be true of more and more businesses tomorrow.

The great change in selling affects practically all industries and all kinds of goods, whether they are what the marketing profession calls "pull-through" or "push-through" products. Pull-through refers generally to mass-produced consumer items, where a sort of siphon is already working. Pull-through products and services are presold by the manufacturer to the final consumer by mass advertising and promotion, which in effect creates a demand that almost literally pulls the goods through the distribution pipeline. Push-through products are wholly new consumer goods for which the siphon has not yet begun to work or, more commonly, they are industrial materials and equipment. Since the latter are usually highly technical in nature, they must be explained to the buyer and they require more personal selling so as to generate in the buyer the idea that he needs the product.

The distinction between pull-through and push-through is becoming less important. The retailer now stocks Kleenex tissues, for example, because he is persuaded that Kimberly-Clark Corp. will maintain public recognition of the brand and will see to it that thousands of boxes are siphoned rapidly and profitably right through his warehouse and off his store shelves. The job of the Kimberly-Clark salesman is to service the account so that the buyer will keep buying. He expedites and consolidates the shipments, keeps track of the retailer's inventory, sees that the goods get the greatest display and promotion possible, keeps himself available in case of any trouble or emergency. The job of the man who sells computers is much the same. The computer is one element in a whole system of mechanical devices and programing techniques, which is sold on the basis of what the customer is persuaded it can do for him.

The salesman's responsibility becomes greater as technology advances and producers offer products of ever mounting complexity. "We are tending toward the marketing of systems and services," says James Jewell, marketing vice president of Westinghouse. "The customers want to buy greater production—not equipment. We take the full responsibility for engineering and installing, and we are moving further into servicing."

This orientation toward the customer's needs is pointed up in a recent book that has received wide attention in the trade—*Innovation in Marketing,* by Theodore Levitt, a management consultant and a member of the faculty of Harvard Business School. Levitt, who speaks for a new generation of believers in "the marketing concept," states flatly that "a strictly sales-oriented approach to doing business can be suicidal. The difference between selling and marketing is more than semantic. Selling focuses on the needs of the seller, marketing on the needs of the buyer. Selling is preoccupied with the seller's need to convert his product or service into cash; marketing with the idea of satisfying the needs of the customer by means of the product or service and by the whole cluster of customer-getting value satisfactions associated with creating, delivering, and finally consuming it."

In this quotation Levitt seems to be oversimplifying the contrast between selling and marketing. Any implication that "the marketing concept" isn't motivated by the seller's desire for profits is, of course, mistaken. While his motives remain the same, the seller now sees marketing as a more elaborate link between production and consumption, a link that has to be carefully constructed and maintained.

Two situations may illustrate the change. In the past, a factory would overproduce the market and unload on the sales force the responsibility for unloading the goods on the customers. In the other situation, the salesmen kept their volume up by selling those products in their line that were easiest to sell—even those that were the least profitable. The incidence of both these cases tends to be diminished by the new trend with its more delicate alignment of markets and production, and its careful analysis of product profitability. The salesman is less often stuck with the necessity of a fast, hard sell. But he is steadily pressed to make the sales where the profit lies. Altogether, the marketing concept has played a vital role in developing the enormous velocity in the flow of goods, a phenomenon that has been described earlier in this series as the "short-order economy" (*Fortune,* August, 1962).

The Mirror of the Markets

There is little doubt that the impact of "the marketing concept" has reduced the stature of the sales manager in scores of companies. He has lost his former autonomy and now reports to the marketing vice president rather than directly to the president. He has less say over such vital matters as pricing and credit policies. The sales force must fit its work into an over-all corporation marketing policy. Furthermore, over the decade, the autonomy of the sales manager has been further trimmed in many companies by the creation of the job of product manager, who has both line and staff authority for a given product or group of products and coordinates production with advertising, research, and field selling.

The marketing concept has had very decided and significant structural effects on sales forces. This can be seen very clearly at General Electric, father of the marketing concept. G.E.'s salesmen used to be essentially product specialists, each selling only the line of a specific manufacturing department, even though it went into a variety of markets. It took time for G.E. to orient its sales forces toward markets rather than products, but this process finally began seven years ago in the company's electrical-apparatus business. Instead of specializing in one product, e.g., cord sets, fan motors, push buttons, the salesman began selling a whole group of products to a particular market—for example, the air-conditioning industry. Early this this year more than a dozen separate departments selling G.E.'s biggest single customer, the government, were reorganized into one defense sales force. In other words, instead of being product-oriented, the sales organizations have become "mirrors" of the markets G.E. serves.

Recently, Westinghouse reorganized its entire 13,600-man field sales organization along somewhat similar lines, in accord with what the company calls the "province concept." The company wants to be represented wherever possible by a "Mr. Westinghouse" rather than by a confusing bevy of different salesmen from various production divisions. (Significantly, in reorganizing, Westinghouse also seized the opportunity to put more salesmen in jobs where they actually meet customers and eliminated virtually an entire "staff" layer of some 104 sales managers who never called on customers.)

The same kind of reorganization has gone on in scores of companies in such diverse fields as motor trucks and optical equipment. At American Optical Co., for example, salesmen who used to be product specialists now sell a line that includes every piece of furniture and equipment for the doctor's office, from lenses to tables.

Thus the kind of man needed for this new kind of sales job has to be a generalist. The trend is away from the "sales engineer," the technically trained salesman, of a few years ago. His successor is a man capable of absorbing stacks of information churned out by the marketing department, and of applying it to his customers' problems. He goes forth armed with a tremendous amount of data on his customers' needs, their products, their corporate organizations, and their supply and delivery schedules.

He is also a man with more executive ability than the salesman of yesterday. A Boston sales manager describes the new salesmen as simply "businessmen who travel." One Milwaukee executive notes that increasingly the new salesman is being given the authority and stature to make important decisions in the field without having to go back to corporate headquarters for an O.K. General Foods has adopted a new title of prestige for its senior salesmen, each of whom lives with one food-chain customer and attends to its needs. They are called "account executives" and they command the services of junior salesmen, who do the routine housekeeping chores of servicing the customers' stores.

In the new order of things there is obviously still a need for hard-selling, aggressive salesmen to open up new accounts, to introduce new and untried products, to sell the wares of new companies that have no national reputation. Since the service-oriented sales staff has turned away from this kind of pioneering effort, the door has been opened to a new kind of specialist, typified by a New York firm called the George N. Kahn Co. This company provides a crew of highly aggressive young salesmen who open up new territories for companies that don't want to retrain their own sales forces for such sporadically necessary missions. (Kahn is not a manufacturer's representative; it works on a flat-fee basis rather than a commission and, after pioneering the sale of a product, expects that the manufacturer will take it back for handling by his own sales staff.) There is now some thought in the top management of a number of companies that the way to deal with this basic problem is to set up special sections of sales staffs with the specific function of going after new business. Thus what has been commonly thought of as the primary function of all salesmen is now becoming the specialty of a few.

The Service Troops

The new salesman has a tremendous advantage over his predecessors. Not only does he have access to much more information about his customers, but he is also backed up by formidable technical and other kinds of assistance. For example, in reshaping its inorganic-chemical sales recently, FMC Corp. (formerly Food Machinery & Chemical Corp.) has beefed up the number of its technical people directly behind the salesmen by some 20 per cent. The present ratio: one technical man to every four salesmen. The great pioneer in this development was du Pont, which years ago saw the close connection between selling and customer service. Today, at Chestnut Run, outside Wilmington, du Pont has an impressive $20-million, campus-like complex of laboratories and workshops, employing 1,700 scientists, technicians, and others devoted to providing sales literature, solving technical problems, providing all kinds of services for customers or potential buyers of du Pont products, and otherwise aiding the sales effort. Companies selling all kinds of goods have developed similar assistance, though, naturally, the more complex the technology, the more elaborate the technical backup.

The development of sophisticated electronic data-processing systems, which was described earlier in this series, is revolutionizing inventory handling, ordering, warehousing, and other physical aspects of marketing. This, in turn, relieves the salesman of a great deal of detail that used to absorb valuable hours of his time—writing up orders and reports, checking whether goods are available and how soon they can be delivered, and performing other niggling drudgery.

At the same time, the computer also introduces an element of impersonality in the relations between a seller and a buyer. Much of today's ordering of goods and materials, from packaged foods to industrial chemicals, is done, as it were, by a computer, which tells the buyer when to reorder; the transaction is handled routinely and a salesman never enters into it. This disencumbering of the salesman releases him to function on a new level of performance, to use his time more creatively. At Allis-Chalmers, which has just set up a department of marketing, an executive says, "Now our salespeople won't get bogged down in a lot of detail that goes hand in hand with selling, like the preparation of presentations, charts, convention exhibits, and whatnot. We'll do all the work, including the training of salesmen, in cooperation with company divisions."

"You Lose One of the Big Babies . . ."

The rise of the new salesman is the result of changes in the marketplace that have drastically altered the relationship of buyer to seller. One of the most significant developments has been the growing importance of the big customer. In almost every line of business, fewer and bigger customers are responsible for an increasingly large part of any given company's sales.

Twenty-five years ago, when independent grocers were an important factor in food retailing, food processors did the bulk of their business with thousands upon thousands of chains and stores. Today, with the concentration of business in the hands of a relatively few big chains, some 300 buying offices throughout the U.S. account for 80 per cent of all food bought at wholesale. Preoccupation with the "key customer" affects every industry, from steel to office supplies. Sighs an officer of the Acme Chemical Co. in Milwaukee, "You lose one of the big babies and you're in trouble."

This whole trend is building up momentum as smaller buyers band together to increase their purchasing power and efficiency by buying cooperatively. It affects suppliers of school equipment, for example, because schools are consolidating on a county basis. Independent hardware stores and even hospitals are doing it.

How this has affected the food business has been fully explored in a new book with a provocative title, *The Vanishing Salesman*, by E. B. Weiss, a New York marketing specialist in the consumer-goods field. Actually, Weiss does not believe that the salesman is vanishing; his point is that the shift to the service-oriented sales function has so greatly altered the nature of personal selling that companies are faced with entirely new conditions in the hiring, training, and organization of salesmen. Weiss also notes that as retail food chains have become bigger and bigger, and their purchases have reached stupendous volume, the position of the individual buyer, once regarded as the salesman's opposite number, has greatly diminished. The buyer in a food chain used to be an important figure; he made the decisions on what the chain was going to buy. Now his power has been usurped by buying committees. The buyer has become merely a technician who interviews the salesmen from the food processor and passes on his findings to his superiors. Says Weiss: "Members of the buying committee tend not to be buying specialists. Moreover, they make decisions covering the entire range of merchandise inventoried by the organization. Since they tend to be at executive levels considerably higher than that of the buyer who appears before them, they are more apt to depend on their own judgment than that of the buyer. And, by the same token, the buyer is not apt to put up much of a battle. . . . In buying committee sessions, it is presumably the majority that rules. But since it is traditional in large organizations for so many committee members to vote with the head of the table, the majority rule prevails more in theory than in fact."

So the man that the seller must get to is the man at the head of the table. And this is true not only in the food field. Throughout U.S. industry, key buying power has steadily risen up through the corporate structure to higher echelons of authority. In industrial selling, an increasing number of purchasing decisions tend to involve bigger and bigger outlays of capital.

In large part this is the result of the rise of what is now commonly called *systems selling*. Instead of buying components from many suppliers, a company often buys a whole integrated system, be it a system for heating and air conditioning, protecting a plant from theft and fire, automating a production line, or handling materials. As technology becomes more complex, users, intent on eliminating technical headaches, are ever more anxious to buy such systems, while suppliers, intent on greater profit, are ever more anxious to design and sell a whole package. Naturally, the final approval for such an expenditure or commitment moves up the line, from the plant superintendent or manager, to the corporate controller or treasurer, perhaps all the way to the president or board chairman.

"The President's Project"

Not only has this created the need for salesmen with sufficient stature to talk to the customer's top management, but it has also drawn top executives more directly into the selling act. In company after company, higher officials now make a very determined effort to get out in the field and call on the big customers, and even to do considerable pioneer work with potential customers. This kind of thing, of course, is not new. Many companies were built by star salesmen at the top, a very good example being the late Thomas J. Watson Sr. at I.B.M. ("What my father used to do when people began to talk about the great complexity of the products," says Tom Watson Jr., the present head of the company, "would be to sweep his hand and say, 'It's all so simple. All it does is add, subtract, and multiply!' ") And in industries where enormous capital investment is required, such as the utility business, intimate and continued contact between seller and buyer at a high level has always been important. But now personal selling by top executives is becoming much more common. Raytheon, for example, has divided up its list of big customers among managers and officers of the company, and assigned each the responsibility of keeping in touch with a few accounts, with a view to bolstering the salesman's efforts.

General Foods was one of the pioneers in this. When Charles Mortimer was president of the company, he started "The President's Project," a series of meetings with customers all over the country. "In the beginning the meetings started out 100 per cent social," explains Wayne Marks, now president of the company. "They were strictly for pleasure—and we invited more than one customer to a meeting. But we found that nothing *happened*. Except that we got acquainted. We didn't find out what to improve in our business operation. So the format was quickly changed."

Now Marks's office sets up his customer-visiting schedule at least a month in advance. The customer is requested to have all his key people at the meeting, and several weeks before the encounter, G.F. sends along a "questionnaire" to elicit comments on G.F.'s performance and suggestions for items to discuss. In the past eighteen months Marks, accompanied by a team of executives and salesmen, has visited fifty-four customers throughout the U.S.

Marks has found the customers "avid" for this kind of contact. Not only does G.F. come out of these encounters (some of them lasting for five or six hours over dinner and drinks) with a fuller idea of what it should be doing—but the customers learn a great deal about their own organizations that they weren't aware of. Says Marks: "Many a meeting, at the end the boss man will say, 'Why don't *we* go out and find out what's happening in our own stores?' At the end of a recent meeting the top man told me, 'I've been frank with you and told you what I don't like about your operations. Would you be willing to report back to us on what you think of us?' "

The "Sellingest" Firm

Personal selling is now a company-wide endeavor, and the contact with the customer takes place at many levels in an organized, formal way. The best illustration of how this has changed fundamentally the relations between buyer and seller is offered by National Cash Register, long known as perhaps the "sellingest" firm in the country. N.C.R.'s founder, the late John H. Patterson, has been called the father of many of the standard techniques of modern selling. He established the first formal training courses for salesmen, the first yearly sales quotas, the first guaranteed sales territories for salesmen, the first annual sales convention. Patterson's earlier sales methods were comparatively crude; cash registers were sold to storekeepers by appealing to their fear that dishonest clerks were pocketing money out of the till. But over the years the company refined its appeals, and forty years ago, when it began selling accounting machines, it even evolved a primitive kind of systems selling. But its big leap came about five years ago when the company introduced, somewhat belatedly as compared with the competition, its first electronic computer.

N.C.R. had to set up a whole new sales force for the computer, and in doing so it made a profound discovery: it was not easy to make a salesman of accounting machinery into a computer salesman. Says one N.C.R. senior salesman: "It was the death of salesmen like Willy Loman. At N.C.R. a few were left behind. They couldn't make the switch. It wasn't that they were too old—some were in their forties. But men's intellectual capabilities get set at various ages, and some *were* too old at that age." The company also found that it had to alter its time-honored compensation system. Normally, the N.C.R. salesman collects an advance that is charged against the commission he makes on his sales. Says marketing director Harry Keesecker, "Computer selling is still incentive selling, but due to the kind of product—sometimes the long time between sales—we have to compensate the salesmen by salary plus commission."

At the same time N.C.R. set up an elaborate organization to give the salesmen technical support. This now includes 325 mathematicians and technical people; the number has doubled in size in the past twelve months. They develop manuals and presentations, help the customer define his problems, train his computer operators for him, set up his E.D.P. system, and produce the programing for it. The support organization also trains the computer salesman, a departure for N.C.R., which years ago built its whole sales-training program around the use of experienced salesmen, borrowed from the field, as instructors. (The total computer sales and support staff numbers about 500 people, as against 2,100 in accounting machines, but the company is supplementing the small computer force by training as many of the accounting-machine men as possible to sell both kinds of equipment.)

The Willy Lomans Are No Longer Feasible

The difference between the old and new eras at N.C.R.—and in salesmanship in general—is dramatically illustrated by the story of how the company landed a rather sensational contract for the sale of a computer to the Dime Savings Bank of Brooklyn, New York, the country's second-largest mutual savings bank. The bank and the company had long-standing ties dating back to 1929, when the Dime bought its first N.C.R. posting machines for the tellers' windows. In subsequent decades the bank bought other N.C.R. equipment. In those years the chief link between the two was an N.C.R. salesman, Anthony de Florio, now district manager of sales for accounting and computer systems, and Karl Stad, who is now vice president of methods and systems at the Dime. The relationship was a cordial one, and N.C.R., which is mainly known for its experience in retailing and banking, was solidly in with the Dime.

In the late 1950's, however, there was a sudden change in the old easygoing ways. The bank decided, in 1957, that it was time to think about tying its entire bookkeeping operations into a computer to keep up with its bounding growth, and Stad was told to set up a task force to study the entire field and to recommend the "ideal" system. De Florio observes, "This was the beginning of group selling. The salesman had to understand the problems and systems of the customer. The staff at the bank had to define what was required. And we at N.C.R. had to be sure that the bank wasn't running away from us in know-how." (To N.C.R., as to many another company, the growing sophistication of the buyer has become an important factor to reckon with.) N.C.R. also had to reckon with competition; every other computer manufacturer came in for the kill at Dime. For the next two years Stad and his team studied the field and enlarged their expertise. By 1959 they had winnowed the choice down to four systems, including N.C.R.'s, and asked the competitors for feasibility studies. (Says de Florio: "By the time you get to feasibility studies, the Willy Lomans are no longer feasible.")

Now the contacts between the company and the bank multiplied. N.C.R. sent teams of technical people from Dayton headquarters to confer with Stad—they submitted a technical proposal two inches thick—and Stad went out to Dayton to talk to N.C.R.'s research people. He was put up at N.C.R.'s plush Moraine Farm, the estate of a former board chairman, which the company now uses to entertain groups of customers and potential customers. (Like du Pont and other companies, N.C.R. uses its factories and laboratories as a sales showcase.) By the end of 1959, Stad decided that N.C.R.'s 304 computer, then just being delivered to the first purchasers, was the one for the Dime.

Thereupon the Dime's board of trustees decided that Stad's decision ought to be second-guessed by an independent consultant in the electronic data-processing field. This, of course, opened up the whole matter again, and brought the competitors back in. Fortunately for N.C.R., the consultant confirmed the decision, and the affair between the bank and the company again resumed, in a deliberate and measured way. The Dime's board selected a committee of three trustees to study the proposal. They went out to Dayton—staying at an even more posh N.C.R. guest house, the old home of Orville Wright—and they talked with everyone from technicians to N.C.R.'s president, R. S. Oelman, and its then board chairman, S. C. Allyn. On the way back in the plane the trustees decided to sign with N.C.R. It was an $800,000 decision, and it was a key one not only to the bank but to N.C.R., which closed some other bank contracts on the strength of the Dime's decision.

N.C.R. was in the middle of a training program for the Dime's employees when, early in 1960, a crisis arose. N.C.R.'s technicians reached the chilling conclusion that the 304 computer would not have the capacity to do what the Dime eventually would require—i.e., a direct linkage from the posting machines at the tellers' windows to the computer without the intermediate use of tabulating equipment. The next model in the design stage, the 315 random-access computer, would do the job—but not the 304. De Florio had to come clean with the bank. "I called up Karl and said, 'Let's have lunch at the Brooklyn Club,'" recalls de Florio, still wincing at the ensuing conversation. De Florio offered to tear up the contract for the 304. The Dime's board accepted the proposal, and the whole computer question was back in the soup again.

Rival manufacturers had another chance to make presentations, and N.C.R. had to start all over again selling its 315 model, then two years from delivery. De Florio kept pounding on one main point: the bank already was using N.C.R. machines at its windows, and any company that finally got the computer contract would have to tie into N.C.R.'s equipment. In the end the argument prevailed; Stad recommended the 315 computer on the grounds that it would be "just as good" as other computers—though no better—and that N.C.R. had "window experience." Along with the computer the bank also agreed to use other N.C.R. equipment in its integrated system, so the total package came to $2 million. Says de Florio, looking back on the whole transaction, "In this kind of selling you can't see everything you buy. A lot has to be bought on faith. Therefore a company likes to work with big companies. Come hell or high water, they have to deliver."

One of N.C.R.'s brightest and most successful young computer salesmen recently expanded this doctrine. "A salesman is important," he remarked, "because the policy makers today come from a previous generation of doing business. They don't have the technical equipment necessary to make a decision about a computer that requires technical sophistication. So the salesman has to take the language of the computer man and turn it into language his customer understands. I used to think that those decisions would be made on a scientific basis—but it's a gross act of faith." The salesman's job, he said, is "to create an environment in which an act of faith can take place."

The "Foot Soldiers" Need Upgrading

There is doubtless still plenty of faith in sales transactions. But as the Dime Savings Bank affair shows, there is a great deal more. And this is the fact that salesmen do not seem to realize when they talk about their jobs. They are still trained to have a kind of emotionalism about their craft, and they carry with them a heavy load of outworn notions about their role. They view selling as both warfare and love, hostility and benevolence. They see themselves as "the men on the firing line," and "the foot soldiers of democracy." The combative nature of selling is stressed in almost every book on the subject, as in one of the most famous and widely sold of all books on selling, *Open the Mind and Close the Sale,* by John M. Wilson, who recently retired as N.C.R.'s sales manager. Wilson speaks of the "tension in every buyer-seller relationship," of the "challenge" in each encounter, of the need for "handling" the customer—though, of course, "in the way he wants to be handled."

This lag in the recognition of what has happened to selling is harmful, because the sales profession is still held in low esteem by the public. Just how low was indicated recently in a survey by *Sales Management* magazine of college students and their attitude toward selling. Selling ranked a very poor fourth, after teaching, law, and medicine, as a choice for a career. Only 6 per cent of the students favored it. (Of seventy-one students whose fathers are in sales, only *five* wanted to go into selling.)

The students did not particularly object to the working conditions in selling; relatively few said they were put off by too much traveling, for example. Nor did many feel that the financial reward was inadequate. The chief objections to a selling career (some even denied that selling *is* a career) were these: "I don't want to force people to buy things they don't need." "Job security is poor." "I'm not extrovert enough." "Selling has no prestige."

One student unwittingly put his finger on the ironic predicament business faces. He remarked that selling simply does not require "a college education or intelligence." The main feature of the new kind of personal selling, of course, is that it does require men who are able and intelligent; the new salesmen, quite obviously, must be recruited from among the better college graduates. But how are they going to be recruited if the better college graduates think selling is beneath them? The experience of Scott Paper illustrates the difficulties business has in luring these men into selling. The company prides itelf on the fact that 95 per cent of its sales staff are college graduates. Each year, to keep the staff replenished, it interviews some 2,000 students, invites about 100 of these men to visit its Philadelphia headquarters, makes offers to about seventy-five—and lands thirty-five or forty of them.

The trouble is that business has signally failed to get across the idea that there has been a tremendous change in selling. (The *Sales Management* poll shows that this generation of students has not grasped one of the simplest and most fundamental changes—i.e., that by and large salesmen are no longer paid on commission but are salaried.) Business has a massive educational job to do. Perhaps as a start it might throw away a lot of the old inspirational literature on selling and let the facts of the new situation do the inspiring.

**If shoppers were informed that
the value of their stamps won't
buy so much as cold cash, would
they still save stamps?**

40

Trading Stamp Tumult

UNTIL ITS LAST FEW weeks, 1966 looked like The Year for trading stamps.
The industry had just crashed the billion-dollar barrier in annual sales,
while surveys showed that nearly 90% of all chain food stores gave stamps
and that more than 80% of all American households saved them. In fact,
a group of stamp companies at one time advertised in a Denver newspaper
that stamps are "as American as apple pie and the ice cream soda."

If so, there is a lot of current unAmerican activity. Today, the whole
industry is becoming unglued by a combination of market saturation, government scrutiny, and bad publicity.

The most dangerous, and least expected, is the bad publicity that blew
in on the wave of supermarket-price protests by housewives. At first, the
loosely organized "lady-cotts" hardly mentioned stamps, venting their frustration of alleged profiteering and games of chance as the cause of high
food prices.

However, after recoiling from the initial blow, the food industry is
appeasing the demonstrators with convincing facts and figures. They've
pointed out, for instance, that the special games of chance [1] account for
less than 1% of the food dollar—usually around .5%. They cite Agriculture Department figures that show food takes less consumer disposable
income than ever before.

Finally, they show that chainstore net profits in 1965 averaged a mere
1.41% of sales and will probably be even less in 1966. As Michael J.

Reprinted with permission of *Sales Management,* The Marketing Magazine (December 1, 1966), pp. 31-34.

[1] Late last month the Federal Trade Commission announced a probe of supermarket games of chance and other promotional gimmicks. The investigation will
examine their impact on food costs and their possible violation of lottery laws.

O'Connor, executive director of the Supermarket Inst., tells housewives, "There's just no more blood in our turnip."

Such arguments don't stop the high-price protesters, but they have caused housewives to look elsewhere for fat in the supermarket price structure. Here's where the spotlight falls on trading stamps. Reliable estimates put their cost at 2% to 3% of gross sales—larger than the average supermarket's net profit.

As the National Commission on Food Marketing concluded after an 18-month study: "We believe the available evidence argues persuasively that the increased use of trading stamps has increased food-store prices by an amount equal to the cost of the stamps"—a notion vigorously denied by the stamp companies—or, as Mr. O'Connor puts it: "If supermarkets were able to cut out stamps and games, they would reduce prices about 2.5% without affecting profits."

Being linked psychologically with the supermarket games of chance hurts the trading-stamp industry. And what hurts even more is that the industry is being asked questions that it would prefer not to discuss publicly.

The big question involves value. Does the consumer pay more for a blanket obtained with trading stamps than she would if it were purchased in a department store for cash? The answer in many cases is yes. The report filed by the National Commission on Food Marketing cited examples that would make any housewife militant.

Among them: A General Electric spray-steam-dry iron, verified by the Federal Trade Commission as costing $14.89 retail at a typical department store. To get that same iron with S&H Green Stamps, the consumer must turn in 7.5 books (representing about $900 in purchases). The cash equivalent of the stamps, according to S&H, is $22.50, or $7.61 more than it would cost to buy the iron in a store.

Or look at it another way: Assume that instead of giving stamps, a food store gave customers a 2% cash discount. This would total $18 on $900 worth of purchases, or enough to buy the iron retail with $3.11 left over.

The case of the iron is no fluke. The National Food Commission's report is full of similar examples: A $139.95 RCA Victor tv set that takes $260 worth of U.S. Green Stamps to obtain; a $39.95 GE vacuum cleaner for $53.60 worth of King Korn stamps; a $26.89 Dormeyer mixer available for $44 in Merchants' Green Stamps; a $13.88 Toastmaster that takes $21.60 in Gold Bond stamps to redeem, and so on.

Other tricks of the trade, though certainly no secret in the industry, are also opening the eyes and mouths of consumer groups. There are only three ways a stamp company can turn a profit. The first is markup on merchandise (that $14.89 iron obtainable for $22.50 in S&H stamps may have only cost the stamp firm $8 wholesale). The second is unredeemed stamps (about 5% of all stamps are lost or destroyed, about $1 million a week).

The third, and least known, is the profit that can be made between the time the stamp company sells a retailer stamps for cash, and the time the stamps are taken to the redemption center for merchandise. During the interim—an average of eight months—the stamp firm may invest the cash in short-term bonds and notes with interest.

All this is perfectly legal and business-like, of course, but it arouses righteous indignation in economically naive housewives. The obvious fact that the merchandise is cheaper without stamps is a shocking revelation.

Washington bristles with concern about the whole thing. No one seems to favor outlawing trading stamps but there is agitation for some sort of "full disclosure" law, much like "truth in lending" or "truth in packaging." Esther Peterson, the President's top adviser on consumer affairs, feels that shoppers should know just what part of their food dollar goes to support trading stamps. "Consumers should at least be aware of the fact that when they shop at a store offering stamps, the merchandise they buy is apt to reflect the retailer's cost of purchasing those stamps," she says.

Some members of Congress feel even more strongly. Rep. Benjamin S. Rosenthal, who heads a newly created "special study unit on consumer affairs," a part of the House Government Operations Commission, indicates his group will probe the food-price trading-stamp issue next year. As a starter, a staff investigator is analyzing chain operations in price-warring Denver. Others threatening an investigation of stamps on Capitol Hill include House Judiciary Committee Chairman Emanuel Celler (D., N.Y.) and Spark M. Matsunaga (D., Hawaii), who heads an agriculture subcommittee.

One Congressman is already crusading to demand "truth in stamps" legislation. Rep. Lester Wolff (D., N.Y.), who speaks widely on the subject, says he'll introduce legislation next year to create a Federal Commission on Trading Stamp Practices. He hopes the commission's activities will lead to legislation requiring that all stamp firms redeem stamps at a stated cash value if the customer wishes. Rep. Wolff also criticizes the Federal Trade Commission for what he considers a "reluctance" to move into the stamp field. He complains that the companies' use of the words "free" and "gift" to describe items in their merchandise catalogues is deceptive and should be challenged.

Actually, the FTC is looking into stamps, but from a different angle. In a case pending against the Sperry & Hutchinson Co., the agency is contesting a couple of common industry practices as unfairly competitive and in restraint of trade. One complaint alleged that S&H has tried to suppress the operation of trading-stamp exchanges (where consumers can swap different brands of stamps). Another charges that S&H has attempted to prevent independent retailers from redeeming stamps for their own merchandise.

The most critical complaint, however, is that S&H has used its economic muscle to stop individual merchants from dispensing more than one stamp for every 10¢ purchase (the standard "rate of exchange" on the stamp market). The FTC says it's none of the firm's business what retailers do with the stamps after they're purchased. The stamp people retort that if merchants are left free to give a stamp for every 8¢ in sales (or 6¢ or 5¢), they will soon find themselves embroiled in uncontrollable stamp wars. This, they argue, will add to a retailer's cost and push up prices at a time when ironically, the FTC itself is concerned that promotions may account for too large a chunk of retail prices.

The FTC is also critical because the stamp business is dominated by a handful of firms. By the agency's estimates, S&H and Top Value control more than 50% of a market of about 300 firms. Blue Chip, Gold Bond, and E. F. MacDonald take up another 25%. King Korn, Eagle, Merchants' Green Stamps, Stop & Save, and Gold Strike bring the top 10 dominance to over 90%. The FTC's companion in antitrust enforcement, the Justice Department, is already moving to force nine California supermarket chains to relinquish control of Blue Chip, charging that the chains first tried to suppress stamps in California, then created a monopoly of their own that eventually grew to 70% of the stamp business in that state.

First it was the specter of market saturation that made the industry edgy and later it was the pending charges of unfair competitive practices and the unsettled antitrust picture. Now, with government and housewives looking into stamps as a possible culprit in food-price rises, many industry observers are forecasting doom. As they see it, if public ire over food prices is trained fully on trading stamps, it could set off a chain of explosions that would blow industry growth and profits to smithereens.

Their reasoning goes like this: Food chains with more than 11 stores account for about 60% of all stamps issued (680,000,000 in 1965). A consumer-inspired move by a few big supers to end trading stamps would trigger widespread cancellations throughout the food industry (particularly among the mom and pops, who generally pay more per stamp than the big volume chains).

This would pave the way for another wave of cancellations among gasoline dealers, who account for more than 20% of all stamps issued. The National Congress of Petroleum Retailers, for example, is overwhelmingly critical of stamps, as are several state associations. Many predict that individual gasoline dealers would quickly desert the ranks of stamp users if only the big-volume users (the supermarkets) would lead the way. If that happened, the stamp industry would be dealt a devastating blow, one from which it might never fully recover.

Not surprisingly, spokesmen for the stamp industry don't quite see it that way. They acknowledge that their share of the food business is probably close to the saturation point but insist it will hold that mark. One of their reasons is that so many chains are now either shareholders or owners of stamp companies.

Right now, industry strategy is to hang on to its share of the food market while at the same time extending its coverage to small department stores, bantam markets, furniture stores, incentive programs, and, most of all, to highly promising foreign markets (Japan's stamp sales jumped 200% last year, England's 100%). Irving M. Axelrod, newly elected president of the Trading Stamp Institute of America, which claims to represent 55% of the industry's volume, predicts confidently that sales this year will grow by about 10%.

A more impartial industry expert, perhaps, is Calvin J. Train, publisher of The Trading Stamp Report, a new industry biweekly that claims to be neither prostamp nor antistamp. "Obviously, these 'ladycotts' and government investigations aren't going to do the industry a bit of good," he says. "But even if things should get bad, you've got to keep the long-range picture in mind.

"The trading-stamp industry has always been cyclical in nature. Before the Depression, stamps were modestly popular, only to plunge into obscurity after 1929. They were popular, too, just before the war, only to be obliterated in a rationed, sellers' market. After the war it was a buyer's market again and stamps took off—from $30,000,000 in merchants' purchases in 1950 to $560,000,000 just 10 years later. Today we may see a decline due to saturation, and competition from discount houses and gimmicks, but in my opinion stamps are here to stay as part of the American scene," because, in his view, "people like them."

For the housewife, Mr. Train says, the stamp has come to represent her private kitty or slush fund. "It enables her to save for a luxury item or gift she probably wouldn't buy if she had to shell out hard cash."

Some statistics support his statement. Example: a 1963 "Study of Supermarket Shoppers," by Burgoyne Index, Inc., asked housewives in six major markets whether they felt shoppers would prefer trading stamps or a 2% discount on prices. The combined response showed 55% in favor of stamps and 45% choosing the price discount.

Just what this may indicate in consumer-conscious 1966 is open to question. For example, another study by Progressive Grocer magazine indicates that 55% of all stamp savers are indifferent to them and do so only because they are shoved under their noses at the checkout counter.

Today the question can be fairly asked: If shoppers were informed that the value of their stamps won't buy so much as cold cash, would they still save stamps? This plus the possibility of "full disclosure" legislation, could turn the large mass of "indifferent" consumers into a rebellious majority. If so, the trading stamp industry's roller-coaster ride to the pinnacle of prosperity could be headed for a swift plunge into another long-term cyclical decline.

E. PRICE DECISIONS

The role of price, then, is to adapt our business system to changes in what society wants from it and in what our scientific revolution and growing capacities make us capable of turning out. The function of price is to direct, motivate, and control this adaptation to change.

41

The Role of Price in the American Business System

JOEL DEAN

THE BASIC JOB of price in the American competitive business system is to do for a free economy what a master economic planning and control commissar does in a collectivist economy. Price rations and allocates inputs (materials, men, and money) to their highest and noblest economic use in producing the goods and services wanted in a free, competitive economy. Price also rations and allocates the output of our economy, using the mechanism of the competitive markeplace instead of wasteful waiting lines or ration coupons. In fact, the efficiency of our market price system in supplying incentives, guidance, and control is more and more recognized, admired, and imitated by our Communist competitors.

The effectiveness of price in performing these vital functions depends in large part upon the responsiveness of price to dynamic changes in conditions and outlook as regards demand and supply. It is the responsiveness of

Reprinted from *Pricing: The Critical Decision*, A.M.A. Management Report No. 66, publication of American Management Association, Inc., pp. 5-11.

price which brings about corrective action. The role of price, then, is to adapt our business system to changes in what society wants from it and in what our scientific revolution and growing capacities make us capable of turning out. The function of price is to direct, motivate, and control this adaptation to change.

Pricing decisions, therefore, need to be adapted to changing conditions, of which the following are important:

1. Technological progress is being speeded up by the revolution in industrial science.
2. The number of new products is growing by leaps and bounds because of research spending on a vast scale.
3. The demand for services, both pure and product-attached, is becoming wider and more insistent because of higher living standards.
4. The ranks of our foreign competitors are being swelled by the entry of new and stronger members.
5. Legal restrictions are being tightened by the present administration in Washington.

Faster Technological Progress

The accelerated rate of technological progress has four important impacts upon pricing decisions:

1. The basic discoveries get more quickly translated into commercial realities and have their effect on the pricing of existing products sooner. Greater fluidity and faster communication of research discoveries among industries and among countries facilitate speedy commercialization. The rapid pace of the research race and the specter of obsolescence motivate prompter introduction of innovations. This acceleration is made practical by advances in innovation economics.
2. The duration of the shelter which the product innovation enjoys in its pioneering stages is shortened. The market power of the new product is more quickly reduced by competitive imitation and improvements. The price elasticity of demand for the novel product changes more rapidly. Insensitive to price in the pioneering stages, it can quickly become highly price-sensitive. The period during which the innovator has wide discretion in setting prices is, therefore, briefer.
3. Commercialization of research—that is, the entry of competitors into a field—is speeded up, thereby forcing the pace of pricing adjustments of the defenders. New entrants in some industries no longer need to spend years building a reputation in order to compete with established firms. Successful drug firms have been created almost overnight through technological innovation, and we have seen the birth of whole industries, such as missiles and electronics, in a single decade.

4. The circle of rivalry of a product is expanding fast. In our technologically advanced, affluent society, there are now many alternative directions of spending of discretionary income. Thunderbirds compete with pleasure boats; trips to Europe with mountain cabins. Greater "shiftability" of demand and response to relative prices (as well as relative promotional pull) generally result from this intensified competition for the consumer's dollar. Broad and rapid changes in the composition of demand are likely as a consequence.

Population Explosion of New Products

Our scientific revolution drives product innovation forward at such a rapid pace that we are experiencing a "population explosion" in new products. The fast proliferation of new car lines by major automobile producers is but one example of the trend toward bigger product families. Bigger families make policies of product-line pricing more delicate, intricate, and important.

Greater population density of substitute and alternative products is another trend which has important pricing consequences. Twenty years ago, for example, there was a sharp three-way choice in foods: fresh, frozen, and canned. Markets were sharply defined and price differentials generally wide. Today the range of choice has been widened and the market segments blurred by the introduction of frozen-uncooked, frozen-completely cooked, frozen-partially cooked, as well as by the multiplication of grades and brands of fresh and canned foods. As a consequence, relatively small price differentials can cause relatively large shifts in consumer patronage.

Another impact of the product population explosion is the rising importance of "target pricing"—that is, tailoring product and anticipated production costs to yield a specified margin or rate of return. Cited by some as a sign of market power and price stickiness, it is actually more often a sign of intense direct and substitute competition. The manufacturer must prove to himself that he can build a product profitably to sell at a given price, because he knows he can't charge any more and still get volume sales. An illustration of this is the experience with compact cars. Target pricing and profit planning do not, however, guarantee success, but they do provide "birth control" pricing which guides new product planning to the *economic* satisfaction of consumer desires.

Increased Demand for Services

The postwar increase in the demand for services has taken two directions, which are difficult to distinguish at the borderline but distinctive in impact on practical pricing problems. These are (1) the increased demand for pure services and (2) the stepped-up demand for services that are built into products.

Pure Services. As far as pricing decisions are concerned, some implications of the increased demand for pure services are as follows:

1. There are likely to be increases in price, because most pure services consist mainly of labor, and productivity gains will consequently be relatively low.

2. These price increases for services (many of which are considered necessities, such as medical services) will contribute to the uproar about inflation and have far-reaching consequences—for example, increased antitrust activity.

3. Our technological ingenuity has not been able to keep pace with the growth in the demand for pure services. However, where manufacturers are able to find cheaper substitutes for these services, pricing discretion will be, at least temporarily, increased. We need only consider the revolution in educational techniques to see this.

4. Insight gained from pricing and price behavior in pure services will have a carryover to product-attached services. Some lessons to be learned are that underlying shifts in composition of demand are occurring; prices are dependent on the rate at which supply can be expanded; the price of a product should be based on the price of substitutes; and an estimate of the future availability of substitutes needs to be built into price policy.

Product-attached Services. Decreases as well as increases in the demand for services built into products are occurring. Services such as credit and delivery in supermarket and in discount-house merchandise are being dropped at the same time that other services are being built into precooked or frozen foods.

In general, the postwar shift in demand toward a richer mix of services has been a gradual one whose impact has been hidden in some industries by the worldwide restocking of durable goods. Hence, the shift, which is not likely to be reversed, may have gone further than is widely recognized.

Shifts in the comparative advantage gained by providing product-attached services at different points along the processing and distribution road confront sellers with altered risks and opportunities in pricing. The direction is usually toward *more* attached service. Technical advances and economies of scale in production reduce the cost of building in more services. Moreover, because the consumer has more money (and therefore places a higher price on leisure) and because there are more working wives, the value of these timesaving services has been increased.

In pricing the bundle of product-attached services, the high opportunity value of the service component can be fully reflected during the period of innovational shelter from competition. As the market power from a pioneered product is eroded by competition, the comparative cost advantage of mass production tends to play a more dominant role in pricing. For the smaller companies in an industry, correct pricing of product-attached services can be a way of existing alongside of much larger competitors who have economies of scale in making the product but have no comparative disadvantage in supplying the associated services.

In pricing, we should recognize that product-attached services constitute a joint product. We should build in services that are economical from both the customers' viewpoint and our own—that is, services that we have a comparative advantage in supplying. We must also price so as to recognize the inelasticity of demand for a built-in service, where it exists. Finally, we should differentiate prices, because elasticities of demand for components of this joint product-service package may vary by customer groups.

A new dimension of pricing is introduced by the manufacturer's discretion in manipulating the size of the service component of his product. First of all, competition in providing services can be discriminatory with greater impunity and greater adaptability to the need of the individual buyer than can explicit pricing. Second, cyclical adjustments of the service component can be more delicate and less disturbing to competitors. Finally, services built into a product are sometimes capable of producing shelter from competition through patents or through peculiar skills which present an unusual pricing opportunity.

The Worldwide Arena of Competition

The power of imports to police domestic prices and impart price elasticity to domestic demand will probably steadily increase. The main causes for the inroads that foreign competitors have made are as follows:

1. The liberalization of foreign trade and the reduction of trade barriers.

2. The narrowing of our margin of superiority in productivity, coupled with the wide disparity in hourly wage rates.

3. The stimulus to investment in new plants and equipment in war-torn economies in West Germany, England, France, and Italy, caused by highly favorable tax treatment of depreciation in those countries.

4. The appearance of new nations which are industrializing urgently. The long-run outlook for American producers is made more gloomy because ordinarily a higher proportion of the gains from higher productivity go to labor in the United States than in rival industrialized nations. This handicap is accentuated by our high tax rates and comparatively unfavorable tax treatment of depreciation.

A number of mistaken pricing attitudes also militate against a satisfactory solution. One is the notion that American technology produces such a wide margin of superiority that we are sheltered from foreign competition and that, therefore, our pricing problem is merely a parochial one. Another is the conviction that the quality superiority of American producers and their ability to adapt products to fit our peculiar needs will always shelter them from foreign competition. Third, there is the idea that passing on higher wage rate is only a problem of public relations—that our prices can go up indefinitely. Fourth, we have the notion that price cuts won't increase total sales of the domestic industry—that is, that American industry faces no price competition and little price elasticity of demand.

Erroneous economic notions like these will be eventually changed by the realities of the marketplace, but the learning process is likely to be a costly one. New competitors may gain a foothold while management, decoyed by questions of "price discipline," loses time that it should be using to ferret out and deal with the real problems—or at least those that management can do something about—the problems of cutting costs and developing new products.

As far as pricing policy is concerned, the basic long-run problem is a national one. It cannot be solved by the pricing policies of any individual manufacturer. Meeting foreign competitors' prices down to the level of our incremental cost is the indicated short-term response. But it is not a long-term solution: our incremental cost may be higher than the foreign competitor's full cost. Therefore, even the best pricing response will only buy time; and time is not worth much unless either the national response or the cost-and-product response of the individual manufacturer produces an ultimate solution.

For the individual manufacturer, non-price actions in the form of research, promotion, wage negotiations, and renewed efforts to increase productivity by mechanization and greater efficiency are more important than pricing adjustments.

The Changing Legal Environment

The legal setting of price decisions is also changing. These changes are particularly perplexing because the laws of economics lead to pricing decisions or policies which are frequently at odds with the Sherman, Clayton, and Robinson-Patman Acts.

Legal changes are susceptible to quicker reversal than are other changes in the environment of the price maker. Pendulum-like, they swing through cycles: from extended policing by government of pricing practices to periods of complacency, when there is renewed confidence in the policing power of intensified competition to force upon businessmen a willingness to keep their own house in order.

The increased concern of the Government is less likely to be expressed by new legislation than by vigorous enforcement of existing legislation. With the intensification of the cold war and a growing recognition of the need to put our resources to their most efficient use, it is possible that Congress may be induced to modify the present pricing legislation which inhibits this optimum use. The Robinson-Patman Act, for example, may deny the consumer, and the economy as a whole, the full benefits of well-established economies of scale. Incidentally, one of the critical differences between our economy and the Soviet economy is belief in economies of scale. In Soviet Russia, there is full faith, and no inhibitions, about complete utilization of savings of size. In our country, in contrast, economies of scale are always suspect and have to fight their way against vigorous government opposition.

Paradoxically enough, at the same time that there is increasing competition in industries traditionally oligopolistic, we find greater Government concern with pricing activities in these industries. Evidence of this is to be found in the drug and electric-industry hearings; the audit of consent decrees, initiated very early in the new administration; and the call to government purchasing agents, military and non-military, to report all instances of price identity to the antitrust agencies.

This paradox is explained by the tendency to confuse the behavior of individual prices with the price level. Holding down the price level is more appropriately the domain of monetary and fiscal policy. Trying to control it through the antitrust division is a mistake. However, it is a mistake of public policy that private business must live with and take into account in its pricing decisions. It must realize that antitrust audits are necessary. A company would do well to conduct seminars in the economies of strictly legal pricing, such as some perceptive manufacturers have inaugurated since the "electrical cases."

A Look at the Future

The economic function of price remains the same: to allocate input and ration output. But the institutional environment for particular pricing decisions is constantly changing. Price will probably perform its economic functions even more effectively in the future because (1) the step-up in antitrust activities will deter collusion and prevent thwarting of the economic function of price; (2) the adequacy of capacity means relatively large shifts in sales may result from small changes in price; and (3) the distorting effect of sharp movements in the over-all price level on the function of relative prices will be reduced.

The need for economically correct pricing decisions will become more pressing. We must face up to the fact of more intense competition where it exists and not be blinded by the "administered price" myth or the "orderly

market" myth. Price behavior is determined by the structure of industries and markets, by supply and demand conditions, and not by wishful thinking. The penalty for incorrect pricing decisions is becoming more prompt and devastating because the catch-up of capacity with demand in many industries will compel more competitive pricing. Moreover, accelerated technological progress will create additional substitute competition and hasten obsolescence. Finally, the rising competence and capacity of foreign manufacturers will police the pricing of more American firms.

Oligopoly is simultaneously becoming more common as the structure of competition and less powerful as a pricing force. The combined effect of (1) scale economies, (2) geographical separation of competitors, (3) quality-strata separation, and (4) specialized products will make oligopoly more and more common in America. It will become the typical economic structure of competition in industries where price making is managerially important.

The tools for making correct pricing decisions are improving. Among these are (1) a scientific approach to the measurement of demand elasticity, by controlled experiments and other objective research; (2) economic and statistical cost research and engineering predictions, which can provide relevant cost forecasts for pricing; (3) electronic data-processing and computer techniques, which speed up and reduce the cost of the analysis of both demand and cost data; and (4) new tools and broader experience which are available for market testing of new products and promotional pricing.

Of all the areas of executive
decision, pricing is perhaps the
most fuzzy. . . . In order to
organize the various pieces of
information and considerations
that bear on price decisions, a
multi-stage approach to pricing
can be a very helpful tool.

42

Multi-Stage Approach
to Pricing

ALFRED R. OXENFELDT

OF ALL THE AREAS of executive decision, pricing is perhaps the most fuzzy. Whenever a price problem is discussed by a committee, divergent figures are likely to be recommended without a semblance of consensus. Although unanimity in marketing decisions is a custom more remarkable in its occurrence than in its absence, agreement in pricing decisions is even more rare.

This article accordingly presents a long-run, policy-oriented approach to pricing which should reduce the range of prices considered in specific situations and consequently improve the decisions which result. This approach, which to the best of my knowledge is new, calls for the price decision to be made in six successive steps, each one narrowing the alternatives to be considered at the next step.

Is this method just another mechanical pricing formula? Hardly, for it is my conviction that the quest for mechanical pricing methods is unduly optimistic, if not downright naive. Nevertheless, many businessmen consistently employ almost mechanical formulas for pricing. They do this even though they scoff at the claim that there are reliable fixed formulas for

Reprinted from the *Harvard Business Review*, Volume 38, No. 4 (July-August, 1960), pp. 125-133.

handling personnel problems or making advertising or capital outlay decisions. Certainly, experience has not produced recipes that guarantee correct decisions in any sphere of business. The best of them only apply under normal conditions, and it is most rare indeed that conditions resembling normalcy prevail.

On the other hand, many discussions of pricing present a long list of factors to be "taken into account," carefully weighed and balanced, and then subjected to a process called "judgment." While a specific price is thus arrived at, this does not alter the fact that intelligent and experienced business executives using the method will arrive at widely different price decisions—all based on the same information.

Yet, even if mechanical pricing formulas are the hope of the optimistic, it would be excessively pessimistic to resign ourselves to a *formless* consideration of all the relevant factors and to a random exercise of judgment. Many things are known about the subject that would be extremely helpful to those responsible for making such decisions.

Sequential Stages

In order to organize the various pieces of information and considerations that bear on price decisions, a multi-stage approach to pricing can be a very helpful tool. This method sorts the major elements in a pricing decision into six successive stages:

1. Selecting market targets.
2. Choosing a brand "image."
3. Composing a marketing mix.
4. Selecting a pricing policy.
5. Determining a pricing strategy.
6. Arriving at a specific price.

The sequence of the stages is an essential part of the method, for each step is calculated to simplify the succeeding stage and to reduce the likelihood of error. One might say that this method divides the price decision into manageable parts, each one logically antecedent to the next. In this way, the decision at each stage facilitates all subsequent decisions. This approach might also be regarded as a process of selective search, where the number of alternatives deserving close consideration is reduced drastically by making the decision in successive stages. Of course, one could arrive at the same result by simultaneously considering all the factors mentioned —but it might require a computer to do so.

While it appears that this approach is applicable over a broad range of industry and trade, the great diversity of business situations precludes the possibility of its being a universally applicable method. No rigid approach, and certainly not the one presented here, offers a guarantee of reaching the best—or even a satisfactory—price decision. It must be adapted to prevailing circumstances; consequently, information, experience, and the application of rigorous logic are required for its optimum utilization.

I. Market Targets

A going concern is "committed," confined, and tied down by several important circumstances which can be altered only over a considerable period of time. It must live with many conditions, even while it may attempt to alter them. Also, an operating business possesses specified resources on which it will strive to capitalize in achieving its objectives. For example, a firm will have:

- A fixed production location, given physical facilities, and a particular production and sales labor force.
- A set of distribution arrangements through which the firm generally sells, including particular distributors with whom it has established relationships.
- Contracts with suppliers, customers, laborers, and lenders of funds.
- A portfolio of customers who have a definite opinion of the firm's reliability, and the quality of its offerings and service.

These commitments and resources of a firm contain pricing implications. Mainly, they determine the type of product that it can make, the type of service it can render, and its probable costs of operation. What is more, these circumstances form the basis for the most fundamental pricing decision that management should make—namely, the types of customers, or market segments, it will attempt to cultivate.

By virtue of its fixed commitments, then, a firm is limited to the several market segments it can reasonably hope to capture. It has customer connections on which it can capitalize, and it has a variety of strengths and weaknesses that limit its choice among potential submarkets for intensive cultivation.

Two examples drawn from the TV set industry will help to clarify this crucial first stage. Certainly, no two firms could possibly exemplify all situations, nor is it possible for an outsider to explain satisfactorily why specific decisions were made in specific cases. However, these illustrations are intended to indicate what factors management must consider if it is to apply the multi-stage approach. They do *not* describe how management reasoned or what would have been the best decision under the circumstances.

ZENITH RADIO

First, consider the pricing problem of the Zenith Radio Corporation at the time it started to produce TV sets in 1948:

- This company, which is one of the two largest TV set producers now, dropped out of the automobile radio business in order to manufacture television sets. (At that time, it was the largest single producer of automobile radios, but this business was not very profitable.) Zenith possessed these resources and was subject to these commitments and limitations that could have influenced its selection of market targets in the TV business—

- It had production facilities in Chicago that had been designed for and used in radio production for many years; its labor force and supervisory personnel were familiar with the electronics business. The firm had substantial manufacturing skills in electronics because of its work for the military during and after World War II. Zenith could assess its manufacturing capabilities as very substantial, but not outstanding.

- Financially, Zenith was also in a very strong and liquid position and could readily have undertaken heavy expenditures at this time.

- But Zenith's outstanding resource was a distributor and dealer organization that was as good as that possessed by any other firm in the nation. Its dealers commanded strong loyalty among their clientele not only in small communities but also in large cities—a most vital fact in view of the technical character of TV and the great power that retailers wield over consumer choices of such products. Here Zenith was helped by the fact that it had acquired an excellent reputation for quality products in radios; for many years, it was the Cadillac of the radio industry. Zenith management, like all other radio manufacturers who entered the television business, decided to sell its sets through the distributor organization it had already created; its distributors, in turn, would sell them mainly to dealers already buying Zenith radios.

- There were also several other peripheral advantages. Zenith was closely identified, in the minds of many consumers, with hearing aids which were widely advertised as much on grounds of moderate price as in terms of high quality. Further, Zenith started to telecast, experimentally, in the Chicago market even before World War II and had some local identification as a telecaster, as well as a manufacturer. Its products were strongly favored in the Chicago market.

In summary, Zenith Radio could count on its strong distributor and retail organizations as its outstanding resource, while recognizing that it did not possess any particular advantage in costs of manufacture or quality of product and, in fact, that its behavior in the television business was necessarily circumscribed by its radio and hearing aid business. Zenith's management would have required very strong reasons to choose as its market targets customers who were very different from those who bought its radios and hearing aids.

Under these circumstances, Zenith management might have decided to attempt to reach customers at almost all levels of income. Partly, it could do this by including "low-end" and promotional models in its line; partly because television sets were sold on installment credit involving modest monthly charges; and partly because, at least in the early years, television purchases were spread rather evenly over all income groups.

On the other hand, Zenith management, as its first step, might well expect to cultivate particularly those consumers who were conservative and quality-conscious, who felt a strong loyalty to particular appliance retailers, and who were located mainly in small cities and towns. On this basis, the Zenith customer targets would not include "snobs" who, at that time, favored the Dumont brand and, to a lesser degree, the RCA set. Also they would not include bargain hunters. Rather Zenith's customers would be the kind of people who feel that "you get what you pay for." (Zenith would presumably capitalize on its strong position in the Chicago area by special measures aimed at that market.)

COLUMBIA BROADCASTING

Now contrast Zenith's position with that of Columbia Broadcasting System, Inc., when it started to produce and sell TV sets under its own brand name in 1953:

CBS resources and commitments were altogether different from those possessed by Zenith, with the result that the two companies could have been expected to cultivate different market targets. Specifically, in the case of Columbia Broadcasting—

- CBS executives were primarily familiar with the management of entertainment talent and the creation and servicing of a network of stations. Although its phonograph record and Hi-Fi phonograph business did involve a type of production and distribution experience, CBS was completely new to major appliance manufacturing and possessed no suitable distribution facilities whatsoever for appliances.

- In addition, CBS acquired production facilities when it entered the TV business that were of relatively poor quality. The size, location, equipment, plant layout, and employee facilities of the Air King firm, which CBS acquired, were widely recognized as mediocre or below. Many people familiar with that company and with the TV industry strongly doubted that Air King's management was capable of establishing a prestige national brand and producing the high quality product needed to support a quality reputation.

- On the other hand, CBS had some genuine pluses in its favor. Its radio and television networks were the largest, and enjoyed great prestige at the time CBS entered the TV set business. Also, by virtue of its telecasting facilities, it could advertise its sets during unsponsored programs at virtually no out-of-pocket cost. It could, moreover, get the advertising support —mainly through testimonials from outstanding personalities like Arthur Godfrey, Edward R. Murrow, Jack Benny, and others—for little or no cost.

To what kinds of customers could a firm with these resources and limitations appeal?

One way that CBS might have adjusted to its particular combination of resources and weaknesses would have been to select as its chief consumer market target the metropolitan customer who is anxious to be associated with prestigeful figures, vulnerable to advertising over radio and TV, prepared to pay a premium price, and relatively unfamiliar with or insensitive to technical performance features. But this market target would hardly have been very large in the first instance; moreover, CBS management must have recognized that many other firms were cultivating this type of customer.

It would appear, then, that CBS was compelled to select its market targets mainly in terms of distributors and retailers, rather than ultimate consumers. Whereas Zenith already possessed a strong distributor and dealer organization, CBS had to construct one. Only after it secured representation on the market could it hope to sell to consumers.

CBS management must have realized that whatever it did in an effort to win distributors and dealers would also influence the kind of customers it could hope to attract. For example, if it had to extend big markups to distributors and retailers to get them to handle its sets (combined with the fact that its production facilities were mediocre), CBS would be compelled to charge a relatively high retail price for its sets. In turn, it would have to rely on intensive advertising to persuade consumers to pay these higher prices and find methods of making its sets appear luxurious and worth the high price.

In addition to having to accept the fact of a relatively high-price product, CBS would feel pressure to concentrate on customers in the large metropolitan centers, because of the need to build large sales volume rapidly in order to get its production costs in line with those of its competitors. Even as early as 1953, the large metropolitan markets were pervaded by severe price competition among set manufacturers and relatively little emphasis on quality and brand loyalty on the part of retailers. Independent distributors were leaving the business because of great manufacturer pressure to gain heavy sales volumes. Hence CBS could not have much hope of obtaining strong independent distributors for its line in most metropolitan markets, but would have to look ahead to a considerable period during which it "supported" both distributors and key retailers to obtain an organization that would distribute its sets.

OTHER CASES

Zenith and CBS have been cited as companies that would have been justified in placing relatively little weight on price in their selection of target submarkets. These companies mainly had to avoid alienating customers by charging prices that were far out of line with other companies' prices. Not all TV set manufacturers could have taken this approach, however. Thus:

Companies like Admiral, Emerson, and producers of private brands were under pressure to cultivate customers who place heavy emphasis on price. Why? Because in some cases they lacked the personnel and financial resources to sustain a claim of quality and style superiority; or, because their experience in the major appliance business before adding a line of TV receivers could have indicated that they had won acceptance mainly among customers who want moderate quality at prices below the average; or, finally, because their chief asset was a very efficient manufacturing organization that could imitate the products of their more progressive rivals at low cost.

Other industries offer clear examples of firms that selected as market targets persons who were not particularly interested in high intrinsic quality or style. Specifically:

- A fairly obvious example is the Scripto pencil, which offers satisfactory performance at minimum cost. Apparently the customers Scripto selected for intensive cultivation were those who would want a pencil to write with and not for display, a pencil they could afford to lose or misplace.

- Some producers of private brands of aspirin likewise have selected as market targets those persons who know of the fundamental similarity of aspirin quality and who actively desire to minimize their outlays for this product.

These examples illustrate a point that may not have been particularly clear in the discussion of the Zenith and CBS examples: *one important criterion in the selection of market targets is customer awareness of and sensitivity to price.*

II. Brand "Image"

Once management has defined the submarkets it wishes to cultivate most actively, it must select the methods it will use to achieve its goal.

Success in the market place for more and more products seems to depend on creating a favorable general image (often vague and formless) of the product or company among prospective customers. The selection and development of this image become of prime importance and have a direct bearing on price, as will be explained subsequently. A favorable image is especially important when one sells consumers' goods, but only rarely is it completely unimportant even in the sales of producers' goods. Buyers' very perceptions are affected by their prior attitudes, the actions and opinions of others, first impressions and early associations. It is a rare firm that can ignore the total impression its potential customers have of it and of what it is selling.

The firm's selection of its company and brand image should be dictated by the types of customers it is trying to attract. Submarkets may be likened to targets at which the seller is firing, and "images" are powerful weapons that can be used to hit the targets.

Almost every going concern has invested—often very heavily—in the creation of a favorable image. Most businesses know what image they wish to achieve and are concerned lest they or their products fail to have a favorable "meaning" to potential customers. At the very minimum, almost every management knows there are certain images that customers might have of it and its product that would prove disastrous.

The type of image a firm can create of itself and its wares depends to a considerable degree, again, on its fixed commitments and resources. With its physical and personnel resources, there is a limit to what it can do to alter the prevailing opinions—for they reflect all that the company was and did in the past. In that sense, the basic commitments limit the type of image a firm can establish, how much time it will require to establish it, and the cost. Even as brand image is frequently an effective weapon in cultivating particular submarkets, price helps to create the brand image. It is for this reason that the selection of a brand image which is consistent with the firm's market targets implies particular forms of price behavior.

Let us carry our original examples a little further. Given the market targets that they might have selected, as explained earlier, what brand image could Zenith and CBS try to create?

ALTERNATIVE QUALITIES

As in the selecting of market targets, every firm has only a few *reasonable* alternatives from which to choose its desired image. For example:

- Zenith already possessed a brand image that contributed strongly to its success in the radio and hearing aid business. Even if another image might have been advantageous for its television business, Zenith's management could hardly afford to injure the bird already in hand. Consequently, Zenith would be obliged to perpetuate for its TV line the brand image it had already established in its other activities. As it happened, that image was altogether suitable for its TV set business.

  To implement this line of thinking, Zenith would be obliged to establish the image of a "premium" product and of a company that was old-time, conservative, and mainly concerned with quality and craftsmanship. Above all, it would seek to avoid high-pressure selling, emphasis on price, and shoddiness of product. In styling, it could pursue a safe policy of including a wide variety of styles, while being especially careful not to alienate its conservative small-town customers with models too far in the vanguard of modern design.

- CBS faced a very different choice with regard to brand image. It, too, could not afford to jeopardize its eminent position in the radio and TV network field, for those activities were very profitable and would always remain its major sources of income. Except for this limitation, CBS had a relatively free choice of brand images.

  CBS could well undertake to be the style leader in the industry. This image would be consistent with relatively inefficient manufacturing facilities, concentration on selling in the metropolitan market, and the necessity of charging a high retail price. It would appear that few brand images other than for advanced styling and for gimmicks would have been consistent with the resources and limitations on CBS at this time.

- In contrast to Zenith and CBS, other TV set producers sought a brand image that did have an important price ingredient. Again, most producers of private brands, Admiral, Emerson, and others, often featured price in their advertising and apparently sought to sensitize prospective customers to price. They could purposely become identified as firms that were not afraid to discuss price and that seemed confident they offered better values than their competitors.

  Many firms outside the TV set industry attempt to establish a brand image that has a heavy price ingredient. Among producers, one finds Caron boasting that its Joy perfume is the most expensive, and Chock-Full-of-Nuts implying much the same thing about its coffee. Without being explicit, some retailers seem to claim that no stores charge more than they—and, strangely, this image is a source of strength. The retail world is full of stores that claim that they are never knowingly undersold; on the other hand, it is difficult to name manufacturers who claim that their product is the cheapest on the market—probably because of the implication that theirs is also the brand of lowest quality. (Automobile manufacturers occasionally claim to be the "cheapest of the low-price three," but none has occupied that position long.)

III. Marketing Mix

The third stage in multi-stage pricing calls for the selection of a combination of sales promotion devices that will create and re-enforce the desired company and product brand image and achieve maximum sales for the planned level of dollar outlays. In this stage, a role must be assigned to price. The role in which price is cast should be selected only after assessment is made as to relative effectiveness and appropriateness of each sales promotion device that might be employed. The short-term gains of certain sales promotion devices may entail injury to the image objectives of the firm. Conflicts of such a nature must be resolved at this stage.

Then, too, a firm might achieve precisely the *desired* image and still find customers very hard to get. It is not enough to establish the desired image; it must be an *effective* image. Furthermore, even though a firm may establish highly favorable impressions of itself and its wares, the company and its products must live up to the image they foster. Not only must its product be "within reach" in price, but it must be accessible by being offered through convenient channels of distribution, and must be sold in outlets where customers like to buy.

The third stage builds directly upon the second. The need to conform to the prior decision about company and brand image greatly limits the number of price alternatives that a price setter can reasonably consider.

The marketing mix decision at this stage need not be translated into specific dollars and cents amounts to be devoted to each sales promotion device; however, it does at least call for crude answers to the following questions:

- How heavily to advertise?
- How much for salesmen?
- How much for product improvement?
- How much of an assortment to carry?
- How large an inventory to hold?
- How best to provide speedy delivery?
- How much emphasis on price appeal?

The composition of a marketing mix (arrived at by answering the type of questions just listed) is admittedly very difficult and highly subjective. But the job is facilitated greatly when answers are subjected to the test of conforming to the desired company and brand image and to the firm's fixed commitments.

Few firms can afford to switch "images," usually because they have invested heavily in them in prior years and should, therefore, not abandon them lightly. Moreover, past images persist and blur any future attempts at image building. Although it cannot easily scrap its brand image, a firm can vary its marketing mix within moderate limits and remain consistent with the image it seeks to create. Thus, the selection of an image sets limits and gives direction to the decision about the elements to be included in the marketing mix. In that way, it facilitates the decision and also increases the likelihood that it will be correct. However, it does not isolate a single marketing mix as the only correct one.

MARKETING THE IMAGE

How might have Zenith, CBS, and other TV set manufacturers composed a marketing mix, if they had reasoned about market targets and brand image along the lines of the foregoing discussion? Let us see:

- In Zenith's case, price clearly would have had to be subordinated as a sales appeal. The company could have placed major emphasis on quality of product, subdued advertising, and reliable service, while placing its product with retailers who would enhance the reputation of the brand. By these measures, Zenith could have re-enforced the image of a high quality and reliable producer.

- In the case of CBS, the role of price in the marketing mix would not have been subject to much control. As explained, it might have been forced to charge a high price; if so, most of its other actions would have been dictated by that fact. It could have relied very heavily on radio and TV advertising to generate consumer preference, and justified its high price by adding externals to the set—particularly attractive styling, an expensive furniture appearance, or special features of some sort. It could not have reasonably hoped to get very much support from retailers who commanded strong loyalty among their patrons.

- Other TV set producers adopted quite different market mixes from those that Zenith and CBS would have selected if they had reasoned along these lines. Some, however, apparently had no conscious marketing mix philosophy and, therefore, seemed to improvise and stumble from one crisis to another. Nevertheless, in their bids for patronage, some TV set producers apparently placed relatively heavy reliance on advertising (including mainly RCA, General Electric, Westinghouse, and Sylvania). Others made strong quality claims (like Dumont and Andrea). Still others placed chief emphasis on styling (Magnavox).

IV. Determining Policy

The fourth stage in multi-stage pricing calls for the selection of a pricing policy. But before a pricing policy can be determined, answers to the following questions must be obtained:

- How should our price compare with "average" prices in the industry? Specifically, should we be 2% above or 4% below the average? And, when we speak of the average, which firms' prices are we going to include in the computation?

- How fast will we meet price reductions or increases by rivals?

- How frequently will it be advisable to vary price? To what extent is stability of price advantageous?

- Should the firm make use of "fair trade" price maintenance?
- How frequently should the firm run price promotions?

These are simply illustrative of the aspects of a pricing policy which management can and should spell out—in proper sequence. By virtue of having made the evaluations and decisions called for in the first three stages, management will find itself limited in the number of choices on these points.

In addition, each company must take account of the valuations placed on its product-service "package" as well as the valuations of rival products by the market segments it is most anxious to cultivate. On the basis of such considerations, plus its target market segments and marketing mix, it will decide whether it can afford to charge much more or less than its rivals.

"BRACKETING" THE PRICE

Before proceeding further, let us summarize. Surely, a price setter would be some distance from a specific price decision even after completing the fourth step. We must ask ourselves whether he would not also have covered considerable distance toward a price decision. By taking account of the firm's basic commitments and resources, the images it desires to establish, its decision about marketing mix, and the selection of a detailed pricing policy, has not the price setter reached the point where he is very strongly circumscribed in the price decision he will ultimately make? To illustrate Step Four, let us carry our two main examples—Zenith and CBS—about as far as they can be taken and see what pricing policy these companies might have adopted:

- If the Zenith management had selected the market targets set forth here and made the same decisions regarding brand image and marketing mix, it would have had little trouble in selecting a pricing policy. It would have felt obliged to charge a price somewhat above the average in the market and to minimize emphasis on price in its advertising. Moreover, it could have varied price relatively infrequently to the consumer—except possibly in some of the large metropolitan markets where neither consumers nor retailers are loyal to anything or anyone, except their own pecuniary interests.

  In Zenith's pricing policy, the preservation of distributor and retailer loyalty would have figured very prominently in its thinking. It would be compelled to sacrifice long-term price advantages in order to protect its distributors and retailers from financial loss due to price change.

- CBS, on the other hand, need not have concerned itself much with dealer and retailer loyalty. It had none and must have realized that it would not have been able to create a loyal distribution structure unless it were willing to make very large financial outlays. If it had reconciled itself to a not-too-loyal distributor and dealer organization, CBS could have conducted sales promotions and varied price frequently and by large amounts. It could have emphasized price in these promotions, but presumably only when combined with strong emphasis on alleged high quality and superior styling. CBS need not have felt obliged to match the prices charged by its competitors, but it could not have afforded to have its retailers' margins be out of line on the low side.

Since it commanded no loyalty from its retailers, CBS was, in fact, compelled to buy their sales support. This it could do, primarily by offering a higher than average margin. (CBS could also have attempted to solve its distribution problem by granting exclusive privileges to a small number of retail outlets. In the case of the TV industry, such a policy has been used successfully by Magnavox. However, this company had already sewed up the strong quality retailers who were capable of producing large volume. As a result, CBS was shut out of this pattern of distribution.)

Although Zenith and CBS apparently would have been obliged to charge more than the average by the foregoing line of thinking, other TV producers were wise to take a very different tack, mainly because of their different resources and commitments. For example, Admiral and Emerson have tended to charge somewhat less than average, while General Electric has not adopted a very consistent price position.

V. Pricing Strategy

It is difficult to draw a sharp line between policy and strategy, but it is possible and useful to make some sort of distinction between them. Policy is formulated to deal with anticipated and foreseeable situations of a recurrent type. However, markets frequently are beset and dominated by *special* situations that basic policy was not designed to meet. For example:

- A Congressional committee might threaten to investigate the company's or the industry's pricing arrangements.
- A sizable firm may have fallen into a desperate financial situation so that it was forced to raise cash through a liquidation of its inventories.
- A large new firm may have entered the market.
- Business may have fallen off precipitately for the entire industry or economy.
- The company may have introduced a model that is either a "dud" or a "sure winner."

Special situations like these ordinarily require an adjustment in price—and the formulation of a strategy to guide management in setting price *during the time that the special* situation endures.

There generally are several strategies which would be compatible with the firm's basic commitments and resources, its market targets, its image objectives, its convictions about the relative emphasis to attach to various elements in the marketing mix, and its specific pricing policies. Others would be incompatible with earlier decisions and therefore might endanger precious values. A threat to one's very survival might justify a scrapping of these, but impetuousness, shortsightedness, or avarice would not. Explicit recognition of these earlier stages of the pricing decision should prevent hasty short-run actions that are painful, but quite common.

No effort will be made to discuss the Zenith and CBS examples in connection with the formulation of a pricing strategy. They have already been stretched far enough to illustrate the application of the multi-stage approach to pricing—especially in the most difficult stages. The reader might, however, speculate about how, within the framework of the approach outlined here, both Zenith and CBS management could have responded to a great pricing crisis in the TV set industry. This occurred in the fall of 1953 when Westinghouse suddenly reduced its TV sets by approximately 20% during the very heart of the selling season. We may speculate that adherence to decisions regarding market targets, brand image, marketing mix, and price policy would have prevented both Zenith and CBS from reducing their prices to the levels set by Westinghouse Electric Corporation.

VI. Specific Price

Here is the final step—the selection of a specific price. At this point, the price setter will usually find himself sharply circumscribed in the specific sums he can charge. Nevertheless, he usually will have some range of price possibilities that are consistent with the decisions made in the preceding five stages of the price decision. How may he best select among the alternatives?

To the extent that he is able, he should be guided by the arithmetic of pricing—that is, by a comparison of the costs and revenues of the alternative prices within the zone delimited by the prior stages of his pricing decision. Once he has taken into account his market targets, brand image, marketing mix, pricing policy, and strategy, he can afford to ignore everything but the calculations of costs and revenues. *The first five stages of decision are designed to take account of the business considerations which may be ignored if one selects price solely on the basis of prevailing cost and revenue conditions.*

It often is impossible to obtain reliable information about sales at different prices; this difficulty is present whatever method of pricing one employs. But the multi-stage policy approach facilitates research and experimentation into demand conditions by limiting the number of alternatives to be considered.

The price that would be established under this multi-stage policy approach would rarely be the same as that set by balancing marginal cost and marginal revenue. The former probably would exclude, as incompatible with the firm's basic commitments and resources, desired brand image, and so on, the prices that would be most profitable in the very short term.

The Advantages

First, this approach breaks up the pricing decision into six relatively manageable pieces. In that way, it introduces order into the weighing of the many considerations bearing on price. This approach, therefore, should increase the likelihood that all major factors will be taken into account and that their large number will not overwhelm the price setter.

Second, this method of pricing reduces the risk that the price setter will destroy the firm's valuable investments in corporate and brand images. Also, it requires the price setter to determine and take into account the limitation on the firm's freedom of decision. In that way, it would discourage the pricing executive from undertaking what he is powerless to accomplish. Similarly, the multi-stage policy approach should militate against a short-run policy of opportunism that would sacrifice long-term values.

Third, the multi-stage policy approach to pricing should be valuable to those executives who are compelled to delegate pricing responsibilities. In the first place, high-level executives are virtually required by the method to make the decisions for several stages, which thus limits their dependence on their subordinates. In the second place, as explained, it simplifies the making of a price decision so that greater success can be expected. Then, too, its use should make it easier for subordinates to raise questions and obtain advice from their superiors, should they be unable to reach a decision.

Fourth, this approach to pricing puts considerable emphasis on the intangibles that are involved in pricing—particularly on the total impression that customers have of the vendor and of the things he sells. Price is far more than a rationing device that determines which potential customers will be able to afford to make a purchase. Generally it is one of the most important actions in creating an impression of the the firm among potential customers. Especially as tangible differences among rival products shrink, these intangibles will grow in significance for marketing success.

The Limitations

This approach does not indicate all the considerations that should be taken into account at each stage in the pricing decision. In other words, the price setter is compelled to isolate the significant factors operating at each stage and weigh them for himself.

Second, this approach does not indicate what price to charge in any specific situation. The most that can be claimed for it is that it narrows down the zone of possible prices to the point where it may not matter a great deal which particular price is selected. As stated at the outset, one must beware of any pricing method that does lead to a single price, for such a method could not possibly take into account all of the special circumstances which are relevant to a price decision and which vary so greatly from market to market and from time to time.

Third, this method does not guide price setters in recognizing the factors that dominate the market at any time and in knowing when to switch basic strategies. Also, there may well be more than one dominant condition which must be considered in selecting a basic strategy.

On balance, then, the multi-stage approach to pricing at best only takes an executive fairly close to his ultimate destination. Although the multi-stage policy approach does not do the whole job of pricing, the part of the job that is left is relatively easy to finish in many cases. Where this is not so, one can only assume that the task would be almost hopeless without the assistance of a method that reduces the pricing decision to a series of relatively manageable steps in a prescribed sequence.

Conclusion

The multi-stage policy approach outlined here differs from usual approaches to pricing in two major respects. First, it demands a long-range view of price by emphasizing the enduring effects of most price actions on company and brand image. One might say this approach constructs a policy framework for the price decision. And, second, it allows the price decision to be made in stages, rather than requiring a simultaneous solution of the entire price problem.

Almost all students of the subject . . . seem agreed on one point: the nature of administered prices is not fully known by policy-makers and the public.

43

Why Corporations Find It Necessary to "Administer" Prices

ROBERT F. LANZILLOTTI

SOME 25 YEARS AGO the distinguished economist Gardiner C. Means coined the term "administered prices" to describe certain industrial goods whose prices are typically rigid, at least for a period of time, and whose sales fluctuate with demand at the rigid price. In contrast to what are sometimes called "market prices," i.e., those that are determined *automatically* by the interaction of demand and supply forces in the market, "administered prices" are formulated in executive offices of companies as a matter of operating policy and financial planning by corporate officials.

The distinctive feature of an administered price situation is that firms, whether acting individually or cooperatively with competitors, have a kind of plenary power to set prices within a considerable range. Market forces, of course, limit the range within which an administered price may be set, but they do not *determine* the price. There is nothing in the supply and demand situation that will *force* a particular price to result.

This condition, where firms enjoy measurable discretion over prices, is found whenever the number of firms in a particular industry or market is

Reprinted from *Challenge: The Magazine of Economic Affairs,* published by Institute of Economic Affairs, New York University, Volume 8, No. 4 (January, 1960), pp. 45-49.

small, or wherever one or two firms account for a predominant share of the market and act as strong price leaders. Typical examples are such industries as automobiles, steel, aluminum, rubber, chemicals, petroleum and electrical equipment.

While recognizing the undesirable competitive implications of these situations, many economists—including Dr. Means—regard administered prices as an *inevitable and indispensable* part of our modern economy. Harvard economist John Kenneth Galbraith goes even further and says: "It is equally inevitable that a great many industries will be conducted by a comparatively small number of large firms. That is the nature of capitalism wherever it is found. A large amount of price administration is thus part of our economic system. Those who deplore it are wasting their breath."

There are other economists of note who contest the validity of this view and hold that administered prices are symptomatic of excessive market power that should be brought under some type of social control. But there is no general agreement among economists regarding either the need or desirability of such measures.

Greater Awareness

Almost all students of the subject, however, seem agreed on one point: the nature of administered prices is not fully known or understood by policy-makers and the public. In order to formulate appropriate and effective national economic policies regarding inflation and full employment, there must be a greater awareness of the way in which administered prices are determined and the nature and extent of their impact on general economic processes.

The limited information available on the actual pricing process suggests that many factors motivate and influence corporate managements. A recent Brookings Institution study of big corporations, whose pricing falls in the administered price category, discloses that corporate objectives underlying price decisions vary from company to company within and among different industries. Most large companies were found to have rather specific long-term goals, such as the desires to:

- Attain a particular "target profit" rate on capital invested in the company.
- Stabilize industry prices, margins and profits.
- Attain a specific percentage or "penetration" of a market.
- Meet or minimize competition.
- Follow the price leader.

A National Industrial Conference Board survey of 155 companies confirms the Brookings finding: "Representative is the statement by a vice president of a general industrial machinery concern that "the basic policy is to establish prices that will return a predetermined volume of sales."

General Motors officials, for example, have indicated in several appearances before Congressional committees that it is their policy to set prices to yield a profit of 15 to 20 per cent *after* taxes on investment. In practice, this means that even though GM output should fall below the company's normal volume (as in 1957-58), or consistently above (as in the 1950-56 period), suggested list prices established at the beginning of the model year will remain unchanged. This is the prototype of administered prices.

Long-range and Inflexible

There are two main sets of factors that explain why managements think in terms of relatively long-range, inflexible prices. First, a firm falling in the administered price group usually will be characterized by one or all of the following features: it is one of a few large producers; it is a price leader; and it sells products in a market or markets that are more or less protected by virtue of the magnitude of capital requirements, the influence of trademarks, brand names and patents, and the control of strong retail organizations.

A second set of special influences is found in the nature of the product, production costs, customer preferences, problems of internal management, control and various public pressures. More specifically, administered prices are traceable to:

- A high capital-to-sales dollar ratio.
- Relatively constant unit costs over wide ranges of output and over long intervals of time (up to a year).
- Rigidity of wage rates and prices of some semifinished materials and intermediate goods.
- Customer preference for stable (rigid) prices that simplify pricing and production planning.
- High cost of frequent price changes for the company.
- Increasing pressure on managements to resort to capital budgeting and profits planning in order to allocate available capital funds to competing uses and to provide for necessary plant expansion. (Projects that offer the best promise of reaching the predetermined profit target over the long term are likely to be given priority in the use of funds.)
- The guarantee of the Full Employment Act of 1946. (Firms, like wage earners, have a reasonable assurance that government action will be taken to maintain incomes and production. Hence, decreases in demand are viewed as temporary, and decreases in price dangerous and unnecessary.)
- Management conception of the corporation as an industry leader vested

with responsibilities akin to those of a public utility. (A U.S. Steel official confided that he was "unable to understand or properly describe the corporation's pricing policy except as something like the approach of the public utilities.")

- This tendency toward public utility thinking is reinforced by the disposition of the community and government officials to appeal to such firms as "pattern setters" for industry generally. In pricing they are expected to restrain themselves from taking full advantage of immediate profit opportunities.

Uniformity of prices among competitors also is typically found in conjunction with administered prices, which means that the force of competition is channeled along lines other than price. This is why profit targets are crucial—to provide a steady flow of funds to help maintain company position in the industry, as well as to mollify stockholders. Plant expansion will be planned with some "built-in" excess capacity so that the company can compete for customers by guaranteeing supplies in times of peak demands.

Thus, administered prices are regarded as necessary to protect producers from the temptation of cutting prices as a means of stimulating sales and operating closer to capacity—an action which corporation executives generally regard as self-defeating.

The wisdom of this thinking, of course, depends upon the responsiveness of industrial and consumer demands to price cuts. It is plausible that in times of declining demand both industry and consumers will postpone those purchases that are postponable; hence, price reductions would not greatly alter the purchases of these buyers. The magnitude of price cuts (i.e., token vs. large cuts) and their impact on buyer expectations must also be reckoned with, however. Experts are divided on this question, and managements feel an administered (rigid) price policy, on balance, is "safer" in terms of their long-run objectives.

Misleading Emphasis

It needs to be noted, therefore, that the expression "administered prices," while an accurate and vivid description of the kind of pricing under discussion, carries a misleading if not faulty emphasis. It would be more accurate and more useful, both to an understanding of management thinking and a guide to public policy, to speak of "administered profits." By doing so, attention would be focused on the fact that our big corporations are *interested in and have the economic power to make administrative decisions that will fully utilize, or underutilize, industrial capacity as necessary to meet profit objectives.*

Even a brief discussion of the problem of administered prices and inflation requires more than just a mention of the importance of the rigidity of costs—and wage costs, in particular. The persistent inflation of the post-World War II period, at times side-by-side with recession, raises the question of whether our economy has developed a new kind of inflationary track as contrasted with the old-fashioned monetary variety.

Although the problem of administered prices would exist even in the absence of unions, the development of strong labor blocks has complicated the problem. The ability of management to administer its prices, on the one hand, has meant less resistance to union demands and, on the other, the level of profits resulting from administered prices has made labor more militant in its demands.

Since the end of the Korean conflict especially, both management and labor appear to have taken advantage of the administered price mechanism to escalate cost and price increases upward in a "staircase" pattern. The rather large area of price discretion available to certain companies has afforded a means by which both management and labor interests could attain their private objectives. The administered price mechanism has provided a rationale for explaining the result to the public.

The decision of the steel companies to "bow their backs" against union demands in the 1959 negotiations was due, no doubt, to concern about the high levels steel prices had already reached and the increasing threat of foreign steel. There is reason to believe, however, that the prolonged stalemate and costly strike was also due in part to the belated recognition by government officials of the administrative nature of wage-price adjustments in our major industries and a desire to do something to bring this inflationary mechanism under control.

The resort to admonitions, pleas and threats at the only real point of susceptibility—prices—reflects official concern over administered prices, but apparent inability to make them serve the economic system. It remains to be seen whether this strange administrative process that has served management and organized labor so well in the past decade will be harnessed and directed in the public interest.

> The price skirmish . . . is of the
> same genera as price warfare,
> although perhaps a different
> species. The differentiation of
> the price skirmish lies, not in its
> intensity but, rather, in the fact
> that it is of limited scope and
> duration.

44

The Price Skirmish—
A Distinctive Pattern
of Competitive Behavior

RALPH CASSADY, JR.

MUCH HAS NOW BEEN WRITTEN in abstract as well as in actual market terms about price warfare.[1] As a result of intensive study of this interesting phenomenon, I have concluded that price wars are a precise type of abnormal

Reprinted from *California Management Review*, Volume VII, No. 2 (Winter, 1964). Copyright 1964 by The Regents of the University of California, pp. 11-16. This article is based in part on a larger study which was supported by the Bureau of Business and Economic Research, University of California, Los Angeles.

[1] Ralph Cassady, Jr., "Price Warfare and Armed Conflict: A Comparative Analysis," *Michigan Business Review*, Nov. 1956, pp. 1-5; "The New York Department Store Price War of 1951: A Microeconomic Analysis," *The Journal of Marketing*, July 1957, pp. 3-11; "Taxicab Rate War: Counterpart of International Conflict," *Journal of Conflict Resolution*, Dec. 1957, pp. 364-368; (with W. F. Brown) "Exclusionary Tactics in American Business Competition: An Historical Analysis," *U.C.L.A. Law Review*, Jan. 1961, pp. 88-134; *Price Warfare in Business Competition: A Study of Abnormal Competitive Behavior* (East Lansing, Michigan: Michigan State University, Bureau of Business and Economic Research, Occasional Paper No. 11, 1963); "Price Warfare—A Form of Business Rivalry," in Cox, Alderson, and Shapiro, eds., *Theory in Marketing* (2nd ed., Homewood, Ill.: Richard D. Irwin, Inc., 1964).

price behavior, and that, just as in international conflict, there are near (cold) "wars" as well as actual (hot) "wars." Thus, some conflicts do not eventuate but are staved off by conciliatory moves on the part of one antagonist or the other before an engagement can take place.[2] While some engagements are completely avoided, some do take place but are only of limited scope and duration.

Further analysis of the genus price warfare reveals a particular species of conflict heretofore not formally recognized. Because of the small segment of the market involved in such conflicts and the promptness of their termination, this type of encounter may be aptly termed a price skirmish.[3]

Such engagements typically are tests of strength which are quickly resolved because one side or the other soon capitulates to the superior strength of its opponent. This paper will examine intensively this special type of abnormal price behavior in order better to understand its precise nature and thus to enhance the knowledge of both theorist and practitioner.

This, then, is a refinement of my previous analyses of price conflicts—an attempt to differentiate two species of abnormal price-competitive behavior and particularly to isolate and examine that which I have chosen to designate here as the "price skirmish."

When abnormal price behavior is examined microeconomically, one discovers many instances of price conflicts which failed to develop into full-blown price warfare because one competitor or the other found it necessary to withdraw. A full-scale price war was thus averted where the conflict was confined to a small segment of the market and was of short duration. The following two case examples are illustrative of price skirmishes.

Expansion of Merchandise Line

Price conflicts are not uncommon in the retail food field and usually involve price reductions and counterreductions on standard-brand canned or packaged items.[4] One of the most interesting price skirmishes which has come to the attention of this writer, however, was one that broke out in upper Manhattan, New York, between two grocery vendors several years ago,[5] involving, oddly enough, the use of green groceries as a com-

---

[2] Cassady, *Price Warfare in Business Competition* . . . , pp. 40-48.

[3] "Skirmish" is defined as: "1. A slight fight in war, usually incidental to larger movements. . . . 2. A slight contest; a brisk preliminary conflict . . . A tentative movement, action, or effort; a flourish. Syn.—See ENCOUNTER." *Webster's New International Dictionary* (2nd ed., unabridged).

[4] See, for example, Cassady, *Price Warfare in Business Competition* . . . , pp. 25-27.

[5] "Fruit and Vegetables Given Away in Price War on Upper Broadway," *New York Times,* Wednesday, March 11, 1953, Pt. II, p. 31.

petitive weapon. Price conflicts rarely revolve around unbranded merchandise since price reductions of such items generally go unchallenged because of the possibility of wide quality variation.

The encounter involving price cutting of fruits and vegetables was precipitated when a merchant who had previously confined his efforts to the sale of green groceries decided to add canned goods. The move was deeply resented by the manager of a small neighborhood supermarket, who evidently considered this an invasion of his territory and thus a threat to his business success. He, therefore, informed his competitor that he intended to resist the move, by drastic means if necessary.

There being no sign of capitulation by early the following afternoon, the first move was made by the supermarket manager who started to undercut the invader on the prices of fruits and vegetables. The initial reductions brought prices approximately to cost or less-than-cost levels. For example, strawberries normally selling at 25 cents a box were reduced to 19 cents, which quotation the invader immediately undercut with a price of 15 cents. When this price was met by the opponent, the invader began giving strawberries away free of charge on a first-come, first-served basis, one pint of strawberries to a customer. Much the same thing happened with tomatoes, bananas, grapefruit, and cucumbers.

The price cuts in the foregoing price skirmish were not publicized except, of course, by word of mouth. Nevertheless it is interesting how quickly news spreads to the consumer in instances such as this. Within minutes consumer-buyers were gathering with two and three shopping bags in order to purchase what was being sold cheaply and to take advantage of the free offerings. Each vendor was attempting to attract customers to his own outlet or, rather, to keep customers from his opponent's establishment. In their attempt to hurt the "enemy," rational action momentarily gave way to emotional behavior, although neither adversary physically attacked the other.

This battle, which broke out at 1:30 P.M., was over by 3:30 P.M. when losses approximated $100 each, at which point reason undoubtedly overcame emotion. Thus, this skirmish ended almost as quickly as it started, apparently because of its costliness in relation to the limited resources of the opposing vendors. The speed of termination undoubtedly was a major factor in confining the conflict to these two establishments and preventing its spread to other neighborhood food stores.

The result of the skirmish developing out of the introduction of canned goods by a greengrocer was that the invader was repelled in his attempt to add the new line. It is interesting that this might have been only a preliminary encounter to a long drawn out action by the invader to gain a beachhead had it not been for the fact that the invader's landlord pointed out to him that the terms of his lease confined his retailing activity to the sale of fresh fruits and vegetables.

Intensive Promotional Activity

Price skirmishes are particularly prevalent in the retail gasoline trade and especially among independent vendors. A common cause of a skirmish in gasoline retailing is the impact of a new entrant who necessarily affects established outlets as he elbows his way into the market.[6] Just as important, perhaps, is the aggressive established vendor who is always looking for opportunities to expand his sales volume by almost any means. Most of the schemes utilized by aggressive competitors involve the use of price reductions or semi-price competitive weapons, such as coupons or premiums, supplemented by publicity effort in the form of large promotional price signs, which have the effect of intensifying price elasticity (i.e., response by consumer buyers).[7]

An excellent example of a price skirmish in motor fuel distribution occurred in the Azuza-Covina district of the Los Angeles, California, area in late May 1964, when a gasoline outlet connected with a discount house operation dropped its price one cent per gallon for regular trade, to 27.9 cents, thus establishing a price one cent below the other independents and three cents below the major-brand stations.[8] The rationale of this move was undoubtedly that the wider differential would attract customers for both the station and the discount house, and that the initiator of the reduction might be able to accomplish this without disturbing the market.

Shortly after the price reduction, the same station offered a weekend special beginning on Friday, consisting of two gallons of gasoline free with every eight or more gallons purchased, presumably for the purpose of stimulating patronage in longer-run terms. This second move brought prompt reaction from an aggressive independent competitor who accepted the challenge by countering the combination price reduction and free gasoline offer. The price of regular-grade gasoline thus was driven down to 21.9 cents, the approximate monetary equivalent of the combination of the lower price and the free offer. This price (10.9 cents ex tax) is as

[6] Competitors usually do not challenge a grand opening special offering in price and/or kind on the part of a new entrant. However, some invaders do not seem to be satisfied with one grand opening—according to one informed industry man, some new outlets may schedule several promotional "openings" in an attempt to woo customers. Such competitive behavior almost surely will bring on a reaction by an aggressive competitor in the form of meeting or beating the aggressor's low-price specials.

[7] If a station blanks out its signs it might be able to get away with a price cut without reactions by others, because a price cut without publicity is a less sharp competitive weapon than one accompanied by price signs.

[8] Data for this section were supplied by a particularly well-informed member of the trade.

low as the independents are likely to go because it is rock-bottom cost (i.e., the Los Angeles rack price). Vendors are reportedly not only conscious of the State Unfair Practice Act but also are reluctant to make a move that could be interpreted as a violation of this law.[9]

The apparent stalemate—which temporarily enhanced volume of both outlets but which was bound in time to bring a reaction by others—continued until the following Tuesday morning when the initial cutter capitulated by restoring his prices, including termination of the weekend offer. This move had the result of permitting the competitor to restore his prices to normal levels. Thus the skirmish was ended.

Normally, one would expect reductions in a price war or skirmish to consist of several small, one- or two-cent, competitive reductions with the result that the price shortly reaches cost levels. A knowledgeable informant reports that in some instances in the southern California market the competitive vendor who reacts to an initial reduction often moves the price directly to the cost level, thus indicating not only an acceptance of the challenge but also a willingness to carry the fight to the finish.

It is important to note, too, that when a cut is made by one seller, heavy consumer response is not immediate and therefore the reaction by the competitor need not be prompt. Actually, the sequence of reaction is that if an independent cuts, another independent will shortly reduce his prices, assuming he is challenging the initial cutter's move, and then, perhaps, several days or even a week hence a countermove may be expected from an aggressive major's outlet. When this happens, unless correction takes place almost immediately, reaction of other majors is apt to follow rapidly.

It should be noted that:

1. A gasoline price skirmish may take place during a weekend (when major company offices are closed) without the risk of triggering a general war.
2. A skirmish in the retail gasoline trade which continues in effect for six or seven days is very likely to end in a general war involving all vendors within the area (including major-brand outlets).
3. Only certain hyper-aggressive major-company suppliers follow independents' cuts directly (i.e., generally those which sell only under their own brands and thus have no hedge against independents' gains resulting from private brand sales).

It is interesting, too, that the rescinding of a reduction by an initial cutter might be accomplished in several ways. The initiator might:

- Go to the competitor and indicate that he is capitulating (not very likely because such a move is usually unnecessary).

[9] See California Unfair Practice ("cost-floor") Act, *CCH Trade Regulation Reporter*, Vol. IV, Par. 30630.07 and 30630.44A (1961).

- Blank out his price signs as a signal of his intent to restore prices (very likely).[10]
- Restore former prices without any announcement (quite possible).

In the gasoline field there is always the danger that a price skirmish will develop into general warfare. For example, in late spring, 1964, an operator of a discount-house-associated gasoline outlet in the Riverside, California, area, which normally would be selling regular-grade gasoline at 28.9 cents, or two cents under the prices posted by major-brand stations, reduced his price one cent, to 27.9 cents, apparently as a countermove to the offering of one-cent-per-gallon coupons by some independent operators. This move was shortly countered by at least one other competitor (presumably a coupon-giving station), and this countermove led to further reductions and counter-reductions.

When the independents' price reached 25.9 cents, one of the non-private-branding major companies moved down to within two cents of the deep-cut operators. This caused other majors in the market to meet the cuts, which, in turn, triggered a horizontal, or spreading, movement to contiguous markets. At this stage, general warfare prevails and the conflict becomes very difficult to contain.

Variation from the Norm

Although price conflicts involving tourist accommodations appear to have been rare or even nonexistent until recent years, several conflicts developed in this field in the fall of 1954, as for example, the one in Miami, Florida. The basic cause of the Miami battle may well have been the tourist slump experienced in the early fall by this vacationland, although there is no evidence that the slump was more than seasonal.[11] Under such conditions, individual operators might be expected to intensify their promotional efforts in order to obtain as much of the limited amount of trade which exists as possible. There is, therefore, a very strong tendency for competitors to resort to price cutting in order to attract custom.

The Miami battle reportedly was triggered by the use of rate signs by

---

[10] According to a reliable member of the trade, major-company salesmen are instructed to watch the price signs of independents and note those which are blanked out. The blanking out of the sign must be interpreted in the light of what has been going on in the market. Thus: if prices have been depressed, blanking out of a sign indicates that an attempt will be made to move up, but when prices have been at normal levels, it possibly means that a reduction is in the offing.

[11] According to the *Hotel Gazette* (Oct. 16, 1954, p. 3), the rate war came ". . . at a time when the resort town usually experiences its worst tourist slump."

price cutters,[12] which, of course, tends to increase the impact of reductions on rivals.[13] Two-dollar (per person for double occupancy) signs appeared in early September, 1954, coincident with the repeal of a Miami city ordinance that had regulated rate signs of motels, hotels, tourist courts, etc.,[14] and with the dismissal of cases against purported violators of the ordinance.[15]

The conflict broke out generally on October 4, 1954, when motel operators along Biscayne Boulevard (U.S. 1) somewhat belatedly reacted to the early September rate cutting of other motel proprietors by dropping rates to $1.50. At that time, daily summer rates for motels along Biscayne Boulevard were reportedly $6.00 to $8.00 for double occupancy.[16] Thus, normal impersonal competitive behavior was replaced by personal conflict in which owner-vendors attempted to inflict damage on one another.

The U.S. 1 Motel Association, which opposed the displaying of price

[12] Basically, the conflict appears to have been precipitated by the reaction of the U.S. 1 Motel Association to the initial reductions. However, the Miami *Herald* reported (Oct. 5, 1954, p. 1): "The price war also has the backing of the Chamber of Commerce, the Miami Hotel Association, AAA and similar groups. . . ."

[13] For the relationship between publicity and price elasticity, see Cassady, *Competition and Price Making in Food Retailing* (New York: The Ronald Press, 1962), pp. 30-31. The basic cause of this phenomenon is that consumers are better informed *re* bargain offerings when a price change is advertised and, therefore, tend to react more promptly and in greater numbers than when such changes are not publicized.

[14] Ordinance No. 4858 of the City of Miami, dated Sept. 15, 1953, was purportedly designed to prevent misleading quotations of rates and frauds against "the unwary traveler." Section 2 made it unlawful to post outdoor price signs unless they included certain specified details regarding rates and accommodations (which would have made it practically impossible to implement).

[15] According to a letter from the Miami City Attorney's office, the ordinance was not presented to the members of the legal staff of the City Attorney's office for an opinion regarding its constitutionality before enactment. After sixty-five arrests and convictions in the Municipal Court, the city was enjoined by the Circuit Court of the State of Florida from enforcing the ordinance against four different motel operators on the grounds that it did not come within the scope of the police powers of the city, and further that it was unreasonable, arbitrary, and capricious for the reason that a motel owner could not comply unless he had someone in constant attendance at the sign to make changes as he rented his facilities.

In view of these developments, the City Attorney explained his opinion to the City Commission that the ordinance was not enforceable and requested its revocation. Consequently, the cause against defendant price cutters was dismissed (*Leonard W. Brown v. The City of Miami*, Stipulation, Motion to Dismiss, and Order No. 170514-I, Sept. 7, 1954).

Subsequently, a new ordinance was prepared which the City Attorney claimed ". . . does not prohibit motels and hotels from advertising and posting signs and does prohibit them from charging prices for accommodations higher than prices posted on signs, and prohibits them from making an extra charge for swimming pool, television, radios, fans and air-conditioning if those are advertised as being available at the motel." This ordinance was designed, ostensibly at least, to prevent fraud rather than to eliminate price signs.

[16] *Hotel Gazette, op. cit.*

signs under normal circumstances, distributed $1.50 signs as tactical weapons for its member establishments.[17] In addition, a spokesman for this group stated that if the original price cutters were to retaliate with a reduction to $1.00, the association's members planned to cut still further.[18] Note that the end in a price conflict is not—as is usually the case in international conflict—destruction of the "enemy" but simply the nullifying of offensive power of opponents, thus protecting competitive positions.

Despite the threats made by the Association spokesman, $1.00 signs were displayed by some motels on the second day of the battle.[19] However, by the third day there were definite indications of the possibility of an armistice resulting from negotiations between the two factions.[20]

Finally, on Thursday, October 7, a month after the first reductions were made and four days after the "hot" action started, the conflict was terminated when five of the motels that had initiated the advertising of the $2.00 rates "agreed to remove their signs." [21] Shortly thereafter, another 35 motels "tore down their $1 and $2 signs," [22] and motel rates were restored to former levels.[23] Again it should be noted that concerted price action to end a "war," or for any other reason, while fairly common in intrastate trade, would not be permitted under federal antitrust regulations applying to interstate commerce.

One final point: There was an implied question in the title of this section concerning the nature of the Miami motel rate conflict. It should be obvious that this engagement had at least one element of a price skirmish—that is, prompt termination. The Miami rate "war" differed, however, in

[17] Such action would seem to border on collusion and would presumably be in violation of the antitrust laws of the state, although such laws are often not enforced with any degree of vigor. See for example, the Note in the *Stanford Law Review* (Vol. II [Dec. 1949], 200) titled, "The Cartwright Act—California's Sleeping Beauty."

[18] Thus: " 'We'll put up 50 cent signs. [In fact if such retaliatory action is taken], . . . we'll put up signs offering free accommodations.' " ("Price War Sparked by Motel Signs," Miami *Herald,* Oct. 5, 1954, p. 1.)

[19] "Motels' Price 'War' Continues; Rates $1," Miami *Herald,* Oct. 6, 1954, p. 1-c.

[20] "Motel Men Seek Peace," Miami *Herald,* Oct. 7, 1954, p. 1c.

[21] "Price War Called Off by Motels," Miami *Herald,* Oct. 8, 1954, p. 1-c.

[22] *Ibid.*

[23] In the Miami rate "war" one hold-out continued at the cut-price level after the agreement was effected. The owner of this motel, on the day following the restoration of rates by the others, reported that an unidentified caller had threatened to burn down his motel unless he removed his rate sign. ("Motel Man Threatened in Rate War," Miami *Herald,* Oct. 15, 1954, p. 1-c.) While one might admire the independence and courage of this enterpriser in continuing to display his signs, the soundness of a decision to adhere to a price so far below market is certainly questionable. It would appear offhand that he could have enhanced his position by displaying a price sign which reflected a smaller price differential between his own and competitors' rates.

at least one important aspect from a price skirmish in that it was not confined to only a small segment of the market, but rather spread rapidly until it covered a substantial portion of the competitive structure in the Miami motel market.

It is presumed in this instance that termination, even with general participation, was possible because of the presence of a strong association which could compel adherence through control of individual and motel-owner behavior. Thus, this was clearly a disciplinary action (likened perhaps to the so-called Korea police action) and not merely a skirmish—it is, in other words, a variation from the pattern set forth in the preceding section and lies somewhere between a skirmish and an all-out war.

Conclusion

In any type of price warfare, and especially in the subspecies known as the "skirmish," corrective forces are inherently contained in the conflict itself. That is, one or more of the adversaries sooner or later must consider termination of the conflict, if only because of limited resources in relation to the expense of continuation. Under certain circumstances, these corrective factors take effect very rapidly and the conflict (or at least the first phase of it) comes to an end. But in other situations, influences in the form of adamance and superior resources are at work which preclude prompt termination.

It might also be inferred that there are conceptually two subspecies of price skirmishes. One is of the isolated border incident type, which may flare up and be quickly extinguished never to flare up again. The second is the preliminary type, which flares up and comes to an end promptly, yet soon breaks out again, sooner or later developing into an all-out "war."

Some marketing taxonomists may detect a third type of price skirmish —a conflict in which the distinguishing feature is the lack of intensity of the encounter. I have described elsewhere a conflict between a major company and a smaller but highly successful independent company in a middle western metropolitan area which was climaxed by a reduction on the part of the major company below the independent company's price.[24] The independent met the cut at once but almost immediately recognized it as a warning that he could not continue to undercut the major supplier. In my view, however, this was not price warfare at all, but, rather, near-war, and if so, it should *not* be classified as a price skirmish.

It should be obvious that consideration of the nature of price skirmishes is simply a refinement of the analysis of price warfare on which I have spent so much research effort. The price skirmish, in other words, is of

[24] See Cassady, *Price Warfare in Business Competition* . . . , pp. 40-42.

the same genera as price warfare, although perhaps a different species. The differentiation of the price skirmish lies, not in its intensity, but, rather, in the fact that it is of limited scope and duration.

In any price conflict there are, of course, management implications. There is the pricing decision that must be made by a vendor who finds it necessary and advisable to increase or regain volume, either because he is a new entrant in the market or because of competitive activities. There is also the pricing decision that must be made by the rival (or rivals) directly affected by the initial price move. The latter is particularly crucial.

There are, finally, decisions that must be made by the peripheral competitors who in time would be affected by the skirmish and, hence, might by their decision to participate or not to participate in the conflict have a determining influence on whether it will develop into a general price war. Certainly sound judgment is requisite on the part of the various decision makers to insure that their actions are based on long-range rather than on short-term considerations.